Catharina Raudvere is Professor of the History of Religions at Copenhagen University, and the author of *The Book and the Roses: Sufi Women, Visibility, and Zikir in Contemporary Istanbul* (I.B.Tauris, 2003), *Islam: An Introduction* and *Muslim Women's Rituals* (both forthcoming, I.B.Tauris).

Leif Stenberg is Associate Professor of Islamology at Lund University, and co-editor, with Birgit Shaebler, of *Globalization and the Muslim World: Culture, Religion and Modernity*.

Library of Modern Religion

1. *Returning to Religion: Why a Secular Age is Haunted by Faith*
Jonathan Benthall
978 1 84511 718 4

2. *Knowing the Unknowable: Science and Religions on God and the Universe*
John Bowker [Ed]
978 1 84511 757 3

3. *Sufism Today: Heritage and Tradition in the Global Community*
Catharina Raudvere & Leif Stenberg [Eds.]
978 1 84511 762 7

4. *Apocalyptic Islam and Iranian Shi'ism*
Abbas Amanat
978 1 84511 124 3

5. *Global Pentecostalism: Encounters with Other Religious Traditions*
David Westerlund
978 1 84511 877 8

6. *Dying for Faith: Religiously Motivated Violence in the Contemporary World*
Madawi Al-Rasheed & Marat Shterin [Eds.]
978 1 84511 686 6

7. *The Hindu Erotic: Exploring Hinduism and Sexuality*
David Smith
978 1 84511 361 2

8. *The Power of Tantra: Religion, Sexuality and the Politics of South Asian Studies*
Hugh B. Urban
978 1 84511 873 0

9. *Jewish Identities in Iran:
Resistance and Conversion to Islam and the Baha'i Faith*
Mehrdad Amanat
978 1 84511 891 4

10. *Islamic Reform and Conservatism:
Al-Azhar and the Evolution of Modern Sunni Islam*
Indira Falk Gesink
978 1 84511 936 2

11. *Muslim Women's Rituals: Authority and Gender in the Islamic World*
Catharina Raudvere and Margaret Rausch
978 1 84511 643 9

Sufism Today

Heritage and Tradition in the Global Community

Edited by

Catharina Raudvere and Leif Stenberg

Published in 2009 by I.B.Tauris & Co Ltd
6 Salem Road, London W2 4BU
175 Fifth Avenue, New York NY 10010
www.ibtauris.com

Distributed in the United States and Canada exclusively by
Palgrave Macmillan, 175 Fifth Avenue, New York NY 10010

Library of Modern Religion, vol. 3

ISBN: 978 1 84511 762 7

A full CIP record for this book is available from the British Library
A full CIP record is available from the Library of Congress

Library of Congress Catalog Card Number: available

Designed and Typeset by 4word Ltd, Bristol, UK
Printed and bound in Great Britain by CPI Antony Rowe, Chippenham, Wiltshire

Contents

List of Contributors

Andreas Christmann is senior lecturer in Contemporary Islam at the University of Manchester. His research interests focus on religious thought and practice in twentieth-century Islam, Sufism and modern Qur'anic hermeneutics. His publications include as co-editor *Studia Semitica* (2005) and *Studies in Islamic Law* (2007) and as co-author *Sufism and Theology* (2007) ed. by Ayman Shihadeh (chapter: 'Reconciling Sufism with theology: Abu l-Wafa al-Taftazani and the construct of 'al-Tasawwuf al-Islami' in modern Egypt') and *Modern and Postmodern Approaches to the Qur'an* (2003) ed. by S. Taji-Farouki (chapter: 'The form is permanent, but the content moves: text and interpretations in the writings of Mohamad Shahrour').

Ron Geaves is professor of the comparative study of religion at Liverpool Hope University and Director of the Centre for the Applied Study of Muslims and Islam in Britain. He began his studies of Islam in Britain in the Community Religion Project at the University of Leeds in 1988 and is the current President of the Muslims in Britain Research Network. He is the author of several books on Muslims in the West, especially Britain, including *Sufis of Britain* (2000) and *Islam and the West Post 9/11* (2004).

Paul L. Heck is associate professor of Islamic Studies at Georgetown University's Department of Theology. He received his PhD from the Department of Near Eastern Languages and Civilization at the University of Chicago, followed by a postdoctoral fellowship at Princeton University's Society of Fellows. His publications focus on Muslim conceptions of the relation of religion and religious knowledge to society and the public sphere. He has recently edited *Sufism and Politics. The Power of Spirituality* (2007).

Heiko Henkel is assistant professor at the Institute of Anthropology at the University of Copenhagen. He received his PhD from Princeton in 2004 and subsequently held a postdoctoral fellowship by the British Economic and Social Research Council (ESRC). His current research focuses on the social conditions that shape contemporary interpretations of the Islamic tradition in Turkey and Western Europe by Muslim practitioners as well as by non-Muslims. He is particularly interested in the repertoire of institutions and disciplines that practitioners employ to shape their life-worlds as Muslim and themselves as pious Muslims.

Gritt Klinkhammer is professor of the study of religions at the University of Bremen. Her main research interests are the sociology of religion, Islam in Europe and the plurality of religious culture in Western societies today. She is the author of *Moderne Formen islamischer Lebensführung* (2000) and the editor of *Dialog auf dem Prüfstand. Kriterien und Standards der interkulturellen und interreligiösen Kommunikation* (2008) and together with Markus Dressler and Ron Geaves *Global networking and locality. Sufis in the West* (forthcoming).

Søren Christian Lassen is external lecturer in history of religions at the University of Copenhagen. His research areas are Sufism and popular Islam in South Asia, as well as Sufi movements and Muslim groups in Western Europe. His studies include *A Meeting Place of Traditions. Ritual Practice and Leadership Strategies in an Islamic Religious Institution in South India* (unpublished PhD thesis from the University of Copenhagen) and 'Growing up as a Sufi. Generational change in the Burhaniya Sufi order' in Ron Geaves et al. (eds) *Global Networking and Locality. Sufis in Western Societies* (forthcoming).

Paulo G. Pinto is associate professor of anthropology and the director of the Center for Middle East Studies at the Universidade Federal Fluminense in Rio de Janeiro, Brazil. He received his PhD from Boston University (2002), *Mystical Bodies: Ritual, Experience and the Embodiment of Sufism in Syria*. He has several publications in English, French, Spanish and Portuguese and is currently working on a book manuscript.

Catharina Raudvere is professor of history of religions at the Department of Cross-Cultural and Regional Studies, University of Copenhagen. Her research interests focus on Turkey and the Balkans, contemporary Sufism and Sufi rituals. She has published the monograph *The Book and the Roses. Sufi Women, Visibility, and Zikir in Contemporary Istanbul* (2002). She is currently working on a book on Bosnian Muslims in Sweden, and a book project, *Muslim Women's Rituals. Gender and Authority in the Islamic World*, co-authored with Margaret Rausch. She has also co-edited a volume, *Turkey in Europe* (2008), with Dietrich Jung.

Margaret J. Rausch is assistant professor at the University of Kansas. She received her PhD in Islamic Studies from the Free University of Berlin in 1997. Her areas of research include: Sufism, Muslim women, ritual and religious educational practices in Morocco, Tajikistan, Turkey and the diaspora. Her publications include *Bodies, Boundaries and Spirit Possession: Moroccan Women and the Revision* *of Tradition* (2000). She is currently completing a book entitled *Embodying Discourse: Ishelhin (Berber) Women's Religious Educational Rituals in Southwestern Morocco*. A second book project is entitled *Muslim Women's Rituals. Gender and Authority in the Islamic World*, co-authored with Catharina Raudvere.

Uzma Rehman received her PhD at the University of Copenhagen in 2007. Her thesis was entitled *Sufi Shrines and Identity-Construction in Pakistan. The Mazars of Saiyid Pir Waris Shah and Shah Abdul Latif Bhita'* (2008). She has published 'Religion, politics and holy shrines in Pakistan', *Nordic Journal of Religion and Society* (2006).

Oluf Schönbeck is a research fellow at the Department of Cross-Cultural and Regional Studies, University of Copenhagen, where he received his PhD in history of religions in 2001. His research interests include contemporary Sufism and devotional rituals and he is presently researching the Lutheran mission in South India.

Leif Stenberg is director of the Centre for Middle Eastern Studies and associate professor in Islamology at Lund University. His research interests are Islam in the contemporary world and he has published several articles on Sufism in Syria and in diaspora. He has co-edited *Globalization and the Muslim World. Culture, Religion and Modernity* (2004).

Simon Stjernholm is currently working on his PhD thesis in Islamology at Lund University. The thesis concerns how Sufism is constructed, communicated and practised in contemporary Britain, with specific focus on the Naqshbandi-Haqqani tariqa in London. He has previously published a research report called *The Struggle for Purity. Naqshbandi-Haqqani Sufism in London* (2006).

Illustrations

Acknowledgements

The project 'Exile and Tradition. Transnational Contemporary Sufism' was run in co-operation between the University of Copenhagen and Lund University in 2005–2007, and was generously funded throughout by The Bank of Sweden Tercentenary Foundation. The project organised the workshop behind the present volume and the editors want to express their gratitude to the Foundation and for supplementary support from our departments, the Institute for Cross-cultural and Regional Studies at Copenhagen and the Centre for Middle Eastern Studies at Lund.

We are thankful to the participants in the workshop who agreed to publish their analyses as chapters in this book.

Catharina Raudvere *Leif Stenberg*

Translocal mobility and traditional authority

Sufi practices and discourses as facets of everyday Muslim life

Catharina Raudvere and Leif Stenberg

In contemporary religious life, Sufism and Sufi ritual practices are one of the few areas where Islam has had an influence on late modern spiritual expressions. Compared to elements from Christianity (revitalised pilgrimage), Judaism (kabbala), Hinduism (ayurveda medicine) or Buddhism (zen and other forms of meditation) that have been adapted and developed in groups outside the traditional religious institutions, Muslim beliefs and ritual practices are usually not shared in present-day trends of private religiosity and spirituality with their little or no interest in established networks and authorities. Hence it is not uncommon to come across the notion of Sufism as something associated with Muslim traditions, but not necessarily with Islam.

Anyone who has tried to search the Internet has come across the enormous amount of matches on contemporary Sufism, ranging from well-established orders (*turuq*, sing. *tariqa*) and their sub-branches, websites of individual masters (*shaykhs*) and invitations to digital repetitive prayer (*dhikr*) alongside Sufi rituals integrated in the numerous variants of New Age practices. All of these aspects of virtual space are of the highest relevance to the study of contemporary religion in order to analyse its movements today; nevertheless, contemporary Sufi life must also be sought after elsewhere. The fellowships and devotional rituals characteristic of Sufism are transformed by born Muslims and converts in urbanisation, by transnational migration and under the impact of national and international politics. Mobility is a key concept in this context as it indicates both mobilisation within movements and the mobility of humans and ideas over national and other borders. Hence fieldwork among groups and networks is needed as well as analyses of local and global charismatic leaders, examinations of books published and spread, and studies of how Sufi activities and teachings in general influence everyday life (Seufert 1997).

Sufism Today presents 12 studies on contemporary aspects of Sufi life, mostly within Muslim communities or about individual Sufi intellectuals. The volume also includes cases from the arenas in digital and social life where Sufi theology and rituals meet and merge with late modern religiosity. Contemporary Sufism dwells and develops between traditionalism in local Muslim communities, in the midst of national and political projects, in transnational movements emphasising the links between diasporas and homelands and in the argumentation in favour or against the notion of a global digital Muslim community (*umma*).[1]

Sufis and Sufism in the transnational flow

Handbooks of religious and Islamic studies often define Sufism in elusive and broad categories such as 'Islamic mysticism' or 'the mystic path of Islam'. It is depicted in ways that can easily lead the reader to believe that Sufism is something separated from Sunni or Shi'a traditions and hereby stands out as apart from everyday life and local conceptions of tradition; it is often used as a contrast to more purist and radical interpretations of Islam.[2] However, there are links between the more radical interpretations and Sufi groups, in terms of practising rituals, building fellowships, establishing authority and legitimacy or when Sufi orders serve as model for mobilisation and structural leadership for Islamic movements. Islamism is more than ideology from the point of view of the followers. Emotional piety practices establish strong bonds between individuals and are not something exclusive to the world of *tariqa*s (Bruinessen and Howell 2007).

The aim and character of almost any academic handbook carries the problem of how to represent the varieties of complex phenomena in a sufficient manner. The concept of Sufism could, on the one hand, easily be deconstructed as too wide an umbrella term, each case being representative only of its own local context; on the other hand, basic features stand out – though not stable or unchanging – in the long and sometimes troubled history of Sufism (De Jong and Radke 1999). Rather than trying to define Sufism from the perspective of theology, the repetitive prayers and strong fellowships in orders and networks could be regarded as constituting stable categories in the everyday lives of practising Sufis.

Idealised presentations of Sufism as the history of pious mystics and orders more or less separated from society in a world of beautiful poetry and rituals, or as abstract outlines of universalist and essentialist mysticism, have played a vital role in the history of Orientalism. As a consequence, many surveys still transmit an image of Sufis as estranged from other Muslims and as generally to be regarded as a challenge to Islam and Muslims. In particular it has been convenient to place Sufis in the dichotomy between orthodoxy, purism and radicalism on the one hand and liberal interpretations on the other. In some accounts Sufis are more or less understood as detached from everyday life in a manner in which they also appear almost at odds with the world. Sufism and Sufis with their sometimes intense rituals can appear exotic, but also by definition connected to something spiritual and otherworldly. Viewing Sufism as exotic and sacred is not only a historical phenomenon linked to the Orientalism of the late nineteenth and early twentieth centuries, it is very much a viewpoint reproduced today. An outlook of this kind exists in many presentations of Sufism on the Internet and in the influential writings of thinkers like Seyyed Hossein Nasr, Frithjof Schuon, Mircea Eliade and William C. Chittick.[3]

The shared basic assumption in the essays presented in this book is that Sufism has more of everyday – and worldly – characteristics and dimensions than is usually underlined.[4] In formal or informal groups Sufi Muslims do not always challenge other forms of Muslim organisational life such as congregations, associations or more loosely connected networks. From local perspectives Sufi gatherings are not by definition in competition with ordinary Muslim communities. On the contrary, they often exist within them in a web of prayer gatherings. Sufi networks link families together or function as an overall structure for business enterprises on a smaller as well as a larger scale.

These issues constituted the platform for the project 'Exile and Tradition', which was run in co-operation between Copenhagen University and Lund University in 2005–2007 and organised the workshop behind this volume. One aim of the project was to document and analyse how Sufi groups in Scandinavia develop and change in diaspora while maintaining their links with Sufi orders in Muslim countries. Being a buzzword in many debates today, Gabriel Sheffer defines diaspora as an academic term:

> a socio-political formation, created as a result of either voluntary or forced migration, whose members regard themselves as of the same ethno-national origin and who permanently reside as minorities in one or several host countries. Members of such entities maintain regular or occasional contacts with what they regard as their homelands. (2003: 9)

In a discussion of the many definitions of diaspora Rogers Brubaker summarises three signifying traits of contemporary diasporas: first the concrete dispersion in space, second the prevalence of an orientation towards a real or imagined homeland and third the boundary-maintenance versus the host society (2005: 5f.).

The comparative focus of the project 'Exile and Tradition' was initially mainly on north-western Europe and with a particular interest in analysing Muslim everyday religious practices in diaspora. Within the framework of the project the editors of the present volume organised an international workshop in September 2006 on the theme 'Exile and Tradition: Transnational Contemporary Sufism' with a broadened regional perspective. The chapters in this book are based on the presentations at the workshop and are all focused on case studies, albeit from shifting theoretical perspectives, all of them highly contextualised. All the essays underline the transformation of contemporary Sufi movements as an important area of research and how the tension between traditional authority and more recent forms of Sufism are negotiated. Transnational is in this respect not only a condition for work-migrant and refugee Muslims who practise Sufism in the margins of European plurality, but has to an increasing extent an impact on ways in which women and young people organise their Muslim activities.

The larger Sufi organisations with their many branches have long been transnational within Muslim societies. The flow of people, commodities, cultures and ideas can be understood as important for the spread of Sufism over the centuries and over the continents. Mass migration after World War II resulted in a significant increase of global contacts, and the exchange in the late modern diaspora has led to growing religious engagement for many individuals. These continuous processes transform local contexts, small groups and associations. In this perspective transnational refers not only to the flow of humans and commodities per se, but also has an impact on social, political, religious, cultural and economic conditions worldwide. This exchange has been nurtured by recent developments in communications like the Internet as well as by urbanisation, international migration and economic globalisation. Sufism and orders are today under the influence of urban lifestyles. Transnational Sufi groups can constitute the backbone of political parties and international business life. Throughout history Sufi revivalism has had apparent political goals and S. A. Arjomand states in his discussion on the political conditions of Islamic movements that Sufism at certain points in history has 'been the agency for the unification of tribes and formation of states' (1995: 181). Sufism was also a source of inspiration for the way in which Hasan al-Banna organised and structured the Muslim Brotherhood (Voll 1991: 393). A similarity in terms of structure between Sufi orders and political parties has also been noted in Morocco. In Morocco's political life, historical as well as contemporary notions on sainthood have played an important role in the process of creating worldly authority (Hammoudi 1997; Cornell 1998). Abdellah Hammoudi notes: 'The formal structures of mass organisations are in fact superposed on network and clientele practices governed by criteria of allegiance and faithfulness akin to those operating in the brotherhoods' (1997: 136). In Kurdish politics, transnational Sufi orders like the Naqshbandiyya and the Qadiriyya have played the role of being the backbone of liberation movements and political parties. For European Muslims the British Sufi Muslim Council (SMC), established in 2006 and supported by the government, is one way of how Sufis, or people attached to Sufi movements, participate in the public debate. The SMC also has the political aim of enhancing the situation of Muslims in Britain.[5]

The very number of labour migrants and refugees in the world today makes it possible to discuss in more concrete terms the transnational contacts and exchange among Sufis on a global scale. In a frequently quoted text Mike Featherstone argued in 1990:

> to point to trans-societal cultural processes which take a variety of forms, some of which have preceded the inter-state relations into which nation-states can be regarded as being embedded, and processes which sustain the exchange and flow of goods, people, information, knowledge and images which give rise to communication processes which gain some autonomy on a global level. Hence there may be emerging sets of 'third cultures', which themselves are conduits for all sorts of diverse cultural flows which cannot be merely understood as the product of bilateral exchanges between nation-states. (Featherstone 1990: 1)

Diasporic Sufi communities may serve as examples of how 'third cultures' emerge and maintain complex relationships with homeland societies while simultaneously developing global contacts crossing the ethnical links and thereby becoming the channels of the cultural flows so often pointed to.

A current of this kind can be the foundation for increased religious and social engagement. As is obvious from the contributions in this volume and in theoretical debates, exchange appears to become accentuated in late modern exile environments. The outcome of economic and cultural aspects of globalisation further fosters this development and opens up for new arenas and new agents. Gender and generation are obvious parameters when visualising the impact of change. Practising Sufism has apparently become an important platform for young people and women to find forms for a contemporary Muslim spiritual life. But rather than the traditional *tariqa*s with their established structures and networks, the more recent branches with charismatic leaders, new ritual forms and other hierarchies are gaining substantial attention. Hybridity and crossover rituals in between the *tariqa*s in diaspora are not to be forgotten, neither are Sufi fellowships without conventional leadership. The space for female agency has apparently grown in globalised Sufism, and young people are seeking opportunities for participation in flatter networks (Raudvere 2004; Stenberg 2005; Bruinessen and Howell 2007).

The study of Islam and the study of Muslims

Research on Muslim everyday life has been a theoretically flourishing field for several decades, and is to a large extent coloured by the perspectives of sociology and anthropology. Many valuable studies have offered highly contextualised analyses based on solid fieldwork. Regrettably, few religious study scholars paid early attention to these contributions, and a certain gap became visible between the social science perspectives and the focus of mainstream Islamic studies. However, the last 15 years have witnessed interdisciplinary exchange on a larger scale when it comes to both empirical data and theoretical debate.[6] Furthermore, recent focus in the media on Islamism as an ideology or Muslims as a social group has resulted in a certain waning interest in the practices of local life. The study of Sufism can bear witness to this development, as was pointed out early on by scholars like Michael Gilsenan (1973, 1982), Nikkie Keddie (1972), Pnina Werbner (2001, 2003), and Pnina Werbner and Helene Basu (1998) to mention but a few, with an impact on religious studies by contextualising religion in its social environment.[7] From a Shi'a perspective Roy Mottahedeh showed how to combine analysis of the individual and the political (1985).

The move from a focus on Islam as a theological concept to an interest in local definitions of what Islam can signify for people who practise it led towards agency and content with the works of Clifford Geertz, Talal Asad and Dale F. Eickelman. The prerequisites of this academic shift have been discussed in depth by Dale F. Eickelman in his groundbreaking textbook *The Middle East.*

An Anthropological Approach (1981), which emphasises that Islam as an abstract category can be understood in a number of ways by the practising Muslims of the world. This stance had a consequence for the academic approach, and Eickelman's and other scholars' works from the 1970s can correctly be described as the anthropological turn in the study of Islam – or rather of Muslims. Eickelman and Piscatori's volume *Muslim Politics* (1996) was likewise a turning point as it shifted focus from ideology to agency. In several studies Talal Asad has underlined the importance of the intellectual history of the study of religion and especially its consequences for the study of Islam. In this context *The Idea of an Anthropology of Islam* (1986) and *Genealogies of Religion* (1993) should be mentioned because of the impact these studies have had on disciplinary self-reflection and on interdisciplinary bridge-building. The latter has also been instrumental in more recent understandings of religion as the result of evolving and changeable discursive practices, intimately linked to power relations.

Many studies in this process deserve to be mentioned. In *Everyday Life in the Muslim Middle East* (1993), a collection of articles edited by Donna Lee Bowen and Evelyn A. Early, religious practice and performance are linked to other forms of cultural expression and social interaction. Thus religion is depicted in their book as a facet of everyday life. The editors write in their introduction how the contributions were selected to 'emphasise life as Middle Easterners live it' (1993: 1) – an aspiration we are happy to try to follow.

Sufism in everyday life

In the present context everyday Islam refers to the interpretations and practices carried out in the drudgery as well as the fluidity of humans' daily existence: more or less routinely performed daily rituals as well as non-ritual actions consciously or unconsciously linked to religion. Henri Lefebvre drew attention as early as in 1971 to the seemingly banal events in daily life that signify the conditions of modern life: 'Everyday life is made of recurrences: gestures of labour and leisure, mechanical movements both human and properly mechanic, hours, days, weeks, months, years, linear and cyclic repetitions, natural and rational time, etc' (2002: 18).[8] The practice of everyday Islam may vary in different groups, but it is always connected to an interaction between religious and social practices to an extent that it is not only problematic, but also unnecessary to separate between the two. From this perspective, religion cannot be separated from culture and society in a realm of its own. Rather, from a constructivist perspective (in the most common sense of the concept) religion in all its varieties is always an outcome of specific cultural and social contexts. Religion is not isolated from the routines and actions that life in general comprises. However, religious symbols, idioms, rituals and theologies may be differently interpreted, understood and utilised than in the theologies of formally educated religious scholars. From a theoretical perspective everyday Islam signifies varying, developing and sometimes creative and innovative locally centred discursive practices founded on how Islam is commonly conceptualised, practised and shared. In sum, a starting point for the perspective of 'Islam' as lived experience is a view in which the context is an important foundation for making sense of the processes that produce Islam.

Everyday religious life, such as Sufi gatherings with their tangible rituals and informal networks, is of greater importance to the majority of individual European Muslims than suicide bombings, female circumcision or overthrowing a regime in the name of Allah. The everyday practice of Islam and the organisation of Muslim communities are connected to daily life in a sense that make catering for informal networks more essential to the individual than power politics on a global level. From this point of departure the project 'Exile and Tradition' studies Sufism as everyday Muslim practice and piety and investigates the importance of its transnational and translocal nature. Peter Mandaville underlines the dimensions of human activity:

> the translocal as an abstract category denoting sociopolitical interaction which falls between bounded communities; that is, translocality is primarily about the ways in which people flow *through* space rather than about how they exist *in* space. It is therefore a quality characterised in terms of *movement*. (2001: 6)

This outlook contests concepts of state, community and identity as closed entities. In the context of contemporary Sufism it is apparent that Sufi orders are becoming translocal in Mandaville's understanding of the concept, far from restricted to a single state only. Not only are various Sufis 'flowing through space', so too are ideas and economies deeply linked to Sufism. The global flow does not mean that all hierarchies are emptied. On the contrary, Sufi communities show many examples of how the conventional *tariqa* structure provides a mode of organising transnational lives. In the wake of migration and globalisation, religion in general is characterised by substantial deterritorialisation (Nielsen, Draper and Yemelianova 2006). Following Olivier Roy's depiction of militants and their relation to a specific country of origin, it can be argued that a Muslim community is more constituted by a shared background of (theological) notions and rituals than merely a lifelong connection to a particular place (Roy 2004).[9]

Sufi organisations have always developed through migration and may be observed from the perspective of translocality and deterritorialisation. Within the Naqshbandiyya branch based in the Abu Nur mosque in Damascus, shaykh Ahmad Kuftaro (d.2004) in his Quranic lessons (*dars*) frequently referred to the possibility of a correct and righteous form of Islam spreading in North America and Europe. In a rhetorical style in which stories and jokes were included he stated that it would be enough to send 100 well-educated *dai's* (missionaries) outside the Muslim world in order to make 'the Americans let their beards fall down'. To this rhetoric Kuftaro usually linked the notion that if he and his foundation had access to a TV channel it would be another device calling the people of the world to a moderate and true Islam. The Ahmad Kuftaro Foundation has for many years been associated with African-American Muslim organisations in the USA, establishing a centre in Baltimore and developing relations with various Muslim organisations in Europe and Asia. In its construction of a worldwide network the foundation has turned into a translocal community founded on the conviction of the global potential of their ideas.

The expressive domains of religion

One of the ambitions of 'Exile and Tradition' has been to provide a study of Scandinavia's Sufi-oriented organisations and communities and to prompt analyses of their relationships to other Muslim groups. The aim of this data collection was to attract attention to otherwise less known aspects of Muslim life in Europe. Some of the shared fields of study in the project were connected to practised piety: informal groups and the mobility in between them, how conventional social and theological hierarchies are contested in diaspora, the variety of prayer meetings in terms of character and context, social memory and legendary history within the groups. One hypothesis was that these present-day informal, and sometimes marginalised, networks will, in the near future, have a substantial impact on the development of Islam in Europe. In an everyday world of social conflicts at many levels, the Sufi communities often appear to stand out as an alternative to more ethnically defined congregations and especially to younger people an alternative arena.

A shared frame was constructed for the collection of data. The model turned out to be necessary in order to underline the many dimensions of everyday religion and the means by which people interpret their religion in words and action. When individuals and small groups are brought forward as interpreting subjects, questions about power, authority and hierarchies are inevitable, and therefore gender, generation and social status have served as basic parameters. In order to identify the individual and collective expressions of Sufism, a model, influenced by Bruce Lincoln's discussion of how to study religion in the contemporary world (2003), was tried out.

A division of four different forms of expressions, or domains as he calls them, proceeds from Lincoln's discussion of Clifford Geertz's and Talal Asad's definitions of religion (Lincoln 2003: 1ff.). Looking into these domains, a consistent alternative to any essentialist understanding of religion is offered in order to identify variety: 'At best, one can try to assess specific movements or tendencies within a tradition at given moments of their development, recognising that each macro-religion encompasses many such groups and tendencies' (Lincoln 2003: 8). Agreeing with the critique of Geertz's definition as putting too much stress on belief and interiority as its site, Lincoln nevertheless argues against Asad's rejection of a general definition of religion and underlines the authority that comes with proficient references to transcendence. In Lincoln's view four domains are necessary elements when religion is to be identified: discourses, practices, communities and institutions. It must be underlined that these forms are not to be understood as hierarchical or contradictory; at an empirical level they overlap. In the perspective of the present project it was essential that the model was based on expressions from various local arenas and that it opened up a more distinct image of possibilities, choices and strategies within otherwise closed cultural and social entities: 'Muslims', 'migrants', 'refugees'. Following Lincoln, data have been collected in order to analyse the four domains as aspects of Sufi expressions.

Discourses are not to be characterised as religious only because they refer to Allah; when they express claims of divine authority and absolute truth this is to be distinguished from ideological, political or literary modes of verbal expression. Or, in Lincoln's words: 'A discourse whose concerns transcend the human, temporal, and contingent, and that claims for itself a similarly transcendent status. Discourse becomes religious not simply by virtue of its content, but also from its claims to authority and truth' (2003: 5). The formation and uses of religious discourses identify, establish and challenge power structures and norms, and are a powerful means to mark positions – on the top or from below. It is apparent that references to Sufism in current Muslim debates serve as an indication of positions taken on radicalism, integration, traditionalism – to mention but a few.

Practices in this perspective are more than rituals and include everyday practice governed by religious norms and ideals. The merging zones between what is considered public and what is private are to be found in disparate fields such as business ethics, spatial aspects of women's rituals or developing piety practices among young people. The least common denominator among Sufis appears to be connections to modes of ritual expressions of a particular kind, rather than concord in theological opinions.

Communities, fellowships and networks seem to be the social hallmark of Sufism throughout history. The Sufi orders constructed identity with reference to the discourses on a blend of hierarchy and belonging expressed in significant rituals. In the contemporary world, Sufi groups have navigated between a defence of tradition and a readiness to adapt to new cultural norms. The establishment of a local community can therefore function as norm keeper as well as norm breaker. Communities form strong links between individuals at a concrete or everyday level (family or formal membership), but also in terms of more emotionally founded religious fellowships. Sufi groups therefore seem to be useful vehicles when moving in translocal circumstances. Community is one of the most frequently used categories when the Muslim diaspora is studied, and then most often it refers to ethnic fellowships of more or less formalised organisations. Sufi communities in diaspora are interesting as they tend to break away from these stable categories.

The last domain, institutions, can be more or less formal and therefore serves a regulating, conserving, modifying or disciplinary function also in local life. Sufi orders are examples of, at least ideally, very formalised institutions whose sub-branches can serve as the very condition for transnational contacts along the liaisons of the *tariqa*. In practice, however, they also generate a web of informal connections between various groups of other Sufi followers, whether they are defined as youth, women or business people.

Diaspora groups are always vulnerable. Both islamophobia and internal power structures can make individuals suspicious of academic studies. As the two parts of the project 'Exile and Tradition' were clearly defined within local contexts and aimed at analysing how individuals participate in networks and groups, it has been important to emphasise the agents as active interpreters and not as victims of globalisation, transnationalism and other macro processes. Featherstone's notion of 'third cultures', as platforms for cultural flows, in combination with Brubaker's notion of the three aspects of diaspora, identify the spaces for moving, merging and mobilising Sufi groups. Even if informal, Sufi communities offer a connection between home and diaspora; on the one hand are the links to conceptions of homeland, traditional authority and shrine devotion, on the other hand many of them show an openness to global cultures and new modes of communication.

* * *

The following essays show how the rethinking of contemporary Sufism takes place in local communities and is made by new agents. Sufi life today is to an increasing extent lived outside the *tariqa* and is more independent in relation to the traditional authorities. Diasporic communities and transnational relationships provide the space for choices and novel life styles unthinkable only 20 years ago. The essays provide cases from a variety of local Muslim communities where heritage and tradition are not necessarily challenged, but nevertheless reinterpreted.

References

Arjomand, Said Amin (1995) 'Unity and diversity in Islamic fundamentalism', in Martin E. Marty and R. Scott Appleby (eds) *Fundamentalisms Comprehended*. Chicago: University of Chicago Press.

Asad, Talal (1986) *The Idea of an Anthropology of Islam*. Georgetown: Center for Contemporary Arab Studies.

Asad, Talal (1993) *Genealogies of Religion. Discipline and Reasons of Power in Christianity and Islam*. Baltimore: Johns Hopkins University Press.

Bowen, Donna Lee and Evelyn A. Early (1993). *Everyday Life in the Muslim Middle East*. Bloomington: Indiana University Press.

Brubaker, Rogers (2005) 'The "diaspora" diaspora', in *Ethnic and Racial Studies* 28:1–19.

Bruinessen, Martin van and Julia Day Howell (eds) (2007) *Sufism and the 'Modern' in Islam*. London: I.B.Tauris.

Bunt, Gary R. (2002) *Virtually Islamic. Computer-mediated Communication and Cyber Islamic Environments*. Cardiff: University of Wales Press.

Bunt, Gary R. (2003) *Islam in the Digital Age. E-Jihad, Online Fatwas and Cyber Islamic Environments*. London: Pluto.

Clarke, Peter B. (ed.) (1997) *New Trends and Developments in the World of Islam*. London: Luzac Oriental.

Cornell, Vincent J. (1998) *Realm of the Saint. Power and Authority in Moroccan Sufism*. Austin: University of Texas Press.

De Jong, Frederick and Bernd Radke (1999) *Islamic Mysticism Contested. Thirteen Centuries of Controversies and Polemics*. Leiden: Brill.

Eickelman, Dale F. (1981) *The Middle East. An Anthropological Approach*. Englewood Cliffs, N.J.: Prentice-Hall.

Eickelman, Dale F. and James Piscatori (1996) *Muslim Politics*. Princeton: Princeton University Press.

Eickelman, Dale F. and Jon W. Anderson (eds) (1999) *New Media in the Muslim World. The Emerging Public Sphere*. Bloomington: Indiana University Press.

Ernst, Carl (1997) *The Shambala Guide to Sufism*. Boston: Shambala.

Featherstone, Mike (1990) 'Global culture. An introduction', in Mike Featherstone (ed.) *Global Culture. Nationalism, Globalization and Modernity*. London:Sage Publication

Geaves, Ron (2000) *The Sufis of Britain. An Exploration of Muslim Identity*. Cardiff: Cardiff Academic Press.

Geertz, Clifford (1968) *Islam Observed. Religious Development in Morocco and Indonesia*. New Haven: Yale University Press.

Gilsenan, Michael (1973) *Saint and Sufi in Modern Egypt. An Essay in the Sociology of Religion*. Oxford: Clarendon.

Gilsenan, Michael (1982) *Recognizing Islam. An Anthropologist's Introduction*. London: Croom Helm.

Hammoudi, Abdellah (1997) *Master and Disciple. The Cultural Foundations for Moroccan Authoritarianism*. Chicago: University of Chicago Press.

Heck, Paul (ed.) (2007) *Sufism and Politics*. Princeton: Markus Wiener Publishers.

Heller, Agnes (1970/1984) *Everyday Life*. London: Routledge & Keagan Paul.

Howell, Julia Day and Martin van Bruinessen (2007) 'Sufism and the "Modern" in Islam', in Martin van Bruinessen and Julia Day Howell (eds) *Sufism and the 'Modern' in Islam*. London: I.B.Tauris.

Johansen, Julian (1995) 'Sufism and politics', *The Oxford Encyclopedia of the Modern Word*, vol. 4: pp. 124–133.

Kafadar, Cemal (1992) 'The new visibility of Sufism', in Richard Lifchez (ed.) *The Dervish Lodge*. Berkeley: University of California Press.

Keddie, Nikki R. (ed.) (1972) *Scholars, Saints, and Sufis. Muslim Religious Institutions in the Middle East*. Berkeley: University of California Press.

Lefebvre, Henri (1971/2002) *Everyday Life in the Modern World*. London: Continuum.

Lincoln, Bruce (2003) *Holy Terror. Thinking about Religion after September 11*. Chicago: University of Chicago Press.

Louw, Maria (2007) *Everyday Islam in Post-Soviet Central Asia*. London: Routledge.

Malik, Jamal and John Hinnells (eds) (2006) *Sufism in the West*. London: Routledge.

Mandaville, Peter (2001) *Transnational Muslim Politics. Reimaging the Umma*. London: Routledge.

Manger, Leif (ed.) (1999) *Muslim Diversity. Local Islam in Global Contexts*. Richmond: Curzon.

Metcalf, Barbara Daly (ed.) (1996) *Making Muslim Space in North America and Europe*. Berkeley: University of California Press.

Mottahedeh, Roy (1985) *The Mantle of the Prophet. Religion and Politics in Iran*. New York: Simon and Schuster.

Nielsen, Jørgen S., Mustafa Draper and Galina Yemelianova (2006) 'Transnational Sufism. The Haqqaniyya', in Jamal Malik and John Hinnells (eds) *Sufism in the West*. London: Routledge.

Raudvere, Catharina (2002) *The Book and the Roses. Sufi Women, Visibility, and Zikir in Contemporary Istanbul* (Transactions 12). Stockholm/London: Swedish Research Institute in Istanbul/I.B.Tauris.

Raudvere, Catharina (2004) 'Where does globalization take place? Opportunities and limitations for female activists in Turkish Islamist non-governmental organizations', in Birgit Schaebler and Leif Stenberg (eds) *Globalization and the Muslim World. Culture, Religion, and Modernity*. Syracuse: Syracuse University Press.

Raudvere, Catharina and Ašk Gaši (forthcoming) 'Between nations and global Islam. Sufi activities and community building among Bosnian Muslims in southern Sweden', in Ron Geaves, Mark Dressler and Gritt Klinkhammer (eds) *Global Networking and Locality. Sufis in Western Societies*. London: Routledge.

Roy, Olivier (2004) *Globalised Islam. The Search for a New Ummah*. London: Hurst.

Schiffauer, Werner (2000) *Die Gottesmänner. Türkische Islamisten in Deutschland*. Frankfurt am Main: Zuhrkamp.

Seufert, Günter (1997) *Café Istanbul. Alltag, Religion und Politik in der modernen Türkei*. München: Beck.

Sheffer, Gabriel (2003) *Diaspora Politics. At Home Abroad*. Cambridge: Cambridge University Press.

Starrett, Gregory (1998) *Putting Islam to Work. Education, Politics, and Religious Transformation in Egypt*. Berkeley: University of California Press.

Stenberg, Leif (1996) *The Islamization of Science. Four Muslim Positions Developing an Islamic Modernity*. Lund: Lund University.

Stenberg, Leif (2004) 'Islam, knowledge, and "the West". The making of a global Islam', in Birgit Schaebler and Leif Stenberg (eds) *Globalization and the Muslim World. Culture, Religion, and Modernity*. Syracuse: Syracuse University Press.

Stenberg, Leif (2005) 'Young, male and Sufi Muslim in the city of Damascus', in Jørgen Bæk Simonsen (ed.) *Youth and Youth Culture in the Contemporary Middle East*. Aarhus: Aarhus University Press.

Stjernholm, Simon (2007) *The Struggle for Purity. Naqshbandi-Haqqani Sufism in Eastern London*. Uppsala: Swedish Science Press.

Voll, John (1991) 'Fundamentalism in the Sunni Arab world', in Martin E. Marty and R. Scott Appleby (eds) *Fundamentalisms Observed*. Chicago: University of Chicago Press.

Voll, John (2007) 'Contemporary Sufism and current social theory', in Martin van Bruinessen and Julia Day Howell (eds) *Sufism and the 'Modern' in Islam*. London: Routledge.

Wasserstrom, Steven M. (1999) *Religion after Religion. Gershom Scholem, Mircea Eliade, and Henri Corbin at Eranos*. Princeton: Princeton University Press.

Werbner, Pnina (2001) *Imagined Diasporas among Manchester Muslims. The Public Performance of Pakistani Transnational Identity Politics*. Oxford: James Currey.

Werbner, Pnina (2003) *Pilgrims of Love. The Anthropology of a Global Sufi Cult*. London: Hurst.

Werbner, Pnina and Helene Basu (eds) (1998) *Embodying Charisma. Modernity, Locality and the Performance of Emotion in Sufi Cults*. London: Routledge.

Westerlund, David (ed.) (2004) *Sufism in Europe and North America*. London: RoutledgeCurzon.

Yemelianova, Galina (2007) 'The growth of Islamic radicalism in Euroasia', in Tahir Abbas (ed.) *Islamic Political Radicalism. A European Perspective*. Edinburgh: Edinburgh University Press.

The politics of Sufism

Is there one?

Paul L. Heck

Networks of Sufism (*turuq*, sing. *tariqa*) took the lead in resisting European colonial powers in the nineteenth century, for example in North Africa against the French and in the North Caucasus against the Russians.[1] Some networks resisted post-colonial states that aggressively sought to secularise local society, for example in the early years of the Turkish Republic and in pre-1982 Syria. And yet local networks of Sufism have pursued ambiguous relations with Islamist republics no less than secularist ones, willingly cooperating with state projects even to the point of allowing state interests to define 'true' Sufism – in Islamist Sudan (under 'Umar Bashir) and secularist Egypt (especially under Nasser, r.1954–1970, but still today) as well as in Iran both under the Shah and the Ayatollah.[2] It is also difficult to speak of a specific approach to politics within a single network. The Naqshbandiyya in post-1982 Syria cooperated with the Ba'thist state to the point of co-option, whereas in neighbouring Turkey its affiliates engaged the Kemalist state in ambiguous ways but not to the point of co-option.[3] In Morocco the Butshishiyya of Sidi Hamza has positioned itself as a mentor to society and counsellor to its royal ruler, whereas the Justice and Charity Group of 'Abd al-Salam Yasin, unofficial offshoot of the Butshishiyya, plays the role of admonisher.

This is not to suggest opportunism but to point to the dilemma of understanding the public outlook of a religiosity that does not link its religious fortunes to a specific political project. No treatises on politics are produced in the name of Sufism as in other circles of Islam. There are no directives on dealing with rulers other than vague exhortations to avoid their company – clearly an ideal and not the reality as history shows. The soundness of inquiry into the politics of Sufism thus remains open to question.[4]

Sufism is itself a complex form of religiosity but constitutes an integral part of Islam.[5] Its widely diverse forms share a common belief in the interior life as the final measure of the worth of religion. It is the spirituality of Islam. Spirituality, however, is not intrinsically indifferent to politics, making it wrong to cast Sufism as quietist in contrast to an activist Islamism. Affiliates of Sufism are not necessarily opposed to the idea of a shari'a-based state (and Islamists are not averse to spirituality per se), but they do not tie the validity of Islam to control of the political sphere.

It is best to speak of the politics of Sufism in terms of *engaged distance* – engaged with society but in principle distant from worldly power. Actual positions will vary according to circumstances, one situation calling for greater engagement, another for greater distance, but both elements must be present in some measure for Sufism to remain true to its own religiosity. Sufism is not about worldly power but character formation (*akhlaq*) as the fruit of the refinement of one's soul (*tazkiyat al-nafs*). There is a continuum between spiritual and material existence, but it is spirit, not matter, that is to guide. Material life is not problematic per se but only when people become excessively attached to it – wealth and power, fame and fortune – and count such things as the final measure of existence. To ensure against ethical waywardness, human activity in the world needs spiritual guidance – sometimes as counsellor and sometimes as admonisher. Whether the body in question is the human body or the body politic, the soul is to be its guide, the individual soul in the case of the human body and the charismatic soul, i.e. the spiritual master (living or dead), in the case of the body politic. Muslim society here is characterised as a body that depends for its ethical reinvigoration on the work of spiritual renewal (*tajdid*).[6] The task of the spiritual master is to be mentor of Muslim society, including its rulers, not holder of the reins of governance – doing so would compromise the spiritual nature of his authority. This advisory capacity (*nush*) can be articulated positively, as counsellor to power, or negatively, as admonisher, as will be seen in the two figures whose respective religious outlooks will be examined here: Muhammad al-Habash of Syria and 'Abd al-Salam Yasin of Morocco.

Muhammad al-Habash, erstwhile disciple of Ahmad Kuftaro (d.2004),[7] is a leading member of parliament in a Syrian state that is secular but still involves itself in definitions of acceptable religiosity.[8] 'Abd al-Salam Yasin, erstwhile disciple of the sheikh of the Butshishiyya, Sidi 'Abbas (d. 1972), openly rejects the Moroccan monarchy's claim to a constitutionally enshrined authority that gives it supremacy over both the political and the religious life. There are thus a range of options available within the spectrum of engaged distance, underscoring the importance of looking at the religiosity of Sufism across a range of national identities, both secular and religious, and in a context of competing forms of Islam, especially vis-à-vis Islamist voices that seek a shari'a-based polity as an essential aspect of Islam.[9] Although Syria has a secularist regime and Morocco a Muslim monarchy,[10] the legacy of Sufism continues to be recognised as an important element of religion in both countries, even if, having undergone a reform of its own, it now presents itself in a modern accent as rational and activist but still basically spiritual.

It is the ethical project of Sufism that compels us to consider the relationship of the spiritual to the political, especially in view of a religious authority that emanates from the spiritual (i.e. non-political) realm. To what degree should the spiritual realm be unmasked as the ultimate standard of ethics? Within the framework of engaged distance, there remains the question of tactic. Worldly considerations can never be overlooked, but there are religious expectations of the ethical efficacy of Islam. The relevancy of religious leadership in Muslim society is predicated upon the ability to show that Islam is in fact guiding Muslim society. What is the best way for spiritual mentors to address a society plagued by corruption and injustice, poverty and immorality: close engagement with worldly powers – presidents and kings – or clear distance from them, including the option of creating an alternative society that ignores national life? Too close an engagement raises questions of worldliness but allows religious actors to speak of the pressing issues of the day in a positive manner with a message that is comprehensible to all and not only the spiritually initiated. Too distant a relationship, articulated as admonishment of worldly power, may enhance the charisma and authority of Islam by emphasising its detachment – and hence innocence – from the corrupt ways of the world, but it can create a spiritual ghetto with a quasi-messianic agenda that may be partly effective as an object of group solidarity and a vehicle of protest but remains unintelligible to the world beyond the spiritually initiated. Spiritual authority, whether embodied in saintly figures and their writings or institutionally in networks of spiritual association, requires distance from this world, making it necessary not to let worldly concerns overtake the priority of spiritual endeavours. And yet the goal of cultivating the inner life is not simply about greater awareness of the other world. It should also bear ethical fruit. The spiritual renewal of the soul, while requiring a measure of detachment from the world, is meant to bring about the ethical reinvigoration of the material realm, i.e. Muslim society.

The idea of renewal is espoused by both our figures in very different ways. Indeed, the legacy of Sufism features as only one aspect of their respective messages, but both seek to ensure the public relevancy of Islam in a modern age. Spirituality in the service of the nation is, then, about bringing the values of Islam to society for the sake of its reform without reducing religion to politics in the process.[11] The danger of 'reducing the call of religion to the institution of state' (*dhawaban al-da'wa fi l-dawla*), as Yasin puts it, is echoed in al-Habash's conception of a complementary but not identical relationship between religion and democracy: 'democracy for the sake of establishing the values of Islam and Islam for the sake of guiding democracy' (*al-dimuqratiyya min ajl iqrar al-qiyyam al-islamiyya wa-l-islam min ajl tarshid al-dimuqratiyya*).

* * *

Muhammad al-Habash (b.1962) promotes a religious message that makes use of the heritage of Sufism not as a network of disciples but as a set of ideas and practices. This is increasingly true across Syria's religious establishment, but al-Habash goes further than most in understanding Islam in the mirror of modern realities.[12] He has no disciples in a formal sense, rejecting as anachronistic the blind obedience that sheikhs have sometimes commanded of their disciples, plundering them of their intellect and will, as he puts it. Rather, he is deeply involved in shaping the national understanding of Islam. It is his message that attracts public attention (although not always public support). He combines his scholarly role with a political one: he is founding director of the Center for Islamic Studies in Damascus and now a leading member of parliament. He writes and lectures extensively for popular audiences, travels widely at home and abroad with the aim of correcting the distorted image of Islam, and participates in a variety of high-level conferences at the international and inter-religious level, such as addressing UNESCO on the education of girls in Islam, representing Syria to EU officials, and participating in events sponsored by the Vatican.

Al-Habash sees the renewal of religious discourse (*al-khitab al-dini*) as essential for the ability of Islam to speak comprehensibly to modern realities – over obscurantist tendencies within the *umma* today.[13] Renewal here means adapting – not succumbing – to contemporary life rather than limiting Islam to a sacred past. He speaks of democracy and human rights as part of the politics of Islam, which is based on the twin pillars of social justice and universal equality and has always affirmed human solidarity and respect for others. The ethical reinvigoration of Muslim society is not a matter of coming up with new values but of presenting its ancient principles in language that is capable of dialogue with other peoples and other religions. Muslims do not need to sacrifice their religious perspective for the sake of engaging the global moment or vice versa. In his view, it is time for Muslims to reconsider suspicions of all that is not explicitly Islam, especially since such suspicions are based on ignorance of the fundamental purposes of Islam (*maqasid al-islam al-kubra*). Islam calls not for separation from others but cooperation in the moral project of building up human civilisation.

This openness does not mean, for example, that al-Habash has no critique of US policy in the Middle East, but he does not put Islam in existential opposition to non-Islam.[14] A chief concern of his is a religiosity of literalism (*zahiriyya*) at play in Islam today, which he sets not against spirituality per se but rather against human comprehension of religion (*fiqh*). Hatred of others in his view is the by-product of the Muslim tendency to reduce religious texts to literal wordings without comprehension of the intentions behind the words or knowledge of the interpretative tradition that adjudicates the meaning and importance of the words. People assume that adherence to literal wordings of religious texts entitles them to assume God's right of judging others, leading them to condemn other Muslims who do not have such a literalist religiosity – a practice known as *takfir* that can justify the spilling of blood of those so condemned. The oft-mentioned warning in Islam against religious innovation (*bid'a*) does not mean that Muslims cannot innovate at all or bring a measure of human comprehension to religion. Indeed, Islam is a message for the intellect (*risalat al-'aql*). The employment of the mind is necessary to bring the values of religion to new situations. Muslims need not wait for a prophet to tell them what to do when it comes to contemporary medicine, economics, fiscal policy, agriculture and irrigation, and legislation in general. The lack of intellectual openness within the Muslim community, al-Habash argues, leads to hatred of others, including other Muslims, as if enemies of God. One example of this, he notes, is a book on the responsibilities of Muslim fatherhood that first appeared as a doctoral dissertation in Saudi Arabia and apparently circulates in some Sunni circles (*al-Thawra*, 14 July 2006). It calls for fathers to teach their children hatred of Shi'is and Sufis. It is this religiosity, he feels, that breeds the radicalism that has so harmed Muslim society.

How has this happened when the Prophet Muhammad spoke of humanity entire as the family of God (*al-khalq kulluhum 'iyal allah*), the most beloved of them to God being those most beneficial to His family (*ahabb al-khalq ila llah anfa'uhum li-'iyalihi*)? He attributes partial responsibility to US 'militarism' and European 'Islamophobia' (*al-Thawra*, 24 February 2006), but the chief cause is the failure of Islam to speak to contemporary conditions, leading naive Muslims to embrace the false notion that religious texts cannot be interpreted (9 April 2005 conference on religious renewal – see his website, www.altajdeed.org/web/). In this view the text is to rule in its literal wording (*tahkim dhawahir al-nass*) without consideration of context or purpose. This in turn requires rejection of the intellect and those who use it to understand the will of God. The key problem is internal to Islam (interview in *al-Sharq al-Awsat*, 3 February 2006), and Muslim leaders are to be faulted for their failure to enlighten Muslims and reject this culture of hatred as anathema to Islam. Muslim leaders can themselves disagree, but that does not release them from the responsibility to tolerate other viewpoints – tolerance in al-Habash's view being the hallmark of Islam (*al-Thawra*, 7 July 2006).

A single theme dominates al-Habash's message – unity: the unity of all Muslims, of all believers, of all humanity. The idea of the oneness of existence, commonly attributed to Ibn 'Arabi (d.1240), is clearly at play in al-Habash's thinking but is nuanced as human solidarity (*wahdat al-wujud al-insani*, lit. the oneness of human existence), which he sees, along with the oneness of God, as the highest purpose of the divine project initiated with God's creation of the human being. His controversial formulation of a Muslim acceptance of all religion that recognises the one God and the Day of Judgment is inspired by Ibn 'Arabi (*al-Thawra*, 12 January 2007).[15] He holds up the tolerance of Ibn 'Arabi over the intolerance of Ibn Taymiyya (d.1328), the darling of Wahhabism and Salafism today, but does not reject Salafism per se:

> It is not reasonable to do away with either Sufism or Salafism ... We need Salafism to preserve the balance of the *umma* according to its scripture (*kitab*) and the tradition (*sunna*) of its prophet, and we need Sufism to preserve the taste and longing and nectar about which the lovers [of God] wrote ... as a light in their hearts.[16]

Islam thus calls for a dialogue not a clash of civilisations, so that the peoples of the world might interact with one another in truth not ignorance. Although not the master of a network of disciples, al-Habash is not unlike those sheikhs who mediate correct states of soul for their devotees. He not only counsels the nation but also models in his behaviour his advice to guide it. His various activities are all oriented to dialogue for the sake of ethically reinvigorating a nation susceptible to the culture of hatred as described above. He engages all: the state, non-Muslims (especially Christians), non-Sunni Muslims, Salafis, secularists, as well as representatives of the so-called West (Europe and the US).[17] He is ready to accept differences within the parameters of the common good, i.e. the good of all, which is God's purpose for His creation. Islam thus seeks to help this world reflect more fully its divinely ordained character.[18] In this sense, Islam has a contribution to make to international policy-making.

In a recent treatise, he demonstrates the compatibility of Islam with the UN Convention for the Elimination of All Forms of Discrimination against Women (CEDAW),[19] which Syria had initially signed with reservations out of concern for possible conflict with shari'a. He expresses high esteem for the UN Declaration of Human Rights while also calling attention to neglected areas of rights, namely the right of children to be born with two parents, the right of parents to receive the honour of their children, the right of women to full financial support, and the right of soldiers to be released from the duty to defend an unjust cause (*al-Thawra*, 12 May 2006). Such rights need fuller elaboration and backing by the international community, a process to which Islam has a positive contribution to make. There is no rejection of others here, no clash with modernity, but quite the opposite – acceptance of others and their points of view insofar as they serve the interests of all. It is in this sense that al-Habash circumscribes the venture of Islam not by particular shari'a precedents that served a past day and age and no longer do so today but rather by universal shari'a principles, which are meant to serve the interests of all and which are relevant for all times and places.

It is this openness, al-Habash avers, that in the past launched Islam to the height of human civilisation and can do so again. For him, despite his castigation of Europe's 'Islamophobia', he sees in the European Union a model for the Arab world with Islam as the guiding agent of justice, equality, unity and righteous action (*al-Thawra*, 16 February 2007), ensuring the welfare of all in reflection of the Qur'an's call for 'a word of equality between us and you' (Q 3:64, where no one is to lord it over others but all affirm common rights and duties). The example of unity as the choice of Europeans after centuries of religious and ethnic strife serves as a backdrop for al-Habash's call to Muslims not to fall into the trap of religious and ethnic conflict (*al-Thawra*, 23 February 2007).

It could be said that al-Habash is simply a mouthpiece of respectability for the Ba'thist regime, someone from within the religious establishment who can make sense of its policies to local Muslims and to the outside world as well. His message of unity and tolerance is meant to strengthen national solidarity – an end shared by a Ba'thist state looking for new formulae of political legitimacy. It cannot be denied that al-Habash has demonstrated his willingness to work within state-defined parameters of acceptable religiosity,[20] but the relationship is more subtle than co-option.[21] There is an exchange of interests – recognition of the state and defence of its policies in exchange for a platform to promote a religious vision. The argument has been made that the Ba'thist state exploits the business establishment for its own interests but in turn allows it to flourish on its own terms, resulting in a measure of independence and unpredictable influence on the socio-economic life of Syria, even if within the parameters set by the Ba'thist state.[22] An analogous situation exists vis-à-vis the religious establishment – its exploitation for state interests but with a measure of freedom to promote its version of Islam that is distinct from Ba'thism, of course, but also from the state version of Islam presented in government schools, which is largely identified with pan-Arabism. Despite overlap, the interests of the state and religion are not coterminous, and al-Habash straddles the two in his desire to engage society for its ethical good.

Al-Habash has openly criticised certain state policies. He calls for the abrogation of article 49 of the constitution that outlaws membership in the Muslim Brotherhood upon pain of death. He led efforts to counter the state's decision to expel foreign students of shari'a from Syria. In his view, secularism has failed as a social system, indicating his reservations about Ba'thist domination of Syrian society. He is a strong spokesman for the compatibility of Islam with democracy – as a way to counter the stringent anti-secularism of radical Islam that threatens Syrian society no less than the Ba'thist state. He argues that the discovery of the will of God can happen through human choices that represent the consensus of the community, consensus after all being one of the sources of positive law in Islam (*al-Thawra*, 9 March 2007); the will of the people can establish common interests that constitute the purposes of Islam for public life (9 April 2005 conference on religious renewal).

In this sense, al-Habash is more accurately looking to broker reconciliation between the Islamic (*islami*) and nationalist (*qawmi*) points of view that sometimes divide Syrian society. He speaks of a Syrian state that is neither religious nor secular but civil (*dawla madaniyya*), and that functions according to alternation of power, parity among citizens, equality before the law and the right of the nation to legislate according to its greatest interests (language now shared by the Muslim Brotherhood). Such talk, even if partly serving the regime, must sound odd to most Syrian ears. The discussion of democracy in terms of Islam and the call for political parties with a Muslim orientation is hardly meant to usher in a revolution but rather to engage Syria's political realities and in so doing call attention to the ethics, values and principles of Islam in Syrian society. To achieve this goal, the responsive participation of the religious establishment is needed (*tajawub al-manabir*), i.e. religiously based public action on behalf of the nation to bring about greater popular awareness of the country's needs and to inspire people to meet them. At the same time, he rejects the idea of Muslim parties that claim to speak exclusively on behalf of Islam, calling instead for political parties with a Muslim orientation (*ahzab dhat marja'iyya islamiyya*).[23] The state has in recent years suggested the possibility of independent parties that are secular, not religious or ethnic, in orientation, but nothing has materialised. Still, one cannot explain the political proposals of Muhammad al-Habash without reference to shifting Ba'thist attitudes towards religion over the course of the last decades and the inevitability of a political future that will include Islam more fully.

In summary, al-Habash combines the interests of Islam and the interests of the nation in a way where religion acts as guide, counsellor, promoter of the affairs of the nation, and also ready arbiter of its symbols.[24] The final goal is ethical reinvigoration of the nation, but in light of his unified vision of existence, al-Habash is able to reach out and work with all parties, including the Ba'thist state, even if careful to preserve his own fundamentally rational and spiritual outlook. He is conciliatory but also reformist. Islam is an essential part of Syrian national identity (*juz' min hawiyyat al-watan*). Religion is not an end in itself, nor is its end a political project, but serves the national good.

* * *

In contrast, the language of 'Abd al-Salam Yasin (b.1928) is not at all conciliatory but challenging and at times militaristic, with not infrequent references to jihad and the army of God (*jund allah*). It is for this reason that he is often categorised under the rubric of Islamism. And yet he makes explicit and frequent reference to Sufism, describes its various elements as well as its relationship to shari'a in his writings,[25] with repeated reference to al-Qushayri, al-Ghazali, and other luminaries of past Sufism. Yasin qualifies his Sufism as Sunni and even Salafi (i.e. in conformity to the Qur'an and Sunna). It is not about isolating oneself from the world in search of the company of angels. Rather, it is practical in nature, endowing the Muslim soul with the ethical vigour to undertake a jihad against worldly powers that have no interest in the earth's dispossessed but only preservation of their own privileged status. The Sufism he promotes is activist with militant leanings.[26] Yasin's religiosity is very Qur'an-centred, but for him the Qur'an is first and foremost God's means of purifying souls from worldly attachments, orienting them totally to the other world (*al-akhira*) as guarantee of the truth of their actions. Knowledge of religion is useless if a person's heart is full of love of the world rather than love of God, making Sufism the key element in forming Muslim society for truly ethical action, i.e. action for God rather than the world, a mistake of which Islamism itself is guilty in Yasin's view. Ultimately, Sufism offers Yasin a hierarchy of holiness, at the top of which Yasin stands as saintly guide (*wali murshid*),[27] with the religious charisma to question the status quo of Moroccan politics and the legitimacy of its royal institution.

The Sufism of Yasin cannot be understood without reference to the Moroccan context where hierarchical authority – political, religious and spiritual – is socially normative.[28] In the first place is the king, who is not simply a secular ruler but also claims religious authority on the basis of his genealogical descent from the Prophet Muhammad, formalised in his title as 'Commander of the Faithful' (*amir al-mu'minin*). To challenge the legitimacy of the monarchy is to challenge not only the nation's political and religious identity but also the charisma (*baraka*) that surrounds the royal family. The task of admonishing such a figure essentially requires a messianic-like figure, as Yasin depicts himself – master of the other world who exposes the fallacies of the master of this world.

At the same time, Yasin, while not in a direct clash with other spiritual masters, operates alongside other spiritual elite who contend for spiritual supremacy over Morocco. Yasin's chief rival in this regard is Sidi Hamza, sheikh of the Butshishiyya, the network from which Yasin split when Sidi Hamza emerged as its spiritual leader after the death of his father, Sidi 'Abbas, in 1972. Yasin chose to forge his own spiritual trajectory and eventually established his own spiritual association, the Justice and Charity Group. Both communities most likely have over 100,000 affiliates, but the Butshishiyya align themselves closely to the monarchy in the role of counsellor. One of their members, Ahmad Tawfiq, is currently head of the Ministry of Religious Affairs, and although the network includes many commoners, it is a favourite of the nation's intellectual elite, such as Taha 'Abd al-Rahman, a widely read author in both Morocco and France whose works use a spiritual language with universal appeal but in a distinctly Muslim accent.[29] The Butshishiyya produce a journal devoted to Sufism, *al-Ishara*, amongst other literature devoted to the spiritual life. Despite a complex history, they are loyal to the royal institution, which looks to them as a pillar of the monarchy.[30]

Hamza's Butshishiyya and Yasin's Justice and Charity Group exhibit a remarkable overlap in spiritual terminology and concepts, and both figures seek to extend their influence into Europe among Moroccan immigrants and European converts, but Yasin's spiritual stature is defined by his rejection – and Hamza's by his support – of the monarchy. As suggested above, the two groups act as two branches of a single spiritual heritage, the Butshishiyya, with distinct approaches to Moroccan society. If Hamza is counsellor to Moroccan society and its rulers, Yasin is admonisher, but both seek to position themselves at the pinnacle of Sufism's saintly hierarchy. Hamza's branch, the official one, speaks – not unlike al-Habash in Syria – of a citizen's politics (*siyasat al-muwatin*) and concern for the higher interests of the country (*al-masalih al-'ulya lil-bilad*) as a religious and ethical duty, including national unity under the banner of monarchy, political stability and social peace (*al-Ishara*, no. 27, 'Fi l-Hayat al-'Amma'). Sufism here is a call to God, freeing one to act ethically in the world, not in ideological confrontation with it (*al-Ishara*, no. 27, 'al-Tasawwuf Da'wa la Muwajaha'). Hamza's disciples see him as guide of their hearts, inspiring work not for partisan interests but for the common good of the nation, which is possible, in Hamza's view, only via the royal institution that God created to ensure Morocco's national unity.[31]

In contrast, Yasin's branch of the Butshishiyya, the unofficial one,[32] sees the royal institution as cause of the grossly disparate class divisions in Morocco and source of the widespread poverty, corruption and immorality that has beset the nation. For this reason, Yasin and his followers refuse to partake in national life as defined by the monarchy. They have formed themselves as an alternative society within the nation,[33] existing, even flourishing, via a well-organised network of cells, called families (*usar*),[34] which provide members with spiritual affiliation as well as economic resources and opportunities that the state fails to provide. This group is hardly otherworldly but has opted out of the national status quo, casting suspicion on the existing order of things if not actually posing a serious threat to the monarchy. Yasin's predictions of an uprising (*qawma*) to overthrow the monarchy and set up the rule of Islam have been ridiculed in various circles; it was scheduled to have happened by the end of 2006.[35] But it should be asked whether Yasin as self-designated master of the other world (as opposed to this one) intended to have such predictions taken at face value, as policy analysts posited, fearing a Khomeini-like revolution in the making. If seen from the perspective of Sufism, his prophecies should be taken as rhetorical not actual – a way to assert his authority symbolically over the nation and its kingly ruler, to cast a spell of ambiguity over the country's political and religious institutions in the eyes of the people and especially his own followers, for whom talk of an uprising is meant not as a call to arms but as an invitation to loyalty.

An actual uprising cannot be discounted, but Yasin has never resorted to violence; his group is very disciplined – and non-violent – in its protest. Yasin is in the last phase of his life, and his successors may take a course different from his in its position towards the state. He calls not so much for political action but more to reconfigure the nature of reality, with the spiritual above the material, the religious above the secular, the word of God above the word of those who fail to recognise Him.

Yasin, unlike al-Habash, divides the world into existential camps – God's allies (*awliya' allah*) and God's enemies (*a'da' allah*).[36] The goal is to awaken the *umma*, destined to be world leader (*imam al-'alam*), and orient it to the next world so that it might restore ethical standards to a world blinded to truth by its materialist pursuits – power and pleasure. It is holy secularity (*laïcité*) that is the religion of the age and that must be deconstructed if Islam is to fulfil its mission of orienting humanity to the face of God, its true nature (*fitra*).[37] Yasin's discourse, which he calls qur'anic (*qur'ani*) and prophetically programmatic (*manhaji*), is meant to prepare Muslims to enter the battle over truth until death, replacing political partisanship with faith as the driver of popular activism. Islam will subdue injustice, liberating Muslims from their current state of subjugation to worldly hegemons, which Yasin associates with the qur'anic term for oppression (*tughyan*). There is good reason, he attests, for dictators, secularists and global powers to be against the introduction of religion into politics, since it threatens the perverse logic on which their exploitation of the downtrodden is based.

There is, however, considerable, and most likely intentional, nuance in Yasin's language (making it rather obscure at times). He denounces the practice of *takfir* where there is no blatant opposition to religion, and while he speaks of the world's infidel powers, the emphasis is on injustice not unbelief. Like al-Habash, Yasin also calls for dialogue, in his case a dialogue with materialism, but in a confrontational, even menacing, tone. His 'dialogue' with the West, with secularity, modernity, monarchy, and even with Islamism, is one that seeks to overpower rather than accept their viewpoints. He is the master, and his rhetoric is meant to help Muslims cast off the pervasive idea of Islam as 'religion of compliance' (*din al-inqiyad*), a concept that serves only the palaces of the world. Muslims are to become more spiritually activist, even spiritually invasive (via jihad) of the ideological boundaries set up by the world as obstacles to Islam's call to God, i.e. otherworldly authority which secularity refuses – indeed is unable – to recognise. Muslims are to confront the mordacious and mighty rule of the world's potentates (*al-mulk al-'add wa-l-jabri*) with a singularity of devotion (*wala'*) to God, His messenger and His shari'a. This will usher in a caliphate that unlike the Umayyad and Abbasid pretenders of the past is a caliphate truly in accord with the prophetic programme (*al-manhaj al-nabawi*), which Yasin will presumably guide.

His political manifesto, *Justice: Rule and Islamists*, is replete with the concepts of Sufism. He outlines the history of Islam's post-colonial awakening (*al-sahwa*) in which the Islamic spirit was linked to national movements in Muslim society. Errors were made, however. The European concept of nationalism at times took over, dividing one Muslim nation against another. Also, the Islamist desire to restore the past led to the mistake of praising the glory of the Umayyad and Abbasid caliphates, which were actually deviations from Islam. The point for Yasin is not to idealise a past that was in fact far from ideal but rather to heed at all times Islam's views about faith in the Lord, in the destined journey to Him, and good acts in this world as evidence of one's ethical character. It is not the past but a life of faith and charity (*hayat bi-l-iman wa-l-ihsan*) that turns individual believers into agents of good works and gives the *umma* the strength to lift itself out of its current abyss.

The chief obstacle is love of the world and fear of death – latent worldliness that plagues the *umma* and leads even its youthful activists to commit misguided and harmful acts. To be sure, the spirit of jihad is alive, enlivened in Muslim youth as the natural response to the oppression of worldly power (*tughyan*). These youth, however, are bereft of true knowledge and have a hostile attitude towards the people of Sufism, seeing them as traitors to Islam (*lam yatamarrasu bi-ahl al-dhikr wa-lam yathiq bi-him wa-la yarahum illa khawanatan li-l-din*). As a result, these youth lack a spiritual perspective and are deprived of guidance to obtain it. They are led to the destruction that the Prophet declared to be the fate of all extremism (*ghulu*). These overly fastidious Muslims are rhetorically skilful but fail to see that religion is not simply about language. (Interestingly, Yasin's criticism of literalists echoes al-Habash's.) Their obsession with the literal wordings of commands and prohibitions (*al-amr wa-nahy*) leads them to condemn others who do not follow the letter of the law, sowing strife (*fitna*) within the *umma*. They are simply ignorant of the fact that shari'a positions are at times contradictory and thus must be carefully ranked and evaluated in accordance with the interests of society. The spiritually near-sighted goal of these extremists is to declare their innocence (*bara'*) of the sins of society while overlooking their own.

The spiritual neglect on the part of Islamism thus demands remedy if the awakening of Islam is to reach its goal. Yasin associates these misguided Islamists with a hadith in which the Prophet predicts the coming of a people whose faith does not go beyond their throats (long taken as reference to Kharijism).[38] For Yasin such people have not introduced Islam into their hearts, restricting it to the material realm, namely eloquence on the tongue, attacking other Muslims perceived to be lax in shari'a adherence. Even if well intentioned in its critique of secularist oppressors, Islamism has a disease of its own, a lack of spiritual perspective, which prevents it from bringing the post-colonial awakening to its prophetic fulfilment. For this disease of the heart to be eradicated, renewal of faith is in order, which can happen in multiple ways (including visits to the graves of past saints, *ziyarat al-salihin*). Key to the process are three elements that are well known from classical Sufism: 1) companionship (*suhba*) of the one whom God has sent to renew the religion (*li-yujaddid al-din*); 2) recollection of God (*dhikr allah*); and 3) honest intention in returning to God, the highest level of honesty (*sidq*) being the honest quest for the face of God (*wajh allah*), a state that produces an ethics of kindness and certainty of faith. The point is the need for a spiritual formation, presumably mediated by Yasin, that comprehends both this world and the next.

This spiritual instruction is not to lead to quietism. Islam, once spiritually renewed, is to advance not by a positive but by a negative engagement with the critical issues of the day – chiefly injustice; *tajdid* here is deployed as a clash with the world, with Sufism acting to encourage antagonism towards the world's secularity that leads to neglect of God and of humanity's needs. Illumination (*tanwir*) for al-Habash is meant to bring about the reconciliation of believers with the world, whereas for Yasin it calls them to separation. Yasin, as noted, is concerned about the Islamist tendency to intra-Muslim strife, but Islam is still to preserve a threatened religion and liberate the wretched of the earth.

Yasin's Sufism approaches messianic proportions – the saint who will save his people by bringing them to God over against a world that refuses to submit to Him alone. The militaristic tone has a purpose fundamentally different from that of Islamism – not to downgrade, replace or even overthrow the monarchy (all three objectives are at play in Morocco's diverse Islamist circles), but to signal an alternative kingdom where justice and charity prevail. Yasin's words are highly political – not, however, in the sense of taking the reins of national governance and ruling the political realm in a worldly sense, but to make the spiritual life of the soul, as formed by his instruction (*tarbiya*), relevant to the political climate of the day, even if as protest. He speaks of a nation of faith and a citizenship of hearts, language essentially disinterested in and dismissive of secular definition of the nation-state. His message, although suggesting a caliphate under his leadership, is compelling not as an actual political project but more so simply as a counterpoint to the national status quo.

Yasin inaugurated his combative spirituality in his famous 1974 letter to King Hassan II, 'Islam or the Deluge', in which he called the king to repent, reminding him of the Day of Judgment to come. A less dramatic letter was issued after his release from prison in 2000 following the succession of Muhammad VI to the throne, entitled 'To Whom It May Concern', in which he addressed the young king as a mentor would, charging him to return the vast wealth that his father's minions had stolen from the people. The fact of a royal institution with prophetic lineage contributes to the quasi-messianic language Yasin attributes to himself – sent by God (*mab'uth*), commanded by him to prepare a force (*quwwa*) with the promise of final victory (*nasr*).[39] In other words, Yasin seeks to unmask spirituality in its full might, in all its power and glory, requiring a position of clear distance from the world. Even if using political language, he recalls the dangers of reducing the mission of Islam, in his view a primarily spiritual affair directed at hearts, to a political project. To be sure, the mission (*al-da'wa*) is political but in a unique way, not attacking but marginalising the state by positioning the authority of the Qur'an above that of the Sultan. The first step is not to overthrow the monarchy and set up an Islamic state, but to neutralise the monarchy, to make it irrelevant, by educating people in Islam as a way for them to opt out of the dictates of worldly power and so withdraw from the domain of political rule for the sake of spiritual guidance.

Withdrawal does not imply passivity. The point is not to construct a new government of worldly character but to live under the otherworldly orientation and heavenly guidance of the Qur'an, which suffices as an agent of the common good. In contrast to the Party of Justice and Development, which is Islamist but in a uniquely Moroccan way, Yasin is not calling for a political implementation of shari'a, i.e. its enactment as national legislation through the electoral process, but rather its spiritual implementation as purifier of hearts through the recollection of God as revealed by the Qur'an. Unlike the leading Islamist group in Morocco, the Movement of Monotheism and Reform, Yasin is not democratic in his use of religion as a tool against the royal state.[40] His goal is the ethical reinvigoration of society apart from and in opposition to the political realities of the nation. Even when it comes to shari'a, Yasin is careful not to define it in worldly terms. Not unlike al-Ghazali, who classified the science of shari'a (*'ilm al-fiqh*) as a worldly – as opposed to otherworldly – science, setting it against the science of the other world (*'ilm al-akhira*) as queen of the religious sciences,[41] Yasin too makes it clear that even shari'a as arbiter of worldly conduct is second to the fundamentally otherworldly purpose of the call of Islam.[42]

It is therefore necessary to reconsider the nature of Yasin's Justice and Charity Group – not as political opposition, at least not in any direct sense, but as an alternative society. The group is mobilised at times as a menacing display of spiritually disciplined strength. Such activity is more than a demand for accountability from the ruling class but acts as the ultimate protest against the political realm by disclosing the existence of another, hidden realm, of which worldly powers must take note: untainted by the impurities of secularity, untroubled by the ideological sophistries of modernism, and untouched by theological error (*dalala*) that unjust rulers force Muslims to accept upon pain of death in order to legitimise the unjust rule. The spiritual authority of the saint functions here in challenge mode, deploying its charisma of sanctity and network of disciples. The power of spirituality is conjured up as an alternative to the world's materiality – engaging it only from a clear distance. The caliphate invoked by Yasin is not to be brought about by the destruction of worldly power but rather by simply ignoring it through the construction of a society based on companionship with the agent of spiritual renewal (*suhbat al-mujaddid*). This in turn leads to spiritual brotherhood with the prophet of Islam. Only this will liberate Muslims from the reigning materialism that blocks realisation of the Islamic awakening (*al-sahwa*). Communism and capitalism, even Islamism, are all cast as materialism and thus inadequate to the goals of Islam, which, to fufill its purpose, i.e. total worship (*'ubudiyya mutlaqa*), must be unobstructed by any barrier of materiality.

The point, then, is not distance simply for the sake of distance – retreat into the spiritual realm – but rather for the sake of the reform (*islah*) of Muslim society: dismissal of politics (*siyasa*) but not of the community (*umma*). Distance here works as a kind of sociopolitical engagement, even if negatively. In actuality, Yasin is obsessed with the monarchy, but his spirituality pretends to obviate its role in Moroccan society. Even if calling for debate and consultation, in the end the only voice that matters is the voice of the holder of power (*wali al-amr*). The fact that Yasin allows no dissent within his own ranks corresponds to the menacing tone he takes to the outside world, whether the monarchy or modernity. Yasin's spiritual voice, similarly to the king's political voice, is not open to question. In contrast, al-Habash relishes a plurality of views. Yasin conceives of leadership chiefly in terms of saintly authority, conflating (his) possession of authoritative religious knowledge with the consent and consultation of his followers. His group is successful (although under increasing scrutiny by Morocco's security forces) not for any appeal to democratic sentiment, which he equates with human passions, but for its effective role as a network of social and moral solidarity, generating charity and services that the state fails to provide and embodying ethical standards that are critical for an environment of mutual trust, something also lacking in local society.

The political allegiance called for by Yasin in this context is to be based, he acknowledges, not on a social contract but on a pact to follow revelation, conflating political power (*sulta*) with privileged access to knowledge of the other world (*al-akhira*), necessitating an imam with the capacity to preserve God's commands from pluralistic and thus divisive interpretation (even if in principle permitting debate and dissent in areas of religion that have not been decisively determined). In this regard, Yasin's agenda is not unlike the king's programme, which seeks to preserve the spiritual security (*al-amn al-ruhi*) of the country by limiting the boundaries of national religiosity to the Maliki school of law, the 'Ash'ari school of theology, and Junayd's school of Sufism. This is evidently not satisfactory for Yasin, who claims that the leader would need to possess qur'anic qualities. For him the leader is to embody the Qur'an, implying that such a leader would serve not simply as a guide to Muslim society but as the very mouthpiece of God – to admonish, even denounce, political society and its rulers for their worldly and self-serving preoccupations.

Yasin's so-called prophetic approach (*al-minhaj al-nabawi*) permits him to alternatively distance himself from a world that does not in his view follow this approach and engage it to remind it that it should. He does avow that Islam is not served by a government that does not submit to Islam, but he also criticises the excesses of Islamists in limiting God's qualities to sovereignty (*hakimiyya*), as if the Prophet Muhammad came for the single purpose of setting up a state. For him, Islamists neglect the fact that Islam, even if inseparable from questions of governance, is also the religion of tolerance and mercy for creation entire. He shows awareness of the inherent danger in getting too close to the realm of worldly power, the pursuit of *dawla* at the expense of *da'wa*. He therefore argues that Islamists, failing to see the rightful priority of internal reform of the heart over political reform of the state, become themselves guilty of a kind of secularism, dealing only with the shell, not the core, of existence. Reform of society does not come about by condemning and attacking it, and Islamists who call for jihad without a preliminary spiritual formation of the heart – believing they are commanding the right and forbidding the wrong – deviate into the error of revolutionary violence, blindly and tragically overstepping the bounds of the legitimate use of power. There is thus a need for the saint, in possession of religious knowledge and authority, to act as the guiding guarantor of the legitimate use of power, preventing indiscriminate violence in the name of religion, which only distorts the image of Islam.

The goal here is not a political project per se but the treatment of the sickness in the hearts of Muslims by spiritual means. Islamism, in Yasin's view a contemporary form of Kharijism (a position shared by al-Habash), is prone to hypocrisy, equating *da'wa* with *dawla*, i.e. failing to maintain adequate distance from the dangers and pitfalls of politics, distance which constitutes the necessary condition for the renewal of Muslim society. Thus they imperil the *da'wa* by reducing it to *dawla*, to a worldly project, when in fact its purpose is always larger than *dawla* – otherworldly destiny (*al-masir al-ukhrawi*). Even if working for the reform of Muslim society, the spiritual cannot be absorbed and swallowed up by the political, i.e. material, realm. Islamism makes this mistake and loses the meaning and purpose of Islam in the process. The call to Islam is to be combined with the state, i.e. Islam is to guide the state, but cannot be neglected or lost for the sake of the state, a scenario that would end by desecrating both religion and politics.

* * *

The two figures considered here, al-Habash and Yasin, share a single outlook, namely the continuum between spirit and matter, although with markedly different emphases. The spiritual is to act as an ethical guide for the material (i.e. the political) – counsellor in the case of al-Habash, admonisher in the case of Yasin – but both act to mediate the goal felt necessary for Islam today: reconciliation of religion with modernity (especially the nation-state) in the case of al-Habash and domination of modernity by religion in the case of Yasin. The two both call for a state shaped by the values of Islam, but al-Habash describes it as a civil state whereas for Yasin it takes on messianic contours. For al-Habash, the current Syrian state, in principle, fulfils the conditions for such a state, attendant to both secular and religious voices, although he would like greater embodiment of the values of Islam in society. For Yasin, in contrast, the state can never fulfil the conditions of Islam unless modelled after the constitution of saintliness; the body politic is to be ruled by the spiritual voice of the Qur'an, almost precluding the need for state institutions, since the voice of the Qur'an, if heeded in the heart, is sufficient to ensure the ethical life of the nation. Yasin casts his political goal as a symbol, the symbol of the other world, which serves his strategy of spiritual distance from the world and is actualised through the spiritual organisation of his followers apart from national politics. It is this spiritual association, alternative society within the nation, that by disclosing its existence acts to protest the way the nation is currently being administered by its political masters – i.e. spiritual protest of material reality. Renewal is articulated not as adaptation but as spiritual mastery. The political order, locally and globally, is to bow to Yasin's spiritual authority for the sake of its ethical good.

The world is in crisis, for both al-Habash and Yasin, and Islam is under threat, necessitating renewal, reform, revival and the return of true religion, but for al-Habash the problem stems primarily from a lack of harmonious unity among the peoples and religions of the world and for Yasin from a pervasive secularity that in its ignorance of religion inevitably begets injustices of the most serious kind. For al-Habash, who is sensitive to the injustices of the world, the solution is to be found in a positive engagement with others, i.e. the realities of the political realm, locally and globally, for the sake of reconciliation. For Yasin it will come about by a negative engagement with political realities, signalled by the prediction of an uprising, in order to make manifest the spiritual realm, unmask it over and above the material one. Both figures pursue a policy of engaged distance, albeit at different ends of the spectrum. They share the ethical sensibilities of Sufism, even if acknowledging the legacy of Sufism in different ways. In both cases, the heart is to be spiritually connected to God – as the ultimate guide for bodies, both human and political, in this material world.

References

'Abd al-Rahman Dhu al-Fiqar, Abu (2004) *Mashayikh al-Sufiyya: al-Inhiraf al-Tarbawi wa-l-Fasad al'Aqdi ('Abd al-Salam Yasin Ustadhan wa-Murshidan)*. Rabat: Top Press.

'Abd al-Rahman, Taha (2005) *Al-Haqq al-Islami fi-l-Ikhtilafal-Fikri*. Al-Markaz al-Thiqafi al-Islami: Casablanca.

Haddad, B. (2004) 'The formation and development of economic networks in Syria: implications for economic and fiscal reform, 1986–2000', in S. Heydemann (ed.) *Networks of Privilege in the Middle East: The Politics of Economic Reform Revisited*. New York: Palgrave Macmillan.

Hamada, M. (2006) 'Sira' 'ala l-Islam al-Sufi wa-Islam al-Jaliyya fi Fransa', *al-Usbu'iyya* 8–14 December, 97: 12.

Heck, P. L. (2004) 'Religious renewal in Syria: the case of Muhammad al-Habash', *Islam and Christian-Muslim Relations* 15: 185–207.

Heck, P. L. (2005a) 'Religion and the authoritarian state: the case of Syria', *Democracy and Society* 4: 4–9.

Heck, P. L. (2005b) 'Eschatological scripturalism and the end of community: the case of early Kharijism', *Archiv für Religionswissenschaft* 7: 137–152.

Heck, P. L. (ed.) (2006a) *Sufism and Politics: The Power of Spirituality*. Princeton: Markus Wiener Publishers.

Heck, P. L. (2006b) 'Sufism – what is it exactly?', *Religion Compass* 1: 148–164 (www.blackwell-synergy.com/doi/full/10.1111/j.1749-8171.2006.00011.x).

Heck, P. L. (2007) 'Muhammad al-Habach et le dialogue interreligieux', in B. Dupret et al. (eds), *La Syrie au present*. Paris: Actes Sud Sindbad, pp. 413–420.

Lauzière, Henri (2005) 'Post-Islamism and the religious discourse of 'Abd al-Salam Yasin', *International Journal of Middle Eastern Studies* 37: 241–261.

Mu'ayyid al-'Uqbi, Salah (2002) *al-Turuq al-Sufiyya wa-l-Zawaya bi-l-Jaza'ir: Ta'rikhuha wa-Nash'atuha*. Beirut: Dar al-Buraq.

Rosefsky Wickham, Carrie (2002) *Mobilizing Islam: Religion, Activism, and Political Change in Egypt*. Beirut: Columbia University Press.

Sa'id Hawwa (1998) *Jund Allah Takhtitan*. MaktabatWahba: Cairo.

Scarfe Beckett, Katharine (2003) *Anglo-Saxon-Perceptions of the Islamic World*. Cambridge: Cambridge University Press.

Teitelbaum, Joshua (2004) 'The Muslim Brotherhood and the "Struggle for Syria", 1947–1958. Between accommodation and ideology', *Middle Eastern Studies* 40: 134–158.

Van Den Bos, M. (2002) *Mystic Regimes: Sufism and the State in Iran from the Late Qajar Era to the Islamic Republic*. Leiden: Brill.

Weismann, I. (1997) 'Sa'id Hawwa and Islamic revivalism in Ba'thist Syria', *Studia Islamica* 85: 131–154.

Weismann, I. (2001) *Taste of Modernity: Sufism, Salafiyya, and Arabism in Late Ottoman Damascus*. Leiden: Brill.

Yassine, Abdessalam (2000) *Winning the Modern World for Islam*. Iowa City: Justice and Spirituality Publishing.

Zarcone, Thierry (2004) *La Turquie moderne et l'islam*. Paris: Flammarion.

Zeghal, M. (2005) *Les Islamistes Marocains: Le défi à la monarchie*. Paris: La Découverte.

Zelkina, Malika (2005) *In Quest for God and Freedom: The Sufi Response to the Russian Advance in North Caucasus*. London: Hurst and Company.

Transnationalising personal and religious identities

Muhammad Sa'id Ramadan al-Buti's adaptation of E. Xanî's 'Mem û Zîn'

Andreas Christmann

The Arabicisation of the Kurdish literary and religious heritage is a particularly brutal case of cultural hegemony and ethno-nationalist repression in Syria's recent past. Since the proclamation of a 'Syrian *Arab* Republic' in 1961 the Kurds of Syria have been forced to become 'Syrian Arab citizens', while those who refused to be Arabicised were denigrated to second-class 'aliens' or shunned – as non-Arabs are not recognised as full citizens by the authorities – as 'non-registered' nobodies (*al-maktumin*).[1] Particular pressure to Arabicise was put upon those Kurds who migrated from the predominantly Kurdish regions of Northern Syria (i.e. the province of Hasaka and the regions of 'Ain al-'Arab and Kurd-Dagh) to the urban centres of Aleppo, Hama and Damascus. If they wanted to integrate into Arab mainstream society they had to completely acculturate their Kurdish identity. Most of them have now become virtually bilingual, although Kurdish can only be spoken in the private domain of their homes inside the cities' Kurdish quarters.

A very prominent case of such Kurdish integration into the urban setting of Damascene Arab society is the career of the scholar Muhammad Sa'id Ramadan al-Buti (b.1929)[2] who represents a class of Naqshbandiya *'ulama* who, from the 1920s and 1930s onwards, had migrated from the Kurdish Jazira in Turkey to Damascus, and who gained prominence and influence after 1963, i.e., after the new *Ba'th*-regime had gradually replaced the *'ulama* from old-established Damascene families with large numbers of Arabicised Kurdish 'newcomers'.[3] Benefiting from state patronage, these Kurdish *'ulama* created extensive networks of student circles and brotherhoods in and around Damascus, through which, unlike many Kurds from North Syria, they made their peace with both the *Ba'th* government and the new nationalist state ideology. And yet these years of forced transformations were not untroubled: the controversial appointment of Ahmad Kuftaru (1912–2004) as the Grand Mufti of Syria in 1964 was fiercely contested; as was the general tendency of the Kuftariya-Order's think-tank, the Abi 'al-Nur School, to formulate the *Ba'th* regime's secular ideology in religious terms.[4] Three more or less violent phases of protest (1964–1966; 1973; and 1979–1982) not only questioned the legitimacy of the *Ba'th* rule but also the claim of the 'assimilated' Kurdish religious elite to represent both the authority of Islamic tradition and the consensus of Sunni mainstream Islam.[5]

In the assessment of Sa'id Ramadan al-Buti's scholarly achievements it has often been overlooked that he had started his career as a scholar and writer before the *Ba'th* party came to power in 1963 and before it was officially illegal to promote Kurdish literature. One of the earliest publications in his astonishingly large oeuvre (over 60 books) is his adaptation of the Kurdish national epic 'Mem û Zîn' by Ehmedê Xanî (1650–1707).[6] His translation of Xanî's original Kurdish poetry into Arabic prose is a small literary masterpiece of modern Sufi literature but, more importantly, it offers us insights into al-Buti's efforts to accommodate his religious and cultural 'baggage' to the standards of his new urban and Arab environment, and to evaporate his foreignness by ostentatiously demonstrating his Arabicised Kurdishness.

To date, the examination of al-Buti's translation of this work has remained minimal and rather superficial. For the most part, his rendition is criticised as not being faithful to the original text.[7] Contrary to this view, this article will endeavour to show that al-Buti's handling of the Kurdish text is actually far more complex, eluding simple classification in terms of right or wrong, authentic or forged. The aim of this paper is to show that al-Buti's reworking of the Kurdish original text is not just an incompetent or random distortion of Xanî's writing. Instead, it is the intentional projection of al-Buti's ideas of a modern, reformed Sufism onto the Kurdish national epic – a selective appropriation of a legacy that can be seen as paradigmatic of al-Buti's reinterpretation of Islam in general.

Context of the reception: Kurdish socialisation and Arabic assimilation

Let us begin with an overview of the biographical context of al-Buti's reception of E. Xanî's 'Mem û Zîn'. When he published his translation in 1957, al-Buti was 28 years of age. It was a time of his life when he went through a deep identity crisis that brought him into collision with both the Sufi tradition of his Kurdish origins and the secularist tendencies of post-independent Arab nation-states. He had studied *tarbiya* (Islamic education) and *fiqh* (Islamic jurisprudence) at the al-Azhar in Cairo and, at the time of this translation, worked as a teacher of Islamic studies at a teacher training school in Homs (1956–1960).[8] Harvesting the fruits of his first publication, he was appointed assistant lecturer at the newly established *shari'a* faculty of Damascus University where his career as a 'scholar-imam' began. For al-Buti, whose ancestors were poor farmers in the rural parts of the Kurdish Jazira, such educational opportunities meant that he had to leave the Kurdish settings of his family environment behind to work in an Arabic urban context that became increasingly liberal and secular during his formative youth. If one is to interpret the autobiographical conclusions he reached in *Hadha Walidi* (1994) as authentic, al-Buti had, up until this time, enjoyed a completely

Kurdish socialisation.[9] Prior to his emigration (1934) from the village of Jilika (on the island of Butan, near the Syrian border town of 'Ain Diwar) and the first few early years spent in the Damascene district of al-Akrad, the most significant influences on the formation of his identity and relationships were his own family and the Kurdish students and learned friends of his father, Mullah Ramadan al-Buti.[10] In addition to his irregular teaching activities, al-Buti's father owned a bookstore and sold Kurdish books to other exiles from the Jazira in order to provide for his family.[11] His father only managed to find regular paid work in 1941, seven years after his arrival in Damascus. Supported by the wealthy and influential Kurdish businessman Abu Sulayman Qarashuli, Mullah Ramadan became interim imam of the al-Rifa'i mosque in the poorer district of al-Harat al-Jadidia. Later, financed by *waqf* monies, he became the mosque's official imam and, as a result of Shaikh Hasan al-Muzayik's recommendation to local government authorities, its approved *khatib*.[12] His father's example shows that a genuine integration of many Kurdish settlers into the urban structure of Damascus only took place after many years of their emigration from Kurdistan.

Al-Buti was first taught at home by his father – as was the custom in his Kurdish homeland. He then went on to attend an Islamic primary school near Suq Sarudja (1936[?]–1939). Due to his exceptional learning abilities, he continued to receive private tuition from Shaikh Hasan Habannaka and Shaikh al-Maradini in al-Maidan (1940–1953). This brought al-Buti into contact with non-Kurdish scholars and the ideology of the Syrian Muslim Brotherhood. However, al-Buti's nostalgic memoirs of his school years, in which memorising the Qur'an, repeating al-Ghazali's *Ihya' 'ulum al-din*, and reciting Sufi poetry all held a central place, show that his religious education was still very much in line with the tradition he was familiar with.[13] A more intense Arabicisation of al-Buti's environment as well as a direct confrontation with secular-nationalistic religious and cultural politics occurred during his studies in Cairo and during his teaching activities in Homs and Damascus. If one is to believe the underlying tone of his writings from this period, this transition was quite a culture shock for al-Buti which resulted in several publications in which he fought his personal 'cultural battle' with modern society. Al-Buti polemicised against the decline of values, cultural decadence, libertinism, hedonism and other modern vices, which he castigated as being the result of a detestable 'Westernisation' of Islam's authentic world views. His tone is that of an admonishing preacher, his vision apocalyptic and his style apologetic. In Cairo, he came across the latest Arabic translations of European neo-conservative critiques of modernity, which reinforced his cultural pessimism and which he then used as an inspiration for his own anti-Western writings. The most significant influence on his world view in this period came from the work of Muhammad Iqbal. Through him, he adopted the belief that a spiritual revolution could be achieved through a *literary* propagation of the true faith. In addition, he also began to argue that the decline in the strength of the Arabic-Islamic nation, and its position as a 'leading civilisation', was caused by a loss of its original purity and immaculacy, resulting from pollution by Western, i.e., Greek-Christian, influences. From this negative analysis, he then went on to claim that the Islamic nation could only become strong again once Muslims were able to defend themselves against such foreign influences.[14]

In this spiritual and existential crisis, al-Buti recalled his Kurdish heritage, particularly from the time when he began teaching at Arabic schools. The literary texts, with which he had grown up as a child, became for him a symbol of harmonious family relationships and of a conservative value system which he wanted to keep intact at all costs. The task now became one of directly influencing the morality and mentality of his Arab students through translating such Kurdish texts into Standard Arabic. Once again he took the lead from Muhammad Iqbal, who reverted to the literary folk tradition of the Punjab and Kashmir, in order to revive the *belles lettres* of Persian and Urdu for pedagogic-reformist ends. Being a Salafi reformer, al-Buti was not so much interested in idealising rural customs as in reviewing and recreating an authentic Islamic textual heritage.[15] Between 1955 and 1965, he translated a series of Kurdish poems, stories, fairy tales, *Adab* precepts and aphorisms into Arabic – always, as he emphasised, from a 'didactical point of view'. For example, he mentions that a story called 'The Mountain Goat' (*al-wa'l*) was told to him by his mother 'for enjoyment and entertainment during moon-lit summer nights', but goes on to state that *he* wants to tell the story in order to teach a 'lesson' (*'ibra*) and to give the reader a 'warning reminder' (*dhikra*).[16] Other translations include biographical and hagiographic writings by Kurdish scholars, e.g. those of Badi' al-Zaman Sa'id al-Nursi, which al-Buti published for the purpose of 'introspection and imitation'. Such publications were an expression of al-Buti's efforts to profile himself as a 'fledgling writer' assisted by literary exemplary models, using their authority to propagate his own views.[17]

Aim of the reception: 'Mem û Zîn' as a poetic and didactic play

In addition to this personal-biographical context, al-Buti's reworking of his Kurdish tradition also had an ideological aim which can be reconstructed with the help of notes that appear in his earlier work. In a journal article published in 1960, al-Buti complained about the lack of authentic Islamic literature to provide young Muslims with emotional and spiritual access to the religion of Islam. In line with his Sufi teachings, he claims that the prevalent rational debates in modernity would not produce morally enlightened persons, but rather intellectual dreamers and rationalist blockheads. It was not sufficient to *comprehend* the meaning of Islam, but – as al-Buti reminds us – to *experience* the spirit of Islam. He suggests a re-examination of traditional views as to how they could be made relevant to the present context for a mission 'based on feeling' (*da'wa wijdaniya*).[18] In another article, entitled 'Language of love' and published in the same period, he pointed out that the language of (true) love causes a resonance in people's hearts, which could carry them beyond the borders of human existence. Only if people were able to transcend their limited, human horizon they would be able to see life from God's point of view. A re-evaluation of all things in one's daily life would be the consequence of such an inspired divine point of view, leading to – according to al-Buti – a personal and social revolution.[19] In an essay about Muhammad Iqbal dating from a slightly later time ('A night with Muhammad Iqbal') he explains that such a resonance of the heart could be achieved through mystic and romantic poetry. One should – concludes al-Buti – create such poetry, or revitalise it by drawing on the Sufi legacy.[20] Finally, in the essay 'On the necessity of an Islamic literature', he wrote that modern Islamic scholars should be able to accomplish a literary and poetic absorption (*istighraqat sha'iriya*) of complex issues of faith, which currently are still not allowed to 'leave the area of the prayer room'. This would require a synthesis of spiritual literature and dogmatic theology:

> Why do we not use the themes of aesthetic literature for our teaching? Why are there no Islamic stories, which appeal to both heart and mind alike? Why is there no literature, in which human nature is portrayed in the light of pure Islam? A literature through which one, with aptness and astuteness, could convey the essence of Islam (*dhatiyat al-islam*) as eternal, divine values? [21]

This quotation can be found in al-Buti's publication *Min al-Fikr wa'l-Qalb* of 1972 which collects essays that al-Buti wrote much earlier, in the 1950s and 1960s. They reveal elements of the *Form and Content Debates* of the Nasser era which aimed at redefining the role of scholars and intellectuals at times of dramatic social and political change. Central to this debate was the demand to place literature in the 'service of society' and to create an 'art for life' and not '*l'art pour l'art*' (*al-fann li'l-fann*).[22] Literati and intellectuals should show their political and social engagement through writing 'committed literature' (*adab multazim*). Such overtly secular reallocation of the role of literature meant that the religious and poetic legacy of Islam was supposed to be re-formulated in order to express purely cultural, ethical and political concerns. Traditional scholars, such as al-Buti, reacted to this restriction by claiming that it was not the predominance of the religious dimension of Islam that was at the root of the social crisis, but the lack of it. Consequently, true social engagement would lie in the revival of spirituality and in the return of the divine sphere – as opposed to the rationalist and positivist *Zeitgeist* in Arab society (in which any 'reference to God' was perceived as the cause of cultural regression and socio-political stagnation).

Against the background of these ideological expositions on the art and manner of appropriation of the traditional, religious legacy, al-Buti's interest in 'Mem û Zîn' and its adaptation become easier to understand. Contrary to many other Kurdish authors who sparked a revival of the literary legacy of E. Xanî in the middle of the twentieth century, al-Buti was solely interested in the mystical-religious contents of 'Mem û Zîn'. In line with the spiritual transformation he propagated, his attention was completely focused on E. Xanî's allegoric projection of mystical perfection, which the latter had achieved within a literary context that transmitted the story as a romantic tragedy. To recap: 'Mem û Zîn' begins with Mem's ecstatic observation of divine beauty in Zîn (during the Newroz festival) and ends with the death of both protagonists, i.e. – from a mystical perspective – with the extinction of God's *mirrored* beauty (in Zîn) and the ultimate devotion of the lover (Mem) to the hidden source of her beauty (God). In contrast to the oral tradition (already filtered by E. Xanî's interpretation), in which Mem mostly appears as a fool in love, an exceptionally gifted scoundrel, or even an amoral loner,[23] the Mem of the literary tradition appears as the model of an authentic mystic, whose consciousness is completely absorbed into God. Mem succeeds in 'elevating' his unrequited earthly love for Zîn through heroically bearing his unfulfilled longing, accepting it as divine predestination. He fills his heart with love for God, renounces his previous existence and is finally united with his true love (God). The dying, tragic hero becomes – in such a (literary-Sufi) interpretation – an ascetic hero, a mystically elevated saint, one of God's dearest intimates (*wali Allah*), who has successfully passed through the stages of *mors mystica*: purification, perfection and enlightenment.[24]

To achieve a literary transformation of key topoi of Sufic love poetry was what motivated al-Buti, in his attack on the secular use of such terminology (e.g. by Jirji Zaydan),[25] to discuss the theme of a romantic love story: inebriation and intoxication (*sukr*) through beholding divine beauty (*nazar ila'l-wird*); mystical ecstasy (*wajd*) and ecstatic speech (*shatahat*) in a state of overwhelming love of God (*'ishq*); suffering and longing of the soul through the pain of separation (*farq*); spiritual purification of the soul (*tazkiyat al-nafs*); experiencing the loss of self (*fana'*) when in unity (*wahdat*) with the loved one (*mahbub*), Allah, etc. In addition there were the theological and ethical themes that the epos also dealt with, for example the question of the meaning of tragedy through no fault of one's own (the problem of theodicy); the question of the role and function of evil; divine predestination and human freedom; the tension between expectations for the 'here and now' and the 'hereafter', etc. Al-Buti almost certainly saw his literary ideal realised in 'Mem û Zîn': literature that could be understood and *experienced*, and which, at the same time, addressed all pertinent issues of Islamic faith.

Reception method: adaptive re-narration

An analysis of the structure of the translated 'Mem û Zîn' shows that al-Buti did not intend to produce a translation that was to reproduce the Kurdish original in Arabic. First of all, he decided not to follow the verse format of Xanî's *Mathnawi*: instead of adhering to the original 61 chapters, containing 2,655 short verses, he wrote 28 chapters in Arabic prose. This genre switch enabled him to create a comprehensive new adaptation of the original text, notwithstanding his assurance in the preface that all he wanted to do was merely to fill 'various gaps' – which appeared inevitably by not making use of the verse format

– 'by relying on imagination'.[26] Al-Buti renders the chapters in such a way that he still manages to portray the essence and the narrative structure of the epic, but which also allows for significant modifications. In his version, for example, al-Buti omitted those parts in which Xanî laments the disaster of political dependency and the suffering of the Kurds as a result of political and cultural repressions. This prelude, known as the *dibacha* of the epic, to which Xanî dedicated two whole chapters (5 and 6), was too nationalistic for al-Buti. He also did not translate the other references to the unfree but proud Kurdistan, which Xanî used as a historical framework for the rest of the poem. Al-Buti might have feared, perhaps quite rightly, that the Arab nationalists among his readers would interpret such patriotic lines as a political affront, committed by a young Kurdish immigrant who, in spite of his ambitions to assimilate, displays sympathies for the call for Kurdish independence, albeit in a literary disguise.

Yet, al-Buti was simply not interested in the public propagation of a Kurdish national state as envisaged by Xanî.[27] What mattered more to him was Xanî's universal (here: pan-Islamic) message that transcended the specific Kurdish context. It was for this reason that the references to Kurdish, Turkish and, in particular, pre-Islamic (Iranian-Zoroastrian) history had to be removed and that those ideas and names that were too distinctly embedded in Kurdish (or Persian and Turkish) history were 'Arabicised'. For example, in al-Buti's 'Mam and Zain', the Newroz Festival is transformed into *'id al-rabi'* (the Spring Festival), Cizre Butan becomes *Jazirat Ibn 'Umar*, *Brazava* turns into *Hafiz*, Mem changes to Mam, Zîn into Zain, etc., etc. Finally, al-Buti left those passages unrendered in which Xanî had referred to folk Islam. They include such things as the belief in the prophet as a miracle worker, the belief in the healing power of the Qur'an's 'talismanic' suras (e.g. *Ya-Sin* and *Ta-Ha*), references to astrology and alchemy, demons, genies, the miraculous figure of *al-Khidr*, the androgynous *Peri* spirits – all such references are absent from al-Buti's version. Significantly, al-Buti also omitted Xanî's literary homage to the epic legacy of Persian love poetry (e.g. Nizami, Jami', Hafiz, Sa'di).

Al-Buti's obfuscation of the literary and historical frame of reference in the original version enabled him to 'domesticate' the 'foreign text' in a consistent manner, ensuring correspondence with the cultural norms of the Arab target audience. This can be illustrated by the following example. In one of the passages of the original version the Kurdish Emir Zain al-Din proclaims the following at the wedding between Taj al-Din and Sati:

'Mem, you be the escort of the bride, I shall bear all costs!'
Both of them [Mem and Taj al-Din] stood up in full regalia,
and in reverence kissed the [Emir's] coat tails.
[940–1][28]

These verses mention two Kurdish customs. One is the tradition of Kurdish rulers to display (or withhold) their generosity during weddings, through which those honoured (or ostracised) gained (or lost) in status and prestige. The other is the tradition of *Brazava* or *Birazav*, in which a high-ranking member of the clan would normally serve as a guard and servant to the bridegroom for the duration of the wedding. This latter custom is also common among Arabs, but there is no equivalent to the former. As a result, al-Buti did not render the first custom of Kurdish rulers, but cleverly mentioned the *Brazava* which has an Arab equivalent. In this way he ensured that his readers were able to associate something 'Kurdish' with their own cultural background, *as well as* to accept it. Where such parity proved to be impossible, radical omissions were made in order to avoid the slightest irritation.

Revision was also necessary in those passages that could potentially be subjected to the widespread criticism of mystical poetry as an enactment of hedonism, libidinous sexual fantasies and unlawful transgressions of Islamic law. This applied to all those parts of Xanî's poetry that reveal the influence of erotic-profane representations of medieval *ghazal* – love poetry. However, al-Buti could not omit the eroticism from a love story and therefore had to manipulate the text at this point. One example is in the scene where the lovers, Mem and Zîn, have an intimate encounter in the garden of the Emir's palace. Following a long and painful separation, they are now finally able to succumb freely to their love and passion for each other. Xanî describes their encounter with a grasp of intimate, gentle eroticism:

Intoxicated by their words, their lips sweetened,
and whose sugar they offered one another.
Fulfilling the demands of their love,
each drank to the fullest.
Their eyes, lips, breasts, necks and shoulders
their cheeks, ears, mouths and chins –
kissed or tenderly bitten –
all the same: stormily conquered. [1556–1559]
They found a pavilion in the garden,
similar to the chalice of Djamchid, revealed to the world. [1565]

...

Here, they both fulfilled the demands of the [love] Sunna,
and when kisses are a duty, who could be surprised, about what took place.
But still: although completely unguarded,
they avoided the final step.
Although they both immensely longed for the other,
they did not cross this threshold.
Although their love was beyond any measure,
their waistlines remained the final frontier.
Love, which expects perfection and water from the purest source,
is closely guarded and tolerates no blemish.
[1569–1574]

The intimacy above 'their waistlines' referred to in the original version seemed too unrestrained and frivolous to the translator. He was aware that this rendition of Mem and Zîn's encounter could be interpreted as spreading sexual immorality, since – contrary to the strict explanation of the *shari'a* – physical contact prior to marriage seemed to be sanctioned here. Even Xanî himself had found this passage problematic and provided a reference to the taboo of below 'their waistline'.[29] Al-Buti's qualms were far more dramatic, since his translation merely recounts a tender touching of hands, a mutual comforting through words, without any additional physical contact.[30] His version was in strict accordance with his understanding of Islamic *Adab* morality, where lovers could declare their love to one another, but should not succumb to it. The translator sacrificed the poetic-sensual charm of the Kurdish original version because of his puritanical belief that love was to be exclusively comprehended in an intellectual-spiritual (and asexual) sense. Through this version, al-Buti rehabilitated Sufi mysticism from the accusation of sexual libertinage. At the same time he followed his own didactic guidelines to convey in an engaging manner the norms of *shari'a* law and Islamic moral virtues by way of writing spiritual literature.

A Salafi critique of mysticism

The last example has made it clear that in his adaptation of E. Xanî's religious-mystical ideas al-Buti has been guided by his intention to censor the dogmatically controversial parts of Xanî's account of Sufism. Al-Buti is a staunch advocate of a synthesis between Sufism and *shari'a* law. Like his father, he cannot formally be associated with any major Sufi order in Syria and, publicly, he denies any links to the Shadhiliya or Naqshbandiya brotherhoods.[31] Instead, he belongs to a modern type of 'reformed' Sufism that scorns the social institution of mystical brotherhoods and stresses the ethical teachings and psychological effects of 'true mysticism' (*al-tasawwuf al-haqiqi*), which does not tolerate allegiance to any particular *Tariqa* or *Madhhab*. A considerable number of his writings criticise the *bid'a*-innovations of mystical orders and yet, at the same time, he defends Sufism as the moral essence (*jauhar al-islam wa-lubbuhu*) of Muslims' life and thinking. His (sometimes quite open) criticism of the locally and nationally powerful Kuftariya clan (which he calls a 'shallow form of Islam')[32] stands in sharp contrast to his ardent defence of Sufism in the light of appeals, based on Wahhabi doctrines, to abolish Sufism altogether.[33] Critique and vindication of Islamic mysticism go hand-in-hand in al-Buti's work – another parallel to Muhammad Iqbal. In order to place the Sufic (spiritual-intellectual) tradition at the centre of Islamic orthodoxy, al-Buti employs two rhetorical strategies. On the one hand, he explains the norms of *shari'a* law in accordance with the standards of Sufi ideals and on the other hand, he redefines the mystic tradition in terms of the criteria used in Islamic law. As a consequence, he subjects his reception of 'pre-modern' mystic literature to specific restrictions and censorship involving those parts that would not be 'acceptable' in reformed Sufism.

Al-Buti faced particular difficulties with the *munajat* part (chapters 1 to 2, the 'invocations of God'). Its stylistic proximity and similarity in content to the controversial *shatahat* commentaries made by Hallaj, Bayazid Bistami or Jalal al-Din al-Rumi gave him serious reasons for concern and was left out altogether.[34] He also avoided controversy about the *na't* prologue, i.e. Xanî's panegyric on the prophet Muhammad (chapters 2 to 4). As this section could have been interpreted both as an expression of monism and pantheism (in terms of Ibn al-'Arabi's cosmology),[35] al-Buti chose to omit the prologue. His overall aim was to remove 'Mem û Zîn' from the 'shadows' of incarnationism (*hulul*), so as to restore the epic in a dogmatically inoffensive manner and to present romantic mysticism in an 'orthodox' light.

One example of this is al-Buti's adaptation of the controversial topic of the *unio mystica*, Mem's experience which forms the key moment in the epic. Against the potential objection that such annihilation in God, through becoming one with God, would lead to nihilism and withdrawal from the world, Mem's loss of self had to be presented without any reference to the doctrine of *wahdat al-wujud*, i.e. a belief in the unity of all existence and the dissolution of divine transcendence. Al-Buti managed to achieve this by describing the unification with God as a testimony to the highest love of God, and the greatest humility in *facing* God, while at the same time emphasising the orthodoxy of the mystics through their non-ecstatic, sober states and rational discourse *after* their mystical union. His portrayal of Mem's gradual dissolving into God, beginning with the vision of God's beauty and ending with the hero's complete isolation and madness, illustrates the pure and devout path from the loss of self to the *unveiling* of God. Mem's confused words in his state of mental derangement, which – 'sensibly' viewed – Sati and Taj al-Din perceive as an expression of mental confusion and madness, are explained in such a way that, parallel to the ongoing *munajat* monologue, they can be seen as an expression of the highest obedience to, and intense *vision* of, God ('I *saw* nothing except Allah – in front of me, next to me, and behind me'). More precisely, al-Buti's message is as follows: ecstasy and delight are not the result of ritualistic meditation practices, but are the final stage of spiritual perfection, a sign of humility and service to God, the climax of the soul's victory over pain and suffering as well as an expression of the acceptance of divine predestination. Unification with God is neither a heretic aberration nor trespassing of the law, but an expression of devout moral conduct and normative practice. In this way, al-Buti managed to provide an interpretation of *wahdat al-wujud* that was neither a philosophical/theological statement of monism nor an expression of disbelief or heresy – (*kufr*). Instead, his interpretation should be regarded as an exclusively positive ethical/mystical appraisal (not as *wahdat al-wujud*, but as *wahdat al-shuhud*).[36] Although he followed the template of Xanî's text, al-Buti consistently changed it 'in accordance' with his own theological position.[37]

Two examples should suffice to show how, as a result of the disappearance of references to the *wahdat al-wujud* cosmology in which Xanî operated, a divergent mystical expression appears. Let us look at chapter 17, in which – in the tradition of neo-Platonic theories about love – both young men, Mem and Taj al-Din, are described as *a mirror image of divine beauty*, and both princesses, Zîn and Seti, are portrayed as *the reflective light of divine attributes*:

Love cannot exist without a man and a woman,
there is no love without a soul.
Love can only exist because of the soul.
Just like the moon cannot shine brightly without the sun.
[699–700]

This verse can be interpreted in terms of the emanation doctrine endorsed by Ibn al-'Arabi, in which the *Divine Essence* or *Divine Being* manifests itself in *divine attributes* in a way that cannot be emulated by human beings – an interpretation that is supported by the cosmological context of the epic in chapter 2.[38] Such attributes, in turn, are referred to by *divine names*, which reflect the beauty of divine attributes. Without such divine names, i.e. without the availability of such a mirror, the divine attributes would be able neither to manifest themselves, nor to reveal their beauty. The language of the poem phrases it in the following way: without both young men (the mirror), the beauty of women (the light of divine attributes) would not be able to manifest itself (a woman not without a man, love not without the soul, the moon not without the sun, etc.). Both mirror and reflections, however, do not just depend on the existence of the Divine Being, but are, in fact, actually identical to it. Xanî put the above verse into the mouth of the princesses' nurse, who wonders how it is possible that two women could fall in love with two girls (as Mem and Taj al-Din appear in disguise on the day of the Newroz Festival). Xanî resolved this tension through referring to the cosmic hierarchy of divine emanation (in which lesbian love would be an ontological defect). Although al-Buti keeps the mirror metaphor in his translation, he omits the cosmological layer and thereby the possibility of discovering the emanation doctrine in 'Mem û Zîn'. Al-Buti's explanation was completely rationally modernist, pragmatic and moralistic (lesbian love is contrary to human reason):

> Surprised by this confession, Helena stared at the floor lost in her own thoughts. Then she looked up and uttered in confusion: 'Yes, Your Majesties. It could only have been a dream, since such a terrible thing only happens in dreams! Nevertheless, when I consider it once more, and no matter how awful this may sound, it may perhaps actually be true that your hearts did just manage to find those two unknown virgins amongst the many young men and women in the festival crowd. *But do both of you not wish to have children some day, and is it also not what those two strangers desire?* [my italics] Would it then not be more likely that both of you have fallen in love with two men? My beloved daughters, how is it possible for a woman's beauty to work, if there is no man to act as its mirror! How

> is it possible for a man to assess his beauty, when there would be no woman for him, to show him its meaning! Does the night's dark charm and restless melancholy not attract precisely those who are possessed by it? Would Shirin be able to carry out her acts without the existence of Khasru, who saw his own likeness reflected in her, finding his strength magnified in her? Who has ever heard of a flower tempted by other flowers, or of a nightingale that sang love songs to other nightingales? No, my darlings, what you have just told me can merely have been a fantasy, an empty dream. Forget all of it and do not become involved in such things!'[39]

As a second example, let us look at the passage from chapter 15, in which Mem describes to his friend Taj al-Din the aches his body and soul suffer after his meeting with Zîn. In this section, Zîn's beauty is considered as a reference to divine beauty, as a physical vehicle for theophany, as a temporary place of divine incarnation. In the following verses, Xanî took the opportunity to use Mem as a witness (*shahid*) to the presence of universal beauty (*mashhad al-husn al-kulli*) and to let him speak about the overwhelming impact of being suddenly struck by divine beauty:

The heart is a place where love resides,
a love which needs an empty space, in which it can be held.
Do not be amazed, when I tell you,
that what took place here, is a form of divine incarnation [in the Kurdish original: hulul].
If this were to be its [love's] original substance, then there shall be no rest for me.
The ruler of love has suddenly become visible.
The spirit swooned, when love overwhelmed me.
She took everything:
Spirit, body, and form.
Soul, liver, heart, my innermost.
Hands, face, feet, back and eyes.
Everything! Nothing is left [as it was before],
My God! Everything is now completely powerless.
Everything is now separated.
Everything screams out: 'Nahnu ashiq' [We love, overcome by passion!]
[634–640]

These lines describe the disintegration of the body in response to the sudden presence of divine love in the heart of a human being. Everything that is not divine (i.e. the outer shell that is our human body) is eliminated by divine theophany (Xanî used the Arabic technical term *hulul*). The love that appears in the human heart is an emanation of divine love ('The ruler of love has suddenly become visible'), because God – as already indicated in the introductory chapter – is its prime cause and ultimate source. A separation between the human and the divine is impossible in the act of love (or as Xanî described it, drawing upon Ibn al-'Arabi: 'No-one loves God, but God' and 'There are no lovers or loved ones, only God').[40] An interpretation informed by the emanation doctrine also suggests itself when looking at other verses in the epic,[41] and the introductory chapters could be particularly read in a pantheistic manner.[42] In some of the verses, Ibn al-'Arabi's terminology is quoted *expressis verbis*.[43] Al-Buti, the translator, had major reservations about such associations. The aim of all presentations of mystical ecstasy was to preserve the transcendence of God as well as the humanity of the mystics, in order to counter the *shirk* objection (cf. the criticisms against incarnationist Sufism as raised, for example, by Ibn Qayyim al-Jawziyya and Ibn al-Jawzi). As a result, Zîn's beauty is merely described as a miracle of divine creation, but not as the *loci* of divine manifestation. Mem's suffering is presented as the consequence of his exposure to divinely created beauty, and not as the *shahid* of divine theophany. Finally, al-Buti makes no reference whatsoever to *hulul*. Instead, he transforms the destructive character of Mem's passion into a twist of fate:

> Finally he looked at Taj al-Din, lost in thought, and whispered: 'You speak of me as I once was, but no longer am today. Nothing of which you speak, can you still find in me. Dear God, I have lost all my strength and fearlessness, and am no more than a shadow of my former self. My body is destroyed by agony and a huge fire burns in my heart. None of my strength has remained, so at least allow me to accept my fate, if you are unable to forgive me.'[44]

Result of the reception: a purification of tradition

In the context of a Reformist-Islamic interpretation, 'Mem û Zîn' is no longer in danger of being vilified as monistic, pantheistic or incarnatory, in al-Buti's translation. Xanî's spiritual proximity to the poetic-ecstatic mysticism of authors such as Jami', 'Attar, Hafiz, Nizami, Rumi and Ahmad al-Ghazali can scarcely be recognised any more. What is apparent is al-Buti's spiritual closeness to representatives of prosaic-sober mysticism, such as al-Qushairi, al-Muhasibi, al-Hujwiri, Abu Hamid al-Ghazali and Ahmad al-Sirhindi. By omitting almost all passages with folklore references, al-Buti avoids the reformist association that Sufism is synonymous with popular Islam and a mixture of particularistic localism and national disintegration (leading to political instability and economic stagnation). Devoid of links to cultural and particularistic (i.e. Persian, Turkish, Kurdish) traditions, the epic – as well as the mysticism it contains – shows no traces of (corrupting) foreign and non-Arab influences. The universal validity of the protagonist's portrayal, realised in the Arabic rendition, is supported by the removal of specific historical references (such as to fourteenth- or seventeenth-century Kurdistan). The resulting characters, who are presented in an archetypical and timeless manner, can therefore easily be transferred by the reader to any period of time: from the early days of Islam and to the present day. In this way, al-Buti's translation retains the 'essence' of the original text and is a fine example of the structure of al-Buti's reception of Sufism: the preservation of the essential core of mystical values combined with the simultaneous purification of all cultural layers formed around this core. From this perspective, al-Buti's version is not really a translation of the Kurdish original text (and therefore should not be measured against it). Instead, it is a piece of Islamic literature that is an appropriate vehicle for transferring religious and mythical norms to the contemporary reader – something that had been intended by Xanî too, but with the difference that such norms have changed since then and what appeared as orthodox to Xanî has become heterodox in al-Buti's eyes.

Aftermath of the reception

Al-Buti's 'Mam and Zain' enjoyed unexpected success (the second edition appeared as early as 1958, followed by numerous reprints)[45] and made the translator known throughout Syria. However, al-Buti produced no further adaptations of mystical poetry whatsoever and his 'literary phase' ended suddenly. Instead, he dedicated himself to other, more 'orthodox' sciences, such as law, theology and Qur'an exegesis, and to the publication of *da'wa*-literature. The 'official' reason given by al-Buti for moving away from the genres of literary translations and Sufi love poetry was the negative reaction he received from some of his audience. On the one hand, doubts were raised as to his authority as a legal scholar, as his competence in the exoteric sciences might be affected as a result of his involvement with the 'obscure' science of esoteric mysticism. On the other hand, objections were raised that his work – in spite of his heavy self-censorship – merely perpetuated current libertine ideas and encouraged young people's obsession with immoral romantic literature (al-Buti's response to these objections came with the publication of *Religion and Love* in 1959).[46] Rather ironically, in a journal article published in 1956, one year prior to the publication of 'Mam and Zain', al-Buti had already noted that readers who lacked the relevant mystical training would be likely to misinterpret his Sufi writings as alluding to profane love poetry. While he repeatedly spoke against the editing of mystical poetry (*Why I do not write about love?*),[47] he himself – paradoxically – carried out such editing (most likely due to intensity of his missionary zeal, as referred to earlier) and, given the anti-Sufi climate of the 1950s and early 1960s, became the target of criticism by anti-Sufi Muslim Brothers in Egypt and Saudi Arabia.

Not only did al-Buti stop any further reworking of Islamic romantic mysticism, he also ended his engagement with the Kurdish literary heritage. Biographically, this breach occurred when he began his career as a university lecturer and when he became part of the network of Ba'thist power relationships, which followed on from his appointment as Dean of the *shari'a* Faculty and as Professor of Comparative Law. He became the imam and preacher of the Masjid al-Sanjaq mosque and later of the Tinjiz mosque. Following his father's death in 1990, he then also became the imam of al-Rifa'i mosque. Al-Buti's assimilation accelerated as a result of the regime's crack-down on the Islamic opposition that occurred in 1979 and 1981. In *fatwas*, he publicly distanced himself from the radical approach employed by the Syrian Muslim Brotherhood and aimed instead at an appeasement with the Ba'th government.[48] During this period, his writings were still characterised by an activist, missionary and polemical tone and style. But contrary to a universal (pan-Islamic) spiritual revolution, he now placed greater emphasis on a stronger internal Islamic revitalisation, in line with the approach taken in Syrian religious politics. During this period, al-Buti polemicised mainly against Wahhabism and radical Neo-Salafism, but he also argued against secular liberalism and the Marxist left, which were both undermining the agreement of a *status quo* struck between the Ba'th regime and its Islamic opposition. In return, he was allowed to establish himself as a national authority and international representative of Syria's Sunni *'ulama*. In 1990, he became the official reader of a series of Qur'an interpretations ('*Dirasat Qur'aniya*') on Syrian state television, his weekly Hadith teachings were broadcast on radio ('*Hadith Usbu'i*' – under the heading of 'Islamic affairs'), and the '*Tabibak*' journal began to publish his *fatwa*s on Islamic social and medical ethics. His broadcasts could be received on four satellite channels (from Qatar and the UAE), which enhanced his reputation within the Arab world and, increasingly so, within Europe. *Al-Hayat* in London printed a series of his articles (*Here and Now – Bain al-hin wa'l-akhar*), his publishing house *Dar al-Fikr* gave al-Buti his own column on its Internet site ('*Kalimat al-Shahr*') and archived his writings. In addition, he was also appointed to several bodies within Muslim organisations (e.g. the *High Council of the Oxford Academy of Education*, the *Royal Society of the Study of Civilization* in Amman, and the *Parliament of the Custodians of Virtue – Majlis al-Umana*'), which all operate on an international basis. In parallel with his increasing media presence, a personal closeness developed between al-Buti and Hafiz al-Asad, Syria's president and head of state at the time. Until Asad's death in 2000, al-Buti was his spiritual adviser and 'confessor', and it was al-Buti who led the funeral prayer on the occasion of Asad's funeral.

Al-Buti's life and public career are nevertheless a case of suppressed identity. At times of increasing anti-Kurdish sentiments among the Arab population and anti-Kurdish propaganda in Syria's state media, in particular in the 1960s and 1970s, it would have been more or less suicidal for a young aspiring 'alim to further publicise his Kurdishness through literary associations with his Kurdish culture, which – after all – was seen as subversive to the goal of a united Arab nation state. Instead, al-Buti's mission was to become 'more Arab than the Arabs ever were' – his flowery, 'Arabesque' style of speaking and writing in Arabic is legend in Syria – and to become the model of a fully Arabicised Kurdish scholar whose Syrian and Islamic identities overrode his Kurdishness. His identity as well as his notion of Sufism became 'trans-nationalised' at the expense of losing the original Kurdish 'flair' that he and his religious upbringing once had.

References

Abd-Allah, Umar F. (1983) *The Islamic Struggle*. Berkeley: Mizan Press.

al-Buti (1972) *Min al-fikr wa'l-qalb*. Damascus: Dar al-Fikr.

al-Buti (1988) *al-Salafiya: marhala zamaniya mubaraka, la madhhab islami*. Damascus: Dar al-Fikr.

al-Buti (1992) *Mamu Zain: qissat hubb nabata fi'l'ard wa-aina'a fi'l-sama'*, 5th edition. Damascus: Dar al-Fikr.

al-Buti (1994) *Hadha Walidi: al-qissa al-kamila li-hayat al-shaikh mulla Ramadan al-Buti min wiladatihi ila wafatihi*. 3rd edn, Damascus: Dar al-Fikr.

al-Buti (1999a) *Ma' al-nas: mashurat...wa-fatawa*. Damascus: Dar al-Fikr.

al-Buti (1999b)*Shaksiyat Istawqafatni*. Damascus: Dar al-Fikr.

al-Buti (2000–2002) *al-Hikam al-'Ata'iya: sharh wa-tahlil*, 3 vols. Damascus: Dar al-Fikr.

Alexie, Sandrine and Akif, Hasan (2001) *Ahmedê Khanî: Mem et Zîn*. Paris: L'Harmattan.

Allison, F. Christine (2001) 'Volksdichtung und Phantasie: Die Darstellung von Frauen in der kurdischen mündlichen Überlieferung', *Kurdische Studien* 1/1: 33–50.

Böttcher, Annabelle (1998) *Syrische Religionspolitik unter Asad*. Freiburg i.Br.: Arnold-Bergstraesser-Institut.

Christmann, Andreas (1998) 'Islamic scholar and religious leader: a portrait of Muhammad Sa'id Ramadan al-Buti', *Islam and Christian-Muslim Relations*, 9/2: 149–169.

Christmann, Andreas (2003) '"I stayed up at night with Muhammad Iqbal": Shaykh Ramadan al-Buti's response to Iqbal's poetry', *Iqbal-Namah* 3/2: 1–8.

Christmann, Andreas (2005) 'Ascetic passivity in times of extreme activism: the theme of seclusion in a biography by al-Buti', in Ph. Alexander, G. Brooke, A. Christmann, J. Healey and Ph. Sadgrove (eds), *Studia Semitica: The Journal of Semitic Studies Jubilee Volume*, Journal of Semitic Studies Supplement 16: 279–303

Conermann, Stefan (1996) *Mustafa Mahmud (geb. 1921) und der modifizierte islamische Diskurs im modernen Islam*. Berlin: Klaus Schwarz.

Chyet, Michael L. (1991) 'A version of the Kurdish romance *Mem û Zîn* with English translation and commentary', in R. E. Emerick and D. Weber (eds) *Corolla Iranica: Papers in honour of Prof. Dr. David Neil MacKenzie*. Frankfurt a. Main: Peter Lang, pp. 27–48.

Chyet, Michael L. (1994) 'Is Mem a hero? An analytical consideration of oral versions of "Mem û Zîn"', *Acta Kurdica* 1: 155–176.

Durre, Abdurrahman (2002) *Şerha Dîwana Ehmedê Xanî: Felsefe û Jiyana Wî*. Istanbul: Avesta Yayınları.

Hassanpour, Amir (1992) *Nationalism and Language in Kurdistan, 1918-1985*. San Francisco: Mellen Research University Press.

Hinnebush, Robert (1982) 'The Islamic movement in Syria', in A. Dessouki (ed.) *Islamic resurgence in the Arab World*. New York: Praeger, pp. 138–169.

Lescots, Roger (1942) 'Introduction', in R. Lescots (ed.) *Textes Kurdes*, vol. 2. Beirut: Memé Alan, pp. iii–xxv.

Lobmeyer, H. G. (1995) *Opposition und Widerstand in Syrien*. Hamburg: Deutsches Orientinstitut.

Rasul, Izzudin Mustafa (1979) *Ahmad al-Khani*. Baghdad: n.l.

Reissner, Johannes (1980) *Ideologie und Politik der Muslimbrüder Syriens*. Freiburg a.Br.: Schwarz.

Rudenko, Margarita Borisovna (1962) *Ahmadî Khani, Mem û Zîn*, Pamiatniki literatury Narodov Vostoka; Teksty, Malaia Seriia. Moskau: Isdatelstvo Bostojnoy Literaturui.

Seale, Patrick (1986) *The Struggle for Syria: A Study of Post-war Arab Politics 1945–1958*. London: I.B.Tauris.

Shakely, Ferhad (1992) *Kurdish Nationalism in Mamu Zin of Ahmad-i Khani*. Brussels: Kurdish Institute of Brussels.

Stenberg, Leif (1999) 'Naqshbandiyya in Damascus: strategies to establish and strengthen the order in a changing society', in E. Özdalga (ed.) *Naqshbandis in Western and Central Asia. Change and Continuity*. London: Curzon Press, pp. 101–116.

Vanly, Ismet Chériff (1992) 'The Kurds in Syria and Lebanon', in Ph. G. Kreyenbroeck and St. Sperl (eds) *The Kurds. A contemporary overview*. London: Routledge, pp. 143–170.

Between home and home

Conceptions of Sufi heritage in Bosnia-Herzegovina and in Swedish Bosniak diaspora

Catharina Raudvere

As an effect of the war in the Balkans in 1992–1995, large groups of refugees with a Muslim background from the former Yugoslavia settled, more or less permanently, in Scandinavia.[1] Scarcely homogeneous, on closer inspection these Muslim communities reveal a lot about the conditions of Muslim life in Scandinavia and the setting for transnational lives in contemporary Europe. Muslims from the former Yugoslavia are difficult, if not impossible, to identify as a coherent group. A long secular tradition, state interventions in religious matters and debates about national identities add to the complexity. As migration statistics in Scandinavia do not record religious affiliation, no exact numbers can be given, and it must be noted from the beginning that only a minority of Muslims from the former Yugoslavia are members of or active in a Muslim congregation. The present chapter will take its departure in a case from Sweden. About 50,000 Bosnian Muslims (Bosniaks)[2] live permanently in Sweden, of whom 8,000 are paying members of a Bosnian Muslim congregation[3] – an unknown number are members of or associated with other Muslim communities. The majority of individuals from Bosnia-Herzegovina with a Muslim background are, however, not members of any Bosniak association with a religious orientation.

The cultural and national networks among the Swedish Bosnians should, though, not be underestimated in their capacity to mobilise, and from an everyday perspective they are impossible to distinguish from many Muslim activities. This blend of cultural, political and religious diasporic[4] activities has also made many turn away from associations, clubs and congregations. Bosniak community building in Sweden, in other words, has turned out to be a double-sided coin: the local groups may very well function as mobilising magnets but also as a reason to reject fellowship based on an identity that mixes nationality and religion. Regardless of religious or regional background, and regardless of personal choices made in diaspora, issues of nationality and identity are themes very much present in the lives of individuals with a personal link to the former Yugoslavia. The suppression of religion during the communist era, the nowadays so controversial mixed marriages (which is still the family background for many individuals) and memories of the recent war give identity and belonging inevitable bonds to religion, but not necessarily to religiosity.

Diasporic lives between home and home

The present study is based on dual fieldwork with two dimensions: the empirical materials have been collected in a Bosniak community in the Swedish diaspora and at places in Bosnia-Herzegovina important to these informants' ways of practising Islam with an apparent Sufi orientation.[5] The result of fieldwork has been analysed from the perspective of religion in transnational communities and in the light of religion as a signifier of national identity (Rudolph and Piscatori 1997). The project began with fieldwork among a group of Bosniaks who have established and developed a Muslim congregation in Sweden's third city, Malmö, in the very south of the country (Raudvere and Gaši forthcoming). The vast majority of its members came to Sweden as refugees during and after the war in the Balkans in 1992–1995. Rather than building on existing diaspora structures and networks new administrative bodies were established, often with the help of Swedish migration authorities and aid organisations. Life at the refugee stations became formative for the future religious and national activities. The present-day Bosniak congregation in Malmö is administratively linked to both Swedish and Bosnian authorities, though these links are very different in character. The Swedish Commission for State Grants to Religious Communities gives economic support through one of the three major national Sunni Muslim organisations in Sweden. This subsidy is, however, small in comparison to the support the Malmö congregation has received from the local municipality. Over the years Malmö City, through its NGO office, has enabled the employment of assistants at the congregation and has taken a very active part in providing premises and supporting cultural and sporting associations with close ties to the congregation. Through the national body of Bosniak congregations in Sweden, the Malmö branch is related to the national Bosnian administration for Islamic affairs in Sarajevo. The formal head of the united Swedish congregations is the Islamic Community of Bosnia-Herzegovina (Islamska zajednica u Bosni i Hercegovini) via its office for congregations abroad in Sarajevo (Ured za bošnjačku dijasporu); this body does not, however, provide any kind of financial support. Its main gate of influence, beside personal contacts with individual imams, are printed materials published by the Islamic Community bought by the diasporic communities and used for religious instruction. There is also the bi-weekly paper *Preporod*, which dominates in more conservative Muslim circles, distributed from Sarajevo to the congregations abroad. *Preporod* is comparatively popular and edifying, and must be considered to be the voice of official Islam in Bosnia-Herzegovina along with the bimonthly journal *Glasnik*. The position of these two publications is mainstream in relation to radical Islam and nationalistic in terms of Bosnian politics. If the Swedish support is mainly economic, the support from Sarajevo is characterised by an informant as theological and national. *Preporod* has no significant theological approach to Sufism. In relation to Sufi-oriented activities, however, the national gatherings at sacred places, *dovišta*, arranged by the

Islamic Community, do take a certain place in the paper. In particular, the gatherings at Ajvatovica every June with the vigils, zikr and votive prayers among the 5,000 participants are presented and reported on as a significant event of particularly Bosniak religious sentiments.

The diaspora congregations are by definition transnational and from an applied perspective they function as membranes for transactions of various kinds: economic, theological, mobilising. Hereby they also constitute means of control (far from always explicitly discussed or consciously executed as such): the Swedish authorities in terms of which Muslim activities are supported and the Bosnian in terms of keeping up a national understanding of what Islam is (Ignatieff 1993). Among the Bosniaks who settled in the diaspora as adults, the conceptions of home, homeland and belonging have evidently changed over time. In time, Sweden has become home as much as Bosnia-Herzegovina, and for the generations brought up in Sweden this is home, embedded in the narrations of what used to be Yugoslav Bosnia and own experiences of transnational travel. Resourceful community building in the 1990s included the establishment of bonds between places of worship. It certainly involved an element of nostalgia in the way it tied conceptions of nation and religion. The prayer locations in Sweden that at first appeared as pale copies of the abandoned places at home acquired in the cause of time a status of home also in terms of piety and with qualities of its own. Jonathan M. Schwartz writes in his book on exile how this position in between is not only a question of loss and lack:

> Homesickness, moreover, is not only looking backwards. It is essentially the searching for a home … homesickness inspired cultural defence and identity, not merely a return to receding past … The search for one's past – Proust's *recherche* – has been confused in translation with *remembrance*. It ought to be possible to distinguish the homesick searching from the nostalgic yearning. (1989: 13f.)

A crucial challenge for the congregation after 15 years of activities in Sweden is to appear not as gatekeepers, but to balance the provision of what its members conceive as stable identities and a ground for personal and collective development. In this respect are Sufi related rituals and Sufi oriented groups among several options to choose from when manifesting belonging.

Sufism as memory, cohesion and possible contact zone

In this chapter various conceptions of and attitudes towards Sufism are analysed as a core element in the understanding of national identity because many (but far from all) Bosnian Muslims conceive of Sufi traditions as the hallmark of a particular Bosnian Islam – even if they never or rarely practise them. The notion of a specific Bosnian Islam appears in many guises. It can serve as the argument that the Bosnian way of practising Islam is European, and it can connect Bosnian Islam to an Ottoman past and a golden age of cultural and spiritual splendour; it can be a stand against present-day Islamic radicalism as well as a front against the secular life-styles and materialism of post-war Bosnia and in diaspora.

The materials from this case study are on the one hand imprints from unique experiences and on the other an indication of processes and events in contemporary times. The individuals in the study are themselves witnesses to decisive political shifts in the history of twentieth-century Europe: the Balkans during the world wars, life behind the iron curtain, and the recent war in the 1990s and the experience of being refugees in Europe after this war and under the impact of economic liberalism. Yet this is a study of everyday diasporic life between home and home in adjustment to new circumstances. Whether these changes are to be regarded as obstacles or opportunities differs hugely between individuals and families. In this context, however, it should not be underestimated that the changes have an impact on religious life as practised too.

Globalisation, migration and transnationality are fundamental conditions for the group, and in the wider study questions are raised about how collectives and individuals at local level relate their religious lives to the huge changes sweeping over the world. It goes without saying that this topic is inseparable from major academic themes like Islam in Europe, globalisation and transnationalism, migration and minority/majority relations. However, these issues are not only at the top of the academic agenda for theoretical reasons, but to an equal extent they constitute the very environment in which the two fields of study are situated. The theoretical discussions are necessary after more than a century of world migration, and the actual living conditions of millions of people affected by these processes in their everyday lives are symptoms of a Zeitgeist that affects us all in a globalised world.

Despite the transnational aspects it is important to underline the two locations of fieldwork as separate in terms of living conditions and the place of religion in public discourse. Still they are tied together by formal or informal links, and are particularly connected in people's memories of the past, dreams of what could have been and their visions for the future. Travelling to and fro is extensive; it is convenient, fast and inexpensive – a huge contrast to refugee life only 30 years ago. Today transnational living conditions rather define the refugees. In obvious ways translocality connects places, but it also makes the different realities of homeland stand out more clearly. The dreams of homeland, origin and authenticity are contested by the ways in which religious practice, life styles and values change at both places. Peter Mandaville points at three themes in diasporic Islam when concluding the fission and fusion in Muslim translocality:

> debates within the Muslim community reveal the nature of the Muslim other; politics, community and gender provide useful indications of some of the ways in which Muslims are rethinking Islam; and … Muslim transnationalism reminds us that these translocal diasporic reformulations can never be viewed in isolation from the rest of the world. (2001: 150)

Travelling might still be an issue of localities, but innovative border zones are appearing where received and transmitted ideas merge into novel constellations of thoughts and ritual practices; processes for which the diasporic Sufi groups are lucid examples. The sources for the present analysis are therefore not theological treatises or official records on the normative aspects of Sufism, but rather semi-formal interviews and field observations, at two locations, some Bosniaks with Sufi affiliations call home.

Sufism in Bosnia-Herzegovina today: a web of popular rituals and an element in identity constructions

Surveys of Islam and Muslim life in the Balkans in general and in Bosnia-Herzegovina in particular regularly stress the impact of Sufism on Bosnian Islam. And rightly so. In the earliest phases of the introduction of Islam in the Balkans the Sufi orders were apparently an effective tool for the mission (Algar 1971; Norris 1993; Malcom 1994; Heywood 1996; Poulton and Taji-Farouki 1997). With their devotional and expressive rituals and the steadfast organisational form, the *tarikat*s provided fellowships and networks that still have an influence over Muslim life in private and in public. During the long Ottoman era, Sufism in its various aspects coloured local piety and the practice of everyday Islam at all levels of society. In rural areas, in small towns and in the districts of the cities, *tarikat*s like the Nakšibendi, Kaderi, Melami, Rufai and Mevlevi with their many sub-branches constituted not only ritual fellowships, but also the bases of political alliances, business relations and the social web for marriages and friendships – and discord (Bringa 1995; Norris 2006).

The historical background is not to be underestimated; it is still visible today in such varied fields as Sufi-oriented theology in present-day debate, the *tarikat* communities as agents within the larger Muslim community and remaining traditional architecture (*tekije*, *turbe*, *zavije*) in rural and urban landscapes – and, perhaps the most important aspect from a transnational perspective, the transmission of legendary history. However, the perspective in this article is mainly on how (the Ottoman) Sufi heritage is conceived today in the construction of national identity and in conceptions of a particular Bosnian Islam.

Sufism is one prism of several in the debates and struggles over what Bosnian Muslim identity is. Therefore, contemporary Sufism in Bosnia-Herzegovina is also influenced by the critical voices of its sometimes strong opponents; it is a complex web of traditionalism and convention, in combination with transnational impulses in terms of theology, mobilisation and entrepreneurship. The revivalism that has been part of Bosniak Muslim life since the early 1980s is even more accentuated in the very apparent struggle over who has the legitimacy to define this 'return' to Islam in Bosnia-Herzegovina after the war: the radicals with their strong purist views on what is conceived as folk religion and Sufi rituals as divergent from authentic Islam, or the defenders of Bosnian Islam referring to tradition and homeland where Sufi heritage to some of the debaters plays a role (Sorabji 1994; Bringa 2002). The revival runs parallel with a transformation in terms of new international groups and orders appearing on the scene competing over followers with the traditional groups. These newcomers are not necessarily in tune with or at all interested in the more national definitions of Sufism or Islam. At their agendas more internationally oriented issues are at stake or a more universalist spiritual approach.

Eight features of importance can be brought forward when drawing the background of the status and situation of Sufism in Bosnia-Herzegovina, not mentioning the historical Ottoman background sketched above.

Bosnia-Herzegovina, like most European countries, has undergone over a century of urbanisation. The very different living conditions in rural and urban areas have a complex social history of their own, but this stratification has certainly had implications for religious life too. The dominating discourse on modernity was, if not anti-religious, at least determined to implement secularism by limiting the influence of the traditional religious institutions. From a Balkan perspective, Sufism, especially its rituals and institutions, was associated with rural life, uneducated *hoca*s and *šejh*s with great authority over people in their vicinity and lack of opportunities for individual choice in religious matters. The contrast was the secular and educated city dweller who did not engage in Sufi networks and who was not likely to practise religion, but if so would do it in private. These stereotypes of traditional religion were shared by most European secularisation and modernisation projects, and were cultivated further in communist Yugoslavia.

A major challenge for present-day Sufi groups is how to contest this dichotomous image of Sufism as the contrast to successful city life when arguing for their theology and ritual life as something in accordance with contemporary life. Apparently some groups are more successful in this than others; and it is not necessarily the old structures that prevail.

The second feature is the shadow of the communist era that still lingers over the Sufi orders and in memories of life behind the iron curtain. Narratives of *tekije* being closed, problems with authorities and lack of possibilities for proper Islamic education are living parts of local legendary history. Belgrade's hostile view of religion in general and Islam in particular deeply affected the Sufi orders and their public appearance, and Sufi ritual life was for long periods mostly performed in private. The Yugoslav politics of religion under Tito could perhaps best be compared to Turkish authoritarianism during the same period – although from a completely different ideological standpoint. The repression was not modelled on Soviet state atheism; it was rather a slow stifling, based on the conviction that modernisation with its mass-education programmes would by necessity be the end of religion. Public religious activities and membership in the communist party were not only socially impossible, but to most people a major contradiction. To a younger generation these conditions are merely hearsay, yet collective memory of these harsh times still has its impact on identity formation in the Balkans as a whole, in Christian and Muslim communities alike. The background in authoritarian secularisation projects is an experience shared – along with the Ottoman background – with the many Turkish Muslim groups, so active in their operations in Bosnia-Herzegovina today. It is also a key to the understanding of how the present-day Muslim groups work vis-à-vis the state, what they expect from authorities and how difference within the Muslim population is conceived (by fellow Muslims and by non-Muslims).

Thirdly, the relationship between the local Sufi fellowships (*tarikat* organised or not) and the official commissions for religious (i.e. Islamic) affairs has for decades been deeply complicated.[6] The attitude of the Islamic Community (ICBH) towards the Bosnian Sufi heritage at large has changed over the last decades, which is very apparent in its relationship to the Sufi orders as important institutions in relation to everyday religious life. There are bitter memories of the dark period during the communist era when the Sufi orders were never formally forbidden by law,[7] but the *tekije* were closed in practice between 1952 and 1977 after a decision made by the Islamic Community. The close links between this directorate of religious affairs and the governments in power are not forgotten and are constantly hinted at even today.

The status of the *tarikat*s today is ambiguous, linked as they are to the introduction of Islam in the Balkan area, and thereby also to the Ottoman Empire and its division of religious groups, *millet*, in a functional multi-religious society. Other factors complicate the relationship to ICBH still further. The global networks of which the Sufi orders are a part make them more independent and turn them into bodies of uncontrolled theological influences from abroad.

The fourth factor to be brought up is the war of 1992–1995. This is not the place to comment on all the damage and trauma caused, that is analysed elsewhere (Sells 1996; Rogel 2004). The war, however, lingers on in the discussion on the importance of marking religious belonging and identity in words and action, in the relationship between people of different religious affiliation and in the popular understanding of citizenship (Poulton 1994; Kepel 2003: 237ff.). The war has apparently made more people ready to signal overtly their religious identity, but has not necessarily made them more religious. More than ten years after the war ended there are comments in private about religion having shown its old role in the midst of the political game. Artistic genres deeply embedded in Sufi traditions have proven to be useful tools when expressing experience from the war and transmitting collective memory. Hymns and narratives with the stories of saints and miracles as their paradigm are transposed to tell of martyrs, heroes and events during the war. Public events with choirs and solo-singers gather substantial crowds, and are later distributed on CDs and DVDs.

Furthermore, Sufism in Bosnia today is affected by the general tendencies of radicalisation and Arabisation (Kepel 2003: 237ff.; Roy 2004: 58ff.). These trends and lifestyle programmes are clearly visible in street life and in the architectural design of the many new mosques erected after the war all over Bosnia-Herzegovina, sponsored by Arabic aid and the sites of intense mission. The clashes between the defenders of radical Islam and people who oppose this trend have even been violent. Some mosques belonging to the Islamic Community are closed outside prayer hours in order not to serve as platforms for the radicals. The radicals on the other hand have interrupted *zikr* and *mevlud* gatherings on the grounds of regarding them as improper folk religion and as a source of superstition. A general influence from the Arab-speaking world, though, began long before the war. Due to lack of opportunities for proper academic training in Islamic theology up until the 1980s,[8] many young men went abroad to receive degrees from Islamic educational institutions, primarily in Saudi Arabia and Malaysia. It is too simplistic merely to state that they all came back with radical and scriptualistic views of Islam. They re-connected Bosnian Islam at different levels to the larger Muslim world, where links to abroad in the 1950s and 1960s had been mainly Turkish. The returnees brought with them not only a world of Muslim learning to be accessed at local level, but also connections to international networks. It is partly on this web of contacts that the substantial global and transnational links of today can be built. These connections were to some extent also an inspiration for liberal and Sufi-oriented circles. It was an update on contemporary Muslim debate and had a reviving impact on local religious life not experienced before in communist Yugoslavia. For the *tarikat* oriented Sufis it meant regular contacts with *šeyh*s abroad and definitively strengthened links to Turkish orders and *cemaat*s.

The transnational contacts cannot be regarded as radicalisation as such, though they are part of an apparent tendency to underline religion as a prime identity and the foremost facet of nationhood and search for roots and authenticity that engages many Bosniaks. The revivalism has two sides that are not always experienced as contradictory: the national belonging and the worldwide *umma*. The aim of the radical missionaries from abroad is to raise awareness of Islam and authentic Muslim traditions. They are indeed successful in their invitation to fellowship on the purist path. The call for awareness, however, also leads people to take different positions, i.e. in defence of what they conceive as Bosnian Islam and in rejection of any foreign attempt to purify it.

A sixth aspect is the role and the status of the *tarikat*s as pious organisations providing space, in all senses, for ritual and devotional procedures. Since the introduction of Islam in the Balkans, the traditional orders have been the foremost way of organising Sufi life. They are traditional in the sense that, by means of legendary history, they claim long genealogies of *šejh*s and connection to specific sacred places (particular historical *tekije* and *turbe*s of holy persons) as the basis for their spiritual authority. The fellowships within the orders are strong and despite all dramatic changes some of them have kept both authority and the capacity to attract. The majority of the followers of the old established *tarikat*s, however, participate as part of a family tradition.

One core agent has already been mentioned, the Islamic Community, which played an important role in defining Sufism out of the public arena in Tito's Yugoslavia. This directorate still exists and has maintained a complex relationship to the government and the state, and in relation to the *tarikat*s. In either way of contact, the Islamic Community represents both. The early 1970s saw an abatement in the suppression of religion and attempts were made to organise an association for *šeyh*s and later a Sufi society. These efforts led to the establishment of the Tarikat Centre (Tarikatski centar) in 1977. After a complicated process this centre is now in association with the Islamic Community. The Tarikat Centre functions as a tool for recognition of Sufi groups and by necessity also as a tool for control. It is therefore not an exaggeration to claim that it constitutes a conservative and restraining force. Only formal *tarikat*s are members.

Today it is primarily the Nakšibendi branches that dominate *tarikat*-organised Sufi gatherings, but the Kaderi should also be mentioned. Among both the Nakšibendis and the Kaderis one traditional aspect of organisation and authority remains, and that is the role certain families still have in some *tarikat* branches and the fastidious influence they seemingly exert with reference to the genealogy they represent. A special characteristic of the *tarikat*s in Bosnia-Herzegovina today is the close link between the traditional orders, limited of space as they were under communism. Sharing rituals and visiting each other's *tekije* is not uncommon, and *šejh*s within different orders are initiated to lead *zikr* among other brotherhoods. This ritual ecumenism is very much apparent and flourishes in diaspora too. The oppression during the communist era, with closed *tekije* and no support from the Islamic community, drew them closer to each other. The repression also forced a privatisation of Sufi rituals. To a great extent homes, and to a lesser extent semi-public spaces, became the location for *zikr*, *mevlud* and *tevhid*. The importance of the private sphere gave women a prominent position as keepers of tradition and as those who carried the social responsibilities for the gatherings. As long as men participated no woman could take the ritual leadership. But Sufi gatherings tended to be mono-gendered events before the Muslim revival and opened up space for women as ritual leaders. Female agency is still at hand in informal Sufi-oriented gatherings, but only to a limited extent within the *tarikat* structures where women either participate from a balcony or at special *zikr* and *mevlud* rituals for women only.

The penultimate factor to be mentioned has a steadily increasing impact on Sufi life in Bosnia-Herzegovina, and the long-term consequences of this development are still to be seen. The traditional *tarikat*s are challenged by more recently established Sufi groups which have made their way into Bosnia-Herzegovina since well before the fall of communism. Even in the early days of Islamic revivalism in the 1980s the new *tarikat*s played an important mobilising role. As newcomers on the religious scene they were neither contaminated by contacts with the communist administration nor regarded as conservative traditionalists. These Sufi groups from abroad have attracted a new generation of followers who are not content with the *zikr* gatherings at home and above all represent a younger generation. Two new Sufi groups with special influence must be mentioned here: the Halidi *tarikat* with its traditional *tekije* activities and offers of spiritual guidance and the Fethullah Gülen groups whose activities in Bosnia-Herzegovina are mainly centred around large-scale educational projects. Both groups have a Turkish background and work with Turkish-based funding. These two groups have also established meeting places and activities in the vicinity of the Bosniak mosque in Malmö. So far there is no real competition, rather a mutual expectant interest.

The last feature with any impact on the status and situation of Sufi-oriented piety in Bosnia-Herzegovina has partly been touched upon already, that is the growing importance of private and semi-private spaces when it comes to how Sufism is practised for the majority who are not members of or in alliance with any *tarikat*. Private homes as the location for zikr and other Sufi rituals have their background in the authoritarian repression, but have turned out to be attractive spaces in post-communist Bosnia-Herzegovina where public religion to such a large extent is involved in conflicts over national identity, radicalism and modernity. In local Muslim discourse *tesavvuf* is not a frequently used term, especially not when compared to the use of precise names for rituals and prayer forms. It is only a limited group of Muslim leaders and imams that can be directly connected to any *tarikat* and their formalised ritual activities. Other imams are known to be either Sufi oriented or in favour of the ritual practices associated with what is conceived as 'traditional Bosnian Islam' (*zikr*, *mevlud*, *dovište* and more small scale visits to *turbe*s), but they do not necessarily give these ceremonies a *tesavvuf* context in a theological sense. Yet another dimension of the spatial aspects of contemporary Sufism is to be added to the picture. The popular independent *šejh*s in urban areas, especially Sarajevo, that operate without claims of links to shrines or genealogies. These are charismatic religious leaders (often imams, but not always) who establish informal groups around them for teaching and (more or less) intense prayers. The explicit references to Sufism are not always there, sometimes even denied when asked about. Though followers refer to these men as *šejh*s, Sufis or spiritual masters when they talk about the intense prayers offered and the *sohbet*s on spiritual development. The reasons for avoiding the explicit *tesavvuf* references are a combination of not wanting to appear as competitors to the orders and wanting to keep their independence as religious teachers outside any theological hierarchy. This freedom provides opportunities to develop another mode of spiritual discourse. The crowds showing up at mosques or meeting halls are apparently familiar with global discourses of spirituality ('New Age') and mirror this in local Muslim traditions. Several of these independent preachers have been on invited tours in Scandinavia arranged by active members of the Bosniak communities.

These eight features with influence in Bosnia-Herzegovina also affect the diasporic Bosniak community in Malmö in the way its members embrace or reject Sufism and as an element in their understanding of what Bosnian Islam can be.

Usually it is the radical influences that are emphasised in the discussions of contemporary Islam in Bosnia-Herzegovina, especially the Arabisation and the purist trends. From the perspective of Sufi activities, however, the Turkish impact cannot be underestimated. Not that the Turkish groups are all liberal in relation to the radicals, but their approach more conventionally matches the nationalist project when they legitimise their presence with reference to the Ottoman past and shared cultural conditions. The Turkish interest comes in many forms and with varied objectives, some of them deeply embedded in the life of the *tarikat*s.

As the examples from the Swedish Bosniak diaspora will show, the organisational framework is of importance to Sufi activities, but more than anything else ritual expressions seem to be the foremost attraction when individuals in late modernity choose their religious lives.

Diasporic Bosniak Sufism in Sweden

The Bosniak congregation in Malmö was established in the late 1990s and had its beginning in the many religious and cultural activities organised in the refugee stations by the refugees themselves.[9] The Muslim work migrants from the Yugoslavian federation who arrived in the area in the 1960s did not organise themselves in religious communities (which would have complicated their relationships with the Yugoslav authorities). A few Yugoslavs with a Muslim background were active in Turkish or pan-Islamic congregations. The rest were either secular or practised their religion in domestic spaces.

When arriving in Sweden the Bosniak refugees had, in contrast to some other Muslim groups, less problems in facing a secular society or multi-religious environments with secular organisations and people with other – or no – religious faiths. Rather, it was the Sufi traits in daily practises that caused some controversies in the contacts with other Muslim groups. The devotional rituals and choirs with young women singing *ilahije* in front of a mixed-gender congregation could appear strange and even shocking.

The road towards possible religious Swedish Bosniak identities though turned out to be bumpy in more ways than one, and not only in the contacts with other Muslims. In relation to the Swedish majority society the Bosniaks had a double stigma as East Europeans and as Muslims (each simplistic category loaded with its own prejudices); in relation to many other Muslims – together with whom the Bosniaks were defined in a lump as 'Muslims' – they lacked the tacit knowledge of Middle Eastern everyday life and proudly kept their own customs. Coming in such numbers over such a comparatively short time the Swedish Bosniak congregations and the associations close to them grew strong, especially as many of them were politically connected with the nationalistic SDA (Democratic Action Party). At the time the party was led by Alija Izetbegović (d.2003), the front figure of the Islamic revival in the 1980s and, to the Bosniaks, the symbol of Bosnia-Herzegovina as an independent state. In the hectic activities during the first years in Sweden political and religious motifs were hard to separate. Influential individuals appeared in several associations. The religious awakening noticeable a decade before the war was brought along in diaspora and its national angle was furthermore underlined. The symbols, narratives and imagery of religion were used as tools in the work for national vocation that was already taking place at the refugee stations. The same community leaders argued for national and Islamic causes. In the wake of the war religious identity became the foremost instrument for many when new identities in diaspora were constructed (Eastmond 1998). It was a trying situation with few conventional roles to fall back on: pious identity, religious leadership and authority were up for (re)construction. Unity, authenticity and survival became the key mobilising concepts of the time. On the other hand, many Bosnians with a Muslim background rejected this combination of strong religious feelings and national sentiments, and disapproved of the category 'Bosniak'. To others the emphasis on cultural heritage and the performance of hymns, legends and rituals were recognised as precious bequests transmitted over time, and now lately over space. It was a legacy identified with something different from non-European Islam and politicised 'Islamist' interpretations: Bosnian Islam was a means of living an authentic Bosnian life. Sufi traditions were parts of this significant form of Islam, though the term *tesavvuf* was hardly ever used. Traditional tunes were rephrased into new texts with direct allusions to the national cause and martyrdom during the war, the narrative framework of legends were used when recounting memories from the war and most importantly the performance of these stories and songs was set in a devotional context with prayers and repetitive choruses from the *ilahije* tradition (Raudvere and Gaši forthcoming). The arenas for this rethinking, in Mandaville's words, were not the conventional mosque activities and formal *idžtihad*, but in cultural associations, voluntary work for Bosnian school classes, music performances and internal aid work. An apparent gender and generation shift was at hand. Other agents of interpretation than imams, *hoca*s and *šeyh*s were voices of Bosniak identity: teachers at the Bosnian schools at the refugee stations (both men and women), leaders of leisure time activities for children and youth, musicians who lead song and folk dance activities.

If the traditional *tarikat*s in Bosnia-Herzegovina are only minor agents on the religious scene as a whole today, their role in diaspora is even less noticeable. According to the Malmö informants there were among the refugees (and to some small extent among the earlier work migrants) a couple of *vekil*s and other respected men, recognised as *šeyh*s by their followers, who led *zikr* at the refugee stations and in the first homes in Sweden. Most of these Sufi leaders have either passed away or returned to Bosnia-Herzegovina. Presently no formal Bosniak *šeyh* resides in Sweden. It is not the institutional aspects of Sufi heritage that attract diaspora. Ritual life is characterised by the hybridity also noticeable in Bosnia-Herzegovina – a consequence, as discussed above, of the suppression during the communist era. Hybridity, though, suits diaspora not only as an aspect of lack of ritual leadership and theological authorities; it opens up for the re-thinking of new agents.

To the extent that there are *tarikat* activities in the Swedish diaspora, they are to a great extent connected to more recently established (or revived) branches of orders – none of which can be distinguished as distinctively Bosniak. What makes them relevant to present study is their capacity to attract young Bosniak followers and their apparent transnational character (Werbner 2003). Recently, meeting-places of a Halidi branch of the Nakšibendi *tarikat* and of a Fethullah Gülen group were established in the vicinity of the Bosniak congregation's mosque in Malmö.

As in Bosnia-Herzegovina, the Swedish Gülen followers are mostly engaged in educational programmes though on a smaller scale, and in Scandinavian dialogue projects with non-Muslim counterparts too. The members of the Gülen group are not necessarily regarded in their local environment as Sufis or define themselves as dervishes for that matter – despite the organisation's obvious roots in the Nurcu movement and further back in Kurdish Nakšibendi branches. The Malmö group has attracted mostly young men of Turkish and Kurdish origin. To the Bosniak community the Gülen group has served as a counterpart to arrange various outwards-directed events. Although the Gülen *cemaat* must be considered a part of a global movement, its activities are to a large extent centred in the more immediate vicinity.

The Halidi group nowadays has a *tekije* of its own and is a much more ethnically mixed group, dominated by younger men. Swedish has therefore become an uncontroversial means of communication. Some Bosniak young men who do not attend the Sufi-oriented ceremonies at the Bosniak mosque a few blocks away, despising it as old fashioned or dreary, attend the silent *zikr* and *hatm-i hacegan* with enthusiasm. The Halidi group is, compared to the Gülen group, much more focused on ritual activities and spiritual training. *Zikr* is performed daily and the meeting place is open between the *namaz* hours. The spiritual training has a direct social aspect too. The young *vekil*, with a Lebanese background, is fluent in Swedish and well oriented in the local community. As he is of the same generation as many of the members of the group, he can take on a role as a brother who, in combination with his religious authority, is a guide in Swedish society.

In both cases the activities in Malmö are on a much smaller scale than those in nearby Copenhagen. The quick communications over the strait make bonding with a larger community convenient. Followers from southern Sweden can easily attend important events and listen to guest speakers from abroad. These two groupings are transnational in the sense that they set up meeting places for Muslims of diverse ethnical background. From a local perspective, this blend of possible new acquaintances is the point where the identification between nation and religion starts to break up. Not that the ethnic identity is forgotten or rejected, but insights in the variations of Islamic practice and different ways of understanding Muslim traditions induce the rethinking of Islam indicated by Peter Mandaville. As the group is ethnically mixed and Swedish is the mutual language, the stress falls on the first compound in the expression Swedish Bosniak identity.

However, the most important aspect of transnationalism is how the groups as a matter of course relate to groups worldwide, find their theological materials on the Internet, encounter mega-star Muslim preachers on satellite TV, and are part of chains distributing printed materials, CDs and DVDs. They move unimpeded between the computer and the TV at home, where choice and flow are the leading words, and the close environment of the *tekije*, where the formal Sufi hierarchies meet with Swedish social relaxed attitudes. New centres for spiritual attention are presented to the followers. It is not so much the tombs and mausoleums of the deceased masters, but the centre of a living guide and his staff. The Halidi group has its spiritual centre outside Urfa, in southern Turkey. Despite living in the era of globalisation, pilgrimage is difficult from both an economic perspective and in terms of taking heart to face the master. Digital media then compensate for the lack of personal encounters for a generation to which the distinction between virtual and social realities is fading.

Private and semi-private spaces as the location of Sufi-oriented ritual activities linger on from the days of communist oppression (Bringa 1995). It has also an apparent gender and generation aspect as it connects to the first factor of conditions for contemporary Bosnian Sufism: modernity, urbanisation and education. If young men can break away from the rituals performed at the congregation without loosening their ties to Bosnianess and if they have social space for seeking individual spirituality in line with the conception of modern individual religiosity – what are the options for young women in terms of Sufi practice (Metcalf 1996; Al-Ali 2002; Raudvere 2002, 2004)?

Teenage girls are active in the choir(s) of the Bosniak congregation and play a significant role at *mevlud* gatherings when their hymn singing alternates with the imam's performance of the *mevlud* text and the Qur'an recitation. They perform in formalised participation as part of holiday celebrations of concern to the congregation at large, where the young women's performances and arrangement of traditional music is now the customary way in which the Bosniak festivals are celebrated in Sweden. The breeding ground for this creativity is the weekly choral practices that provide freer social space for the young women and themes can be developed over time. The choral activities are creative and leave room for female initiative and artistic enterprise. The paraphrasing and reformulation of classical works brings the *ilahije* tradition alive as the results formulate a collective memory. The limit is the nationalistic religious traditionalism of the congregation. For adult women there is less ritual space within the mosque premises; elderly women only seem to attend the weekly *zikr* gatherings under the imam's guidance. Private homes remain the prime space for women's Sufi-oriented rituals.

* * *

The case from the Bosniak community in Malmö indicates the complexity of transnational Muslim life in Europe. On the one hand the ethnical bonds and the connection to homeland, memory and family are strong and constitute the foundations of individual identity. On the other hand the options for pious choices and strategies are many in late modern society. Small groups compete and traditional religious authority is not to be taken for granted. In many ways today's Sufi activities among the Bosniaks contest clear distinctions of inside and outside the formal congregations. The earlier so-firm grip of a combined national and Muslim identity is less obvious among younger people associated with the congregation. Gender and generation are apparently the parameters that set the limits for options and possibilities in the search for spiritual expressions of contemporary mode. Sufism does not appear to be conceived primarily as a theological stance, but as a means of expressing loyalty and belonging to a cultural legacy without contradicting one's identity as a Swedish Bosniak.

References

Al-Ali, Nadje (2002) 'Gender relations, transnational ties and rituals among Bosnian refugees', *Global Networks* 2: 249–262.

Algar, Hamid (1971) 'Some notes on the Naqshibandi Tariqat in Bosnia', *Die Welt des Islams*, NS 13: 168–203.

Bringa, Tone (1995) *Being Muslim the Bosnian Way* Princeton: Princeton University Press.

Bringa, Tone (2002) 'Islam and the quest for identity in post-communist Bosnia-Herzegovina', in Maya Shatzmiller (ed.) *Islam and Bosnia. Conflict Resolution and Foreign Policy in Multi-Ethnic States*. Montreal: McGill-Queen's University Press.

Eastmond, Marita (1998) 'Nationalist discourses and the construction of difference. Bosnian Muslim refugees in Sweden', *Journal of Refugee Studies* 11: 161–181.

Greenberg, Robert (2007) *Language and Identity in the Balkans. Serbo-Croat and its Disintegration*. Oxford: Oxford University Press.

Heywood, Colin (1996) 'Bosnia under Ottoman Rule, 1463–1800', in Mark Pinson (ed.) *The Muslims of Bosnia-Herzegovina. Their Historic Development from the Middle Ages to the Dissolution of Yugoslavia*. Cambridge, Mass: Harvard University Press.

Ignatieff, Laurence R. (1993) *Blood and Belonging. Journeys into the New Nationalisms*. London: BBC.

Kepel, Gilles (2003) *Jihad. The Trail of Political Islam*. London: I.B.Tauris.

Malcolm, Noel (1994) *Bosnia. A Short History*. London: Macmillan.

Mandaville, Peter (2001) *Transnational Muslim Politics. Reimagining the Umma*. London: Routledge.

Metcalf, Barbara (ed.) (1996) *Making Muslim Space in North America and Europe*. Berkeley: University of California Press.

Norris, Harry T. (1993) *Islam in the Balkans. Religion and Society between Europe and the Arab World*. London: Hurst.

Norris, Harry T. (2006) *Popular Sufism in Eastern Europe. Sufi Brotherhoods and the Dialogue with Christianity and 'Heterodoxy'*. London: Routledge.

Poulton, Hugh (1993) *The Balkans. Minorities and States in Conflict*. London: Minority Rights Publications.

Poulton, Hugh and Suha Taji-Farouki (eds) (1997) *Muslim Identity and the Balkan State*. London: Hurst.

Raudvere, Catharina (2002) *The Book and the Roses. Sufi Women, Visibility, and Zikir in Contemporary Istanbul*. Stockholm/London: Swedish Research Institute in Istanbul/ I.B.Tauris.

Raudvere, Catharina (2004) 'Where does globalization take place? Opportunities and limitations for female activists in Turkish Islamist Non-Governmental Organizations', in Birgit Schaebler and Leif Stenberg (eds) *Globalization and the Muslim World. Culture, Religion, and Modernity*. Syracuse: Syracuse University Press.

Raudvere, Catharina and Ašk Gaši (forthcoming) 'Between nations and Global Islam. Sufi activities and community building among Bosnian Muslims in southern Sweden', in Ron Geaves, Mark Dressler and Gritt Klinkhammer (eds) *Global Networking and Locality. Sufis in Western Societies*. London: Routledge.

Rogel, Carole (2004) *The Breakup of Yugoslavia and Its Aftermath*. Westport, Conn.: Greenwood Press.

Roy, Olivier (2004) *Globalized Islam. The Search for a New Ummah*. New York: Columbia University Press.

Rudolph, Susanne H. and James Piscatori (ed.) (1997) *Transnational Religion and Fading States*. Boulder, Colo.: Westview Press.

Schwartz, Jonathan M. (1989) *In Defence of Homesickness. Nine Essays on Identity and Locality*. Copenhagen: Akademisk Forlag.

Sells, Michael (1996) 'Religion, History, and Genocide in Bosnia-Herzegovina', in G. Scott Davis (ed.) *Religion and Justice in the War over Bosnia*. London: Routledge.

Sorabij, Cornelia (1994) 'Mixed motives. Islam, nationalism and *mevluds* in an unstable Yugoslavia', in Camillia Fawzi El-Sohl and Judy Mabro (eds) *Muslim Women's Choices. Religious Belief and Social Reality*. Oxford: Berg.

Werbner, Pnina (2003) *Pilgrims of Love. The Anthropology of a Global Sufi Cult*. London: Hurst.

Continuity and transformation in a Naqshbandi *tariqa* in Britain

The changing relationship between *mazar* (shrine) and *dar-al-ulum* (seminary) revisited

Ron Geaves

The majority of Muslims in Britain originate from South Asia where Sufism maintains a strong presence. It is argued that the Barelwi tradition originating in the organisational ability of Ahmad Reza Khan Barelwi (1856–1921) to defend and justify as normative the mediatory custom-laden South Asian Islam that is closely linked to the inspiration, leadership and intercession of Sufis, both living and deceased, was and remains the dominant group amongst British South Asian Muslims.[1] The efforts of Ahmad Reza Khan to establish a movement that could counteract the reformers of Deoband and those influenced by them such as the Muslim missionary movement, Tabligh-i Jamaat and the more hardline anti-Sufi Ahl-i Hadith, resulted to some degree in the institutionalisation of diverse Sufi movements and their allies.[2]

Although not all Sufis of the subcontinent were to affiliate or identify themselves as Barelwis, many of the dominant *tariqas* (Sufi orders) were to do so, especially those such as the Indian Naqshbandis and others who considered themselves to belong to the more moderate forms of Sufism that abided by the Hanafi *fiqh* (jurisprudence). Inevitably, the struggle to claim the mantle of being the normative form of Islam, the *Ahl-as Sunna wa-Jamaat*, or traditional Sunni Muslims, would lead many of the *pir*s (Sufi masters or spiritual leaders) into a political and religious conflict complicated by the various positions taken by these competing movements towards the struggle for Indian independence and the creation of Pakistan.

Not only did these movements relocate themselves in Britain with the mass migration of South Asians in the 1960s and 1970s, they also brought with them existing rivalries, strategies, leadership patterns, worldviews, beliefs and practices which were all replicated in British mosques throughout the second half of the twentieth century. Thus the *pirs* entering Britain amongst the economic migrants were not only charismatic leaders renowned for their piety and links to established *tariqas,* accepting *bai'at* (the formal vow of allegiance) from individuals in traditional Sufi manner, but also significant leaders of the Barelwi tradition keen to establish powerful centres in the new location and compete for the hearts and minds of British Muslims, challenging and fighting their old rivals, all now labelled under the pejorative label of Wahhabi. Consequently, such figures as Pir Wahhab Siddiqi in Coventry, Pir Marouf in Bradford and Sufi Abdullah in Birmingham were to become significant regional leaders with considerable skills in micro-politics. In addition to building mosques, representing the Muslim community in local council issues such as racism, education and housing, and the traditional role expected of a *pir* to lead a *tariqa*, both Pir Wahhab Siddiqi and Pir Marouf were to attempt to create national organisations of Barelwi *ulema* (Muslim clerics) to replicate the situation in Pakistan and India, respectively the *International Muslim Organisation* and the *Jamaat al-Sunnat*.

These various roles of the South Asian Sufis *pirs* in Britain were to complicate the traditional role of the charismatic Sufi *sheikh* based on spiritual authority. The British *pirs* were brought into the arena of community politics, competing claims of leadership, representation of their respective communities to the civic frameworks of British society, in addition to their spiritual leadership of the *tariqa*.[3] As leaders of Barelwi organisations they were faced with a different relationship to the *ulema* than that described by Pnina Werbner under the heading of 'ambivalences of authority, where she describes a conflict between the ulema's learning and religious expertise based on sacred text and knowledge of the law and the *pir*'s charismatic authority. As she summarises, 'the maulvi preaches, the *pir* blesses' (Werbner 2003: 257). This chapter will explore the complexities of Sufi charismatic authority in the British context in relation to traditional forms of South Asian Sufi organisation, beliefs and practices, focusing on the relationship between *mazar* (shrine) and *dar al-ulum* (seminary) in a Naqshbandi *tariqa*, the first to experience the loss of a first generation *pir* and the succession of his son, a British-born second-generation Muslim. In doing so it hopes to elucidate a number of issues around continuity, representation, tradition and authority in circumstances of rapid change and uncertainty.

The first-generation leadership

In July 1997, a significant event in the history of the South Asian Sufi presence in Britain took place in the city of Coventry in the East Midlands. Onlookers would have observed a procession of Muslims along the Stoneygate Road, slowly weaving its way towards Nuneaton over ten miles away. The procession consisted of a line of cars which stretched for five miles as it was escorted by police outriders on motorcycles. On the *urs* of their father who had died in 1994, the four sons of Pir Wahhab Siddiqi mentioned above had chosen to move his remains from where he was originally laid to rest in Coventry to a new location in Nuneaton.

The original resting place of their father had been unusual and controversial. As the most prominent leader of Coventry's Muslim communities, with a following that extended around the Pakistani diaspora worldwide, Coventry City Council had been open-minded enough to allow his body to be entombed in the front room of the small terraced house that had been the original house used as a mosque and place of teaching on Stoneygate Road, the area around which the South Asian migrants had first established themselves in the city in the 1960s and remain to this day. So the old mosque which was situated only several hundred yards away from the new purpose-built mosque in Eagle Street became the site of the first Sufi *mazar* in Britain, possibly in Western Europe and North America.[4]

But Pir Wahhab Siddiqi had always been controversial amongst the *pirs* and leaders of the Barelwi tradition who had arrived in Britain alongside the South Asian migrants. Disappointed by political developments in Pakistan which resulted in the division of the nation, he decided to leave Pakistan in 1972 and migrate to Britain. Unlike many of the migrants he did not come for economic reasons as the family were wealthy and well-established in Lahore. On arrival in Britain, he established himself in Coventry where he financed his religious activities and maintained his family through buying and selling property. His background was very different from the typical uneducated *pirs* of rural Pakistan. Pir Wahhab Siddiqi was a visionary, belonging to a branch of the Naqshbandi *tariqa* that prided itself on both the spiritual and intellectual achievements of its historic leaders.[5] In his vision of Sufism there were no 'ambivalences of authority' between mystic and scholar but rather he bemoaned the lack of scholarship in both *ulema* and *pir* and perceived such figures as al-Ghazali (d.1111) or Ahmad Sirhindi (d.1624) as role models for Sufi and ulema, combining experiential knowledge of God with intellectual study of Qur'an, Hadith and *fiqh*.

Primarily, Pir Wahhab Siddiqi was concerned that the new community in Britain should transcend old ethnic and religious divisions inherited from the subcontinent. He instinctively felt that these traditions would not be acknowledged by the young generation of British-born Muslims who were the future of the community. He also felt that the first-generation Muslim migrants were badly out of touch with their new situation in Britain. He was concerned with the quality of scholarship amongst the imams in the mosques, the lack of knowledge of English and, above all, the level of both secular and religious education in both generations of subcontinent Muslims. As a qualified *alim* (singular of ulema) he knew that very few of the subcontinent *pir*s had thoroughly studied Islam and achieved *alim* status. He also realised that the British mosques actively maintained the deep ethnic and religious divisions of the subcontinent. In all of these issues he pre-empted the concerns of both moderate Muslim leaders and government that were to emerge post 7/7.

In his time opportunities for radical partners beginning to forge new identities for British Muslims were few and far between and it is not surprising that after the Salman Rushdie protests at the end of the 1980s, he linked himself with the Muslim Parliament established by Kalim Siddiqi. The Parliament had many shortcomings, not least its support for Ayotollah Khomeini and his *fatwa* (a legal interpretation and pronouncement) on Rushdie, but at least it was an attempt by educated Muslims to bypass the mosques and establish a new leadership for the Muslim community from across the ethnic and religious divides. According to Sheikh Faiz Siddiqi, his eldest son and successor, his father also had personal reasons for his support of Kalim Siddiqi which involved honour and ties of friendship.[6]

However, it was increasingly the arena of education that absorbed the *pir*. He felt strongly that the next generation of imams should be the natural Muslim community leaders. In order to achieve this they should be equally educated in both professional and religious spheres. He foresaw that the success of Islam in Britain would involve Muslims becoming both materially successful and capable of promoting their faith in the midst of a secular and religiously pluralist society. His vision was a united Muslim community led by imams who also worked as lawyers, accountants, doctors and engineers. He felt that the mosques were the places to establish this new vision of Islam in Britain because of the influence which the imam can have through the *Juma'a qutba* (Friday sermon). He began by setting out to achieve his goals with his own four sons who would one day inherit his work. Pir Faiz ul-Aqtab Siddiqi claims that his father's vision arose from his desire that his children would not be pure clerics nor lose their faith to the secular life in Britain.[7] It is this clear focus on mosque leadership that places Pir Wahhab Siddiqi in the mainstream of Muslim community development and demonstrates the allegiance of Barelwi *pirs* with the ulema of their tradition. Unlike many of the second-generation Muslim leadership in Britain who have established organisations that are independent of mosque leadership, the *pir* knew instinctively that any major developments within the community would need to have the support of the mosques and that eventually the British-born generation would inherit the religious infrastructure established by their parents and grandparents.

Pir Wahhab Siddiqi succeeded with his own children. The eldest son attended London university, qualified as a barrister and then studied to be an *alim* at al-Azhar in Egypt where he was disappointed by the low standard of education. Two more sons qualified as solicitors and the fourth became a doctor. All four had also been educated by their father himself at his fledgling *dar-al-ulum* in Coventry. He then used his success with his own children to encourage Muslim parents to send their children to the school. The essence of the message was to combine the knowledge of *din* (religion) and *dunya* (world). This challenged the Dars-i Nizami training, for imams taught in the *dar al-ulums* of South Asia which either rejected secular subjects and taught only *manqulat*, the traditional religious curriculum (Deobandi approach), or maintained both religious and secular but focused on an outmoded curriculum consisting of *ma'qulat*, the rational sciences made up of Greek philosophy and Aristotlian logic (Barelwi approach). The *pir*'s vision was the replacement of the old-style traditional *ma'qulat*, abandoned by the Deobandis, with a modern secular curriculum that would prepare young *alim* for the role of leadership in a contemporary Western environment.

The final goal of Pir Wahhab Siddiqi was to establish the first Muslim university in Britain providing both secular and religious education. In the early

1990s, he purchased a large Victorian estate in Nuneaton to fulfil this dream. The site comprised of an old English country house set in 62 acres of park land. Unfortunately the *sheikh* was already ill and died in 1994 before seeing the completion of his vision.

The transferral of authority

The procession that took the body of their father from Coventry to Nuneaton was fraught with risk. Spiritually a deceased Sufi is regarded as more powerful than when physically alive. From the grave he intercedes on behalf of petitioners before Allah, acts as a conduit for miracles and is venerated by his generations of *murids* down through the ages until the final day of judgment. The tomb is usually the final resting place until that event. Even the smell of decay from the body could endanger cherished beliefs concerning the *pir*'s ability to resist the normal ravages of the body and his power to dominate even nature itself. This is to say nothing of the emotional toll on the close family who were experiencing a second funeral.

The death of the *pir* and the inheritance of the Hijazi Naqshbandi *tariqa* by his sons was important for the development of Sufism in Britain. For the first

The building that houses the tomb of Pir Wahhab Siddiqi. It is constructed to traditional South Asian architectural style and dimensions. The outer walls contain verses of the Qur'an and the inner walls are transcribed with the silsilah in addition to Qur'anic verses.

time a South Asian *tariqa* introduced into the country through migration was to move from first-generation leadership to second-generation British-born Muslims. The *tariqa* could now be described as a genuine British-based Naqshbandi Sufi organisation. Stephen Barton (1986: 102) had once written that the traditions of this kind of Islam could not be maintained in Britain because the focus would always be on shrines in the subcontinent. He considered that this would always hinder the development of an emergence from local ethnic identities to a uniquely British form of the tradition. Although this had to some extent been overcome by the arrival of resident British *pirs*,[8] no-one had foreseen the possibility of shrines duplicating the traditional focus around the *mazar* in a British context. The procession allowed Pir Wahhab Siddiqi to be placed in his final resting place until the Day of Judgement. The new shrine location at the college in Nuneaton is a purpose-built mausoleum similar to those found in South Asia and designed to traditional specifications.

In 2000 I wrote that the four sons of Pir Wahhab Siddiqi represent a *uberliefurung* (handing on or moving forward) in the development of the Muslim community in Britain.[9] The procession which moved the location of their father's *mazar* from Coventry to Nuneaton was symbolic in that it changed the actual location of sacredness from the mosque to the college. At that time I presented it diagrammatically in order to represent the physical and symbolic shift. The original and traditional structure in Coventry was as shown in diagram A. The relationship between mosque and supplementary school is identical to that found in most mosques of subcontinent origin throughout Britain. The unusual factor which makes this a unique Sufi mosque is the location of the *mazar* (shrine) adjacent to the mosque.

Diagram A

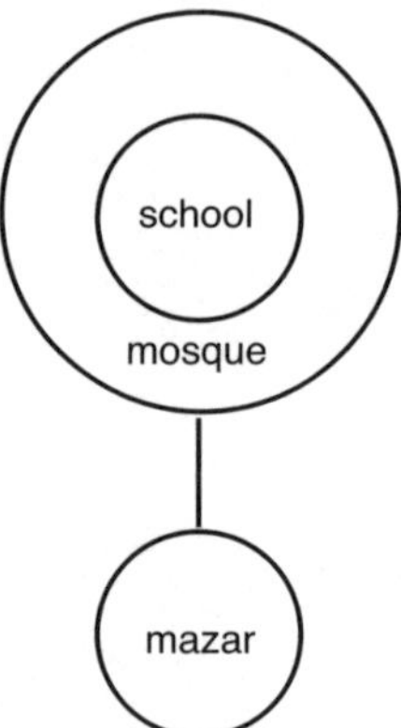

The presence of the *mazar* near to the mosque provided both physical and symbolic authority to the mosque and the community around it. Muslims from the area could attend prayers and then enter the *mazar* as supplicants without leaving their physical location. Thus religion, ethnic background and tradition were all located in one geographical space. The mosque was controlled by the committee who represented local Muslims of the first generation. The procession to the college changed the sacred geography from that represented in diagram A to the following in diagram B.

The college is no longer subsumed under the authority of the Coventry mosque but contains within its grounds both a mosque and the *mazar*. It thus becomes a complete environment of prayer and education, and the location of the shrine will create a new sacred space for pilgrims. The attraction of the college education will bring Muslims from all over the world to the new location and thus could transcend local ethnic communities.

Diagram B

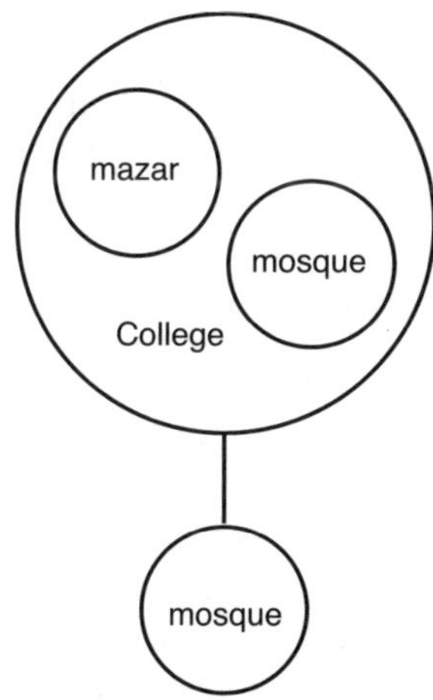

The leadership of the new sacred space is in the hands of the inheritors of the *tariqa* and not the old mosque committee. In diagram B, the Coventry mosque has become a satellite of the college. The college authorities will provide the imam and the guest speakers for occasions at the mosque. The local Muslims who live around the mosque will now have to make a pilgrimage to the college in order to make their supplications to the deceased *pir*. This will be particularly noticeable at the *urs* (religious gathering and celebration marking the day of death of a Sufi) which will take place every July in the college grounds.[10]

The mosque

The inheritance of a branch of the Naqshbandi *tariqa* by British-born second-generation Muslims provides a unique opportunity to explore the changing relationship between tradition and innovation as the Muslim community evolved in Britain. In this case, the college provides the opportunities for innovation whilst the mosque maintains the tradition. The new leaders of the *tariqa* are adept in both worlds. They are familiar with the demands of British life arising out of their experience of university and working in their professions, but they also have unique insight into the workings of the older generation Barelwis who still form the leadership of the mosque and its committee.

The mosque remains a centre of worship and community activities for the traditional Muslims of the *Ahl as-Sunnat wa Jamaat* belonging to the Hanafi school of law. The subcontinent Hanafis are some of the most conservative Muslims in the world and will consider any innovation with a great deal of suspicion. The mosque is also the centre of followers of a branch of the Naqshbandi *tariqa* and caters for their spiritual activities. In this respect tradition is followed carefully. As in other subcontinent mosques which have allegiance to a *tariqa*, the emphasis is on *dhikr* (remembrance of Allah's names). Pir Wahhab Siddiqi had permission from the four major subcontinent *silsilah*s (chains of authority) to perform *dhikr*, but the form combines both *dhikr-i khafi* (silent or quiet) which is traditional amongst Naqshbandis, and *dhikr-i jali* (loud) which is traditional to both Qadiris and Chishtis. There are also monthly *Giarvaan Sharifs* in which the great Sufis of the past, particularly Sheikh Abdul Qadir Jilani, are remembered through prayer, *dhikr* and sermons. Two *urs* are celebrated; one to the young sheikh's grandfather and now another to Pir Wahhab Siddiqi. *Milad-i Nabi* (birthday of Muhammad) is celebrated as an important part of the religious calendar and the tradition of a procession through Coventry is maintained. This is normal amongst urban concentrations of South Asian Barelwis and has been described by Pnina Werbner (1996) as 'stamping the feet of Allah' on Western soil. However, the processions also function to mark out a territory of influence to a particular *pir* in the context of Britain. This is not to say that each *pir* will not have *murids* (followers) or even mosques in other cities but the place of residence becomes a kind of fiefdom of influence. There are also celebrations in remembrance of Abu Bakr Siddiq and Hazrat Ali Talib, the original founders of all the Sufi *tariqa*s according to Muslim belief. However, surprisingly there is no *urs* to Ahmed Riza Khan Barelwi, the founder of the Barelwi movement which is traditionally maintained by his supporters in South Asia. The mosque is plain compared to some Barelwi mosques in Britain but displays the usual '*wa Allah*' and '*wa Muhammad*' on each side of the *minbar* (the niche that directs worshippers towards Makkah). In all ways this is a mosque that maintains the traditions of Barelwi forms of Sufism.

The college

It is here that the innovatory vision of their father can be carried out to fulfilment. The college is an interesting blend of tradition and adaptation. Young children who are taught at the school traditionally kiss the hand of the *pir* when he wanders the grounds or enters the buildings to teach. The *pir* is also the college founder and a practising barrister. Conversations with him are likely to lead to discussions on the future of Islam and religion in general in a postmodernist Britain. The school teaches the traditional *Dars al-Nizami* curriculum used since the late middle ages to train the *ulema* in the subcontinent, but this is combined with GCSE studies at both levels. A recent addition to the

The main college building which houses the student's classrooms, bedrooms and the offices of staff.

curriculum is the teaching of RE in accordance with the British national curriculum.[11] The children wear the traditional *juba* (white gown) and head covering during the day time but change to Western clothes if they wish in the evening. Both football and cricket matches take place with local state schools. The college provides a course which introduces the students to all the varieties of *aqida* (correct belief) within Islam and hopes one day to have sufficient scholarship to undertake *ijtihad* (independent reasoning). At present the school only has male students but the *pirs* are aware that the issue of female students will eventually have to be resolved.

Although already functioning as a school, the vision remains to create the first Islamic university in Britain providing both religious and secular education. The expansion plan which will turn the school into Hijaz College Islamic University has already begun but moves slowly. The new buildings combining teaching rooms, library facilities and accommodation blocks are now complete, but it is evident that there is much to be done before an Islamic university could be considered on the site. The challenge for the moment is to maintain one of the only two Barelwi *dar al-ulums* in the UK, ensuring that the students are able to take their place as the next generation of British-born and educated imams in their tradition, ready to serve the hundreds of Barelwi mosques in the country.

The tomb of Pir Wahhab Siddiqi. It is covered with layers of traditional cloth, usually green, brought as offerings by pilgrims and supplicants. The large image of the turban at the head of the tomb is typical of the Turkish style and indicates the Sheikh's authority over his spiritual domain that remains in death.

The *mazar*

The overriding symbol of this complex relationship between tradition and innovation must be the presence of the *mazar* of Hazrat Allama Pir Muhammad Abdul Wahhab Siddiqi in the college grounds.

As the college develops and attempts to carve a reality out of the *pir*'s vision of the future for Britain's Muslim population, every success will be attributed to the mercy of Allah and the *baraka* (divine power) that he has given to Britain's first deceased Sufi lying at peace in his *mazar*. The prospect exists of students graduating from the college in secular subjects such as law or accountancy whilst traditional followers of Barelwi tradition seek intercession and perform *du'a* (independent prayers of supplication) at the shrine of a deceased Sufi as Muslims have done all over the Muslim world for nearly 13 centuries. The relationship between the students of the *dar al-ulum* and the *mazar* is one for future investigation but there is no doubt that in the domain of tradition, construction and the regulation of moral behaviour, the religious narrative of the grand-sheikh's spiritual dominion and baraka over the complex and its residents and extending outwards into the wider world will be of considerable significance to this particular Muslim educational establishment. As noted by Iram Asif, there are students who visit the grave and feel affection for the *pir* in his tomb, believing him to remain alive and powerful.[12] The mausoleum is treated with great respect and, along with the presence of a living *sheikh*, forms the locum of sacrality within the college grounds and elevates the *dar-al-ulum* beyond the realm of religious education to a location of theophany.

New developments

Nearly fifteen years on from my first visit, I have to remind myself that the sons of Pir Wahhab Siddiqi are approaching middle age but they still represent the generation of British-born Muslims; a generation marked by crisis as they have lived through an increasingly degenerating situation in the Middle East and the advent of home-grown terrorism in their midst. Various political initiatives have taken place as this generation has carved out its own spaces for leadership and British Sufis have not been absent from these manoeuvres. Although many of the traditional South Asian *pirs* have remained apart from the national political arena, there have been attempts by younger Sufis to form umbrella organisations that can compete with the MCB (Muslim Council of Britain) as it appeared to lose favour in government circles. These tended to take place amidst discourses as to who represented moderate Islam in Britain. However, once again these types of political activities tended to take place outside of the mosques and the Barelwi *ulema* that control these religious institutions.

As a second generation Sufi *pir* and a Barelwi, Sheikh Faiz ul-Siddiqi is uniquely positioned to bridge this gap but would he want to place himself in the frontline of Muslim politics, an arena that might jeopardise his role as a spiritual leader? The main change that had taken place was in the *pir*'s presence at the *dar al-ulum*. A new building had been constructed, containing living quarters, office and a reception area for visitors, and is known as the 'Blessed Seat', a literal translation for the Punjabi '*gaddi*', a term used across religions to indicate the presence of a living saint or holy man leading a religious movement. The *sheikh*'s presence changes the dynamic of Hijaz College yet again. It can no longer be described as a college which contains a *mazar* in its grounds. The presence of a living head of a Naqshbandi *tariqa*, the shrine containing the remains of his predecessor, an area demarcated for the graves of *murids* who want to be buried in close proximity to their *sheikhs*, a *dar-al-ulum* for the religious education of pious students and a mosque for worship all indicate the siting of a traditional South Asian Sufi *dargah* in Britain.

Other key Urdu or Punjabi Sufi terminologies had been changed to Anglicised forms. The *pir* had become the 'Blessed Guide' and his father was the 'Blessed Supreme Guide'. *Kalifas*, the representatives of the *pir*, were 'Blessed Envoys' and the traditional annual *urs* had become the 'Blessed Summit'. The Anglicanisation not only marked out the *tariqa* as one which was changing its territorial space from South Asia to Britain, but also appeared to have something of 'branding' associated with it.

The land put aside for the Garden of Remembrance where followers will be able to be buried near their sheikh, maintaining the closeness of master and disciple even after death.

In addition, the *urs* too had lost something of its traditional format. Advertised as a 'Blessed Summit on Realisation', a number of questions were posed such as 'Does science have all the answers?'; 'What is my place within the universe?'; 'Where do I belong?'; and 'Do I work to live or live to work?'. Several speakers were addressing these themes and the literature advertising the event contained no South Asian languages. Except for the unmistakeable evidence of a Sufi-orientated event such as *nasheeds* (devotional songs), *dhikr* and *auraad* (prayer litanies), there was something of the feel of a Muslim youth summer camp popularised by the Wahhabi-orientated or Maududi-influenced reform movements.

The *sheikh* has also accepted leadership of a new initiative from the *ulema* that arose out of national meetings responding to the crisis created by the Danish cartoons. Sensitive to public reaction to demonstrations in which Muslims were observed in violent or aggressive protest, over 600 members of the *ulema* met and formed the Muslim Action Committee to campaign against and form responses to incidents perceived to be Islamophobic. The MAC instituted and formalised a Campaign for Global Civility.[13] Mosques and Muslim organisations were asked to sign up to a declaration of global civility embodied in a charter which encapsulates the core values of mutual respect and acknowledging differences with dialogue. The idea behind the campaign was to help

Muslims discover the moral high ground when reacting to perceived insults and to avoid mutual recrimination and demonisation. Although based on the ideals of mutual respect that should hallmark a civil society, the *sheikh* admits that the inspiration arose from traditional *adab* or manners practised historically by Sufis. In agreeing to take the leadership of this campaign, Sheikh Faiz continues his father's tradition of activism and remains nominally the head of the IMO (International Muslim Organisation) founded by Pir Wahhab Siddiqi.[14] However, he recognises that the role of such organisations that sought to create umbrella bodies of national leadership in the 1970s is defunct. He would like to revive it but as a grass-roots community organisation involved with specific projects intended to resolve deep-rooted problems and issues such as gender, islamophobia, unemployment, underachievement, honour killings, incest and various family problems.

The role of the traditional South Asian *pir* is being challenged by the younger generation leadership. Sheikh Faiz believes that in the contemporary British context the traditional *pir* will become extinct. He argues that the power of the *pir* and the *ulema* has diminished amongst Muslims in Britain to be replaced by the authority of the community-led organisations. The new role of the *pir*, he insists, is moral leadership. Although he acknowledges that the authority of the *pir* remains located in the *ijaza* (authority) manifested in the *silsilah,* he argues that it is relevance to people's lives that is more significant in today's society. He has given up the traditional role of the *pir* counselling petitioners seeking miraculous intervention for the problems of daily life, although it continues for older murids who expect it as part of their relationship with the guide but is carried out by one of his brothers. These transformations would suggest an awareness of the shifting boundaries located in the new non-Muslim contemporary environment of twenty-first-century Britain, but also have their historical roots in the traditions of reformed Sufism acceptable to most Muslims of South Asian origin regardless of their allegiance to various Islamic movements.

Concluding remarks

The young British *sheikh* will encounter difficulties. His activities will be observed by Barelwi elders with great caution and even suspicion. The innate conservatism of traditional Muslims will not sit easily with change and nor will it seem natural to many of them to be led by the younger generation. The older generation *ulema* may consider the innovations undertaken by the young *sheikh* as undesirable.

The combination of *mazar* and *dar al-ulum* can be problematic for student intake. Traditionally, first-generation parents have seen the *mazar* as a place of sanctity, an enchanted realm where problem children can be sent for guidance and rehabilitation based on an encounter with the supernatural. This may conflict with the educational aims to create young Muslim leaders able to combine traditional Muslim scholarship with British mainstream education, to recreate traditional Sufism in the Western environment and provide new leadership acceptable to the mainstream. A school can only handle so many problem students before it becomes something else – a place for special needs pupils.

The ethnic and religious factions that dominate the organisation of the *Ahl as-Sunnat wa Jamaat* could destroy the vision of a British Muslim university. Each group of *murids* is obsessively loyal to their own *sheikh*. This can prevent them from acknowledging other *sheikhs* or participating in projects that could benefit the whole community. The rhetoric of unity is being raised in Britain but the reality still seems far away. In 2000 I wrote that the Hijazi Naqshbandis in Britain had chosen education as the means to transcend narrow ethnic boundaries. In fulfilling their father's wish to be buried in the grounds of the new college, they also performed a physical and symbolic act which transformed the spiritual geography of their *tariqa*.[15] The sons of Pir Abdul Wahhab Siddiqi, as representatives of British-born, British-educated Muslims, have different concerns from their parent's generation. In simple terms, they look forward to the development of the community in Britain, rather than back to the past and the preservation of traditions and customs of the subcontinent Muslim village. In this respect, even their heritage as children of a *pir* who was raised in Lahore in comfortable middle-class circumstances does not predispose them to cling to village traditions.

But even the dynamics of community development have changed since the arrival of the first-generation migrants and their consolidation activities. The young *sheikh* and his brothers are faced with the challenge to keep up with transformations amongst their own generation. More typically the British-born generations have moved away from the mosque-based organisations to establish their own bodies that operate away from the traditional mosque leadership that has failed to tackle the issues of the young. This is also true of young Sufis who are more likely these days to find their inspiration amongst their peers on the Internet or by listening to travelling *sheikhs* of their own generation from Damascus.[16] The Hijazi Sufis remain allied to the mosque-based Barelwi traditional leaderships and co-operate to a large extent with their *ulema*. However, they are no respecters of age in itself and often demand fresh thinking of the tradition-bound elders. Innovations in that most traditional of subcontinent Barelwi activities, the *urs* celebrations, have already lost the support of many that previously attended the *dargah* on that special occasion. The innovations do not seem to be radical. There are fewer speeches, especially those that are 'table-thumping and triumphalist' by eminent speakers from the Barelwi tradition, so loved and familiar to the older generations. However, the prevalent mood is one of reflection and piety but only the younger generation seem to attend. Alienating the older generation Barelwis has a material implication. Finances are tight when so much of the work has to be achieved by donation. The *tariqa* is trying to take a middle path, remaining a mosque-based organisation but relating to the second- and third-generation British Muslims. The danger is losing the loyalties of both and becoming too innovative for the elders and the *ulema*, too traditional for the young who pursue their own visions of British Islam.

The role of the *sheikh* will be key in this arena of the spiritual economy where gaining an edge over the competition is paramount to survival. It is here that charisma will play its part in the process. In the historic process of the waxing and waning of Sufi movements identified by Pnina Werbner, the charismatic *sheikh* has played a significant role in creating or revitalising global Sufi *tariqas*. This charisma has been traditionally associated with Sufi belief in the *sheikh*'s intimacy with the divine. Sheikh Faiz al-Siddiqi is aware that his relationship with Allah has to remain paramount amidst all of his activities. He has used his considerable leadership skills to establish institutional and bureaucratic mechanisms that free his time for the demands of his spiritual life. He is aware that his leadership will be based on his moral example, his ability to demonstrate knowledge and sincerity. It is his piety and knowledge of Islam that will be examined and prove crucial to the success of the college and the fame of the *dargah*. To some degree his move to the *dargah* already demonstrates a renunciation of worldly life in favour of working for the message of Allah to be promoted in Britain with maximum impact. The *dargah* forms a kind of Islamic microcosmic territory insulated from the outside world in many ways, but aware that it needs to be relevant for the demands of young Muslims living in twenty-first-century Britain.

Sheikh Faiz adopts a self-effacing attitude in his encounters with others and sees self-reformation as central to becoming a truly pious person but also as the necessary beginning to transforming society and human life within the framework of Islamic life. There is no doubt that he is a Sufi. The *tariqa* manifests such characteristics as observance of exoteric religious obligations, supererogatory devotions and ascetic practices such as retreat (*chilla*) combined with individual initiation and spiritual guidance from a guide. However, one is able to see signs of the convergence that has taken place amongst second-generation British Muslims. I have already mentioned the transformation of the *urs*, but Sheikh Faiz's manifestation of Sufi principles into his own life suggests a form of Sufism acceptable historically to the South Asian reformist movements such as the Deobandis and Tabligh-i Jamaat. As stated by Dietrich Reetz regarding the reformer's view of Sufism:

> but in right measure and form Sufism was seen as an indispensable element of true Islam shaping a moral and pious character, a necessary supplementation for theological students, but also for salvation in general. (Reetz 2006: 35)

Reetz argues that Sufism remains an aspect of the nineteenth-century South Asian reform movements, particularly Tabligh-i Jama'at, in spite of a strong anti-Sufi rhetoric especially with regard to shrine and *pir* veneration. However, I would argue that the convergence goes in both directions. Young Sufis in Britain are learning from the reformers.[17] Sheikh Faiz's moderate Sufism and personal piety can enable him to work with Deobandi leaders but the presence of the outer manifestations of Sufi sacred space maintain a clear Barelwi identity. It can be argued that as long as the tomb is not an object of pilgrimage, it clearly abides by the rules of reformed Sufism as defined by the Deobandis,[18] but *barakat* is not absent from the site of Hijaz and new tales of the shrine are being recounted, some of which tell of miraculous incidents or the ability of the location to transform lives.[19]

The first British-based *tariqa*, led by British-born Sufis of South Asian origin, will develop within a territory demarcated by shifting boundaries in which tradition and transformation, allies and rivals, active participation and withdrawal, scholarship and piety will need to be constantly negotiated. Iram Asif, in her study of Hijaz, utilises the theoretical concept of 'invented tradition' first developed by Eric Hobsbawn (Asif 2006: 11). It is true that the contemporary form of the Hijazis exists as a set of practices and organisational structures which are heavily dependent on continuity with an historic past, a reference to old situations which consist not only of tacitly accepted rules and rituals of Sufi values and norms of behaviour heavily reinforced by repetition, but also historic relationships with rival Muslim movements that have existed for the last 150 years. As stated by Asif, the Principal of Hijaz College and guide of the *tariqa* embodies certain patterns of behaviour which personify Islamic values as interpreted by Sufis, but all of this will be heavily tested by the new location and rapidly changing responses of British Muslims to new contexts. The claim of continuity to the past may become increasingly irrevalent and, as described by Hobsbawn, demonstrate the pecularity of invented traditions, that is the fictitious nature of their relationship with tradition.

References

Asif, Iram (2006) 'Hijaz College: students of Islamic Sciences in contemporary British society', MA Dissertation. Centre for Theology and Religious Studies: Lund University.

Barton, Stephen (1986) *The Bengali Muslims of Bradford*. Community Religions Project Monograph Series: University of Leeds.

Gaborieau, Marc (2006) 'What is left of Sufism in Tabligh-i Jama'at?', *Archives de Sciences Sociales des Religions*, July–September: 53–72.

Geaves, Ron (1996) 'Cult, charisma, community: the arrival of Sufi Pirs and their impact on Muslims in Britain', *Journal for the Institute of Muslim Minority Affairs, Institute of Muslim Minority Affairs* 16(2): 169–192.

Geaves, Ron (2000) *Sufis of Britain*. Cardiff: Cardiff Academic Press.

Geaves, Ron (2002) *The Sufis of Britain*. Cardiff: Cardiff Academic Press.

Geaves, R. A. (2006) 'Learning the lessons from the neo-revivalist and Wahhabi movements: the counterattack of new Sufi movements in the UK', in Jamal Malik and John Hinnells (eds) *Sufism in the West*. London: Routledge.

Geaves, R. A. (2008 forthcoming) 'A case of culturl binary fission or transglobal Sufism? The transmigration of Sufism to Britain', in R. A. Geaves, Markus Dressler and Gritt Klinkhammer (eds) *Global Networking and Locality: Sufis in Western Society*. London: Routledge.

Malik, Jamal (1998) *Colonisation of Islam: Dissolution of Traditional Institutions in Pakistan.* Delhi: Manohar.

Metcalf, Barbara Daly (1982) *Islamic Revival in British India (1860–1900).* Princeton: Princeton University Press.

Reetz, Dietrich (2006) 'Sufi spirituality fires reformist zeal: the Tabighi Jama'at in today's India and Pakistan', *Archives de Sciences Sociales des Religions*, July–September: 33–51.

Sanyal, Usha (2005) *Ahmad Riza Khan Barelwi*. Oxford: Oneworld.

Werbner, Pnina (1996) 'Stamping the earth with the name of Allah: Zikr and the sacralising of space among British Muslims', *Cultural Anthropology* 11(3): 309–338.

Werbner, Pnina (2002) *Imagined Diasporas among Manchester Muslims: The Public Performance of Pakistani Transnational Identity Politics*, World Anthropology Series. Oxford: James Currey Publishers.

Werbner, Pnina (2003) *Pilgrims of Love*. London: Hurst.

A translocal Sufi movement

Developments among Naqshbandi-Haqqani in London

Simon Stjernholm

The aim of this article is twofold. A first goal is to describe and contextualise the developments which have taken place within a Naqshbandi-Haqqani community in London in the last couple of years, with reference to the socio-political framework.[1] My description and contextualisation are meant to manifest the theoretical outlooks briefly outlined below, and have direct implications for my second goal, which is to view Sufism not as something qualitatively different from other Muslim expressions or social activities in a general sense, but instead to have an approach that considers how religiously motivated actions can be framed by the social context, regardless of what those actions might be. Hence, a specific 'ethnography of Sufism' which has been proposed by some scholars, implying certain methodological and analytical limitations, is not suitable to this endeavour (Draper 2002: 8–10). Moreover, creating a strict dichotomy between fixed categories such as 'political Islam' and 'Sufism' will not significantly deepen our understanding of contemporary forms of Islam in Western Europe, but rather strengthen the contentious positions taken by some Muslim groups on these issues.

The developments and activities among the attendees to a Naqshbandi-Haqqani Sufi priory in north London in recent years have come to raise questions regarding collective identity, individual needs and translocality. The relationship between shaykh and *murid*, 'disciple', has been developed into a complex interaction where ongoing negotiations concerning the content and form of the *tariqa*'s activities continuously take place.[2] The individual qualities and needs of participants influence the shaykhs and their agenda, which can be seen as a result of the complexity of society in late-modern Western Europe and the kinds of relationships this fosters. At the same time, political initiatives referring to 'Sufi ideology' are becoming a key aspect of the tariqa's activity, along with public events where spiritual experiences are performed in a popularised manner. To comprehend these developments and activities I will briefly present some theoretical concepts which will help understand the key processes regarding this Sufi movement.

The word *movement* is consciously chosen as I view the Naqshbandi-Haqqani as a social movement in line with the thoughts of Alberto Melucci, whose concept of *collective identity* and its relation to individual needs are central to this article. Melucci defines collective identity as an interactive process consisting of shared cognitive definitions, active relationships and emotional investments (Melucci 1996: 70f.). Consequently, collective identity is not a fixed state that 'is' one way or the other, nor an objective 'thing' simply to be internalised. Instead, each participant's own investment in and contributions to the foundational relations of a movement have a role to play in shaping this identity. The process of collective identity has effects on *what* a movement and its actions are, *how* these actions are performed, and on the explanations as to *why* the answers to the previous two questions are that way. If one accepts this view of collective identity and applies it to a Sufi movement like the one in focus here, it becomes important to consider not only the shaykhs' statements and stances, but also individual responses to the above questions from those partaking in the movement's activities.

In addition, Saba Mahmood and Peter Mandaville offer explanations of 'the political' which are not limited to the inclusion of actions within a set structure of politics concerned with states, nations or institutions. Rather, social activity, because of its relational qualities, is also political, in that it is an ongoing negotiation concerning how, why and where one should act in a certain way. This negotiation is not confined to concrete attempts of persuasion (e.g. political debates or public demonstrations), but also includes social activities involving ethics and attempts to reform the self, engaged as it is in a negotiation regarding what 'the good' is, and why (Mahmood 2005: 32–35; Mandaville 2004: 9–11). Mandaville states regarding *political identity* that it:

> must be seen as a product of the constitutive relationships with both internal *and* external 'others'. It is therefore an assertion of belonging to one group and not to an*other*, but one which can be made only after an internal negotiation about what it *means* to belong. (…) We should therefore be devoting ourselves to the task of understanding the contexts in which particular political identities come into being and the circumstances which mediate boundaries of inclusion/exclusion. We should not be asking an identity *what* it is, but rather *why* and *how* it is. (2004: 105)

The similarity in Mandaville's approach to that of Melucci's regarding identity can be traced to their mutual focus on the *relationships* and the *negotiation* of meaning, a focus which is central in this presentation. I wish to stress in my presentation. Mandaville also adds valuable insights regarding the *translocality* of spaces and movements. In my view, translocality has great significance for understanding the Naqshbandi-Haqqani movement. By translocal space Mandaville means:

> an abstract (yet daily manifest) space occupied by the sum of linkages and connections *between* places (….) Translocality is hence about recognising forms of politics situated not within the boundaries of a territorial space, but rather configured across and in-between such spaces. (2004: 50)

Shaykh Kabbani surrounded by murids after dhikr in the priory, November 2006.

As will become clear, flows of information, ideas, practices and meanings through, between and across geographical spaces are vital to the Naqshbandi-Haqqani movement. This means that although the tariqa exists in varying localities affected by their specificities, there are fundamental links and connections between them through the movement of people, communication techniques, etc., which make these localities interdependent.

A very brief introduction to the Naqshbandi-Haqqani

From the centuries-long tradition of the Naqshbandi Sufi tariqa, many offshoots have developed in various local environments.[3] In the early 1970s, the Turkish Cypriot Muhammad Nazim al-Haqqani received permission from his then dying shaykh, Abdullah ad-Daghestani, to take responsibility for his branch of the tariqa and specifically address the supposed lack of spirituality in Europe (Damrel 2006: 117). Thanks to the resurging spiritual quest happening in Britain at that time, but also to the group of Turkish Cypriot immigrants living in London, he managed to establish a group of 'seekers of truth', a term which signifies that the classification 'Muslim' is not the first priority in many individual cases. The group consisted of both Muslims by birth who pledged allegiance to Nazim as their shaykh and converts or truth-seekers who found him to be a living Sufi saint. In time, the movement was able to establish more stable mosque-based activities in London as well as smaller circles in other parts of Britain, a development which has been described by Tayfun Atay (1994) and Mustafa Draper (2002). Shaykh Nazim travelled extensively throughout the world and was able to establish groups of followers of varying sizes in many locations. It seems his main focus was on Western Europe, North America and, to some extent, Central Asia and the Middle East. In the latter, however, success was more difficult to obtain due to the long-established Muslim (and Naqshbandi) activity (Nielsen et al. 2006). However, his message appealed to people in traditionally non-Muslim parts of the world. Britain remained one of the strongholds of the movement, which is why Shaykh Nazim used to spend a few months there every year until recently.

Furthermore, he sent his *khalifa*, 'deputy', and son-in-law, the Lebanese Shaykh Hisham Kabbani, to the USA in the early 1990s. Kabbani has since started publishing houses and organisations of different kinds, founded a number of websites and engaged in political debates (Damrel 2006). The tariqa, though disparate due to its large and rapid spread, has been taken as an example by scholars to illustrate globalisation and contemporary developments of Sufism. Emphasis has been put on the messages of the shaykhs and how these indicate modern influences, as well as on Shaykh Nazim's charismatic appeal (see, for example, Schmidt 2004; Westerlund 2004; Böttcher 2006). To a lesser extent, the particular activities of the movement's participants have come into focus, especially combined with an analysis of the processes whereby these activities are framed, explained and legitimised. These activities include practices not traditionally associated with the Naqshbandi tariqa, popularised ways of conveying a spiritual message, public political initiatives, the use of communication techniques in various ways, and multiethnic participation dissimilar to most Muslim communities in Britain (see, for example, Geaves 2000; Lewis 2002: 13–23; Fetzer and Soper 2005: 50).

The priory to which I will refer in this article is located in a rather plain and ethnically diverse neighbourhood in the north of London. It was bought and given to the tariqa in the early 1990s and it has been used regularly to house people, not only the shaykh when he came to London. It is sometimes referred to as 'the *derga*' by the attendees.[4] Several attendees have complained to me about it presently not being utilised to its full capacity. The large building used to be a Christian convent, which explains the cross on one of its gables and phrases in Latin written on its walls. Some of the attendees to the priory live close by, but many travel lengthy distances to get there from around and outside London. The priory contains a prayer hall, washing facilities for men and women, another large hall that is used for martial arts training (see below), a small restaurant in the basement and accommodation where visitors can stay. The attendees with whom I have had contact are, almost exclusively, males of various ethnic origins. The majority of them are between 20 and 40 years old. Although women and girls do attend *dhikr* and prayers at the rear end of the priory, it is difficult to speak at length with them, and at tea gatherings after dhikr only males are present. This article therefore only deals with male, fairly young attendees as far as material based on personal conversations is concerned.

Socio-political framework and public activities

In July 2006, the Sufi Muslim Council (SMC) was established and officially launched at the House of Commons in London. The then Secretary of State for Communities and Local Government, Ruth Kelly, was among the guests, a fact which was rapidly made known to the interested public and affiliated individuals through mailing lists and websites. The aim of the SMC is to represent 'the silent majority of moderate Muslims' in Britain, and the means of achieving this are mainly by taking a high profile in denouncing extremism and promoting Sufism as the true, peaceful, democratic and moderate Islam.[5] The SMC's claim to represent the silent majority, however, has been questioned, since its links to the broader majority of Muslims in Britain appear vague. The SMC is closely related to the Naqshbandi-Haqqani tariqa and Shaykh Hisham Kabbani, who has become known in the USA through his various organisations and his official condemnation of 'extremism'. In 1999 he famously accused 80 per cent of US mosques as being run by extremists in a speech delivered at the US State Department (Damrel 2006: 120).

In 2004 a conference was arranged in Washington, DC, by The Nixon Center, at which Shaykh Kabbani and several representatives of a number of US universities explored the theme 'Understanding Sufism and its Potential Role in US Policy'.[6] Kabbani, as well as the other participants, promoted a view of Sufism as moderate, traditional and accepting of differences. These qualities were contrasted with the alleged negative qualities of 'Wahhabism', a term which in the report came to symbolise many forms of reformist interpretations of Islam. Sufism was portrayed as having the inherent power to bridge religious, cultural and ethnic differences. To meet the articulated task of balancing the impact of Saudi-promoted 'extremist' Islam in various parts of the world, with specific focus on Central Asia, the conference participants concluded that the encouragement of Sufism was of great significance. The Naqshbandi tariqa and its Haqqani branch were specifically mentioned in a positive manner, with special reference to Uzbekistan and Chechnya. Kabbani and the other participants suggested that US policies should include: (1) the preservation and refurbishment of Sufi shrines, thus protecting them from attacks from reformist Muslims who strive to purify Islam from what they see as non-Islamic practices; (2) assistance in preserving, translating and publishing classic Sufi texts that otherwise risk being destroyed or forgotten; and (3) help to create the political space for Sufi activities to play a more prominent role in Muslim societies (Baran 2004). The kind of idealised (and ideological) image of Sufism which dominated this conference fits the purposes of the SMC well.

In the British context, the representational Muslim bodies have had trouble balancing between recognition by the government and legitimate representation of the Muslim communities. Problems have arisen due to ethnic, sectarian and ideological differences – problems that are not limited to Britain but can largely be generalised to most Western European countries. In later years, the Muslim Council of Britain (MCB) has emerged as one of the strongest and most active representational bodies for Muslims. It was created in the mid 1990s in response to the then Conservative Home Secretary Michael Howard's request for a credible organisation with which he could deal that would represent Muslims in Britain (Birt 2005: 99). Since then Muslims have also increasingly participated in existing political parties, and several Muslims have entered the House of Lords. The MCB has been caught in a difficult situation, though, being criticised both for being too closely affiliated to the government (e.g. when the bombings of Afghanistan started in November 2001) and for not taking a firm enough stance against extremism and political manifestations of Islam. Thus it seems that both the Muslims who actively engage in the MCB's activities and the governmental bodies are somewhat disillusioned with it (Birt 2005: 94–97; Fetzer and Soper 2005: 51).

The SMC effectively targeted a sensitive spot when it clearly and without hesitation condemned religious extremism, violence and 'Wahhabi' doctrine, instead putting forward concepts such as tolerance, religious dialogue and 'Sufi ideology', a term which has not been distinctly defined. Despite its lack of precision, the SMC was welcomed by the political establishment. Because of this, it was also taken in by the media, as was the case for example after an incident when Home Secretary John Reid was interrupted and verbally attacked while speaking in a predominantly Muslim neighbourhood of London about the importance of controlling one's children's education to prevent them from 'fanatics who are looking to groom and brainwash children' and subvert them into becoming terrorists.[7] Mr Reid was strongly criticised by the high-profile Muslim radical Abu Izzadeen, who was previously part of the now illegal group al-Muhajiroun. The same evening on BBC's Newsnight, an ally of Mr Izzadeen, Anjem Choudary, was debating the topic of extremism with Haras Rafiq, the representative of the SMC. Obviously, the two had very different opinions regarding what the correct Muslim stance regarding the British state and its policies towards Muslims home and abroad should be.[8] Whereas Mr Choudary defended Abu Izzadeen's harsh criticism of the government's policies regarding Muslim communities, Mr Rafiq rather adopted the Home Secretary's position. Rafiq stated that there indeed are extremists who pose a threat to children's well-being, adding that actions such as Abu Izzadeen's make all Muslims look like fanatics. As with what happened in relation to Kabbani's above-mentioned controversial statement on extremism in the USA in 1999, the SMC has been criticised by Muslims and non-Muslims alike for its close links to both the neo-conservatives in Washington, the New Labour government of Britain and Islam Karimov, the president of Uzbekistan who was sharply criticised by Human Rights groups but who is a political ally of both Britain and the USA.[9]

When Kabbani came to Britain again in March and April 2007, a new meeting was arranged at the House of Commons. This time, a musical group called Naqshbandi Ensemble (see below) accompanied Kabbani in representing the 'voice of the silent majority'. Again, Ruth Kelly attended the meeting, if only for a short time.[10] This meeting was held at a time when Ms Kelly had just formulated a new government stance towards Muslim communities in a government action plan and in an article in the *New Statesman*, signalling that instead of merely keeping in contact with representational organisations of various kinds, relations should also involve people who are actively engaged in Muslim education, youth work and mosque governance with the aim to 'win the battle for hearts and minds' (Kelly 2007). It remains to be seen if the SMC's unhesitating political support of firm action against extremist tendencies among Muslims will compensate for weak representative capacity.

However, the SMC is not discussed very much by the priory attendees I have spoken to, but merely mentioned when speaking of the role of Shaykh Kabbani, or referred to as a tool against 'Wahhabis' who are portrayed as having 'hijacked' mosques and Muslim organisations throughout the world. It seems that the SMC does not actively involve many more people than Kabbani (when in Britain) and Haras Rafiq. In addition, the magazine that was launched simultaneously with the SMC, entitled *Spirit the Mag*, has not yet had a second issue.[11] The first issue's cover featured Amir Khan, the young English boxer of Pakistani background, and the pop singer Chico. Chico had become fairly well known in Britain after having participated in the TV talent show 'The X-Factor'. His single 'It's Chico Time' had topped the British chart for two weeks (effectively pushing Madonna's latest single down the chart). Chico was the first Arab to top the British chart, and received media attention because of his previous employment as a goat herder in Morocco and a stripper in London. In several interviews, he emphasised how his life had changed when coming into contact with Shaykh Nazim as a spiritual guide. His role as spokesperson of the Naqshbandi-Haqqani has been cemented at the two events entitled 'Celebrating Spirituality' which took place in relation to Kabbani's visits to Britain in 2006, in March (Manchester) and November (London).[12] Chico performed a few songs seemingly written especially for this audience, and in London he delivered a speech in which he elaborated on the topic of his personal salvation and the direct role that Shaykhs Nazim and Kabbani had played in this process. The music of the songs he performed in these settings was not particularly 'sufic', but rather a mixture of r&b beats and melodies similar to Arabic pop songs. The lyrics, in contrast, were of more interest in terms of Sufism, since in the song 'Mawlana', which translates as 'master', he sang phrases such as:

Sultan al-Awliya
Saint of Saints
Jewel of the Crown
Revivor of the Faith

I need you to understand
He's my ego slayer
When the devil comes calling
I only have to say a prayer

Mawlana
Shaykh Nazim al-Haqqani
Mawlana
Shaykh Hisham al-Kabbani

Through lyrics like these, Chico uses a terminology that is recognisable to the audience as sufic. He sings of 'ego slaying' and the great centrality of the shaykhs, both of which are dominant themes in the shaykhs' *sohbet*s or 'speeches', in the tariqa's literature and in conversations between murids. Practically all the activities of the murids are said to be aimed at killing the ego. The incorporation of a character such as Chico into the public events arranged by the tariqa shows a positive attitude to popularising the Sufi message of spirituality through concepts, practices and terminology that are not specifically Muslim, e.g. pop music. At the event in November 2006, it was apparent that the younger people in the audience especially had listened to Chico's songs and were able to sing along. At the end of the show, Kabbani even urged Chico to perform his pop hit, a song that sparked dancing and singing by several young attendees. It was apparent that Chico and Kabbani enjoyed a warm relationship, solidified onstage by the talk Chico gave about how he had previously been lost and without a direction in life, but how it had all changed when he came into contact with the shaykhs.

Two other musical acts, Naqshbandi Ensemble and Seela, were also performing that evening. Seela are from Scotland and used instruments such as guitar, flute, saxophone and drums to accompany their vocals. The tunes they played were moderately groovy variations on Arabic-inspired melodies, and the lyrics were mainly repetitions of prayer-like invocations of Muhammad and expressions of faith in God. Moreover, a few whirling dervishes accompanied them on the stage. Naqshbandi Ensemble, on the other hand, used only drums as accompaniment, which gave them a more traditional appearance than Seela. They performed songs in Arabic, French and English. A few of the members had, to my knowledge, travelled together with Shaykh Kabbani from the USA. In the priory it is also possible to buy CDs of the lead singer of Naqshbandi Ensemble. After their performance, Chico took to the stage. The central role of these musical performances at the event shows a willingness on Kabbani's and the organisers' behalf to convey their message in a manner attractive to the

A whirling murid onstage during Seela's performance at 'Celebrating Spirituality', November 2006.

young. This might not perhaps be equally satisfying to the older murids who are used to a more old school 'shaykh-style' behaviour from Shaykh Nazim. It is possible that a generation rift might develop between younger and older age groups among the attendees, caused by this popularising tendency. Efforts aimed at ensuring that the interests and needs of all age groups are met will probably be necessary in order to maintain their sympathies to the tariqa.

To the 'Celebrating Spirituality' event in March 2006, the organisers had invited guest speakers to represent Judaism, Buddhism and Christianity.[13] This inter-religious approach is not an entirely new phenomenon. As Draper has shown, there has previously been a tendency to play down the 'Muslim' agenda in favour of a more general 'spiritual' one (Draper 2004: 148). An interesting point, though, is that when Kabbani delivered his speech at the 'Celebrating Spirituality' event in November and used a general spiritual vocabulary rather than an Islamic one, he was interrupted by Muslim religious chants which praised and invoked Muhammad and the shaykhs of their Naqshbandi *silsila*. A number of individuals started these loud chants, which the attendees completed with the formulaic phrase *sallu Allah 'alayhi wa sallim*. Shaykh Kabbani, too, had no choice but to concur with this, although it meant he was interrupted while addressing the audience. Effectively, Kabbani adopted a more Muslim terminology and frame of reference to comply with these verbal interruptions. This might indicate that even though the shaykhs express an ambition to transgress what is seen as 'Muslim' tradition, to encourage an inclusive spiritual atmosphere, the attendees perhaps do not always agree on the need to do so. The example from 'Celebrating Spirituality' is illustrative because it challenges the way power relationships in Sufism have commonly been described, i.e. as being strictly hierarchical. It seems that the common attendees have a degree of influence on the tariqa's activities and discourse, which indicates a significant development. The content and form of activities are continuously negotiated through the social interaction that takes place in relation to the various activities that the attendees engage in, as in the above example. Even though the idea that all murids should imitate the shaykh's example is commonly accepted, there are points on which disagreements occur as to how this imitation is best pursued. In the priory various aspects of the shaykhs' teachings are often discussed and seemingly non-controversial interactions such as greetings and signs of respect (e.g. kissing a brother's hand or calling a fellow brother 'shaykh') sometimes lead to lively conversations regarding correct behaviour and interpretations.

Recent years' developments at a Naqshbandi-Haqqani *priory* in London

Tayfun Atay (1994) distinguished three ethnically defined subgroups of the Haqqanis in London: one Turkish (and Turkish Cypriot), one South-Asian, and one mainly consisting of ethnically British converts. The divisions, in Atay's account, were largely due to cultural dissimilarities. Even though ethnic backgrounds might still play a crucial role to some murids, and subgroups defined partly or mainly by ethnicity probably still exist, many emphasise the multiethnic participation in their activities. Some attendees quoted Kabbani as having said, regarding their dhikr, that they 'look like a Benetton commercial'. The activities I have witnessed have all been attended by a very ethnically diverse crowd. However, I have been told that a number of the attendees who are able to do so meet in homes on other occasions during the week to perform dhikr.

As mentioned above, the shaykh used to spend a few months with his followers in England each year, during and around Ramadan. This is one of the major differences regarding the contemporary local activities of the tariqa: due to his age, Shaykh Nazim does not travel anymore, according to attendees at the priory. Instead, the murids travel to the shaykh's home in Cyprus. Some of them have even attempted to live there permanently, though their family situations have made it impractical. The journeys to Cyprus are an important feature of Naqshbandi-Haqqani discourse in London; the journeys are talked about, the people who return from a journey are affectionately greeted and asked about the latest news. I have also heard homecomers recount 'miracles' the shaykh allegedly performed during their stay. At times, collections of pictures from certain individual journeys to Cyprus have been displayed on the wall, illustrating the various situations (although familiar to most murids) that are part of daily life at the home of Shaykh Nazim. Speeches by the shaykh are also transcribed, translated and posted via an online mailing list directly from Cyprus. In 2004, during my stay in London, the shaykh's wife passed away, whereupon a large number of murids immediately went to Cyprus to comfort the shaykh. According to some attendees to the priory who have visited Cyprus since then, this loss has had an effect on the shaykh's strength and might also be one reason for him staying in Cyprus. Another reason, apart from age and grief, for the shaykh not to travel to Britain anymore could be the reported disappointment among some murids regarding the prophecies Shaykh Nazim had made for the year 2000. Shaykh Nazim had, for a long time, been elaborating on the significance of this year, promising that the Mahdi, a messianic figure in Sunni Islam, was due to come and initiate the apocalyptic end of this world (Damrel 1999; 2006). When nothing happened many who had anticipated the Mahdi's arrival and prepared for it in various ways became disillusioned and sceptical (Nielsen et al. 2006). Some participants of the Haqqani group in Birmingham had prepared a safe house. Others talked of escaping to the mountains with supplies or going to Damascus or Lebanon. When, in August 2000, Shaykh Nazim started to travel again he did not come to Britain, where some had left the tariqa out of disappointment, though others were merely reluctant to talk about these matters and kept focusing on their own spiritual path (Draper 2002: 159–161).

My own research indicates that Shaykh Nazim at present does not travel elsewhere either, to the effect that Shaykh Kabbani has taken over the main 'travelling shaykh' role of the tariqa. Kabbani's position as main khalifa, however, is disputed among some murids. Evidence of this can be seen on various websites on the Internet, and I have witnessed discussions among murids in London who express the view that he does not possess the same spiritual qualities as Shaykh Nazim. One murid told me that Kabbani is a great organiser – he founds organisations, writes books, engages in debates and meets politicians – but he cannot provide the same spirituality, the same love and humility. He does not have the same natural ability to attract people. The murid stressed that he said this 'with all due respect', and that different shaykhs are tools of Allah in various ways. He felt that Kabbani has a crucial role to play, albeit not the very same role of attracting people as Nazim's.

Despite this, Kabbani's visits to England have the effect of summoning the various branches of the tariqa in the country, especially to the 'Celebrating Spirituality' events of 2006. In relation to the event in November, there was a regular Thursday evening dhikr in the priory in north London. When Kabbani was introduced as dhikr was about to begin, the man who introduced him informed the attendees that Shaykh Nazim had recently said in a sohbet in Cyprus that anyone who wishes to approach him and become his murid must come through Shaykh Kabbani. The same information was repeated from the stage the following evening at 'Celebrating Spirituality'. The mere fact that this was said is in itself strong evidence of Kabbani's disputed position. This particular dhikr was much more crowded than on regular Thursdays, since

Shaykh Kabbani addressing the audience at 'Celebrating Spirituality', November 2006, with the evening's musicians lined up behind him.

many people had come from various parts of the city as well as from other parts of Britain and Europe. Drums were used during the dhikr, and more people than usual were whirling in the midst of the crowd in the manner usually associated with the Mevlevi order of Turkey. This has become a standard feature of the weekly dhikr in the priory. Each Thursday dhikr I have witnessed has involved between two and four whirling dervishes. This could be explained by an alleged relation to the Mevlevi tariqa in Shaykh Nazim's family (see Böttcher 2006 for details), but that explanation alone seems reductionist in my view. In the process of shaping a 'Sufi ideology' and distinguishing oneself from what one calls 'Wahhabis', well-known elements of Sufi practices are incorporated into this otherwise Naqshbandi-oriented tariqa. The murids who whirl have explained this practice to me as not being contradictory to their spiritual belonging, but instead as increasing their feeling of love for Allah and the purifying effect of dhikr. It could, however, also be viewed as a means of attracting new sympathisers through this eye-catching ritual. The dhikr most attendees engage in, however, does not involve whirling. Dhikr is led by one of the elderly men of the tariqa, who has other senior attendees on each side of him. Then there is a large circle of men sitting on the floor in which the whirling takes place. Behind the circle others sit next to each other in rows, and in the back of the hall are the women, who take active part in the dhikr, but in the back of the hall. The dhikr leader starts repeating certain phrases in Arabic and the others join in. Each phrase is repeated melodically for a fixed number of times – the instructions for dhikr can be read in a Naqshbandi guidebook published by Kabbani.[14] The ritual is ended with a *du'a*, 'prayer', that often blends Arabic with English and sometimes includes blessings on the royal family of Britain.

Other developments include the activities that are arranged with the priory as a base. The community has long had trouble utilising the priory to its full capacity, given that it is a huge building complex (Geaves 2000: 155). For example, since my first visit to the priory in November 2004, one of its main rooms has been used weekly as a martial arts training hall. This shows a great contrast to Shaykh Nazim's negative attitude towards sports, which Atay (1994: 190) reported as part of his rejection of modern society at large. It is not any random form of martial arts that is being practised, though. A murid of Turkish Cypriot origin is teaching classes on Wednesdays (for adults) and Thursdays (for children) in *Silat*, a martial art originating from south-east Asia that, according to the instructor, has been practised for a long time in the Muslim environment of Malaysia.[15] It is supposed to be both physically and spiritually beneficial. The physical aspects should be obvious, given the benefits of physical exercise in general. The spiritual benefits, however, concern the constant struggle the murids are engaged in with their *nafs*, 'ego'. The movements in themselves, according to the instructor, engender humility when repeated over and over again, which is good for controlling the *nafs*'s urge for attention. One murid who had come into contact with the tariqa through Silat also explained that some movements are similar to those of *salat*, the daily prayers. Moreover, 'wrestling' (which Silat is compared to) in general is described as being more beneficial than boxing, since the wrestler is dependent on the movements and the 'flow' of the opponent, and effectively has to move *with* the opponent instead of *against* him/her (Stjernholm 2006: 50–53). This requires that the participant is in harmony with him/herself in order to control the ego's wish to compete and win. According to the instructor, Shaykh Abdul Hamid (who used to be Shaykh Nazim's deputy in London) has said that 'if you cannot train Silat [because of practical reasons], train Aikido'. Many of the attendees to the priory train in Silat, both within the priory and in other sports centres where a Silat master who also sometimes leads dhikr in cities near London teaches classes. During recent years Silat has also emerged as a missionary, *da'wa*, force. A young man whose parents are Indian Hindus told me of how his interest in martial arts had brought him in contact with the tariqa. At the time we spoke he had not yet met Shaykh Nazim. He was present when Shaykh Kabbani visited London, although there was no opportunity for him to meet Kabbani personally. I have also observed one of the Silat instructors bringing young men from his classes with him to the priory on several occasions. This highlights an important development: the ability of this local branch of the tariqa to attract new followers without them meeting the shaykh for a long time. Of course, the new ones are encouraged to visit the shaykh in Cyprus, but it seems that some also consider themselves to be his murids without ever having met him, simply by reading his and Kabbani's books and taking part in the activities in the priory.

In addition to the spiritual sporting activity of Silat, so called 'sacred archery' events have been arranged a few times on rugby grounds on the outskirts of London, where shooting techniques 'according to the sunna' are taught, and men, women and children are encouraged to take part (Stjernholm 2006: 53f.). The choice of these specific sports is explained by stating that these physical activities, along with horse riding, were practised by Muhammad. Engaging in these activities is seen as part of the endeavour to imitate the Prophet, the most perfect man who ever lived. However, no specific hadiths in support of this statement have been related to me by any attendee, although a book entitled *Sacred Archery: the Forty Prophetic Traditions* has been published by a publishing house connected to the tariqa and is sold at the events mentioned above.

Individual narratives of engagement

In a small flat in the northern part of greater London, a man in his mid-thirties told me a metaphor used by Shaykh Nazim. The recounting of Shaykh Nazim's sayings is a common practice among the attendees, which means that a shared language of symbols, emotionally charged phrases and frames of reference is produced. Thus, language use becomes a shared cognitive definition, to cite Melucci, and one aspect of a person's behaviour from which the attendees are able to recognise fellow brothers. The point of this particular metaphor was as follows: the ego is like a horse. Some people have Arabian thoroughbreds, some have wild horses and others have donkeys. No matter what kind of horse you have it must be tamed. If the horse is tamed properly, you can move forward with great pace and in a state of grace. But if the horse is not tamed you cannot ride it. Likewise, if you tame and control your ego you can be a truly good, humble and successful person, but if not the ego will control you and ride you. Likewise, you have to learn the proper ways to tame your own ego, to ride your ego like a horse, or your ego will 'ride' and control you instead. The man who recounted this story is one of the regular attendees to the priory, and one of the whirling participants in the dhikr. He wanted to illustrate the meaning of his activities as a Naqshbandi, which in his opinion all boils down to controlling your ego. He felt that reminding himself of stories such as the above recounted in his daily life was helpful in his effort to be a better person, both privately and at work.

This man's father, who is of Turkish origin, had been one of the first in London to start following the shaykh in the 1970s, after previously leading a non-religious lifestyle. The man told me how he had noticed many changes in his father's behaviour after he started being a murid of the shaykh. He had met the shaykh many times during his adolescence, but had not taken any affirmative steps to becoming an active participant in the tariqa himself, not until, that is, after a long period of 'wild' living with lots of parties, drugs and sexual relations, when he had nowhere to live and as a consequence was given an offer to stay in the priory. Although he had no real intention of becoming part of the Naqshbandi community, he felt a very strong attraction to Shaykh Nazim during the time the shaykh was in London. Simply the fact that the shaykh let him and others stay in the priory without asking anything in return impressed him. He listened to the shaykh's talks (despite being sceptical about the bits about Islam and Allah) and witnessed the humility and wisdom with which the shaykh approached the people who were there to see him. Gradually he came to the conclusion that 'Islam is perfect, it's the bloody Muslims that put you off!' He stayed in the priory for five years and adopted an 'Islamic lifestyle', including regular prayers, growing a beard and wearing the type of clothes worn by the shaykh. The clothes, he said, have a spiritual quality in themselves. He blamed the people that represent Muslims in British politics (e.g. the MCB) for not wearing clothes like these. In his opinion, it proved that they were not really spiritual people, but only nominal Muslims. In the long run, though, it did not work out to wear the turban, robe and wide trousers 'in the *dunya*', in the 'worldly everyday life'. But even though he shaved off his beard and started wearing Western-style clothes at work, only slipping into the 'Naqshbandi outfit' when attending the priory, the shaykh's teaching of Islam still provides a backdrop to practically everything he does. For example, in his work within social care concerning youths with special needs and problematic backgrounds,

Onstage dhikr which concluded the 'Celebrating Spirituality' event in November 2006, with Chico standing behind Kabbani and members of Naqshbandi Ensemble sitting on each side of him.

he felt that he made everyday use of his experiences with the shaykh – in how he approached them with respect, love and humility. He further described the weekly dhikr and the whirling as a much-needed 'purification' of his heart in what he thinks is a depraved environment.

This man's personal narrative resembles that of other attendees to the priory. Most of the men I have talked to describe their initial contact with Shaykh Nazim as an awakening, regardless of their religious or non-religious upbringing. One man, an ethnically British convert, compared his first three meetings with the shaykh to the biblical story of Eli and the boy Samuel, and recounted it as follows: God is calling on Samuel during the night, but Samuel believes it is Eli who is calling him. Not until the third time does Eli realise that it is in fact God who is calling the boy. Likewise, not until the third meeting with Shaykh Nazim did this murid realise that he had to follow the shaykh. But it was not an easy choice even then: 'I wanted to fornicate', he said, and explained that he had to get married before actually becoming a murid of the shaykh and living as a Muslim – which, for him, made Jesus and Muhammad 'walk hand in hand'. Many of the attendees refer to their previous lives as dark periods, when they lived sinful and unconscious lives. This is put in contrast to their present lives after having found 'a true guide', 'a living saint' who, even though they may still experience hardship, guides them on their spiritual path. Although these examples concur with the accounts given by many converts of their spiritual awakening (see Köse 1996: 153), they are worth paying attention to because they are part of shaping a collective identity. Furthermore, similar storiies are told by attendees who are Muslims by birth but who have also had a spiritual awakening and a new sense of belonging with Shaykh Nazim.

It is obvious that murids who have been 'with the shaykh' for a longer period of time have more authority in the priory than the newer ones. They dress very self-consciously, with elaborate details regarding both their dress and social conduct (how they move and talk, how their hands are being kissed, how they are sometimes referred to as 'shaykh') distinguishing them from others. Since 'knowledge' is very much connected to individuals and their experiences, those who have had the most contact with Shaykh Nazim are more knowledgeable than those with less experience. It is my impression that since the shaykh stopped travelling to see his murids, and is therefore more difficult to build a personal relationship with, this concept of 'knowledge' has become more developed, meaning that narratives of first-hand experiences of the shaykh are key elements in the interaction between participants. The travels to Cyprus have thus become essential in the lives of the murids.

The use of media and the Internet

Hand in hand with this development goes the distribution of translated speeches and video clips from the shaykh, which make him accessible to those who cannot be in his physical presence. Speeches have for a long time been edited and published in books, but are now also quickly translated and spread through mailing lists. As noted above, this takes place at the shaykh's home in Cyprus. There have been collections of money on a mailing list for the purchase of a new laptop computer for the translator there. Information regarding Shaykh Kabbani's visits is also spread through the Internet, and DVDs are distributed of certain dhikr and sohbet gatherings. The above-mentioned 'Celebrating Spirituality' events are also available on DVD. In February 2007 there was also a table in the priory where a DVD series of speeches by Shaykh Nazim from 2003 onward was sold. At that time the number of DVDs was about 170, but according to the man who sold them, many more were on the way.

The number of video sites utilised by the Haqqanis on the Internet has increased, some of which are based in the USA and a few in Britain. However, one must be careful when equating the increased number of available sources on the Internet with the actual influence they have on individual participants' lives. Live video streams of dhikr and speeches are sometimes broadcast. Video clips are also posted on the globally popular video site YouTube, where the viewer can subscribe to the video posts by a specific user. The above-mentioned SMC events in the House of Commons can, for example, be viewed on YouTube, along with many other events related to the shaykhs. Many of these clips involve Sufi rituals from various places, Kabbani visits, Shaykh Nazim's home in Cyprus, interfaith messages at conferences and the like, and celebrations of Muhammad's birthday (*mawlid*). In fact, the Internet activities related to the Naqshbandi-Haqqani tariqa have become so widespread that it is almost impossible to avoid their websites and other materials if you use words like 'Sufism', 'shaykh' or 'dhikr' in your search. As in the case of the SMC, the degree of attention it thus receives is not proportional to its representative capacity. Yet the efficiency with which keywords like those mentioned above have been claimed by Haqqani activists on the Internet is remarkable, and is without doubt useful in shaping the translocal 'Sufi ideology' which Kabbani is promoting.

Concluding remarks

The developments relating to the Naqshbandi-Haqqani priory in London which have been described in this article indicate that there are certain processes and important elements to consider in analysing the movement. This is crucial not least because the tariqa finds itself in an important period, most obviously because Shaykh Nazim is ageing and will eventually pass away. His authority as Grand Shaykh persists, but increasingly Shaykh Kabbani seems to aim at taking his place as he is now acting as main khalifa. What will happen when Shaykh Nazim passes away is open to debate, especially since the attendees appear to be divided with regard to Kabbani's capacities. As his responsibility has grown, so has the negotiating aspect of the relation between shaykh and murids in London. Individual qualities and needs of participants are incorporated into the tariqa's discourse and activities, for example through the common practice of

Silat training and the popularisation of the Sufi message through pop music. Kabbani himself has also given the activities in Britain his personal touch when establishing the SMC and fostering relations with the government.

A few important aspects of the tariqa need to be highlighted here, with specific relevance to its presence in London. First, the translocal character of the movement should be emphasised, since translocality is essential to its activities and structure. In fact, one could say that its translocal character is a precondition of the tariqa's current state of affairs. The tariqa exists in many different geographical spaces, yet the attendees' loyalty to Shaykh Nazim unites them. Nielsen et al. have suggested that 'the tariqa only fully exists where Shaykh Nazim is' (Nielsen et al. 2006: 113). Even though they conclude that translocal is an 'appropriate term' to describe the tariqa, my reading of Nielsen et al. indicates that their notion of the tariqa being non-existent when the shaykh is not present misses out on the validity of the movement's attendees themselves. Different activities persist in Shaykh Nazim's absence and take novel forms both because of local attendees and because of Kabbani's influence. Furthermore, the local attendees travel to see the shaykh and bring back stories from their meetings with him, as described above. Sohbets and news of the shaykh's utterances are rapidly spread to the local attendees through the Internet. Thus, many local parts of the movement can knowingly share the same news feeds, interpretations of events and symbolic stories. The translocality of the movement, in other words, has direct influence on the individual attendee and, in some cases, provides the very possibility to *become* or continue to be a participant attendee.

The 'Sufi ideology' that Kabbani has been speaking of can be understood in terms of a collective political identity, in the meanings of Melucci and Mandaville, that has certain emotionally charged symbolic keywords and practices that differentiate it from what is denounced as 'extremism'. Yet it is not only Shaykhs Kabbani and Nazim who fill this identity with meaning, but to a large extent also the attendees through the kinds of processes I have described above. The struggle by individuals to 'purify' their lives, be truly 'spiritual' and kill their egos is part of this collective political identity. Each person's daily life is a struggle for personal salvation and well-being, as well as for the ideological definition of 'Sufism' and 'spirituality' that is part of the activities the tariqa's attendees are engaged in. This struggle manifests itself in, for example, Silat training, dhikr and other spiritual exercises, good moral conduct, promoting the tariqa on the Internet and partaking of the material published there, and dressing in the 'Naqshbandi outfit' which brings blessings and distances oneself from other Muslims. These actions are all contributions to the kind of collective identity in Melucci's definition above, which is why they are crucial to include in the analysis of a movement such as the Naqshbandi-Haqqani. Issues and activities like those described and analysed in this article make the Naqshbandi-Haqqani in London a dynamic and illustrative Muslim movement to take into consideration when reflecting upon contemporary Islam in Western Europe.

References

Atay, Tayfun (1994) 'Naqshbandi Sufis in a Western setting', unpublished thesis for the degree of PhD, School of Oriental and African Studies (SOAS), University of London.

Baran, Zeyno (ed.) (2004) 'Understanding Sufism and its potential role in US policy', Conference Report available online at www.nixoncenter.org.

Birt, Jonathan (2005) 'Lobbying and marching: British Muslims and the state', in Tahir Abbas (ed.) *Muslim Britain: Communities Under Pressure*. London: Zed Books.

Böttcher, Annabelle (2006) 'Religious authority in transnational Sufi networks: Shaykh Nazim al-Qubrusi al-Haqqani al-Naqshbandi', in Gudrun Krämer and Sabine Schmidtke (eds) *Speaking for Islam: Religious Authorities in Muslim Societies*. Leiden: Brill.

Damrel, David (1999) 'A Sufi apocalypse', *ISIM Newsletter* 4.

Damrel, David (2006) 'Aspects of the Naqshbandi-Haqqani order in North America', in Jamal Malik and John Hinnells (eds) *Sufism in the West*. London: Routledge.

Draper, Ian K. B. (2004) 'From Celts to Kaaba: Sufism in Glastonbury', in D. Westerlund (ed). *Sufism in Europe and North America*. London: RoutledgeCurzon.

Draper, Mustafa (2002) 'Towards a postmodern Sufism: eclecticism, appropriation and adaptation in a Naqshbandiyya and a Qadiriyya tariqa in the UK', unpublished thesis for the degree of PhD, University of Birmingham.

Fetzer, Joel S. and J. Christopher Soper (2005) *Muslims and the State in Britain, France, and Germany*. New York: Cambridge University Press.

Gabourieau, Marc, Alexandre Popovic and Thierry Zarcone (eds) (1990) *Naqshbandis: Historical Developments and Present Situation of a Muslim Mystical Order*. Istanbul: Isis Yayimcilik.

Geaves, Ron (2000) *The Sufis of Britain: An Exploration of Muslim Identity*. Cardiff: Cardiff Academic Press.

Kabbani, Shaykh Muhammad Hisham (2004) *The Naqshbandi Sufi Tradition: Guidebook of Daily Practices and Devotions*. Michigan: Islamic Supreme Council of America.

Kelly, Ruth (2007) 'Time for a British version of Islam…', *New Statesman*, 9 April.

Köse, Ali (1996) *Conversion to Islam: A Study of Native British Converts*. London: Kegan Paul.

Lewis, Philip (2002) *Islamic Britain: Religion, Politics and Identity among British Muslims*. London: I.B.Tauris.

Mahmood, Saba (2005) *Politics of Piety: The Islamic Revival and the Feminist Subject*. Princeton: Princeton University Press.

Mandaville, Peter (2004). *Transnational Muslim Politics: Reimagining the Umma*. London: Routledge.

Melucci, Alberto (1996) *Challenging Codes: Collective Action in the Information Age*. Cambridge: Cambridge University Press.

Nielsen, Jørgen S., Mustafa Draper and Galina Yemelianova (2006) 'Transnational Sufism: the Haqqaniyya', in Jamal Malik and John Hinnells (eds) *Sufism in the West*. London: Routledge.

Schmidt, Garbi (2004) 'Sufi charisma on the Internet', in David Westerlund (ed.) *Sufism in Europe and North America*. London: RoutledgeCurzon.

Stjernholm, Simon (2006) *The Struggle for Purity: Naqshbandi-Haqqani Sufism in London*. Uppsala: Swedish Science Press.

Syamsiyatun, Siti (2007) 'A daughter in the Indonesian Muhammadiyah: Nasyiatul Aisyiyah negotiates a new status and image', *Journal of Islamic Studies* 18/1: 69–94.

Westerlund, David (2004) 'The contextualisation of Sufism in Europe', in David Westerlund (ed.), *Sufism in Europe and North America*. London: RoutledgeCurzon.

One foot rooted in Islam, the other foot circling the world

Tradition and engagement in a Turkish Sufi *cemaat*

Heiko Henkel

In one of his famous analogies, the thirteenth-century poet and scholar Mevlana Jalal ud-Din Rumi urges his fellow Sufis to be like compasses: to circle with one foot the countries of the world but to stay rooted with the other foot in Islam. This compass analogy captures well a feature that characterises many branches of Sufism, today as much as in the past: the commitment to explore and engage with society across cultural and geographical borders – and, by implication, with social change and diversity – and yet to stay rooted within the Islamic tradition.[1] Focusing on one prominent Turkish Sufi branch, this chapter explores the particular way Sufi Islam seeks to secure and rebuild the practitioner's connection to the sources of Islam while at the same time engaging in and with society. While most of the paper focuses on Turkey, I shall begin in Australia.

Continuity and rupture

On 4 February 2001, at about 4.20pm, the driver of a pick-up truck on the highway between the Australian towns of Dubbo and Peak Hill lost control of his caravan trailer. The trailer hit a car travelling in the opposite direction, killing two of the passengers. The local Australian newspaper identified the victims as 'Professor Dr Mahmud Esad Coşan, an internationally renowned Muslim scholar, and his son-in-law Dr Ali Uyarel.'[2] As the paper reported, the two had been based in Brisbane (Australia) for the past three years.

News of the accident made it to Turkey within hours of the event and caused grief and alarm among tens of thousands of Coşan's followers. For a week or so the event dominated the headlines of Turkey's national press. Here in Turkey, Prof. Coşan was indeed well known, but his fame, and the attention the news of his death generated, had little to do with his academic accomplishments. What galvanised public attention in Turkey was the fact that Coşan had been the leader, or sheikh, of one of Turkey's best known and perhaps most influential Sufi brotherhoods: the Iskenderpaşa branch of the Naqshbandi *tarikat*. Coşan had settled in Australia after being forced into exile in 1997 during the so-called 'postmodern coup', in which Turkey's staunchly secularist military had

5 ŞUBAT 2001 PAZARTESİ

akit

175.000 TL

Esad Coşan Hocaefendi vefat etti

HAKK'A YÜRÜDÜ

SON TAVSİYELERİNDEN BİRİ

Din; cihad ile, cehd ile, sa'y ile, gayret ile, fedakârlık ile, hizmet ile, cesaret ile, kahramanlık ile ... durur... Tembellik

İŞTE KAMPANYA★★★

Osmanlılar

www.osmanlilarsilah.com

Hürriyet

Türkiye Türklerindir

8 Şubat 2001 Perşembe

Kurucusu: Sedat Simavi 1896 - 1953

Fiyatı: 200 bin TL

Prof. Mahmut Esad Coşan Avustralya'da vefat et

Gurbette vuslat

● Elim bir trafik kazası geçirdi

28 Şubat sürecinde yurtdışına çıkmak zorunda kalan ve 1997'den bu yana Avustralya'da yaşayan Nakşibendi tarikatı liderlerinden Prof. M. Esad Coşan, gurbet hayatı yaşadığı Avustralya'da trafik kazasında hayatını kaybetti.

● Coşan, hastanede kurtarılamadı

Prof. Coşan'ın otomobili, başkent Sydney'e 5 saat mesafedeki Dubbo yakınlarında karşı yönden gelen kamyonla çarpıştı. Kazadan ağır yaralı kurtulan Coşan, kaldırıldığı hastanede ahirete irtihal etti.

● Kaza, sevenlerini üzüntüye boğdu

Coşan'ın damadı Prof. Dr. Ali Yücel Uyarel'in de olay yerinde öldüğü kazaya yol açan kamyon sürücüsünün uyuduğu belirlendi. Coşan ve damadının ölümü, Avustralya ve Türkiye'deki sevenlerini üzüntüye boğdu.

GÜRKAN GÜRBÜZ / SÜLEYMAN ÜNAL'IN HABERİ 4-5'TE

Esad Coşan sevenlerini üzdü

Prof. Dr. M. Esad Coşan'ın vefat haberinin duyulmasından sonra, sevenleri Coşan'ın Küçükçamlıca'daki baba evine akın ettiler. Yakınları Coşan'ın Avustralya'da toprağa verileceğini açıkladılar.

● Prof. Dr. Mahmut Esad Coşan

Mehmet Zahid Kotku'nun en yakınıyd

İslam ahlakının yerleşmesi ve gelişmesi için çalışan Esad Coşan, Kotku'nun isteğiyle 1977'de hadis sohbetlerine başladı ve hocası Kotku'nun vefatıyla 80'de hizmetleri üstlen

Esad Coşan Hocaefendi

Alimin ölümü,

ZAMAN

5 ŞUBAT 2001 PAZARTESİ

ALBARAKA TÜRK "Faizsiz Kazanç"

...'e gönderilen ka ...aniye'ye defnedil

Sezer'in görüşünü

Ecevit, "Sayın Cumhurbaş name hakkında

TÜRK

5 Şubat 2001 Pazartesi

Nakşibendi se

Milliyet

AYRINTILI HABER

Esad Coşan trafik kurbanı

Nakşibendi tarikatı yasta

Nakşibendi tarikatının kolu olan "İskenderpaşa Cemaati" lideri Esad Coşan, Avustralya'da geçirdiği trafik kazasında can verdi

ŞERİF ERTÜRK Melbourne

İskenderpaşa Cemaati'ni şoke eden kaza, Avustralya'da, Sydney'e 600 kilometre uzaklıktaki Dubbo kenti yakınlarında gerçekleşti.

Prof. Dr. Mahmud Esad Coşan ile beraber araçta bulunan damadı Prof. Dr. Ali Yücel Uyarel de ölürken aracı kullanan Cevdet Taşkın isimli şoförle cemaat mensubu Hüseyin Kara yaralandı. Kaza, bir ziyaret için Dubbo'ya giden Coşan'ı taşıyan araca karşı yönden gelen bir kamyonun şerit değiştirerek çarpması sonucu meydana geldi. Damadı olay yerinde ölürken, Coşan yaralı olarak Dubbo Devlet Hastanesi'ne kaldırıldı.

Çabalar boşa gitti

Ancak yapılan tıbbi müdahalelere rağmen Coşan, kurtarılamadı. Olayın Türklerin yoğun olarak yaşadığı Melbourne ve Sydney'de duyulmasından sonra cemaat üyeleri araçlarla Dubbo'ya hareket etti. Son bir yıldır Queensland eyaletine bağlı Brisbane'da yaşayan Coşan, zaman zaman çeşitli ülkelerde de konferanslar veriyordu.

Ziyarete gitmişti

Coşan'ın, son zamanlarda yatırımcıların gözdesi Dubbo'ya, burada ticaret yapan bazı cemaat üyelerini ziyaret için gittiği öğrenildi. Cenazeyi almak üzere Esad Coşan'ın oğlu Avustralya'ya giderken cenazenin bugün karayoluyla Sydney'e, buradan da uçakla yaşadığı Brisbane'a götürüleceği bildirildi.

Tam 20 yıldır cemaat lideri

Coşan, bir yemekte Mesut Yılmaz ve Türkeş'le birlikte görülüyor.

Tarikat yasta

NAKŞİBENDİ tarikatının kolu olan "İskenderpaşa Cemaati"nin lideri Prof. Dr. Esad Coşan, Avustralya'da geçirdiği trafik kazası sonucu yaşamını yitirdi. Coşan ile araçta bulunan damadı Prof. Dr. Ali Yücel de öldü.

CEMAATİN şeyhi M. Zahid Ko...ku'nun damadı olan Coşan, s...yasilere yakın biri olarak tanın...yordu. Coşan'ın 1997'den be... yaşadığı Avustralya'da defn...dileceği öğrenildi. ■ ŞERİF ERTÜR...

Dubbo'dan bildiriyor... 17'de

Osmanlı arşivlerinde araştırmalar yapan Hanefi Bostan'ın bu konudaki yüksek lisans tezi, "**Said Halim Paşa**" adıyla yayımlanmıştır. (İrfan Yayıncılık, 1992. Adres: Çatalçeşme Sok. Defne Han, No: 27 / 14, Cağaloğlu, İstanbul)

Said Halim Paşa, Mısır Valisi Kavalalı Mehmet Ali Paşa'nın torunudur. 1864 Kahire doğumludur. Böyle Hıdiv ailesinden geldiği için "**prens**" unvanına sahiptir.

Avrupa'da okumuştur. Türkçe ve Arapçadan başka, eser yazacak düzeyde Fransızca ve İngilizce bilirdi.

★★★

SAİD HALİM, Osmanlı'da yüksek bürokratik görevler üstlenmiştir. Kendisini şahsen tanıyan yazar Eşref Edib'in deyimiyle, Batı'da "**fikir serbestisine sahip bir alemde yetiştiği**" için, İstanbul'daki "**muhit - i istibdad**"a u-

Press coverage in the aftermath of Prof. Coşan's death, February 2001.

forced the resignation of the then prime minister Necmettin Erbakan, and had started a severe clampdown on religious Muslim organisations which it considered a threat to Turkey's secular order. A few days after the fatal accident, tens of thousands of mourners (and one anthropologist) attended Coşan and Uyarel's funeral service at Fatih mosque in Istanbul and accompanied them on their last journey to Eyüp cemetery.[3]

Coşan's death and the attention it generated bring a number of issues into focus. Most obviously, the event demonstrates the continuing importance of Naqshbandi-Khalidi Sufism in Turkey and Turkish Islam – despite the fact that Sufi organisations in Turkey have been outlawed for more than 70 years.[4] The enormous outpouring of grief shows the strong attachment many people felt to Coşan; it also indicates the significance of Esad Coşan's leadership regarding the exceptional dynamism and creativity that has characterised the Iskenderpaşa *cemaat*'s reinterpretation of the Sufi tradition and the relationship of Islam to secular modernity. Substantial coverage in the secularist media and president Sezer's high profile intervention (vetoing the burial of Coşan at the grand Süleymaniye mosque's officially 'closed' graveyard) reflect, however, the anxious attention given to the event by the secularist public and the state. The often very hostile commentary by secularist observers also raises the question of which role Sufi brotherhoods may play in a modern liberal democracy. The attention paid to Coşan's death points to the particular conception of 'tradition' in Sufi Islam, at the centre of which stands the spiritual lineage of the Sheikh, the *silsila*. The *silsila* both counters and enables the geographic and intellectual mobility of Sufi practitioners. At the same time, Coşan's death highlights its potential fragility. What, then, was the continuing importance of the Iskenderpaşa *cemaat* under Coşan – and perhaps of Sufi *cemaats* more generally?

The *cemaats*: institutional matrix of Muslim civil society

An often mentioned characteristic of Sufi brotherhoods is their ability to generate far-reaching and closely knit social and economic networks, and to provide followers with effective avenues for upward social mobility. This is certainly the case with the Iskenderpaşa *cemaat*.[5] Since the 1980s, a substantial line-up of businesses that are tied, one way or another, to the *cemaat* provide followers with employment, business contacts and investment opportunities. The *cemaat* also helps followers to find work in companies implementing Islamic business standards, and allows consumers to imagine themselves engaged in 'ethical consumption' (not unlike those of us who purchase 'fair trade' coffee in 'ecologically sensitive' supermarkets).[6] Moreover, these business enterprises generate substantial revenues that the *cemaat* uses to fund its many social projects. Given the increasing political influence of the (post-) Islamist parties both on the municipal and subsequently on the national level since the 1980s, these networks also facilitate the promotion of followers into positions in the (especially municipal) bureaucracy and in publicly owned companies.

Related to these more tangible aspects of upward social mobility is another important domain of the *cemaat*'s influence: its role in fostering a religious Muslim avant-garde. Ersin Gürdoğan gives a fascinating autobiographical account of how a group of young men, newly arrived from small Anatolian towns in Istanbul in the 1960s, find in the networks of the *cemaat* an 'invisible university' (*görünmeyen üniversite*) gathered around Coşan's predecessor Zahid Kotku.[7] Gürdoğan and his friends are drawn to Kotku because they feel he offers them an intellectual framework with its privileged understanding of the universe, as well as a practical way of life deeply rooted in the Islamic tradition and yet intensely engaged in the social and intellectual issues of the day. The young men I met in Istanbul a generation later had similar things to say about why the *cemaat* was so attractive to them. First of all, it was the extraordinary wisdom and leadership of the *hocaefendi* (the *cemaat*'s sheikh, lit. 'esteemed teacher'), but also the company of a group of senior members of the *cemaat* (including Gürdoğan) and a peer group that confirmed the extraordinary stature of the *cemaat*'s leader. Corresponding to the emphasis on the extraordinary personality of the *hocaefendi* is the emphasis they put in developing and disciplining their own person, again in a similar way to what we read in Gürdoğan's narrative.

This concern for the development/disciplining of the self (*nefs*) reflects the traditional Sufi concern for the 'disciplining of the self' (Turk: *nefs terbiyesi)* as the central object of Sufi self-discipline. In keeping with the *cemaat*'s Naqshbandi-Khalidi heritage, an *ethical* project of self-shaping is thus closely aligned with the *cemaat*'s *moral* project of regulating social relations in line with precepts derived from the Islamic tradition (the sharia, in other words). As Yavuz (1999) points out, the *cemaat*'s energetic and innovative reform project cannot be understood outside of the context of Turkish modernity – and, I would add, Turkish secularism. Theirs is, in many ways, a distinctly 'republican' Islam. At the same time, the Iskenderpaşa *cemaat* is clearly 'stretching the borders of Modernity', as Yavuz writes. In fact, it stretches these borders in two directions. On the one hand, the *cemaat*'s interpretation of Islam has contributed to incorporate into distinctly modern ways of life many of those who have long considered Islam as modernity's great alternative. On the other hand, the *cemaat*'s high-profile engagement within the institutions of modern Turkish society make the old secularist proposition that Naqshbandi brotherhoods are 'naturally' opposed to, or even outside, the Republic's modernising project increasingly untenable. To paraphrase Georg Stauth (2001), the Iskenderpaşa's interpretation of Islam is both motor of and challenge to modernity. But the perhaps paradoxical relationship of the *cemaat* to the Turkish Republic's secularising and modernising project clearly needs some closer consideration.

To be sure, this concern with shaping the Muslim self through religious practice is neither specific to the Iskenderpaşa Naqshis nor to Sufism. Talal Asad (1986, 1993) has pointed out that projects of self-shaping are central to the Islamic tradition, and Saba Mahmood (2001, 2004) and others have shown their importance in current revival movements. The emphasis on regulating social relations according to Muslim moral precepts is, of course, characteristic of a great many Islamic revival movements. What is noteworthy, however, is the way in which this and other *cemaats* have brought these concerns into play in the context of Turkey's secularised and increasingly liberal society.

The *cemaat* facilitates an institutional and intellectual framework in which followers are encouraged to educate themselves in – and shape themselves according to – the principles of the Islamic tradition as it is interpreted in the *cemaat*. The *cemaat*'s leader together with its senior members and the individual's peer group are available to mentor, support and criticise this continuing process of learning and self-cultivation, and of interpreting contemporary society from a religious Muslim point of view.[8] This active role in fostering a process of self-formation often takes on the role of encouraging and helping students to graduate through the notoriously unsupportive Turkish school and higher education system, for instance in the form of bursaries, student hostel places and extra-curricular religious education.

At the same time, the *cemaats* provide followers with fora in which they can calibrate their endeavours of Muslim self-cultivation and can deliberate, test and develop both their formal religious training and their endeavours to 'Islamise' (Turk: *Islamlaştırmak*) modern society. As was the case with other *cemaats*, in the 1980s and 1990s, the Iskenderpaşa *cemaat*'s publications gained importance as fora with an audience both inside and outside of the *cemaat*. Among these were a range of widely circulating journals like '*Islam*' and 'Women and Family' (*Kadın ve Aile)* which in the 1980s and 1990s made the *cemaat* an influential part of Turkey's expanding Muslim public sphere.[9] But equally importantly, groups like the Iskenderpaşa *cemaat* encourage and help followers to pursue careers in public administration and municipal companies, private businesses, the education sector, etc. In this way, these organisations can become important places in which the *cemaat*'s members can gather experience and show their talents. The *cemaats* thus provide and facilitate an institutional infrastructure in which followers can emerge as 'organic intellectuals' rooted in the wider Muslim revival movement, and endeavour to contribute to it as an intellectual and pious Muslim avant-garde.[10] The Sufi project of self-shaping is here thus immediately connected to gaining authority in the public deliberation of Islamic precepts. It offers the Sufi practitioner the means to gain authority within a religious Muslim (and perhaps wider) public – and it is this public who evaluate the authority of these intellectuals' contributions. The *cemaat* itself provides a sheltered space for this endeavour (a mini public?), but is by no means a closed space, nestled as it is in wider overlapping public arenas (Turkish Muslim public, the Turkish national public, transnational Muslim public and the emerging global public sphere).

The multi-faceted role of tradition in Turkish Sufi Islam

In this formation of a Muslim avant-garde, the engagement with Islamic traditions plays a multi-faceted role. Most generally and obviously, the Iskenderpaşa *cemaat* considers itself both part of a Turkish and a universal Muslim community, and thus its publications and social activities, as well as the daily practice of followers, are permeated with explicit and implicit references to the Islamic tradition (Henkel 2005, 2007). These very wide horizons are narrowed by the *cemaat*'s position within the Sunni-Hanefi legal school (which in Turkey sets it apart most importantly both from Alevi groups and neo-Sufi circles). They are also centred on a radically more specific and concrete tradition which defines the *cemaat*'s Sufi character: the lineage (or *silsila*) of the *cemaat*'s sheikh. Esad Coşan is considered to be the fortieth link in a line that connects him with such important Sufi figures as Zahid Kotku, his immediate predecessor (d.1980), who is reported to have played a crucial role in encouraging Necmettin Erbakan to form Turkey's first 'Islamist' political party in the late 1960s, and Ahmed Gümüşhanevi (d.1893), who established this Naqşbandi branch in Istanbul and acted as an influential spiritual advisor to Sultan Abdulhamit II. Among the other prominent figures in the *silsila* are Mevlana Khalidi (d.1836), who introduced the silent zikir and the social activism that still characterise the *cemaat*, and Baha ad-Din Naqshband (d.1389), the eponym of the Naqsbandi *tarikat*. Ultimately, of course, the *cemaat* traces its *silsila* back to the Prophet himself.[11] Through his successive roles as disciple (*mürid*) and then master (*mürșid*), the sheikh provides a material, quasi-familial bond through the *silsila*, even though this bond takes on a somewhat mythical character for the earlier links in the chain. Most crucially, this historical link is said to enable a spiritual link between the individual actor and the prophet through the mediation of his (or her) sheikh (and the sheikh's *silsila*).[12] The *silsila* thus not only provides a distinct sense of continuity that relativises, and to some extent supersedes, the ruptures caused by historical events such as the foundation of the Turkish Republic or an individual's displacement through migration, it also defines an authoritative centre of interpretation for the individual's engagement with Islam.

From this securely anchored vantage point, then, the *cemaat* draws on numerous Islamic sub-traditions in its interpretation of Islam and society.

Tasavvuf

The Iskenderpaşa *cemaat* has placed great emphasis on the cultivation of the traditional Sufi practices of *tasavvuf* aimed at disciplining the self in order to purify it from worldly desires and so to achieve closeness to the divine. In his 'sohbets' (lit. 'conversations', but better described as lectures or sermons delivered in person or circulating as audio or video recordings, or on the Internet) which became the main interface between Coşan and his followers, Coşan presses home again and again the point that it is a person's own *nefs* that is his most dangerous enemy.[13] *Tasavvuf* provides the individual with a method of disciplining this *nefs* (*nefis terbiyesi*). But to reduce Coşan's message to this stark project of self-discipline would be misleading. The theme of love both for the creator and the prophet also plays a prominent role and, in line with long-standing Sufi tradition, Coşan's sohbets are filled with different and often paradoxical definitions of what Sufism is.[14] At the end of one of his sohbets, Coşan works himself towards one of those classical tropes, suggesting that '*tasavvuf* is to worship as if one saw God' (1996: 331).[15] If we remember that ideally all human practice should be an act of worship, this means that to be a good Sufi means to live life as if one saw God.[16] In order to achieve such an exalted state, the Sufi practitioner must purify himself through a lengthy and arduous process, the eventual success of which is by no means guaranteed. In any event, success can be achieved only with the guidance of the sheikh, through which the link with the divine is established.

But while the central persona of the sheikh is of crucial importance for the *cemaat* and its trajectory, the role of the sheikh has changed considerably in the twentieth century. Perhaps the most consequential decision of Esad Coşan was to take the opportunity offered by Turgut Özal's government after 1983 and lead the *cemaat* in building a substantial range of business ventures.[17] This very worldly element of the *cemaat* is consistent with the Naqshbandi-Khalidi commitment to integrate Sufi practices into social life and its scepticism towards ascetic withdrawal. A prominent example is the adoption of the silent *zikir* (*zikir* or *dhikr* is the meditative repetition of Gods name practiced by many Sufis) in favour of the more ecstatic practice of communal rhythmical chanting. I was told that this silent zikr fits better into a modern lifestyle as it can even be performed, if needs be, in front of the computer at the office.

Annemarie Schimmel has suggested two tendencies within the history of Sufism, based on classical scholarly Muslim texts: on the one hand, the mystic strand tends to renounce the world in order to rid the practitioner of worldly attachments; while on the other hand, the prophetic strand suggests that the Sufi has the responsibility to use his insights to help others to lead better lives (Schimmel 1985: 20). The Iskenderpaşa *cemaat* is firmly rooted in this second tendency. The degree of worldly engagement of the *cemaat* under Esad Coşan, however, has not only met with approval. Critics from other *cemaats*, including former followers of Coşan's predecessor Kotku, have claimed that Coşan had come to act more like a 'merchant' rather than a Sufi sheikh, referring to his endeavours to build and expand the business holding of the cemaat at the cost of providing a creative guidance rigorously grounded in the Islamic tradition. Whatever the merits of this critique, it underscores the observation that the role of the sheikh has changed.

In other aspects, Coşan's leadership of the *cemaat* continues a longer historical trend. Although the Iskenderpaşa Naqshis have maintained the central role of the sheikh and the *silsila* as the centring principle of their *cemaat*, the relationship between the sheikh and his followers has substantially changed over the course of the twentieth century. Historically, relationships between sheikhs and their disciples have varied, of course. Nevertheless it is probably safe to say that a defining feature of Sufi practice has been the (claim of) absolute authority of the sheikh over his disciples. With the re-emergence of Sufism in the Turkish Republic, however, this has changed. When Abdülaziz Bekkine and his successor Zahid Kotku began gathering ambitious young men around them in the 1950s and 1960s, they could neither offer them a stipend nor a Sufi lodge to live in. As already mentioned, what they could offer their followers was spiritual and intellectual guidance and the encouragement to become active and successful members of the Turkish society. During those years, the sense of a close relationship among the followers developed, and the Sufi brotherhood became a *cemaat*. When Kotku died and Coşan took over, he was the first sheikh not trained in the Ottoman system. He was not an *alim* (a Muslim scholar educated in and certified by the traditional system of formal religious education) but a professor of Persian and Arabic literature, educated at a Turkish state university. Coşan openly expressed his gratitude towards senior members of the *cemaat* who helped him lead the *cemaat* and emphasised the importance for the *cemaat*'s members to use their own critical thinking even in their relationship with him. If this made the sheikh appear as 'primus inter pares', it became even more accentuated in the transition from Esad Coşan to his son Nureddin. Although I was told that members of the *cemaat* admire Nureddin's spiritual depth, it is also recognised that Nureddin, who holds an MBA in management from a college in New York State and was president of the *cemaat*'s business ventures in the 1990s, was in many ways less prepared for the task than his father. And not only was Nureddin (b.1963) comparatively young when he took over the leadership of the *cemaat* but he also cultivated a distinctly youthful image: he appeared at his father's funeral in an 'Italian' designer suit and open shirt, wearing designer sunglasses, and he reportedly refused the offered hand kisses (presumably as a sign of humility). The appearance so struck the Turkish media that *Milliyet* named him the 'Millennium sheikh'. It is perhaps no surprise, then, that he is reported to distribute *bereket* (blessings) to his followers by SMS messages.

In his study of the cultural foundations of Morocco's authoritarian political system, Abdellah Hammoudi (1997) suggests that the rigidly hierarchical relationship of the Sufi sheikh and his disciples provides the cultural scheme on which current political relations in Morocco are modelled. Given the strong position of powerful individuals both in the Ottoman and Republican Turkish political systems, this observation is certainly pertinent for Turkey as well. It should be noted, however, that in contemporary Turkey power is vested in a cluster of institutions with complex and often antagonistic interests and ambitions (most importantly the modern state apparatus, but also, and increasingly, in a vast number of civil society organisations) rather than in one central figure at the apex of a tightly integrated social hierarchy. Aside from being a Sufi sheikh and tied to this capacity, Coşan was the leader of one such organisation. As was the case with other Turkish *cemaats* since the 1980s, his *cemaat* was engaged in a variety of ventures which were directed by a 'holding company', a well-established business model in Turkey. The function of these enterprises was partly that of generating economic funds, partly that of creating 'Muslim spaces' in Turkish society (Henkel 2007).

Fiqh – the legal tradition

A second Islamic tradition central to the *cemaat*'s conception of Islam is the Muslim *fiqh* (*fıkıh* in Turkish, often called Islamic law or jurisprudence), by which Muslim scholarly discipline considers which practices are obligatory or forbidden, allowed or discouraged, according to the sources and methods of the Islamic tradition. In other words, the Muslim fiqh is concerned with defining the rules of the sharia, although due to the heightened public sensitivity concerning the use of language, the term sharia (*şeriat*) is seldom found in Turkey. Unlike other branches of Sufism, the Naqshbandi-Khalidiyye lineage strongly emphasises the importance of fiqh as a crucial element of Sufism. *Cemaat* members have repeatedly used the classic phrase '*şeriat-tarikat-hakikat*', which suggests that adherence to the sharia (however it is interpreted in a given context) forms the basis on which the path of Sufism may lead to achieving righteousness, and clarifies the relationship between Sufism and Islamic law (or fiqh). This commitment has greatly contributed to the fact that 'secularists' in Turkey commonly view Naqshbandi *tarikas* as particularly 'conservative' (*muhafazakâr*) or 'reactionary' (*irtica*).

Significantly, however, there is today a close alignment of the *cemaat*'s interpretation of Islam with what one could call the contemporary Turkish Sunni orthodoxy, as represented by senior scholars at the official Turkish Directorate of Religious Affairs and the semi-official Institute for Islamic Research (ISAM) in Istanbul.[18] It is thus no coincidence that ISAM's recently published two-volume *Ilmihal* ('Muslim catechism') (Karaman et al. 2000) emphasises the important role of *tasavvuf* in the Islamic tradition, without, however, mentioning the significance or even existence of Sufi *cemaats*. This position is also apparent in the Ilmihal's emphases on Muslim 'legal culture' (*fıkıh kültürü*) as the matrix inside which commitment to Islam can be sustained, on the cultivation of Muslim '*ahlak*' (morality/subjectivity), and on the central role of the prophet's exemplary life as a model for today's believers. Most importantly, the Directorate's *Ilmihal* interprets the sharia as a legal/moral system distinct from *and yet compatible with* secular state law. While the relationship between the Republican state and Sufi *tarikats* (and activist Islam more generally) is often contentious, here we can see a substantial convergence with sections of the state, if not with the state per se.

Sunna

The quasi-legal connotations of the Muslim *fiqh*, which aim at establishing a coherent moral framework for the entire Muslim community, together with the introspective disciplines of *tasavvuf*, form converging aspects of a single socio-religious project. But how are these components connected? To understand how what one may call the moral and the ethical components of the Islamic project are related in everyday interpretative praxis, it is useful to consider a third component of the *cemaat*'s engagement with the Islamic tradition: its emphasis on the interpretation of the prophet's *sunna*, the Prophet's life-practice and sayings as transmitted in the *hadith* reports. As is well known, from early on in the Islamic tradition, hadith reports constituted the second source (after the Koran) for Muslim interpretation of how to live according to God's command. In the late Ottoman Empire, however, it was Sheikh Gümüşhanevi of Istanbul, one of Coşan's well-known predecessors, who re-emphasised their importance and made the reading and exegesis of hadith his central occupation. His voluminous collected edition of hadiths marked the beginning of a hadith's renaissance that still endures today.

The emphasis on hadith-based reasoning implies an open-ended process of deliberation in which actors can refer to a wide range of different hadith reports to support their own interpretation of proper Islamic practice. The polysemantic process of hadith exegesis thus marks a different trajectory from the tendency of modernist Islam to codify moral and legal norms, and to tie their enforcement to the authority of the state. Proficiency in hadith interpretation is a much valued skill amongst members of the *cemaat* as it gives concrete clues as to how to judge today's dilemmas of practical morality. An important part of Coşan's communication to his *cemaat* took the form of hadith commentary. He gave weekly lectures, or sohbets, in Istanbul, but also spoke at conferences and while visiting members of the *cemaat* in Turkey and abroad.[19]

The *cemaat*'s concern with *tasavvuf*, fiqh reasoning and hadith exegesis converges thus towards its members' endeavour to shape themselves (their *nefs*) in the spirit of the Islamic tradition. This Sufi endeavour is conjoined with the attempt by many of those affiliated with the *cemaat* to achieve leading positions in other fields: as businessmen, political commentators, academics, etc.

Secularism, the state and the autonomous self

The significance of the Iskenderpaşa *cemaat*'s innovative engagement with secular society for a wider discussion of contemporary Islam is seen more clearly when we consider for a moment a recent proposition by Talal Asad concerning the way law and morality are conceptualised in late nineteenth- and early twentieth-century Egypt (2003).

In an interesting discussion on the central role of family law in the legal reforms of the era, Asad notes that the focus on family law must be seen as a profoundly modern concern, directly linked to the emerging forms of modern governance in colonial Egypt and elsewhere (Asad 2003). While all Muslim reformers examined by Asad share these modern concerns, Asad argues that it is the change in the way some of them come to locate moral authority that marks the decisive shift from a classical to a secularised interpretation of Islam. Asad takes Muhammad Abduh (often seen as a founding figure of Islamic modernism) to exemplify the classical Islamic position. Abduh's position appears clearly in the way he writes about the preconditions for a judge to adjudicate the sharia. To dispense judgments in the spirit of Islam, Abduh writes, the judge (and, by extension, anyone claiming authority in interpreting Islam) cannot simply apply a catalogue of 'rules'. Rather, only a person educated and formed in the spirit of the Islamic tradition, and knowledgeable about the deeper meaning of Islamic justice, is able to properly adjudicate Islamic law.

Ahmad Sefwat, writing about 20 years later than Abduh, approaches the issue in a distinctly different way (Asad 2003: 235ff.). In contrast to Abduh, Safwat seeks to separate what he sees as the *legal* and the *moral* dimensions of the Koran. Having established the possibility of clearly separating these two domains, Sefwat then entrusts the legal dimension of the sharia to the regulation by the state through its legal system, and the moral dimension to the conscience of the citizen. Asad juxtaposes this approach to Abduh's, for whom the interdependent disciplines of the sharia (ibadet/ritual, muamalat/social relations, *tasavvuf*/Sufi techniques) are indispensable for generating the ability of judgment in the spirit of the sharia: 'Together' Asad writes, they 'occupy the space that Ahmad Safwat would pre-empt for the legislative authority of the sovereign state and the moral authority of the sovereign subject' (ibid.: 251). Between the 'classical' position taken by Abduh and the position developed by Sefwat, Asad locates the advent of secularism in the Muslim Middle East.

Asad's writing on Islam and secularism is admirably perceptive and nuanced. And yet it seems to me that a closer look at the Iskenderpaşa *cemaat* complicates Asad's analysis of secularism as a social formation tied to a Kantian ethics (as apparently is the case with Ahmad Sefwat). For my interlocutors, moral authority is by no means simply split between the legal authority of the state and the conscience of the autonomous citizen. In fact, the *cemaat* clearly seeks to foster what Asad describes as a 'classical' approach to moral authority. Just as Asad points out for Abduh, the Iskenderpaşa Naqshis strongly emphasise the central importance of the disciplining function of living according to Islamic precepts (including ritual and social obligations). As for Abduh, it is only the individual formed by the Islamic tradition who can interpret the tradition in its authentic sense. In other words, moral authority is vested in the individual educated in *and shaped by* the Islamic tradition, most powerfully exemplified in the persona of the sheikh. And yet, it is hardly disputable that the Iskenderpaşa Naqshis operate in a highly secularised environment. But more than that, they have clearly come to embrace the Republic's political framework and accepted its legislative authority. This is evident, for instance, in Sheikh Kotku's constructive engagement with the Republican state in the 1960s and in 1970s, as well as in Esad Coşan's alignment with Turgut Özal's reforms and his call for a 'real secularism' in Turkey in the 1980s and 1990s.[20] This is also clear from many conversations I had with people affiliated with the *cemaat* who sharply criticised the authoritarian constitution of many Middle Eastern countries (also in cases where this is justified with reference to Islam), with the argument that it stifles Muslim public discourse and thus obstructs the ongoing interpretation of the Islamic sources.

One can therefore perhaps best characterise the *cemaat*'s approach by pointing out that its members assume the moral autonomy of the individual – but they tend to draw different conclusions from this assumption than Ahmad Safwat and reformers like him. The immensely successful project of 'Islamising' the everyday life, that has characterised the Islamic revival movement at least over the past quarter of a century, can only be fully understood if one recognises that this autonomy is perceived both as opportunity (in that practitioners can choose to commit themselves to an Islamic way of life rather than one tied to other social projects) and challenge (in that the dominant institutions of society tend to support and shape moral commitments in tension or conflict with Islamic moral precepts). The endeavour of building lifeworlds is thus a project that recognises – and responds to – the conditions under which the moral commitment of individual actors is shaped. For the Iskenderpaşa Naqshis this project of self-shaping (of *nefs terbiyesi*) does not require the institution of the sharia as state-law. And so their 'classical' approach does not contradict either the perception of the individual as autonomous citizen or the legal authority of the state (although, as with other moral projects, this loyalty is clearly not unconditional; see Henkel 2004).

The example of the Iskenderpaşa *cemaat* indicates that the redistribution of authority suggested by Asad is, at least in the Turkish case, more complex than he allows for. For one, neither in theory nor in practice did the Republican state restrict its project to executing legal sovereignty over its citizens; it sought instead to implement an encompassing 'moral' project that aimed at producing subjects with a particular set of qualities. This Republican project did not deny religion a place (as was the case in the early decades of the Soviet Union), but sought to control and harness it for the state's own agenda; similarly, accommodation with the state's project of secularism did not necessarily mean the bifurcation of moral authority, as Asad suggests. The 'place' of the Islamic tradition within Turkish society thus remained, and remains today, ambivalent and contested. Moreover, while the dissolution of the Ottoman 'millet' system in the Turkish Republic (which assigned each citizen to one of the religio-ethnic communities of the empire) formally disassociated the individual from any particular religious tradition, this did not necessarily end their attachment to particular religious traditions. Many Muslims remained *committed* to an interpretation of Islam which, with the emphasis on an (in principle) all-encompassing code of conduct, maintained a quasi-legal corrective to this formal autonomy.

Conclusion

Today the Iskenderpaşa *cemaat*, like other Turkish Muslim organisations, operates precisely within the space opened by the formal separation of a state-controlled legal system (formally disconnected from religious authority) and the realm of private morality. In fact, it could be said that it is this autonomy (increasingly unencumbered by inherited political loyalties, social constraints and customary interpretations of Islam) that enables the self-shaping endeavours of the Sufi tradition to take new forms. And in Turkey's emerging public sphere – made up of equally autonomous (although morally committed) individuals – the success of this self-shaping is especially fruitful.

Rumi's admonition that Sufi practitioners should both 'circle the world' and experience it in its diversity, and yet stay rooted in the Islamic tradition, aptly captures the socially engaged character of the Iskenderpaşa *cemaat* under the leadership of Mehmed Kotku and Esad Coşan. Whether actually abroad for reason of work or political exile or in Turkey, members of the *cemaat* have sought to counter the challenges posed by social contexts often indifferent or hostile to Islam by weaving Islamic ways of doing into their everyday life following the injunctions of the Islamic fiqh, by studying the example of the prophet as transmitted in the hadith collections, and by seeking spiritual purification under the guidance of their sheikh. The framework of a Sufi *cemaat* thus 'roots' the Muslim practitioner in the Islamic tradition in a manner that is both akin to other kinds of Muslim *cemaats* and yet distinct. The example of the Iskenderpaşa *cemaat* shows the potential of this framework to be extraordinarily dynamic and innovative in the way it enables the practitioner to bring the Islamic tradition to bear on his or her life. And yet, the catastrophic death of Coşan, along with that of his designated successor, also demonstrates the potential fragility of the Sufi framework over time. If we look at the *cemaat* not in isolation but as one node embedded in the much wider web of Muslim civil society organisations, however, even this fragility points to the strength of Turkey's Islamic revival movement and suggests that the organisational framework of the Sufi *cemaat* may well continue to play an important role in grounding religious Muslims within the Islamic tradition.

References

Alger, Hamid (1989) 'Der Nakşibendi-Orden in der republikanischen Türkei', in Jochen Blaschke and Martin van Bruinessen, *Islam und Politik in der Türkei*. Berlin: Berliner Institut für vergleichende Sozialforschung (Edition Parabolis).

Alger, Hamid (1990a) 'A brief history of the Naqshbandi Order', in M. Gaborieau, A. Popovic and T. Zarcone (eds) *Naqshbandis: Historical Developments and Present Situation of a Muslim Mystical Order*, Istanbul-Paris: Éditions Isis.

Alger, Hamid (1990b), 'Political aspects of Naqshbandi history', in M. Gaborieau, A. Popovic and T. Zarcone (eds) *Naqshbandis: Historical Developments and Present Situation of a Muslim Mystical Order*. Istanbul-Paris: Éditions Isis.

Asad, Talal (1986) *The Idea of an Anthropology of Islam*. Washington DC: Center for Contemporary Arab Studies.

Asad, Talal (1993) *Genealogies of Religion: Disciplines and Reasons of Power in Christianity and Islam*. Baltimore: Johns Hopkins University Press.

Asad, Talal (2003) 'Reconfigurations of law and ethics in colonial Egypt', in *Formations of the Secular: Christianity, Islam, Modernity*. Stanford: Stanford University Press, pp. 205–256.

Coşan, Esad (1996) *Islam, tasavvuf ve hayat*. Istanbul: Seha Nesriyat.

Gaborieau, Marc, A. Popovic and T. Zarcone (eds) (1990) *Naqshbandis: Historical Developments and Present Situation of a Muslim Mystical Order*. Istanbul-Paris: Éditions Isis.

Gürdoğan, Ersin Nasif (1996) *Görünmeyen Üniversite*. Istanbul: İz Yayıncılık.

Hammoudi, Abdellah (1997) *Master and Disciple: The Cultural Foundations of Moroccan Authoritarianism*. Chicago: The University of Chicago Press.

Henkel, Heiko (2004) 'Rethinking the dâr al-harb: social change and changing perceptions of the West in Turkish Islam', *Journal of Ethnic and Migration Studies* 30(5): 961–978.

Henkel, Heiko (2005) 'Between Belief and Unbelief lies the Performance of Salāt: Meaning and Efficacy of a Muslim Ritual', *Journal of the Royal Anthropological Institute* 11(03): 487–507.

Henkel, Heiko (2007) 'The Location of Islam: Inhabiting Istanbul in a Muslim way', *American Ethnologist* 34(1): 57–70.

Karaman, Hayreddin, Ali Bardakoğlu and Yunus Apaydın (2000) (eds) *İlmihal*, 2 vols. Istanbul: Islam Araştırmaları Merkezi.

Manneh, Butrus Abu (1990) 'Khalwa and râbita in the Khâlidi Suborder', in M. Gaborieau et al. (eds) *Naqshbandis: Historical Developments and Present Situation of a Muslim Mystical Order*. Istanbul-Paris: Éditions Isis.

Mahmood, Saba (2001) 'Rehearsed spontaneity and the conventionality of ritual: disciplines of the salāt', *American Ethnologist* 28(4): 827–853.

Mahmood, Saba (2004) *Politics of Piety: The Islamic Revival and the Feminist Subject*. Princeton: Princeton University Press.

Navarro-Yashin, Yael (2002) *Faces of the State: Secularism and Public Life in Turkey*. Princeton: Princeton University Press.

Özal, Korkut (1999) 'Twenty years with Mehmet Zahid Kotku: a personal story', in E. Özdalga (ed.) *Naqshbandis in Western and Central Asia: Change and Continuity*. Istanbul: Swedish Research Institute in Istanbul.

Özdalga, Elizabeth (ed.) (1999) *Naqshbandis in Western and Central Asia: Change and Continuity*. Istanbul: Swedish Research Institute in Istanbul.

Schimmel, Annemarie (1985) *Mystische Dimensionen des Islam: Die Geschichte des Sufismus*. Köln: Diederichs Verlag.

Stauth, Georg (2001) *Islam, Motor or Challenge of Modernity*. Hamburg: Lit Verlag.

White, Jenny B. (1999) 'Islamic Chic', in Çağlar Keyder (ed.) *Istanbul: Between the Global and the Local*. Lanham: Rowman and Littlefield.

Yavuz, Hakan (1999) 'The matrix of modern Turkish Islamic movements: the Naqshbandi Sufi Order', in E. Özdalga (ed.) *Naqshbandis in Western and Central Asia: Change and Continuity*. Istanbul: Swedish Research Institute in Istanbul.

Creativity and stability in the making of Sufi tradition

The Tariqa Qadiriyya in Aleppo, Syria

Paulo G. Pinto

The notion of Sufi order (*tariqa*, pl. *turuq*)[1] was considered by most of the scholarship produced until the 1990s as the main unit of analysis of Sufism as a social and historical phenomenon in the Middle Eastern societies.[2] The Arabic word *tariqa*, which is usually translated as 'Sufi order', refers to two distinct albeit complementary realities: the set of doctrines, rituals and initiation practices that constitute a particular mystical path; and the institutionalised constructs of a particular mystical tradition. While it is empirically observable that the religious discourses and practices in the Sufi communities are informed by the supra-local normative references that define the mystical tradition of their *tariqa* – such as doctrinal and poetic texts, oral narratives, saintly figures and ritual performances – there is also a great amount of local variation regarding the boundaries, content and uses of such tradition.

Religious practices and doctrines that are referred to, by Sufis and non-Sufis alike, as being specific to a particular *tariqa* can be present in Sufi communities linked to other *tariqas*. So, while the ritual of the *darb al-shish* (piercing the body with skewers) is seen by most Muslims in Syria as being peculiar to the Rifa'iyya order, it is also practised in some *zawiyas*[3] linked to the Qadiriyya and the Naqshbandiyya throughout northern Syria.[4] Similarly, the self-image that was created by the *shaykhs* of the Naqshbandiyya, which attribute to this order more sober forms of ritual, such as the silent *dhikr*,[5] and text-centred *shari'a*-oriented religiosity, does not hold truth everywhere. In the *zawiya* of shaykh Hassan al-Naqshbandi, the main centre of the Naqshbandiyya in the Kurd Dagh, the Kurdish region north of Aleppo, the *dhikr* includes the chanting of songs praising the Prophet accompanied by the sound of drums. Also, the religious authority of shaykh Hassan is linked to his capacity for performing miraculous deeds and dispensing *baraka* (grace/blessings) rather than his ability to produce a discursive exegesis of sacred texts.

The social organisation of the *tariqa* is linked to the rise of regional and transnational Sufi networks through the creation of new local communities or the incorporation of pre-existing ones under the religious authority of a *shaykh*. The degree of homogeneity in the ritual and doctrinal features of a Sufi network's various communities is directly linked to the level of material and/or symbolic dependency that their *shaykhs* have in relation to the leading *shaykh* of the *tariqa*. The particular codification of the mystical path by a Sufi *shaykh* is likely to be faithfully emulated in a new community founded by his *khalifa* (deputy), as the religious authority of the latter is directly linked to the religious teachings and the *baraka* that he received from the master.[6] As these ties weaken, ritual and doctrinal variations are likely to arise. This process can unfold in cycles of expansion and fragmentation as the *shaykh* and his community may break free from an existing network and, eventually, begin a new one while still claiming to belong to the same *tariqa*.[7]

Therefore, rather than a stable ritual and doctrinal tradition or a clearly bounded moral community, the *tariqa* is better understood as a classificatory idiom used to connect particular configurations of Sufi religiosity to idealised codifications of the mystical path. While the *tariqa* is widely used by the Sufi *shaykhs* as a tool for legitimating their religious authority and mystical constructs, it seems to have little impact on the configuration of the religious identities of the members of the Sufi communities. The Sufis whom I met during my fieldwork in Aleppo defined their links to Sufism through their affiliation to a particular *shaykh*,[8] as from their point of view he embodied the esoteric truth (*al-haqiqa al-batiniyya*) of the mystical path beyond the apparent divisions between the *tariqas*.[9]

Instead of approaching Sufism from the point of view of the Sufi orders, we should focus on the processes that allow the production and enactment of particular constructs of the Sufi tradition in each local community. The emergence of local forms of the Sufi tradition depends on the capacity of the *shaykh* to embody the mystical path and enact it as a constitutive element of the power relations that he establishes with his followers. Therefore, the religious authority of the Sufi *shaykh* and the power relations that sustain it are central elements in the process of production, circulation and reproduction of any particular configuration of the Sufi tradition.

Concerning this point, it is useful to bring in to the analysis Talal Asad's reflection on the role of power in defining religious tradition in Islam. Asad defines tradition as 'discourses that seek to instruct practitioners regarding the correct form and purpose of a given practice that, precisely because it is established, has a history' (Asad 1986: 14). Thus tradition is a normative framework that links conceptually the past and present of religious practices through the establishment of power relations with exemplary, pedagogical or corrective qualities, which Asad define as 'orthodoxy'. According to him, 'wherever Muslims have the power to regulate, uphold, require, or adjust *correct* practices, and to condemn, exclude, undermine, or replace *incorrect* ones, there is the domain of orthodoxy' (Asad 1986: 15).

Asad's analysis aptly highlights the role of power relations in the definition and delimitation of religious traditions. However, it is less useful for the understanding of the actual functioning of the various normative codifications of the mystical path that can be found in contemporary Syrian Sufism. As there is no fully integrated or homogeneous field of power relations connecting the various Sufi communities that claim affiliation to a particular *tariqa*, the discrete forms that the mystical tradition can take are shaped by the disputes to define the sources and forms of a legitimate exercise of power. Also, while the implementation of a particular codification of the Sufi tradition is related to the capacity of its carriers to impose or affirm their power, it is also shaped by the capacity of others to evade or resist it, or to give it a new meaning.

The limitations of an analysis solely focused on power relations are clear when we look at the case of the *tariqa* Qadiriyya in Aleppo. This *tariqa* has a hierarchical organisation that was inherited from the Ottoman past according to which the old Qadiri *zawiyas* in Aleppo remain under the religious authority of the *shaykh* of the zawiya al-Hilaliyya.[10] The position of *shaykh al-mashayikh* of the Qadiriyya in Aleppo is hereditarily transmitted among the *shaykhs* of the Hilali family. Until today the *shaykh* of the zawiya al-Hilaliyya determines the doctrinal and ritual content of all public activities of the *zawiyas* placed under his authority. This hierarchical organisation of power allows a high level of stability in the production, delimitation and circulation of local constructs of Qadiri tradition.

However, the relatively homogeneous distribution of a particular construct of the Qadiri tradition among the *zawiyas* affiliated to the *shaykh al-mashayikh* did not result in similar modes of religiosity or Sufi identities among them. The two main Qadiri *zawiyas* in Aleppo, the zawiya al-Hilaliyya and the zawiya al-Badinjkiyya, have profound differences in relation to their religious life. While the Sufi community in the zawiya al-Hilaliyya is defined by the commitment of its members to text-centred forms of religiosity and religious identities based on shared moral dispositions, the community in the zawiya al-Badinjkiyya is defined by *baraka*-centred forms of religiosity and religious identities based on individualised religious experiences.

The differences that exist between religious communities that share the same construct of the Qadiri tradition show that the analysis of the role of Sufism in informing and shaping the constitution of religious communities and identities in contemporary Syria cannot be limited to the distribution of power. It must seek to understand how the exercise of power is embedded in the forms of codification, transmission and enactment through which the various Sufi traditions are communicated and experienced. The specific combination of religious idioms – such as doctrines, rituals, images and symbols – into which each construct of the Sufi tradition is codified delimits a particular range of possibilities for its communication, interpretation and enactment in different contexts.[11] While the discursive meanings that are pedagogically transmitted in texts, rituals and public discourses generate a common set of shared meanings, values and cognitive capacities among the members of a particular Sufi community, the iconic metaphors that are transmitted through the ritual manipulation of concrete symbols produce embodied dispositions and religious experiences that individualise them according to their level of initiation in the mystical path.[12]

Another important issue is how these religious idioms are enacted as disciplinary practices.[13] Specific aspects of the tradition can be emphasised, suppressed or given a new meaning according to the context – such as a sermon (*khutba*), religious lesson (*dars*) or ritual gathering (*hadra*) – and the audience addressed, which can vary from the group of disciples (*murid*, pl. *muridun*) to an anonymous crowd. The transactions over meaning[14] and experience through which normative codifications of Sufism are crossed by divergent ritual performance and layers of esoteric meanings are the analytical keystone for the understanding of how stability and creativity are both constitutive elements in the transmission and circulation of the Sufi tradition.

In order to demonstrate these propositions I will analyse the processes that allow the emergence of discrete forms of religiosity in the zawiya al-Hilaliyya and the zawiya al-Badinjkiyya.

Creating tradition: the emergence of the Qadiriyya as a centralised Sufi order in Aleppo

The *tariqa* Qadiriyya in Aleppo has its main centre at the zawiya al-Hilaliyya, a late-eighteenth/early-nineteenth-century Ottoman building located at the neighbourhood of Jallun in the Old City of Aleppo (al-Ghazi 1999: 56–57). The Hilali family has held the title of *shaykh al-mashaykh* of the Qadiriyya in Aleppo since the early nineteenth century. The current *shaykh*, Jamal al-Din al-Hilali told me in several interviews that the religious authority acquired by the members of his family over the Qadiriyya in Aleppo was the result of both their excellency in religious knowledge and their spiritual and genealogical descent from ʻAbd al-Qadir Jailani, the 'founding-saint' of all Sufi orders.[15] The Hilali family also acquired the hereditary title of *shaykh* of the *tariqa* Khalwatiyya after shaykh Ibrahim al-Hilali was initiated in this *tariqa* in Cairo during his studies in al-Azhar in the late eighteenth century (Zarcone 2000: 445–446). Since then, the *shaykhs* of the Hilali family combine the function of *shaykhs* of both *tariqas* in Aleppo.

The Hilali *shaykhs* were already part of Aleppo's religious establishment by the end of the nineteenth century, when they managed to extend their authority over the main Qadiri *zawiyas* in the city. Until the twentieth century the affiliation to the Qadiriyya or the Rifaʻiyya was not only a source of religious identity, but also a form of religious distinction that positioned the individuals into networks of solidarity and circuits of power. Therefore, the notable families of Aleppo did transmit hereditarily the affiliation to these *tariqas* as part of their cultural capital[16] and the urban elite was split into 'Qadiri' and 'Rifaʻi' families (Gonnella 1995: 152; Meriwether 1999: 52–53, 58). Although there is no evidence of direct interference of the Ottoman state in the process of centralisation of the Qadiriyya in Aleppo, the role of the Qadiri *shaykhs* in organising local forms of governance within the Ottoman polity might have fostered the process.[17]

The religious prestige of the Hilali *shaykhs* in Aleppo's religious and social establishment allowed them to attract to the Qadiriyya even *shaykhs* who were affiliated to other *tariqas*, as was the case with the *shaykhs* of the Badinjiki family. The Badinjkis were originally *shaykhs* of the Rifa'iyya in the rural region east of Aleppo, but at the end of the nineteenth century the great-grandfather of the present *shaykhs* moved to Aleppo and made a *bay'a* (oath of allegiance) to the *shaykh* of the Hilaliyya, adopting the Qadiriyya. Since then, the Badinjki family has presided over a large Sufi community centred in the zawiya al-Badinjkiyya, which is located at the premises of the old al-Turnata'iyya mosque[18] in the neighbourhood of Bab al-Nayrab.

The narratives that were called upon by the current shaykh Badinjki in order to explain to me the adoption of the Qadiriyya by his great-grandfather show that the acceptance of the authority of the *shaykh al-mashayikh* was an important point in the transition from the rural to the urban milieu.[19] Even the acquisition of the *al-Turnata'iyya* mosque, which gave an urban base to the religious activities of the Badinjki *shaykhs*, is attributed to a miracle (*karama*) performed by the Hilali *shaykh* of that time (Badinjki 2006: 146). The personal connections that were created between the Badinjki *shaykhs* and the Hilali family constituted a pathway for their incorporation into Aleppo's religious establishment.

The zawiya al-Badinjkiyya in the popular neighbourhood of Bab al-Nayrab, Aleppo.

The Hilali *shaykhs* valued textual forms of religious knowledge as the main element in their codification of the Qadiri tradition. Their intellectualist approach to mysticism was expressed also in their use of ascetic disciplines from the Khalwatiyya, such as the *khalwa* (solitary retreat), as a pedagogic device for learning and the development of reflexive forms of religious subjectivity in the process of initiation into the mystical path.[20] The current shaykh Hilali defines Sufism as a mystical discipline firmly based on the *shari'a*, as, in his words, 'all mystical truth (*haqiqa*) that does not confirms the *shari'a* contains heresy *(zandaqa)*' (al-Hilali 2001: 10). Therefore, for him, the Sufi path can only be taught to those who already have a deep knowledge and practice a strong observance of the *shari'a*. Also, the tradition of the zawiya al-Hilaliyya requires its *shaykhs* to master religious and secular sciences. Shaykh Hilali complied with this ideal, receiving his education on Sufism and on the *shari'a* from his father, the previous *shaykh*, as well as studying medicine in Germany and Italy. These ideals reflect an intellectual understanding of Sufism based on the mastering of encyclopedic knowledge and on the theoretical elaboration of mystical concepts.

While the religious ideals of the Qadiri tradition codified by the Hilali *shaykhs* were successfully imposed on the *zawiyas* under their religious authority, they were challenged by the attraction that Salafi or modernistic versions of Islam and secular Arab and/or Syrian nationalism had among large parts of

The individual cells for khalwa *(retreat) in the main hall of the zawiya al-Hilaliyya.*

Aleppo's urban elite in the twentieth century. When confronted with the sociological change in his audience towards more popular strata,[21] the grandfather of the present *shaykh* decided to discontinue the initiation of disciples in the mystical path (*tariqa*). Shaykh Hilali implicitly referred to the intellectual and social skills necessary for a long and elaborated initiation in the mystical path, when he commented that his grandfather stopped issuing certificates of religious studies (*ijazat*) because there was 'a complete absence of competence (*kafa'*) [among the disciples]'[22] (Hilali 2001: 10).

Still today the present shaykh Hilali does not have disciples, despite the fact that the renewed interest in Sufism in Syria has created a social environment favourable to the recruitment of members of the middle and upper classes. He insists in limiting the mystical initiation to his own son in order to reproduce the family position as *shaykhs* of both the Qadiriyya and the Khalwatiyya. He explained to me in a conversation the causes of this refusal to re-open the mystical path:

> People are ignorant of the *shari'a*. So how can we teach them the *tariqa*? Only when people live according to the *shari'a*, Sufism can be taught again, but we won't live to see this happening.

However, the refusal of the *shaykhs* from the Hilali family to transmit the tradition of the *tariqa* through mystical initiation did not affect their leadership over the Qadiriyya in Aleppo. In reality it might actually have enhanced the charismatic power of their religious *persona* for, as many informants pointed out, they became the embodiment of the ideal of 'tradition' as a pristine and authentic form of cultural heritage, which is a central element in Aleppine identity. The construct of Aleppo's urban identity as connected to 'tradition' – which is often expressed through the public display of religious identities and practices – is particularly present among the trading families of the *suq al-medina*, Aleppo's bazaar.[23]

As most members of the Qadiri *zawiyas* under the authority of the Hilali *shaykhs* are recruited among the old trading families and their associates and dependents, the 'traditionalist' take that shaykh Hilali has on Sufism resonates well with the cultural ideals that inform the Aleppine identity of his followers. This symbolic capital allowed the Hilali *shaykhs* to maintain the centralised hierarchical organisation of the Qadiriyya under their authority until today. A similar organisation existed for the Rifa'iyya in Aleppo, but it collapsed and broke into autonomous *zawiyas* in the twentieth century. Notwithstanding the stability of the organisation and power structure of the Qadiriyya in Aleppo, it coexists with processes of religious variation that are inscribed in the forms of transmission and appropriation and enactment of the Qadiri tradition in each *zawiya*.

Transmitting tradition: mystical initiation, textual knowledge and moral counselling

Both shaykh Hilali and shaykh Badinjki agree that the only way to have access to the esoteric dimension of the *tariqa* and become a 'true Sufi' is through the process of mystical initiation (*tarbiyya*) under the guidance of a *shaykh*. As it was explained above, the practices of initiation were discontinued in the zawiya al-Hilaliyya, where they are reserved for the older son and future successor of the current *shaykh*. However, this resolution was not followed in the zawiya al-Badinjkiyya, where the *shaykh* continues to accept the oath of allegiance (*bay'a*) of new disciples and initiates them into the esoteric knowledge of the Qadiriyya.

This creates a breach in the doctrinal consensus that, according to shaykh Badinjki's own words, defines the 'true tradition' of the Qadiriyya, in opposition to the new Qadiri *zawiyas* that were created in Aleppo in the last two decades and are not affiliated to the centralised organisation of the *tariqa*.[24] Shaykh Badinjki justifies the continuation of the initiation of disciples and the practice of *khalwa* (retreat) in his *zawiya* by claiming that his ancestors had received both the Khalwatiyya and the Qadiriyya from *shaykhs* other than the Hilalis.[25] Shaykh Hilali is dismissive of shaykh Badinjki's claims, but recognises that there is nothing he can do to stop his activities. When I asked shaykh Hilali about the differences between his *zawiya* and the *Badinjkiyya*, he said that:

> They [the Badinjkis] are not very dedicated and do not study anything. For example, shaykh Badinjki says that the *khalwa* is a symbolic thing and if you do not eat during a working day you have done it. That is wrong, the *khalwa* includes fasting, studying and solitude for forty days! He says that he initiates his disciples, but he does not offer them either the correct knowledge or the right mystical initiation.

Beyond the disputes between shaykh Hilali and shaykh Badinjki, the fact is that the disciplinary practices of mystical initiation constitute a mode of transmission of the Sufi tradition that is central to the configuration of the moral community in the zawiya al-Badinjkiyya, while in the case of the Hilaliyya, they are restricted to the legitimisation of religious authority. As it was said before, the initiation into the esoteric (*batini*) aspects of the *tariqa* is reserved for the disciples of shaykh Badinjki.[26] What differentiates between a disciple and an ordinary follower of shaykh Badinjki, or even a simple member of the *zawiya*, is the fact that the former took an oath of allegiance (*bay'a*) in which he/she[27] voluntarily recognised the absolute authority of the *shaykh* and vowed to follow his advices and orders uncritically.

During the ceremony of taking the oath, shaykh Badinjki holds the future disciple's hands within his own hands and recites with him praises to God, Quranic verses, the names of God and the ritual formula of the oath. After that, shaykh Badinjki whispers the disciple's personal *wird* (mystical formula) in his ear, which he must repeat alone or, when with other people, silently, until he can accede experientially to the mystical knowledge encoded in it. The personal *wird* – which can be one of the 99 names of God or a verse from the Quran and has its content known solely by the *shaykh* and the disciple – constitutes an important disciplinary practice in the process of mystical initiation as it provides the disciple with a reflexive arena in which he/she can gradually fashion an individualised religious subjectivity.

The recitation of the *wird* also inscribes the master/disciple relation in the process of subjectification fostered by the mystical initiation. Shaykh Badinjki is the main source of religious knowledge for his disciples, the highest instance of evaluation of their progress in mastering the discipline of the *wird* and the guarantee that the mystical experiences of the disciple are in accordance with the esoteric tradition of the *tariqa*. Therefore, the disciplinary effect of the *wird* on the subjectivity of the disciple reinforces the hierarchical links that connect shaykh Badinjki with each of his disciples. This articulation between religious individuation and hierarchical relations centred on shaykh Badinjki's religious *persona* is present in all disciplinary practices that constitute the process of mystical initiation in the zawiya al-Badinjkiyya.

The process of initiation under the guidance of shaykh Badinjki comprises several stages that express the transition from exoteric to esoteric forms of knowledge. In the early stages the disciples are obliged to study the Quran and Islamic jurisprudence (*fiqh*). Shaykh Badinjki requires them to enrol in the courses on *fiqh* ministered in the state-owned *madrasas* or at the university in order to learn what he calls the 'exoteric path' (*al-tariqa al-zahiriyya*). After the disciple proves to have a satisfactory intellectual proficiency in religious sciences, shaykh Badinjki introduces him to the study of texts written by the great Sufi mystics. In the beginning of the initiation the focus is on more pedagogical classical treatises, such as the *al-Risala al-Qushayriyya* or al-Ghazzali's *Ihya' 'Ulum al-Din*. There are also contemporary texts such as *Haqa'iq 'an al-Tasawwuf*, a manual that was written in 1961 by the Aleppine shaykh 'Abd al-Qadir 'Isa and reprinted in several editions ever since. This text stresses the role of Sufism in shaping the public order in a Muslim society through its moral reform of the individuals. The more esoteric Sufi texts, such as those of Ibn 'Arabi, are introduced only in the more advanced stages of the initiation.

Gradually the study of texts is combined with mystical exercises, such as those performed during *khalwa*,[28] in order to provide the disciples with the body techniques and emotional dispositions necessary to reach the experiential dimension of the Sufi path. The disciplinary effect of the mystical initiation over the existential dimensions of the disciple's being is expressed in his correct manifestation of experiential states during the performance of the *dhikr*. These emotional and corporeal manifestations are evaluated both by the *shaykh* and the other participants in the ritual according to the models presented by the Sufi tradition, as well as those set by previous performances. These evaluations individualise and position each disciple in the mystical hierarchy of Sufism.

After the dhikr, *the participants engage in informal albeit intense conversations on religious and profane topics in the courtyard of the zawiya al-Hilaliyya.*

While there is no formal initiation path open to the members of the zawiya al-Hilaliyya, the fact that most of them have a relatively high cultural level, having completed at least secondary school, has allowed the emergence of individual and collective voluntary efforts to acquire a deeper knowledge of the Sufi doctrinal tradition. There are several forms of appropriation of the doctrinal categories and norms encoded in the Sufi treatises, which range from individual practices of reading to the creation of study groups. For example, a group of ten members of the zawiya al-Hilaliyya, all merchants in the *suq al-madina*, gather regularly in the shop of one of them to read and discuss passages of Sufi texts.

In this group the most frequently used texts are *al-Risala al-Qushayriyya* and *Haqa'iq 'an al-Tasawwuf*. The pedagogical character of these texts allows a more homogeneous distribution of doctrinal categories and religious knowledge among the members of the group through reading or exegetical commentary.[29] Therefore, the shared doctrinal understandings that are produced in the religious debate are an arena for the constitution of a moral community that has a more egalitarian aspect than the one in the zawiya al-Badinjkiyya. However, as shaykh Hilali refuses to coordinate the religious education of his followers in a system of initiation into the esoteric dimension of the Qadiri tradition, there is no authoritative selection and systematisation of a coherent corpus from the large universe of Sufi texts. As a result, there is no homogeneity in the readings of the different groups within the Hilaliyya and their members share only very broad and general doctrinal concepts and values.

The activities of both *shaykhs* as guides of their communities are also important arenas of transmission of their particular codification of the Qadiri tradition. They inscribe Sufi categories and values as practical dispositions that inform the everyday life of their followers through moral advice, religious healing and the mediation of conflicts. Despite the similarities in the religious principles that are manipulated by shaykh Hilali and shaykh Badinjki in their role as religious leaders, the meaning and disciplinary effects of their activities are shaped by the practical context in which they take place. A clear example of this happened in the spring of 2000, when I was in shaykh Hilali's office:

> A man in his 30s entered the room and, after the usual exchange of greetings, asked an audience with the *shaykh*. Once seated, he told shaykh Hilali that he was troubled by the fact that his wife wanted him to install a satellite dish in his house. He said that he was reluctant to do so because he had two daughters and the satellite TV channels could expose them to what he defined as 'immoral programs and Christian beliefs'. Shaykh Hilali told him that technology could be used for good or for evil, but had no moral quality in itself. The man replied by saying, 'but those innovations bring disturbance'. Shaykh Hilali interrupted him and said 'And many good things too. See the computer, for example, you can use it for searching immoral things in the internet, or you can use it to install softwares with the Quran or all the Hadith collection of al-Bukhari. I have a computer myself and I study better with it. If you give your daughters the right education, according to the principles of the *shari'a,* they will distinguish between good and evil. But if you do not do it, don't blame a machine for the consequences'. The man remained silent for a while, thanked the *shaykh* for his advice, asked for his blessing and departed.

The goal of this discursive strategy is to induce the listener to commit himself to a systematic inward reflexivity, which aims at the internalisation of normative religious principles as embodied cognitive, emotional and practical dispositions. Shaykh Hilali told me on another occasion that he used the Sufi notions of *muhasaba* (accountability) and *sidq* (correctness) in order to produce in his followers a sense of morality and responsibility framed by the *shari'a*. Thus, he adapted Sufi disciplinary practices, such as the reflexive evaluation of thoughts and actions in relation to a religious code, in order to internalise a set of moral dispositions that guide the processes of taking action and making choices.

Despite shaykh Hilali's focus on *shari'a*, his religious leadership is not limited to his role as an *'alim*. Many people come to him for discussions and for his opinion on religious or mystical experiences that they had during the performance of the *dhikr* or in other contexts, such as dreams, visions or premonitions. Shaykh Hilali explains the meaning of these experiences in terms of the Sufi tradition. His explanation is accompanied by a demonstration of his mastering of the textual tradition of Sufism, as he usually uses books from his library to indicate the passages that legitimate his interpretation. This 'textual education' of shaykh Hilali's followers allows the *shaykh* to discipline mystical experiences and to shape and control the shared understandings of Sufi mysticism that circulate in his community.

Shaykh Badinjiki is also known as an *'alim* by his followers, although his reputation is not as widely recognised as shaykh Hilali's. His position as a leader involved with the local politics of Bab al-Nayrab creates a social context for the construction and enactment of his religious *persona* that is very different from that of shaykh Hilali. He is not an interpreter of the *shari'a* who aims to translate it into a systematic social discourse or principles of individual morality, but rather a religious authority that uses his knowledge in order to mediate conflicts and dispense justice. For example, in the case of a dispute over the debt that a widow had contracted with the baker of her neighbourhood, he decided that her adolescent son should work as an assistant to the baker for a salary lower than the average. Therefore, as shaykh Badinjiki explained to me in a later conversation, the amount of money would be gradually paid, while the boy would earn some money and learn some working skills for his future.

Shaykh Badinjiki's religious *persona* has strong charismatic features, which include the capacity of performing miraculous or extraordinary deeds that are understood by his followers as the expression of his *baraka*. Shaykh Badinjiki's *baraka* has several sources, the main one being the esoteric knowledge of the divine reality (*haqiqa*) that he acquired through his initiation in the Sufi path. He also benefited from the *baraka* that was believed to be passed hereditarily in his family. Another important source is the relic – a hair from Prophet Muhammad – that is held in his *zawiya*. This relic is exhibited on special occasions, such as the two *'Aids* or the *Layla al-Qadir*, when it produces an epiphany of *baraka* for the participants in the *dhikr*. The regular display of shaykh Badinjiki's *baraka* allows him to connect the religious experiences of each one of his followers with the embodied elements that constitute his religious authority.

The codification of the Qadiri tradition shared by both shaykh Hilali and shaykh Badinjiki is differently embodied in their religious *persona* and enacted as constructs of authority that connect them with their followers. The moral order informed by this tradition also varies according to the disciplinary practices that are mobilised to produce and shape the religious subjectivities of the members of the two *zawiyas*. The Sufi community in the zawiya al-Hilaliyya is defined by relatively horizontal and egalitarian ties defined by doctrinal categories and moral values shared by its members. On the other hand, the members of the zawiya al-Badinjkiyya are religiously individualised through mystical experiences validated within the hierarchical relation of master and disciple that defines the Sufi initiation.

Performing tradition: ritual, symbols and religious experience

The religious order which inform the organisation of the *zawiyas* is expressed in ritual gatherings called *hadra,*[30] which mark the collective religious life of their Sufi communities. The *dhikr* is the main ritual in these gatherings. It constitutes another important context of transmission of the Qadiri tradition, as well as the main arena where the religious knowledge and embodied capacities are publicly expressed and collectively evaluated.

Both *zawiyas* follow the ritual model that is established by shaykh Hilali and transmitted to the other *shaykhs* during a weekly meeting in the zawiya al-Hilaliyya. While the form and symbolic content of the ritual is practically identical in both *zawiyas*, the religious order or subjectivities that are produced and dramatised in it are very different. The *dhikr* is composed of singing and the recitation of poems praising God, Muhammad or the members of his family (*ahl al-bayt*). Each one of these sacred figures personifies a set of moral and emotional qualities, and constitutes concrete symbols that express discrete aspects of the divine reality (*haqiqa*). The meaning of these symbols is given primarily through an experience of emotional and physical identification with them, as they work as 'a set of evocative devices for rousing, channeling and domesticating powerful emotions' (Turner 1995 [1969]: 42–43).

The dhikr *in the zawiya al-Badinjkiyya.*

The main emotional theme in the *dhikr* ritual is 'love' (*hubb*), which connects the various stages that are demarcated by the evocation of discrete sacred figures, such as Prophet Muhammad, his daughter Fatima, his son-in-law Ali, or his grandson Husayn. In this codification of the Qadiri tradition there is no canonic definition of 'love', but rather an elaborate system of classification of its emotional and physical manifestations in hierarchically organised mystical states (*ahwal*, sing. *hal*). The classification of the discrete forms and manifestations of love is taken from the normative models that are fostered in the sermons, speeches and texts that compose the universe of doctrinal discourses of the *zawiya*.

The *hadra* in both *zawiyas*[31] begins with the recitation of the *wird* by the *shaykh*, which is repeated in unison by all the participants.[32] After the recitation of the *wird* the *shaykh* stands and the participants are organised in concentric circles with him as the focal point. The places near the *shaykh* are always occupied by people who have an important rank in the hierarchy of the *zawiya*. In the middle of the room, the singers (*munshid*, pl. *munshidun*) sit in two parallel rows, linking the *shaykh* to the three main singers who sit facing him.

The main singer stands and the *shaykh* starts the utterance of '*la 'ilah 'ila Allah*', accompanied by body movements from right to left. The *dhikr* starts with the first part of the Muslim profession of faith, the *shahada*. All the participants in the *dhikr* imitate these utterances and bodily movements. Then the singer recites poems about God's love and praising the Prophet, while marking the rhythm by beating the outer side of his hand. After a while, the *shaykh* changes the chant to 'Al-lah' and the body movement to a front–back rocking, while the singer continues to sing praises to the Prophet accompanied by the chorus of the other singers.

The music and the chanting go in a *crescendo* and the bodily movements become faster and more exaggerated. As the emotional mood of the ritual is gradually heightened, the singer's voice becomes more and more intense. Some people abandon themselves in the flow of movements and utterances of God's names, closing their eyes or crying. Suddenly, the *shaykh* stops the movements and the music. Those who were carried away by the emotion of the ritual take the time to regain their senses and all sit on the floor to hear the *sama*' (spiritual concert).

During this part of the *dhikr* only the singers have an active role and the rest of the participants quietly listen to the music in order to be enraptured by it. Some people pray silently. Others enthusiastically utter expressions of approval, such as '*ya 'ayni*' (lit. Oh my eyes), '*Allah*' (God), '*na'm*' (yes), whenever the singers show excellence in their performance. The singers take turns singing praises to the Prophet and his family. This is one of the most emotional moments of the *dhikr*, for it evokes the strong devotion that the Sufis feel to the family of the Prophet (*ahl al-bayt*), as well as the protective and intercessory role that its members have for the believers.

The last part of the *dhikr* consists of songs about the Prophet and chanting of '*Allah Hu-Ma*', accompanied by a semi-circular movement of the body from the right to the left. This part of the *dhikr* has a very joyful mood, with vigorous movements and loud intonation. Then, at a sign of the *shaykh*, the movements cease to be performed and everybody starts repeating loudly '*la 'ilah 'ila Allah*'. At this point, the *shaykh* moves to the centre of the room under the cupola and everybody follows him. The main singer sings a last song, which ends in a chorus of '*ya mustafa, ya habib Allah*' (Oh Chosen One, Oh Beloved of God) sang together with back and forth movements, marking the end of the *dhikr*.

Usually, most people leave at this point, but some participants stay to listen to the *da'wa*. Shaykh Hilali told me that it is a prayer related to all the Muslim community, which includes the recitation of the *shahada*, in opposition to the *dhikr* which he defined as concerning the relationship between the individual and God. Therefore, the *hadra* leads the participants through a pendulous movement, which includes a progressive religious individualisation based on mystical experiences and the restatement of their insertion in the larger Muslim community (*umma*).

The emotional and existential states induced in the participants during the *dhikr* are collectively classified as discrete manifestations of 'love', which is both a doctrinal category and the dominant symbol[33] in the *dhikr* ritual. However, 'love' as it is constructed in the ritual condensates various levels of discrete and, even, disparate meanings, such as purity, lust, passion and contemplation, and its esoteric meaning is given by the cluster of feelings and sensations that is delimited by this term in each context.

Hence, the symbolic meanings of 'love' vary with the discrete experiential configurations that ground it in the emotional and sensorial states that were induced by the engagement of the participants in the *dhikr* ritual. Therefore, despite 'love' being a category used by the members of both Sufi communities to communicate and classify their religious experiences, its discrepant meanings reflect the little commensurability of the cognitive, emotional, sensorial and organisational realms that are expressed and created in the ritual performances of the two *zawiyas*.

The ritual performance in the zawiya al-Hilaliyya aims at a high degree of ritual precision and aesthetic refinement, in order to induce a sense of harmonious order in the participants. During the *dhikr*, the performance of the songs and their corresponding movements are tightly controlled by shaykh Hilali. The importance of the performative aspects of the ritual for the *dhikr* was explained by shaykh Hilali as deriving from 'a direct relation between music, rhythm and dhikr'. When describing the experiences induced by their engagement in the ritual performance of the *dhikr*, the participants of the *hadra* of the Hilaliyya usually used notions, such as *nisam* (order), '*aql* (reason) or, referring directly to the aesthetic aspect of the ritual, *jamal* (beauty). The mystical path is experienced as the orderly and harmonious progression towards the divine reality, which is often described by the members of the Hilaliyya as being the mystical meaning of 'love'. An ethnographic example can be seen in the speech of a 35-year-old merchant of the *suq*. When I asked why he was a member of the Hilaliyya, he said:

> I have been in other *zawiyas*, but I stayed in the Hilaliyya because only there you feel order (*nizam*), the dhikr has limits (*hudud*) that guide your soul to God and that protect it against deviations. In this *dhikr* you feel the meaning of God's love. God loves order, otherwise … only chaos would exist.

By contrast, the emphasis on shaykh Badinjiki's *baraka* through the performance of *karamat* (miraculous deeds) or religious healing during the *dhikr* and on the hierarchical distinction of the participants in the ritual creates a very different context for the experiential construction of 'love' as a religious reality.

The sensations and feelings that the emotional dimension of the ritual induces in the participants are horizontally shared through the collective repetition of coordinated movements or through the unified utterance of the name of God. However, as the *dhikr* becomes more emotional, they become fragmented in a multiplicity of loosely coordinated individual manifestations, which are perceived as directly linked to the *shaykh*'s mystical *persona*. The *shaykh* is thus ritually invested as the ultimate source of the mystical states experienced by each of the participants in the ritual. A young man in his twenties, who worked as an employee in a cloth store in the *suq*, summarised this, saying that:

> During the *dhikr* I can feel God's love (*hubb Allah*) in my heart. It comes from the shaykh's *baraka* and it gives strength to my soul.

The direct link between the participants and shaykh Badinjiki allows the dissolution of their individual differences into his mystical *persona* and their integration into his religious community. This makes the understanding of 'love' to be linked to individualised experiences of high emotional content oriented towards shaykh Badinjiki's guiding figure. In the Hilaliyya as the ritual performance aims at the collective creation of a religious order, the mystical experiences are understood as the embodiment of its various existential levels by the participants. Therefore, 'love', as an experiential category, is connected to themes of harmony and orderly connection between body, society and the universe. These examples show how the ritual mobilisation of concrete symbols for the codification, transmission and enactment of a shared Sufi tradition allows the emergence of divergent processes of religious subjectification.

Conclusion

The examples of the zawiya al-Hilaliyya and of the zawiya al-Badinjkiyya have allowed us to tackle the processes that inform and shape the dynamics of emergence, transmission and enactment of a particular codification of the Qadiri tradition as a shared religious context in two Sufi communities in Aleppo. While both *zawiyas* share a doctrinal and ritual system that was adopted as the normative model for the legitimisation of discourses, practices and identities within the religious universe of Sufism, they also present profound differences within these same domains.

In order to understand this apparently paradoxical dynamic, the analysis enquired how power was exercised, which religious vocabularies were used to codify tradition and which disciplinary practices shaped the religious subjectivities of the members of these Sufi communities. The charismatic character of religious authority, the combination of doctrinal and iconic/imagistic forms of religious codification and the central role of mystical experiences in the constitution and affirmation of Sufi subjectivities appeared as defining elements of the Qadiri tradition in both *zawiyas*. These elements allowed the constitution and spreading of the Qadiri tradition as codified by the *shaykhs* from the Hilali family, but they also constituted the well-spring from which processes of creative variation constantly emerged.

The charismatic character of Sufi religious authority is implicitly inscribed in the very distinction between the exoteric (*zahiri*) and esoteric (*batini*) truths which organises the transactions in religious knowledge within the realm of Sufism. This religious epistemology allows the inscription of individual creativity in the core of institutionalised processes of transmission of the Sufi tradition. If shared knowledge always remains attached to superficial and potentially illusory realities there is always the possibility and, even, the need for their 'correction' by esoteric illuminations. Thus, while shaykh Hilali and shaykh Badinjiki legitimate their religious knowledge by inscribing it in a chain of transmission (*silsila*) that is to a certain extent common to all Qadiri *shaykhs*, they also constantly affirm the uniqueness and superiority of their esoteric knowledge and mystical powers.

The articulation between shared religious knowledge and esoteric revelations that is inscribed in the religious *persona* of the *shaykhs* is reflected in the combination of discrete religious idioms in the codification of the Qadiri tradition. Doctrinal discourses of dogmatic or pedagogic character coexist with ritual performances and initiation practices. The esoteric dimension of the religious knowledge is transmitted through the manipulation of concrete symbols – such as 'love' as a lived experience or the Prophet and his family as iconic codifications of emotional sensibilities and moral values – in ritual performances and disciplinary practices. The fact that concrete symbols have multiple layers of meaning, which are reached not only through the intellectual decoding of their cognitive content but also by experiencing the emotional and existential realms that they evoke, prevents a durable homogenisation and stabilisation of their meaning to emerge.

Shared doctrinal categories, such as 'love', have their meaning constantly transformed and dislocated by the new configurations of their existential reality which emerge in the ritual. As the members of both *zawiyas*[34] see these experiential realms as directly connected to the esoteric dimension of the Qadiri tradition, ritual performance becomes a privileged arena for constituting and disciplining Sufi subjectivities. The emphasis on the performative aspects of ritual inscribes creativity and improvisation at the core of the arena for normative disciplining and affirmation of Sufi subjectivities. Therefore, divergent dynamics of subjectification can emerge and be consecrated as normative models among Sufi communities that have a common ritual and symbolic idiom, as is the case with the Hilaliyya and the Badinjkiyya.

From the example of the *tariqa* Qadiriyya in Aleppo we can conclude that the understanding of the dynamics of a particular codification of Sufism can only be reached by enquiring into the processes that shape its appropriation and enactment in the religious life of local communities. The analysis showed how both stability and creativity are constitutive elements of the codifications of the Sufi tradition that compose the *tariqa*. This approach opens up possibilities for a more complex and dynamic understanding of Sufism as a social phenomenon, as it focuses on the processes that inform and shape the constitution, expansion and local adaptations of its doctrinal and ritual traditions, rather than assuming the homogenous replication of its idealised codifications.

References

Asad, Talal (1986) *The Idea of an Anthropology of Islam*, Washington: Georgetown University, Center for Contemporary Arab Studies (Occasional Papers Series).

Asad, Talal (1993) *Genealogies of Religion: Disciplines of Power in Christianity and Islam*, Baltimore: Johns Hopkins University Press.

Badinjki, Nabhan (2006) 'Muqabala al-Shaykh Nabhan Badinjki', in 'Abud 'Abd-Allah al-'Askari (ed.) *Al-Turuq al-Sufiyya fi Suriya: Tasawwrat wa Mafhuma, Qira'at fi Waqi' al-Hal*, Damascus: Dar al-Namir.

Barth, Fredrik (1987) *Cosmologies in the Making: A Generative Approach to Cultural Variation in Inner New Guinea*, Cambridge: Cambridge University Press.

Barth, Fredrik (1990) 'The guru and the conjurer: transactions in knowledge and the shaping of culture in south-east Asia and Melanesia', *Man*, New Series, 25(4): 640–653.

Bourdieu, Pierre (1997) *Outline of a Theory of Practice*, Cambridge: Cambridge University Press.

Chih, Rachida (2000) *Le Soufisme au Quotidien: Confréries d'Égypte au XXe Siècle*, Paris: Sindbad/Actes Sud.

Douglas, Mary (1996 [1970]) *Natural Symbols: Explorations in Cosmology*, London: Routledge.

al-Ghazi, Kamil (1999 [orig. 1922-1926]) *Nahr al-Dhahab fi Tarikh Halab*, Aleppo: Dar al-Qalam al-'Arabi bi-H alab, 3v., v.

Gilsenan, Michael (1973) *Saint and Sufi in Modern Egypt*, Oxford: Oxford University Press.

Gilsenan, Michael (2000 [1982]) *Recognising Islam: Religion and Society in the Modern Middle East*, London: I.B. Tauris.

Gonnella, Julia (1995) *Islamische Heiligenverehrung im Urbanen Kontext, am Beispiel von Aleppo (Syrien)*, Berlin: Klaus Schwarz Verlag.

al-Hilali, Jamal al-Din ('Abd al-Qadir) (2001) *Al-Tariqa al-Qadiriyya wa al-Dhikr al-Qadiri*, Aleppo: Zawiya al-Hilaliyya.

al-Hilali, Jamal al-Din ('Abd al-Qadir) (2006) 'Liqa' ma' al-Shaykh al-Duktur Jamal 'Abd al-Qadir al-Hilali' in 'Abud 'Abd-Allah al-'Askari (ed.), *Al-Turuq al-Sufiyya fi Suriya: Tasawwrat wa Mafhumat, Qira'at fi Waqi' al-Hal*, Damascus: Dar al-Namir.

Hoffman, Valerie (1995) *Sufism, Mystics and Saints in Modern Egypt*, Columbia: University of South Carolina Press.

'Isa, 'Abd al-Qadir (1993 [1961]) *Haqa'iq 'an al-Tasawwuf*, Aleppo: Maktaba al-'Irfan.

Luizard, Pierre-Jean (1990) 'Le Soufisme Egyptien Contemporain', *Egypte/Monde Arabe*, 2: 35–94.

Meriwether, Margaret (1999) *The Kin Who Count: Family and Society in Ottoman Aleppo*, Austin: Texas University Press.

Pinto, Paulo G. (2006) 'Ritual, mysticism and Islamic law in contemporary Syrian Sufism', in Alfonso Carmona (ed.) *El Sufismo y las Normas del Islam*, Murcia: Editora Regional de Murcia, Colección Ibn 'Arabi.

Rabo, Annika (2005) *A Shop of One's Own: Independence and Reputation among Traders in Aleppo*, London: I.B.Tauris.

Seurat, Michel (1989) *L'État de Barbarie*, Paris: Seuil.

Trimingham, J. Spencer (1998 [1971]) *The Sufi Orders in Islam*, Oxford: Oxford University Press.

Turner, Victor (1967) *The Forest of Symbols: Aspects of Ndembu Ritual*, Ithaca: Cornell University Press.

Turner, Victor (1995 [1969]) *The Ritual Process: Structure and Anti-Structure*, New York: Aldine de Gruyter

Werbner, Pnina (2003) *Pilgrims of Love: The Anthropology of a Global Sufi Cult*, Bloomington & Indianapolis: Indiana University Press.

Whitehouse, Harvey (2000) *Arguments and Icons: Divergent Modes of Religiosity*, Oxford: Oxford University Press.

Zarcone, Thierry (2000) 'Un Cas de métissage entre Qadiriyya et Khalwatiyya: *Dhikr* et *Khalwa* dans la Zawiyya al-Hilaliyya de Alep', *Journal of the History of Sufism, Special Issue: The Qadiriyya Order:* 443–455.

Sacred spaces, rituals and practices

The *mazars* of Saiyid Pir Waris Shah and Shah 'Abdu'l Latif Bhitai

Uzma Rehman

In South Asia, where multiple religious and cultural traditions have co-existed for centuries, Sufi *mazars* have been functioning as centres of devotional practices for people adhering to diverse religious and cultural backgrounds.[1] Sufi *mazars* also perform multiple functions that basically link the spiritual world with the mundane desires of the people and their day-to-day business. In this regard, they not only create a sacred space for devotional expressions, but they also play financial and social roles as well as occupying an important place in the local cultural landscapes.

As religious and sacred institutions, Sufi *mazars* are visited every day by multitudes of people for various motives. A large majority of pilgrims and devotees visit the *mazars* in order to perform rituals or participate in social activities that are part of the daily life at the *mazars*. Devotees perform rituals at the *mazars* of two eighteenth-century Sufi poets/saints, Shah 'Abdu'l Latif Bhitai (hereafter, Shah Latif) in Bhit Shah, Sindh, Pakistan, and Saiyid Pir Waris Shah (hereafter, Waris Shah) in Jandiala Sher Khan, Punjab, Pakistan, for a variety of purposes. The essay provides a description of the rituals performed at the two *mazars* and an interpretation of the purposes that these rituals may serve, as well as the meaning they carry for the devotees and pilgrims. By employing Ballard's (1999) panthic, dharmic and kismetic categories, the essay analyses these aspects of the devotees' religious experience at the *mazars*.

The essay is structured in the following way: First, it provides brief accounts of the saints' biographies and of their *mazars*. Second, it briefly discusses how the space of the *mazars* is sacralised through ritual performance. It then explains various rituals performed at the *mazars* of Waris Shah and Shah Latif such as the *mach* (fire) ritual, the *dhammal* (devotional dance), the *ziyarat*, the calendrical rituals, prayer and devotion, healing and vow rituals. Finally, the essay uses Werbner's (2003) notion of 'sacred exchange' in order to analyse the mainstream and routine rituals (such as *langar*) and annual *'urs* celebrations at the two *mazars*.

References to the legendary history

Shah Latif (1689–1752) was born in a *Saiyid* family in the Hala Haveli about 80 miles from Bhit Shah (Hyderabad district, Sindh). His great grandfather Shah 'Abdu'l Karim Bulri was thought to be a great Sindhi saint and poet. His father, Shah Habib, claimed much respect among the people of the area and was thought to have received education in spiritual matters. His poetry, known as *Shah-jo-Risalo* (the book of Shah), is popular among the Sindhis – be they educated or illiterate. According to popular narratives, Shah Latif spent a few years of his youth travelling in the company of Hindu *yogis*. Compelled by his spiritual ordeals, he came to a solitary place covered in sand and settled on a *bhit* (literally, sand dune) – a place where he settled and spent the remaining days of his life and where he is thought to have composed his poetry. The *dargah*[2] of Shah Latif is situated in Bhit Shah (Hala Taluka) about six kilometres east of Hala, north-east of Hyderabad, Sindh.

Waris Shah (1722–1798) is said to have been born in a *Saiyid* family that also followed the tradition of *piri-muridi*.[3] Waris Shah is said to have never married nor did he have any children. As a young man, Waris Shah is thought to have travelled to southern Punjab, settling for some time in a town called Malka Hans. There he wrote his famous *Hir*, based on the fifteenth-century Punjabi legendary story of *Hir-Ranjha*, in a mosque in 1766. The *mazar* of *Waris Shah* is situated in Jandiala Sher Khan, a small village on Hafiz Abad Road, and is located 15 kilometres from Sheikhupura in central Punjab. The present structure of the Waris Shah Memorial Complex was built and completed in 1983, almost 200 years after the saint's death.

Mazar rituals: an anthropological study of space

Scholars such as Kim Knott turn to social, cultural and religious theories of space for analysing 'the location of religion' in contemporary societies, especially the ones that have been increasingly secularised. While analysing the ritual aspects of space, Scott suggests that 'sacred space is not stimulus for ritual; ritual, as sacralising behaviour, brings about "sacred" space. Ritual *takes place*, and *makes place* in this sense' (Smith 1987: 26; cited in Knott 2005: 43). 'Sacred place is ordinary place, ritually made extraordinary' (Knott 2005: 96). In his study of rituals, Smith (1987: 103) contends that a place is made meaningful due to the ritual activity that takes place there. He suggests that it is the focus, attention or special interest marking the ritual that 'explains the role of place as a fundamental component of ritual'. In this way, 'place directs attention'. Drawing on Knott's and Smith's analyses of space, I argue that the ritual activity is the primary factor that lends a place its sanctity. In other words, if there were no rituals or no ritual subjects, the *mazars* would be mere structures without 'sacred' life.

Ballard (1999: 9ff.) says that grounded in the spirit of the Protestant Reformation, a Eurocentric understanding of what religion might entail ignores the fact that religious experience can include a number of varied dimensions that may have different meanings for different groups of people. Ballard explains that 'in sharp contrast to contemporary processes of religious polarisation, there is a powerful sense in which Punjabi religion has historically manifested itself in a sense of spiritual inspiration which flows freely across current ethnic and religious divisions, and is consequently quite specifically *unbounded*'. Although Ballard's argument about a singularised Eurocentric understanding of religion may seem a tilt towards generalisation, it does point out the lack of emphasis in Western scholarship on indigenous understandings of the Punjabi religious life. While this essay is also related to Sindh, Ballard's argument is well suited to analyse the ritualistic practice at the shrines of Waris Shah and Shah Latif.

In order to gain a close understanding of Punjabi religious life, although these dimensions can also be easily found in other parts of South Asia including Sindh, Ballard makes a useful distinction of four elements, namely: panthic, dharmic, kismetic and qaumic.[4] He derives three out of the four dimensions from Mark Juergensmeyer's study of the rise of the Ad Dharm movement amongst the untouchables of the Punjab. The panthic dimension of popular religious practice in Punjab refers in English to 'the mystical and spiritual dimension of religious ideas and practice'. Ballard uses a definition of the term *panth* that is applicable to the religious activity across conventional distinctions of Hindu, Sikh and Muslim. He states that although the panthic traditions of Punjabi religious life have distinctive features in terms of teachings of panthic masters and backgrounds of panthic followers, they all share a similar goal; that is, to gain awareness of and have contact with the ultimate beyond the physical world.

Ballard defines the dharmic dimension of the religious experience as 'the divinely established set of rules to which all activities in the existent world, whether amongst humans, animals or even the Gods themselves, should ideally conform'. However, Ballard considers a 'straightforward equation' between the concept of *dharma* and its Western interpretation as a concept of morality misleading. Ballard explains that, if one pays more attention to the popular social conventions according to which Punjabis *actually* organise their lives, the differences between Hindu, Sikh and Muslim modes of behaviour begin to 'shrink dramatically'.

Ballard adds another dimension to the popular Punjabi religious life and identifies it as kismetic (from the Persian word *qismat*, fate), which refers to the devotees' aim to pray to the saints for their mediation in order to get their assistance and tap into their powers not only to face severe and unexpected adversity such as death, serious illness, infertility and other forms of personal affliction or experience of war, flood, famine and other similar disasters, but also to reverse and change such situations. Thus, by invoking the assistance of 'living *Babas* (persons recognized for having saintly qualities), *Sants* (saints), *Pirs* (Muslim saints and spiritual guides) and *Yogis* (Hindu ascetics)' and those who visit the shrines of 'long-dead' saints, many of the devotees try to make sense of their experience with adverse circumstances in their lives.

In the following sections, I will use the panthic, dharmic and kismetic dimensions of popular religious life in Punjab in order to analyse the rituals performed at the *mazars* of Waris Shah and Shah Latif. While recognising that these are in fact overlapping, hard-to-separate categories in practice, this essay suggests that the rituals performed at the two *mazars* are primarily an expression of the kismetic dimension of religious practice, although the panthic and dharmic dimensions are also playing a role. In other words, the majority of devotees visiting the *mazars* of Waris Shah and Shah Latif appear to perform rituals for gaining access to the saints' spiritual *baraka* (Divine grace bestowed on saints), seeking material and mundane benefits.

The panthic dimension of religious experience at the *mazars*

On the evening of the first Monday of every lunar month, a *mach* (fire) ritual is performed at Shah Latif's *dargah*. This ritual is not only associated with Shah Latif's tradition, but it is also performed at several other *mazars* in South Asia. At Shah Latif's *dargah*, the ritual starts when a group of around 65 *faqirs* (devotees) gather in the large courtyard of the *dargah* and make a fire with hay and dried branches from trees. Once the fire has been lit, the *faqirs* start to walk around it in circles. While they move, they keep repeating the words '*Aa-Hē*' (in Sindhi, meaning 'He [God] Is'). This practice is similar to other Sufi rituals related to *zikr* (repeated chanting of words of praise and glorification to God). The *sajjada-nishin* (saint's descendant or custodian) of the *dargah* sits on a prayer mat inside a raised place in the courtyard with a fence around it facing the *faqirs*. After half-an-hour, the ritual comes to an end and the *sajjada-nishin* moves towards the tomb and sits down with his face towards the closed door of the tomb-chamber and does prayers in which a large crowd of devotees join him. Following this act, a *faqir* distributes sweetmeats weighing about 40kg among those who are present at the *dargah*.

Although the *mach* ritual may be attended by devotees and pilgrims present at the *dargah*, its active performance is limited to the *faqirs* who on the one hand may be fulfilling a tradition of the saint, while on the other hand they may attempt to gain a spiritual experience. However, the fact that the ritual is observed by a large majority of devotees and pilgrims, and that the ritual ends with the distribution of sweets among those present at the *dargah*, points to a collective sharing in the blessings associated with the performance of the ritual. The *mach* ritual seems to have a spiritual importance for the *faqirs* of Shah Latif's *dargah*. Through the practice of *zikr*, they attempt to attain a deep spiritual experience and a connection with God.

Dhammal is a devotional dance performed at several *mazars* in Punjab and Sindh which can be seen as an expression of panthic religious experience. Devotees may perform the devotional *dhammal* dance in order to gain a personal spiritual experience through the ecstasy it induces in them. They may thus try to make sense of their place in the world by gaining a deep spiritual experience through bodily movements.

Every evening after the *Maghreb* prayer, *dhammal* is performed at the eastern end of Shah Latif's *dargah*.[5] This *dhammal* session starts when the *dhammali* takes his position at a gallery along the eastern boundary wall of the *mazar*, beating the drums following a traditional practice. Some devotees and pilgrims present on the occasion dance to the beat of the drums. Usually it is the male pilgrims who perform the *dhammal* but women also join in. Some women perform the *dhammal* as a fulfilment of their vows made to the saint or as a gesture of thanks to the saint for granting their petitions. During the *'urs* at Shah Latif's *dargah*, *dhammal* rituals are performed with extraordinary zeal and intensity. Several small groups of pilgrims and devotees were observed performing *dhammal*. Some devotees wore ankle bells while dancing. One could hear the sound of ankle bells mixed with the sound of a *dhol* (drum) from several directions. One group of devotees performing the *dhammal* included a young male devotee aged between 18 and 22, an elderly woman aged between 50 and 55 and other male devotees of various age groups. A young male college student performing the *dhammal* had travelled from another Sindhi town. Usually, those who dance belong to humble backgrounds. However, its performance may not be limited to devotees of particular social backgrounds. At the *mazar* of Waris Shah, apart from the annual *'urs*, *dhammal* is a rare sight. However, the *dhol* is played at the *mazar* on the first Thursday of every lunar month. Unlike Shah Latif's *dargah* where the *dhammal* has become a regular feature as part of the ritual routine, at Waris Shah's *mazar* it is performed mostly on special occasions or depends on the individual choice of devotees and pilgrims.

Devotees not only perform rituals at the *mazars* of Waris Shah and Shah Latif to gain personal, spiritual experience, but they also perform rituals in keeping with social and moral norms or in line with what Ballard calls the dharmic dimension of religious practice.

The dharmic dimension of religious experience at the *mazars*

Ballard (1999: 21) defines the dharmic domain of religious practice in Punjab as 'the divinely established set of rules to which all activities in the existent world, whether amongst humans, animals or even the Gods themselves, should ideally conform'. The dharmic dimension of religious practice in Punjab entails a systematic order of social conventions and rules. *Ziyarat* (visitation) to shrines may be considered in itself a religious norm according to particular practices among Muslims of South Asia. Although non-obligatory in essence, *ziyarat* to shrines is considered a practice that complements and reinforces faith in a systematic religious and social order.

In Pakistan, Sufi *mazars* are associated with the devotional culture. Some Muslim devotees consider it a part of their faith to visit the tombs of saints. A large number of devotees consider the saints as their spiritual guides, and seek their blessings and guidance in their daily lives. Visitation of *mazars* may be a religious duty for some. Others are advised by their *pirs* (spiritual guides) to visit regularly certain *mazars*. Some devotees seemed to believe that one learns etiquette, respect, humility and other moral lessons by visiting the *mazars*. Others claimed that through *ziyarat* to Sufi *mazars* they learn the lessons of brotherhood, friendship, devotion and humility. A male transvestite devotee described this at Shah Latif's *dargah*:

> I learnt [*adab* or manners] from the *darbars* (another term used for *mazars*) and the *Saiyids* say that we should not lie to anyone ... That one should serve one's mother and father and do good things, work hard and take care of brothers and sisters and respect them so one would not need to come to the *darbars*. I have now come to know this. That is why I am praying that I should prepare for my return to home ... my mentor taught me to visit the *darbars*, do good deeds, find the vision, share your sorrows with the king of kings.

The *mazars* allow diverse devotional and religious expressions. While some pilgrims perform the Islamic ritual of *namaz*, others recite from the Qur'an or count prayers on rosary-beads. Inside the tomb-chamber at Shah Latif's *dargah*, the general practice is to enter through the western door to the tomb-chamber, walk several times around the tomb from right to left, always having the tomb to one's left, and then exit through the eastern door. However, on a day when the tomb-chamber is less crowded, some pilgrims do not follow this order. Besides, the number of circles one makes around the tomb also depends on the pilgrims' wishes. Some complete the circle once, others twice and yet others seven times. Devotees and pilgrims offer their greetings to the saints and recite the *Fatiha* prayer at the tomb. Some sit by the tomb, pleading the saint for his intercession, or just stay quietly with their eyes closed to establish a 'communion' with him.[6]

Certain ritual acts such as the circumambulation of the tomb, lighting of the clay lamps and prostration before the saints' tombs are shared by devotees of Muslim, Hindu and Sikh backgrounds. However, this is mostly relevant in the case of Shah Latif's *dargah* and not in Waris Shah's *mazar* for the simple reason that there are practically no Hindus or Sikhs living in Jandiala Sher Khan or anywhere nearby. Although ritual acts such as lighting clay lamps and prostrating before the saint's tomb may be performed at the *mazar* of Waris Shah, one seldom observes devotees with Hindu, Sikh or Christian backgrounds in the *mazar*. One might, however, expect Christians to visit the *mazar* of Waris Shah since they form almost 25 per cent of the total population of Jandiala Sher Khan and are the largest religious minority in Sheikhupura. It appears that Christians visit the *mazar* less frequently. However, this does not stop the children from the Christian families who visit the *mazar* quite often playing together with the children from the Muslim families in the *mazar*'s grounds.

At the shrines, ritual behaviour such as emulating the saints, though voluntary in their character, may be considered as part of the dharmic dimension of religious experience. Devotees at the *mazars* of Waris Shah and Shah Latif commonly express their wish to emulate the saints. Using the information passed down through generations, some devotees attempt to adopt what they believe to have been the saints' habits, their spiritual discipline and their ideas in their own lives. Some devotees try to emulate the saints' appearance. For example, the *faqirs* of Shah Latif's *dargah* usually dress in black since they believe that the saint used to be dressed in black, the colour of mourning. Similarly, some devotees of Waris Shah try to take on an appearance in keeping with the memory of the saint preserved in paintings depicting his profile with a beard, long hair reaching his shoulders, clad in a long loose shirt with an opening to the left side joined together with buttons, and a white turban.

Some devotees even add the saints' name as a suffix to their own names. For example, a devotee of Shah Latif had added the suffix 'Latifi' to his name. Similarly, a devotee of Waris Shah had added the suffix 'Warsi' to his name. The practice of emulating the saints and one's *murshid* (spiritual master) can be traced back to the companions of Prophet Muhammad, who tried to emulate him both in his words and actions. Ever since, a common practice among Muslims has been to emulate the Prophet's *Sunnah*, the tradition which is interpreted as the Prophet's actions, his habits and his appearance. Similarly, the early Sufi mystics are considered to have followed the spiritual *Sunnah* of the Prophet.

Calendrical rituals performed at the *mazars* of Waris Shah and Shah Latif are rooted in local cultures. Such rituals often include mourning or celebration practised across religious traditions. Although some rituals of mourning or celebration performed in the *mazars* may have an Islamic background, some Hindu and Sikh devotees perform them too. For example, Muslim and Hindu pilgrims bring newly wed members of their families to the *dargah* of Shah Latif. These rituals are usually officiated by the *kunji-bardar faqir* (the *faqir* who bears the key to the tomb-chamber) or other *faqirs* of the *dargah*. For example, it is a custom among Sindhi Hindus and Muslims to tie the corners of the wedded couple's dresses together. They bring the wedded couple after the marriage ceremony has been performed in order to untie their dresses before the tomb. This is believed to bring the couple luck and blessings from the saint. These rituals performed on an elaborate scale are usually observed at Shah Latif's *dargah*. Although newly wed couples may be seen in Waris Shah's *mazar*, they mainly visit either in order to receive the saint's blessings or for recreation, and there are no specific rituals performed on this occasion. A major part of the wedding rituals are also performed at the *dargah* of Shah Latif. It should be noted, however, that during my visits to the *mazar* of Waris Shah, I did not observe Christian families from the village visiting the *mazar* after their weddings.

The kismetic dimension of religious experience at the *mazars*

Ballard states that the belief that spiritual masters are imbued with siddhic powers, their power obtained through intense meditation and discipline, is shared among all the panthic traditions of Punjab. These powers possessed by spiritual masters from various panthic traditions become even more effectively available after death or their union with the highest source of all powers at their tombs.

Ballard says that resorting to spiritual guides and visiting a shrine in search of solace not only amounts to a useful occupational therapy but also that the act of visitation itself provides relief from stress. By visiting the shrines the devotees try to make sense of the 'trials and tribulations of their everyday lives'. The devotees visiting the *mazars* of Waris Shah and Shah Latif may also engage in certain rituals in order to gain earthly benefits, solutions to the problems that they may be surrounded with, or prevention of misfortunes.

The majority of devotees visiting the shrines of '*Babas*, *Saints*, *Pirs* and *Yogis*' (saintly persons from various panthic traditions) 'are primarily concerned with gaining supernatural assistance in the face of adversity'. Ballard calls this dimension of religious practice kismetic. In other words, it can be argued that the majority of devotees of Waris Shah and Shah Latif visit their *mazars* in order to pray to the saints for earthly gains:

> *A female devotee*: Yes. Something is troubling me. I am joining my hands before him (the saint) and request him for his help that he may listen to my request…May Allah also give you children, a daughter or a son…if one comes here then one has to take something from here …may he not send us back empty handed.[7]

Most devotees are drawn to a saint's *mazar* by his reputation for possessing healing powers. The overarching phenomenon that directs the course of healing is the saint's spiritual *baraka*.

Healing rituals performed in the *mazars* of Waris Shah and Shah Latif are all-pervasive features of the *mazars*. The physically sick and the mentally and psychologically tormented are brought to the *mazars* to seek a cure. Healing rituals are performed with the help of a ritual specialist, usually a member of the descendants' families or leaders of certain groups of devotees, or by the pilgrims themselves. For example, the *sajjada-nishin* of Shah Latif's *dargah* leads periodical rituals where he acts more as a supervisor than as a ritual specialist. Due to the government control of the *mazars'* administration, there is no longer a fixed position of *mujawir* (caretaker), the person who receives the pilgrims at the tombs, as is the case in other self-autonomous *mazars* where they lead the rituals. In Shah Latif's *dargah*, this function is often performed by a *ragi faqir* and an employee of the government department of *auqaf*, inside the tomb-chamber, to direct pilgrims in the performance of their rites. This is not the case in the *mazar* of Waris Shah where rituals are mostly performed without ritual specialists.

A young devotee offers his greetings to the saint (Waris Shah) with his two little nephews.

Healing rituals are mediated by both male and female descendants of the saints at their residences outside the premises of the *mazars*. Usually the descendants are visited by their *murids* (disciples) for healing, but also by ordinary pilgrims who may either have had previous knowledge of their healing powers or may have been directed to them upon visiting the *mazars*. However, all healing rituals are performed in the name of the saints by tapping into the spiritual power that is thought to emanate from the saints' tombs.

In Shah Latif's *dargah*, healing rituals are mediated by the *sajjada-nishin*, his mother, other female members of his family and some close devotees and *faqirs* of the *dargah*. The general practice at Shah Latif's *dargah* is that the aspirant *murids* or pilgrims explain their problems and make requests for healing. The *sajjada-nishin*'s female *murids* contact either his mother or sister-in-law. In the case of Waris Shah's *mazar*, usually, the *sajjada-nishin*, his cousin and brother-in-law, or other male members of their family perform the healing rituals, while the women from their families facilitate the rituals by handing out ritual prescriptions to the *murids*.

Ritual specialists subscribe to various methods of healing and particular intangible means, formula or amulets which the ritual subjects may use or take home as a prescription or a blessed article. These include several methods. *Dam-pani* (lit. breath-water) is a traditional method where the ritual specialist whispers Qur'anic verses and blows on a glass of water and gives it to the ritual subject. Another method is *dam* (lit. breath-blow) where the ritual specialist whispers the Qur'anic verses or formula and blows on the patient's face and body. These methods are used in order to heal a ritual subject from physical and psychological ailments or in order to prevent malignant forces from harming the person.[8] There is only a slight difference in the way these rituals are performed at the two *mazars*. The *sajjada-nishin* of Shah Latif, his family members and *faqirs* of the *dargah* use black strings (masses of black thread which work as amulets) as a means of healing rituals, while the *sajjada-nishin* of Waris Shah's *mazar* and other members of his family resort to the traditional *dam-pani* (breath-water) or *dam* (breath-blow) methods for healing sick disciples or pilgrims.

Each year during the third day of the *'urs*, masses of black strings are kept inside the relic cloak of Shah Latif so that they absorb the spiritual *baraka* believed to reside in the cloak. These are then distributed among the aspirant devotees and *murids* throughout the year. The *sajjada-nishin* and the women of his family recite verses from *Shah-jo-Risalo* or special prayer formulas from the Qur'an, blow on the strings and then pass them on to the aspirant devotees along with instructions for their use or a religious formula that they are told to repeat. The women of the *sajjada-nishin*'s family also give recipes to cure certain kinds of illnesses, psychological problems, etc. Recipes for certain ailments such as dog-bites include two-and-a-half leaves from a tree in the *dargah* that are said to have healing properties.[9] If the person is healed from his/her physical/psychological ailment, he/she offers a gift, usually in the form of money, to the ritual specialists.

Rituals of healing and vow at Shah Latif's *dargah* are mostly shared by pilgrims of diverse religious backgrounds. Sometimes, however, prescriptive formulae are adjusted according to the devotees' religious backgrounds. Occasionally, ritual specialists recite the Qur'anic verses, but they do not hand out a copy of the pages of the Qur'an to non-Muslim devotees as they would do in the case of their Muslim *murids*. Instead, when dealing with Hindu devotees, the ritual specialists at Shah Latif's *dargah* recite verses from the saint's poetry or some general prayers commonly used by the Sindhis. For example, either a member of the *sajjada-nishin*'s family or a *faqir* of the *dargah* recite a famous verse from the *Sur Yaman Kalyan* (Melody of Peace Through Self Conquest) of *Shah-jo-Risalo*. The verse reads:

> You are the healer, You are the Friend; A balm that brings my pain to an end;
> O Beloved, within my body's frame; Are sorrows and pangs, without a name; O Master, this patient before You stands; O Lord, cure such with Your healing hands.[10]

Rituals of healing are also performed by the *faqirs* of the *dargah*.[11] The key bearer *faqir* performs a collective prayer every evening once the door to the tomb-chamber has been locked from outside. Due to the importance of his job as the key bearer *faqir*, he is also considered to have been blessed by the saint with spiritual power and his prayers are seen as effective. Similarly, the leaders of various groups, mainly *ragi* or *tamrani faqirs*, also mediate healing rituals.[12]

Healing rituals are also performed without the help of a 'ritual specialist' or an officiating authority. Pilgrims and devotees perform rituals themselves with

A female devotee sits in front of the singing faqirs *at Shah Latif's* dargah *expecting to be healed from her ailment.*

the help of the information passed on to them through friends, neighbours and other family members or popular stories about the saints' healing powers.

A female pilgrim from a village near Jandiala Sher Khan told me how she believed in the saint's healing power. Visits to this *mazar* have been a tradition in her family. Another elderly woman resident of Jandiala Sher Khan said that she has been visiting the *mazar* for the last 22 years and had been recently cured in her eyes after she turned almost blind. She claimed that her eyes were cured without any medical treatment, only with the help of the saint's blessings. While it is difficult to assess whether these rituals actually bring about any healing effect, it is the devotees' belief that they do. By communicating their wishes, their worries and anxieties to the saints, devotees appear to achieve a kind of psychological relief. Ballard calls this 'therapeutic relief' in his explanation of the kismetic dimension of the religious experience.

One may ask why devotees visit the shrines for healing purposes instead of visiting public health authorities. Due to the deplorable state of healthcare in Pakistan, especially in rural areas, and due to lack of economic resources, some devotees may resort to the shrines in order to gain access to the saints' intercessory powers as well as the systems of healing that were found in the premodern era. However, for others, it may be a matter of faith in the saints' spiritual *baraka*. Others yet, who have strong financial backgrounds and can afford to pay for proper treatment, may combine both medical treatment and a vow at a saint's *mazar*. Some devotees visit several shrines for healing or cure as if the chances of success may be greater if one visits more than one shrine.

The choice between using the help of a 'ritual specialist' and performing rituals individually may depend on the severity of the physical or psychological ailment of the patient. If the pilgrims suffer from serious illnesses, they are advised by the ritual specialists to visit medical doctors. Less educated pilgrims may rely entirely upon the advice of ritual specialists rather than taking independent steps. There seem to be multiple healing options available to the pilgrims and given their economic and social backgrounds, pilgrims may choose between them. Other unmediated and individualised rituals performed at the two *mazars* include the ritual vows.

Ritual vows (in Urdu, *mannat man-na*) are all-pervasive phenomena at the two *mazars*. The majority of devotees and pilgrims visit the *mazars* with the intention either of making vows the first time or as a repeated practice, or as a way of thanking the saints for having granted their previous requests by making offerings to them.

Raj and Harman (2006: 3ff.) remark that devotees visiting the shrines of deities, saints and other holy beings across South Asian traditions take vows in order to 'seize control of their own perceived spiritual and existential fate'. By taking ritual vows, devotees strike a 'deal' with the saints whereby they promise offerings in multiple forms, i.e. 'money, ritual activity, devotion, service, a willingness to undergo pain', in return for the assistance of the saints in the face of adversity. Ritual vows at the *mazars* of Waris Shah and Shah Latif are usually aimed at healing, marriage, fertility for bearing children, economic prosperity, solution of legal problems or other difficult situations. Other reasons which may not be material but have to do with personal well-being are peace of mind, psychological help, exorcism, dream interpretation with the help of senior devotees or *faqirs* of the *mazars*, confession of sins, etc. Yet, it would appear as if most vows are based on mundane and material requests that are common among the majority of pilgrims.

At the time of making their petitions, pilgrims and devotees tie rags, strings of various colours or small pouches on the trees and walls or windows located close to the tombs. These pouches contain hair from first-born babies, gathered at the time of their first head-shaving. In Shah Latif's *dargah*, most devotees tie their votive rags and strings on the dried thin branches of a tree planted at the north-western end of the *dargah* and protected by a fence. Some hang small Chinese locks along the wooden fence enclosing the tomb of the saint and his nephew. Devotees tie strings, rags or attach locks as a token for the saint to remember their requests.

After making a vow, the votive subject may have to keep fasts during a particular period, perform a cyclical formula of recitation, perform *zikr*, read from the Qur'an or perform an act of charity. If the devotee believes that the petition has been granted, he/she makes the journey to the *mazar* in order to perform the promised ritual of gratitude. This is a sacrificial moment when an offering is made. Once the ritual of gratitude is performed, the votive subject may make a new vow. This cycle appears to repeat itself especially in cases where the devotees believe their wishes have already been fulfilled. Those whose petitions are perceived as not having been granted may choose to seek the assistance of another saint. If they believe that their requests have been granted, pilgrims untie their vow rags, strings and locks.

Often the practice of making vows is handed down from one generation to the next. A woman who worked in the fields surrounding Jandiala Sher Khan, and visited Waris Shah's *mazar* quite regularly, told me that many of her requests as well as those made by her brother and other family members had been fulfilled, and they are blessed by the saint in all aspects of their lives.

In exchange for requests being granted, pilgrims present offerings of several kinds to the saint. A local family visiting the *mazar* of Waris Shah told me that they visited in order to fulfil their vow as their buffalo had recovered and was giving milk again. They brought a special dessert (rice and milk) to the *mazar* to distribute it among those present at the *mazar*. A pilgrim family visiting the *dargah* of Shah Latif from Balochistan sacrificed two lambs for their little son's *'aqiqa* (a Muslim custom of animal sacrifice for newborn babies) and distributed the meat among the poor. Another family from a small locality just outside Lahore visited the *mazar* of Waris Shah. After the devotee's wife was cured from her sickness and their daughter had married, the family visited the *mazar* led by a music band. They came with offerings in the form of large quantities of cooked food and decorated green silk sheets for the tomb of the saint, and were accompanied by a large number of relatives, neighbours and friends thanking the saint for fulfilling their requests.

While it may seem that pilgrims and devotees to these *mazars* mostly related that their wishes had been granted, there were also instances where devotees reported that their requests were not granted:

> *An elderly male devotee:* Unless one has strong belief, one's prayer is not accepted either.
> *Another elderly male devotee:* Only if one has strong faith and one comes to a saint's abode, he listens to the prayer, if not the first time, then surely second or third time. It is all about faith.[13]

During my fieldwork, I met pilgrims of Muslim and Hindu backgrounds who wished to pray to the saint at Shah Latif's *dargah* to find a wife for their sons, brothers or themselves. An elderly female Hindu pilgrim, who believed in the spiritual power of the saint, visited the *dargah* in order to pray for her son's marriage. According to some of my Muslim and Hindu respondents, Sindhis belonging to particular local castes have to pay a large amount of dowry in order to get their sons married. The price for a prospective wife or daughter-in-law is decided by negotiation, but still turns out to be higher than the majority of ordinary Sindhis can afford. Thus, in a society where there are wide gaps between the rich and the poor, devotees resort to the saints and ask them for help in order to resolve their economic difficulties.

Rituals and 'sacred exchange' at the mazars

Werbner (2003: 110) points out that acts of charity performed at Sufi shrines may be explained in various ways such as service, the love of God, merit or for God's forgiveness. At the *mazars* of Waris Shah and Shah Latif, rituals also become the means by which devotees and the management of the *mazars* express their goodwill and provide service. Some rituals have been performed at the *mazars* for centuries and over time have become part of the routines of the *mazars*. These rituals may be analysed from two perspectives. On the one hand, devotees participate in these rituals for panthic or kismetic reasons. On the other hand, since these rituals involve persons in official positions such as the *sajjada-nishins* or people from the management of the *mazars*, there seems to be an element of 'sacred exchange' present on these occasions. The people in official positions control and manage these rituals while devotees and pilgrims participate in them and make offerings for various reasons discussed above.

The daily rituals at the *mazars* of Waris Shah and Shah Latif commence with the opening of the door to the tomb-chamber in the morning and end with the closing of the door at stipulated times. Upon opening the door to the *mazars*, the person in charge usually lights up oil lamps and incense sticks. Usually, this duty is performed by appointed devotees or staff members who have either been associated with the *mazar* for a long time or are descendants of the devotees previously in charge of the keys to the *mazars*. Then the person in charge of opening the door, devotees or pilgrims voluntarily sweep the floors of the tomb-chambers and other parts of the *mazars*. Devotees may be fulfilling a vow by sweeping the *mazar* or serving the pilgrims. Pilgrims start to arrive early in the morning. Most of them are local residents. Some local devotees visit the *mazars* to greet the saint before starting their day. Others recite from the Qur'an or repeat some religious formula. Although performed according to a particular routine or schedule, the daily rituals of the *mazars* are largely informal and voluntary.

Sharing the sacred space of the *mazars* also includes partaking of the blessed food distributed there. Distribution of *langar*[14] is a common exercise in the South Asian *mazar* tradition. The tradition of *langar* is said to have been originally sustained by the saints themselves as an organised step for the welfare of the people (Naqvi 2001). It may be argued that devotees participate in charitable acts and food distribution in order to gain personal and spiritual satisfaction by making a symbolic sacrifice of a part of themselves, or they may seek the saints' supernatural assistance through these acts.

Food offerings distributed in the *mazars* are of two kinds: a) the daily *langar* arranged by the *Auqaf* administration of the *mazars*; and b) the food offered by devotees and pilgrims as charity or thanksgiving offerings made to the saints as a result of the fulfilment of their petitions.[15] Although the money spent on the *langar* in certain *mazars* is supported by the *Auqaf* administration, it is mostly sustained by the donations made by pilgrims and well-to-do devotees.

Examples of rich devotees of saints contributing with large amounts of money to the upkeep of the *mazars*, their repair and renovation, the *langar* and serving the devotees and the pilgrims are found in all parts of Pakistan. It is not only devotees and pilgrims who pay their donations to the *mazars*, but also the local governments that announce large chunks of monetary donations to the *mazars* each year:[16]

> *A male devotee*: ... thousands of people are sitting here and are getting food, tea etc. You can't even imagine who made your tea. Who would he be and where has he come from ... there are two of our friends who are sitting by the stove ... we are friends here and this is our *murshid*'s (spiritual master's) *mela* (festival). We have to perform our duty and have to perform our friends' duty. And then the enjoyment part. Everyone finds enjoyment in one thing or the other ... Here these [friends] find enjoyment in this.

The system of *langar* differs from *mazar* to *mazar*. Whereas *langar* is distributed twice a day at Shah Latif's *dargah*, there is no such tradition in Waris Shah's *mazar*, where the major part of food distribution comes entirely from pilgrims and devotees. There is a manifold increase in the number of people distributing and receiving food at the *mazars* during the monthly rituals and annual *'urs* celebrations:

> *A male devotee*: During the five six days of the *mela* (fair), hundreds and thousands of people, including beggars and other [marginalized] people, visit [the *mazar*] and in one way or the other earn their livelihoods. He (the saint) is like a king. The way his *langar* (public kitchen) runs, even a king cannot do it ... his *langar* has been running for the last 250 years ... people who cannot afford food, get to eat chicken and meat here. What could match such charity? Even after his (the saint's) death, his *faiz* (the flow of the divine grace) continues ... The biggest *faiz* is to feed the hungry or provide livelihoods.

The female members of the Hindu *Bagri* (low caste) migrant community who have settled in Bhit Shah visit the *mazar* during the daytime, beg and get their share of *langar* distributed at the *dargah*, while the male members bring the food for the family in the evenings. Charity performed at the *mazars* of Waris Shah and Shah Latif and in their surroundings seems to serve as a social security net.

Werbner (2003: 114) points out the hierarchical nature of religious giving or sacrifice among Muslims. She also mentions that at Sufi shrines, the *langar* food is only partaken of by the poor as queuing up for the food is considered 'unpleasant' and 'degrading'. Whereas there may be some truth in this statement, it is not a feature that may be applied to all Pakistani *mazars*. Certainly, the devotees of both poor as well as rich backgrounds partake from the food distributed at the *mazars* of Shah Latif and Waris Shah. However, *langar* distribution may also depend on the *mazars*' management roles. For example, it is entirely up to the *Auqaf* department as to how much funding it makes available for the food distribution.

The annual *'urs* celebrations at the *mazars*: multiple devotional and social activities and 'sacred exchange'

Werbner contends that pilgrimage to the annual *'urs* and the voluntary labour or service vested in its preparation

> are texts which are at once personal and performative. Each pilgrim re-enacts his or her own text, her or his annual visit and contribution to the growth of the lodge. Each personal text reflects on all the prior personal texts, as a series of reflexive memorials of positive action. (2003: 127)

Thus, the gifts, amulets and blessings charged with the saints' spiritual *baraka* that devotees take along have to be understood as 'tokens of moral renewal energising this mundane world of the here and now in which pilgrims live their daily lives'.

The annual *'urs* celebrations mark the death anniversary of the saints. These annual celebrations held at Sufi *mazars* are an important part of the cultural heritage of South Asia. The village fairs are considered regular features of the local social life, combining reverence for the saints with recreational festivities. During these annual celebrations, pilgrims and devotees take part in activities related to art and music, rituals, entertainment, economic opportunities, charity, spiritual and moral training, among others. Since celebrations include a combination of ritual and recreational, scholarly, literary, commercial and trade activities, they interest pilgrims and visitors from a variety of backgrounds. Rural fairs also have a large appeal to local populations due to their folkloric, art and trade-related activities. The annual *'urs* celebrations at the *mazars* of Waris Shah and Shah Latif are large-scale social and cultural events for those who live near the *mazars* or in surrounding villages, as well as those who travel from far off areas of the country.

The *'urs* held at Shah Latif is a significant devotional and cultural event which is attended by thousands of pilgrims, devotees, scholars, artists, folk singers, musicians, media representatives including TV and newspaper journalists and reporters, foreign journalists, politicians, diplomats and other foreign delegates from abroad, as well as those present in Pakistan.[17] Activities related to the *'urs* start a few days prior to the actual day of the *'urs* and continue until a few days after the *'urs*. The *'urs* is inaugurated by a government dignitary. The inauguration is performed first by giving '*ghusl*' (bath) to the tomb and laying *chadars* (sheets of silk cloth usually in green, red and black colours embossed with silver and gold verses from the Qur'an) on it.

During the *'urs* celebrations at Shah Latif's *dargah*, inside the tomb-chamber, pilgrims perform a variety of rituals. Some recite aloud from the Holy Qur'an; others sing the poetry of the saint; others meditate or sit quietly; and yet others prostrate before the tomb. Other pilgrims distribute sweets to those present in the chamber. There are constant loud chants of prayers and slogans in

Devotees and pilgrims enter the room where Shah Latif's tomb is situated in order to pay their respects to the saint, while others sit outside facing the tomb-chamber.

honour of Prophet Muhammad. Hazrat 'Ali and Shah Latif are also heard, with devotees wishing that their memory may live for ever. Devotees present on the occasion jointly respond to these slogans. On the third day of the *'urs*, an important ritual is performed at Shah Latif's *dargah* in which the *sajjada-nishin* clads himself in the traditional cloak of the saint and performs a traditional prayer. This ritual is awaited by thousands of pilgrims who are eager to catch a glimpse of the saint's dress and other relics taken on by the *sajjada-nishin*.

Women seemed to outnumber the men during the annual *'urs* celebrations at Shah Latif's *dargah*. In their article on women's agency in mosques and shrines, Mazumdar and Mazumdar (2002: 172) describe the relationship that women devotees have with a saint as 'deeply personal, emotional, and devotional'. They also term women's 'weeping, cajoling and pleading with the saint to intercede on their behalf' as a relationship that contains 'love and affection, happiness and ecstasy, pain and sorrow, and even at times frustration and anger'. On the third day of the *'urs* at Shah Latif's *dargah*, while women perform ritual circles around the tomb, they chant aloud in Sindhi communicating their wishes and petitions to the saint. Such emotionally charged scenes occur quite frequently throughout the *'urs*.

For many, *mazars* serve as a source of livelihood. During the three days of *'urs* celebrations there is an environment of a rural fair where people sell and buy, play and listen to music, make and sell food, and run public transport between Bhit Shah and other towns and villages. For vendors, non-professional artists and entertainers, their presence fulfils a double function: they visit the *mazars* to give their greetings to the saints as well as earning their livelihood there:

> *A male devotee and a food vendor*: We (the devotee seemed to refer to himself and his fellow vendors) come every year for our livelihood. We are not educated. We don't know what he (the saint) is. Allah knows better. Now he is gone. How would we know about it? We leave after we have earned our livelihood. We go to the *dargahs* to earn our livelihoods. We sleep on the ground. We don't have beds or *char-pa'i*. We sit here and eat here and sleep here too. Every year and [during] all the *melas* this is how we live.

Given the large numbers of people present for the *'urs* celebrations at the two *mazars*, the question of law and order is always present. Each year, the local police stations, municipal and provincial governments and security departments (in Sheikhupura and Hyderabad cities) prepare a line of action for meeting any incidents of violence. There have been in the past incidents of theft and pick-pocketing during the *'urs* either inside the *mazars'* premises or in their surroundings. These security arrangements are planned much ahead of the annual *'urs* and are implemented by several uniformed police officers. Although the police act as representatives of local government departments, some of them appear to be as much devoted to the saints as other pilgrims.[18] During the *'urs* at Shah Latif's *dargah*, groups of young volunteer scouts[19] helped to maintain order among pilgrims, especially during the performance of rituals related to *Muharram*.

Every year in the month of July (usually 23–25), and 9–11 of *Savan*, the fifth month of the Punjabi (Sikh) calendar, the *'urs* of Waris Shah is celebrated at the Waris Shah Memorial Complex. According to a rough estimate, the number of pilgrims visiting the *mazar* daily during the annual *'urs* reaches up to 100,000 (*Daily Times*, 26 July 2007). The rituals performed during the *'urs* tend to be informal and may be categorised as predominantly recreational. The three-day *'urs* is inaugurated by the government officials. Rituals performed by the government officials include '*ghusl*' (ritual of bathing the tomb) and Qur'an - recitation. The main events at the *'urs* include the *Hir*-recitation competition, *mushaira* (a competition of reading poetry by the poets themselves) of Punjabi Sufi poetry, *kabaddi* matches (wrestling in the South Asian style), horse-dancing, and a rather elaborate fair with a circus, stalls selling food and sweets, stalls providing medical treatment, etc. Usually, an old Punjabi feature film '*Hir-Ranjha*' is played during the annual *'urs* in Jandiala Sher Khan (*The Nation*, 20 July 2000). To mark the end of the yearly *'urs* activities, a minister of the Punjab Provincial government or the Chief Minister of Punjab himself lays a floral wreath at the tomb. *Dhammal* and *langar* (communal meal) are important features of the *'urs* (*The News*, 25 July 2005).

Devotees approach the mausoleum dancing to the rhythm of drum beats. Young boys dance *dhammal* at the *mazar* while *dhol* (beating of drums) competitions are held (*The News*, 30 July 2005). A local NGO called '*Waris Parhia*', established by some local residents, runs the *langar-khana* for the devotees during the *'urs* days and raises funds for *'urs* preparations (*The News*, 3 August 2005). During the *'urs*, some devotees even show their devotion for the saint by inflicting pain on themselves or humiliate themselves. For example, it was reported that a young male devotee walked to the *mazar* of Waris Shah from a long distance, carrying chains weighing more than 60kg tied to a ring around his neck. The devotee has been performing this act for the last seven years following his *murshid*'s (spiritual master's) instructions. Another male devotee roamed around the *mazar*'s premises 'with his head smeared in a layer of dung from the buffalos of the village', since to him all the buffalo in Jandiala Sher Khan belong to Waris Shah.

The *'urs* at Waris Shah's *mazar* is considered to be a reflection of all shades of the Punjabi culture and 'one of the few secular festivities that now exist, with all the trappings of the *mela*' (Naqvi 2005). The fact that the *'urs* is held according to the Punjabi calendar (instead of the Islamic lunar calendar) shows its historical significance in the local Punjabi religious culture. A newspaper report reads that not long ago Sikhs used to dance *bhangrha* (Punjabi folk dance) at the annual *'urs* of Waris Shah's *mazar* (*The News*, 4 August 1995). All in all, the atmosphere during the annual *'urs* celebrations at Shah Latif's *dargah* is said to be more like a fair rather than a religious occasion. Devotees at the *mazar* who are either engaged in singing the saint's poetry or listening to it seem to place more importance on the meaning and style of rendition of the poetry.

During the annual *'urs* celebrations, the physical space outside the *mazars* reflects the space inside. The towns of Bhit Shah and Jandiala Sher Khan undergo a temporary transformation during the annual *'urs*. Due to their festive contexts, the annual *'urs* celebrations held at the two *mazars* also indirectly involve the entire towns of Jandiala Sher Khan and Bhit Shah and the surrounding areas who otherwise may claim to be independent from the presence of the *mazars*. The original population of the towns increases manifold. There is a common feeling of jubilation and celebration among the local residents. Many local residents receive guests from other parts of the country. Some residents of Jandiala Sher Khan and Bhit Shah related to me that the annual *'urs* celebrations at the *mazars* of Waris Shah and Shah Latif, respectively, are a part of the community life of the towns and are important occasions for festivities, devotional experience and recreation. The significance of these annual celebrations for the local residents as well as pilgrims from far-off areas must be seen in terms of continuity of the multicultural and multireligious environment of Punjab and Sindh.

Conclusions

The essay discusses how devotees perform rituals at the *mazars* of Waris Shah and Shah Latif out of a variety of purposes which may be categorised as panthic, dharmic and kismetic. It provides a description of the rituals performed at the two *mazars* and an interpretation of the purposes that these rituals may serve, and the meaning they carry for the devotees and pilgrims. Through the performance of rituals, devotees and pilgrims try to make sense of who they are and what their place in the world is. Not only that. Through ritual performance, the devotees also attempt to improve their situation. Employing Ballard's panthic, dharmic and kismetic categories the essay analyses the devotees' religious experience at the *mazars*. It was explained that devotees perform rituals at the two *mazars* for various reasons such as gaining a deep spiritual or gnostic experience, fulfilling the social norms and conventions that are part of the systematic order of the society, or tapping into the mysterious powers of the saintly beings either in order to gain material and earthly benefits or to face adverse circumstances in their lives. By performing rituals out of a variety of motives, the devotees and the pilgrims try to make sense of who they are in moral, spiritual and religious terms and what their place in the world is.

Although devotees at the *mazars* may perform rituals in order to gain all the above-mentioned dimensions of religious experience, the ethnographic data from the two *mazars* shows that the majority of devotees and pilgrims perform rituals for the purpose of attaining access to the saints' spiritual power for mundane and earthly benefits, which is related to the kismetic dimension of religious experience. There may be a variety of reasons for this. The majority of devotees and pilgrims visiting these *mazars* have poor backgrounds which mean that they have limited access to opportunities related to health and education, and lack in economic stability. In order to cope with the problems in their lives, devotees and pilgrims resort to the saints' *mazars* in order to ask them to intervene on their behalf and help them improve their life conditions. Further, by requesting the saints' help in return for ritual performance, devotional expressions and offerings, the devotees seek relief from their mental stress and physical ailments. Another reason why the kismetic aspect of religious experience is more prevalent in the *mazars* is that it seems to respond to the devotees' most urgent needs related to their material and earthly lives.

Whereas the panthic, dharmic and kismetic dimensions of popular religious life may also be represented at the annual *'urs* celebrations at the two *mazars*, the intense devotional and social activity observed in the *mazars* on these occasions are better explained in terms of 'sacred exchange'. Devotees 'shed their mundane persona' by providing voluntary services to their fellow pilgrims, participating in the distribution of food, making offerings of food, money and other gifts to the saints which are then transferred to the poor and the deserving, and thereby take on a symbolic nature imbued with the saints' spiritual power.

References

Allana, G. (1980) *Selections from the Risalo,* Karachi: Cultural Wing, Education Department, Government of Sindh.

Ballard, Roger (1999) 'Panth, Kismet, Dharm te Qaum: continuity and change in four dimensions of Punjabi religion', in Pritam Singh and Shinder Singh Thandi (eds) *Punjabi Identity in a Global Context*, New Delhi.

Daily Times (2007) 'Celebrating the poet of love', 26 July.

Ewing, Katherine Pratt (1984) 'The Sufi as saint, curer, and exorcist in modern Pakistan', *Contributions to Asian Studies*, XVIII: 106–114.

Knott, Kim (2005) *The Location of Religion: A Spatial Analysis*, London.

Mazumdar, Shampa and Sanjoy, Mazumdar (2002) 'In mosques and shrines: women's agency in public sacred space', *Journal of Ritual Studies*, 16/2: 165–179.

Naqvi, Ather (2005) 'One among many', *The News*, 30 July.

Naqvi, Imran (2001) 'Langar', *Nawai-Waqt*, Sunday Magazine, 13 May.

Pinto, Desiderio (1995) *Piri-Muridi Relationship: A Study of the Nizamuddin Dargah*, New Delhi.

Raj, Selva J. and William P. Harman (2006) *Dealing with Deities: The Ritual Vow in South Asia*, New York.

Rehman, Uzma (2007) 'Sufi shrines and identity-construction in Pakistan: the *Mazars* of Saiyid Pir Waris Shah and Shah 'Abdu'l Latif Bhitai', University of Copenhagen, Denmark.

Smith, Jonathan Z. (1987) *To Take Place: Toward Theory in Ritual,* Chicago.

The Nation (2000) '*Mela* Waris Shah', 20 July.

The News (1995) 'Waris of Punjab', 4 August.

The News (2005a) 'Waris Shah shrine turns into a pilgrimage site', 25 July.

The News (2005b) 'Remembering *Heer*', 3 August.

Werbner, Pnina (2003) *Pilgrims of Love: The Anthropology of a Global Sufi Cult*, Karachi.

Encountering Sufism on the Web

Two Halveti-Jerrahi paths and their missions in the USA

Margaret J. Rausch

Islam is like clear water poured into different vessels.
It takes the color and shape of each vessel

al-Junayd al-Baghdadi

The contemporary transnational expansion of Sufi orders can be viewed as continuity rather than novelty in many respects. The proliferation of Sufism, and Islam more generally, crossed the borders of empires and religio-cultural traditions throughout history.[1] The current spread of Sufism to the Americas and Europe parallels its historical expansion in several ways, with travel, community-building and oral and written text production in local languages playing a crucial role in the transfer and exchange of dogma and practices in each phase.[2] Muslim migrants to distant frontier regions, driven, historically and more recently, by the pursuit of economic advancement, imported their Sufi traditions after their relocation became more permanent. The 'transplanted' Sufi orders provided familiar communal structures and a sense of home in exile.[3] In other instances, Muslim wayfarers seeking spiritual exchange imported Sufi dogma and practice into non-Muslim settings.[4] In both cases, the new Sufi communities that formed became channels for the proliferation of Islamic knowledge in the non-Muslim environment, giving rise to educational initiatives, for which women's participation as scholars, teachers and ritual leaders has been highly significant.[5] The subsequent influx of local converts fostered the integration of elements of the surrounding religio-cultural heritage into the dogma and practices,[6] resulting in local variants commonly referred to by geographical designations such as South Asian, Turkish and North African Sufism. Similarly, the more recent transplantation of Sufi orders in Europe and the Americas has entailed varying degrees of adaptation to the new environment, with gender and hierarchy constituting significant points of contention for some members. An important component of the adaptation process has been the use of the Internet, which can affect the dimensions of the orders' communities and educational potential. Their websites have become important sources of information about the orders and their mission, as well as Islam and Sufism in general, to potential newcomers and scholars alike.[7]

The expansion of the Istanbul-based Halveti-Jerrahi[8] Sufi Order to the USA gave birth to two very distinct New York-based branches, both of which maintain elaborate websites.[9] Shaykha Fatima Fariha al-Jerrahi, the American convert to Islam Phillipa de Menil Friedrich, is the current spiritual head of the Nur Ashki Jerrahi Sufi Order[10] (NAJSO) based at the Masjid al-Farah, the Mosque of Divine Ease, in New York City. Founded in 1983 by Shaykh Nur al-Anwar Ashki al-Jerrahi, the American convert to Islam Lex Hixon (d.1995), the NAJSO currently maintains subsidiary circles throughout the USA and Mexico, as well as in England and Australia. The native-born Turk Shaykh Tosun Bayrak al-Jerrahi al-Halveti is the founder and current leader of the Halveti-Jerrahi Order of Dervishes (HJOD), based at the branch's New York *dergah*, or Sufi lodge, in Spring Valley with branches in Argentina, Australia, Brazil, Canada, Chile, Italy and Spain, as well as in various urban centres in the USA. Both branches trace their lineage back to Pir Nureddin al-Jerrahi, who founded the Halveti-Jerrahi Sufi Order as an offshoot of a Turkish branch of the larger 'transnational' Halveti (Khalwati) Sufi Order in 1704. In spite of their shared lineage of origin, their geographical proximity and their common source of inspiration and guidance, the nineteenth shaykh of the Istanbul-based Halveti-Jerrahi Sufi Order, Muzaffer Ashki[11] Ozak al-Jerrahi (1916–1985), these two branches differ from each other in significant ways. These differences, which led to their development into two entirely separate entities,

Grand Sheikh Muzaffer Effendi and Sheikha Fariha sitting together after a meal in Yonkers, NY in the early 1980s.

resulted from personal choices made by their founders, and in the case of the NAJSO, by the founder's successor, Shaykha Fariha, regarding the extent and forms of the branches' adaptation to various aspects of the American religious, cultural, socio-economic and political environment.

Drawing on data found on the branches' websites, secondary sources (Webb 1995; Blann 2005; Hermansen 2000, 2004 and 2006) and statements by current members, as well as preliminary fieldwork findings, this article investigates these differences. It examines the statement of mission, outreach, declaration of lineage, instruction, ritual and approach to gender and hierarchy of the two branches, as they are articulated through the texts and images on their websites as well as through the logistics of their ritual evenings. It explores the means and degree of their adaptation to the American context as well as of their preservation of the legacy of their spiritual inspiration and guide Muzaffer Effendi. Furthermore, it sheds light on the use of websites by Sufi orders to create a virtual presence, to reach out to potential newcomers and to proliferate their approach to Islam and Sufism among Muslims and non-Muslims worldwide, as well as on their usefulness to scholars as research tools or objects.[12]

Muzaffer Effendi and his legacy

The NAJSO and the HJOD can be considered two significant, but distinct, components of Muzaffer Effendi's legacy. The spiritual and intellectual development of Muzaffer Effendi began with long and thorough training in the Islamic sciences, in particular in the Qur'an and *ahadith*, the officially compiled exemplary words and deeds of the Prophet Muhammad.[13] Continuing with his immersion in Sufism, it constituted a lifelong process lasting until his death in 1985. As his biography demonstrates, he was both firmly rooted in his perspective and willing to make revisions to this perspective, as long as the revisions were not in contradiction with his fundamental beliefs, which were based in the *shari'a*, the way of the Qur'an and *ahadith*. His own recollection of his initial hesitation before entering the Sufi path provides evidence of the degree of caution with which he approached this step. Though life changing, this step did not diminish the centrality of the *shari'a* to his life and beliefs, but rather 'sweetened' his relationship to it. Taking place officially under the guidance of two Turkish Sufi shaykhs, from 1949 until the death of the second in 1966, this second phase of his spiritual development was enhanced by his contact with foreigners from a variety of religious backgrounds, whom he enthusiastically welcomed into the Halveti-Jerrahi *tekke* in Istanbul beginning in the early 1970s,[14] as well as by his interaction with Americans, whom he met during 14 visits to the USA between 1978 and 1984.

Muzaffer Effendi's initial visit to the USA was made possible by Phillipa de Menil Friedrich, later Shaykha Fariha, and Tosun Bayrak, later Shaykh Tosun, both of whom met him in Turkey in the 1970s.[15] Tosun Bayrak, a former New York City-based artist[16] who had become disillusioned[17] by what he perceived as the ego-inflation that accompanied his artistic success, established a Sufi study group in his home in Spring Valley in 1976, assisted by his wife Jemila, an American convert to Islam. Both studied with Muzaffer Effendi in Istanbul in the 1970s and received the shaykh crown from him. During his initial visit, Muzaffer Effendi performed a *dhikr*, or Sufi remembrance ritual, on Lex Hixon's radio programme 'In the Spirit', together with the Turkish dervishes he had brought with him and Tosun Bayrak, who served as his interpreter during his visit. After the programme, Tosun Bayrak invited Lex Hixon, who had spent much of his life studying various forms of spirituality both as an academic field, culminating with a PhD in World Religions from Columbia University, and as an individual pursuit, studying with masters in several religious traditions, to accompany the group to Spring Valley. The encounter between Muzaffer Effendi and Lex, both of whom shared a profound love for all of humanity and a lifelong commitment to spirituality, resulted in an intense bond that transformed both men emotionally and spiritually, according to statements by both men and by those who observed their interaction. Muzaffer Effendi invited Lex to accompany him on the *hajj* in 1981. Their relationship opened Muzaffer Effendi further to different channels of spiritual energy and led Lex Hixon to focus more on one channel, that of Sufism, and Islam. In one conversation between the two men, Muzaffer Effendi acknowledged the accuracy of Lex Hixon's depiction of spirituality as a tree with many branches, but expressed his preference to remain in the 'trunk'. During his visits, Muzaffer Effendi spoke publicly and performed *dhikr* in a variety of venues throughout the country. He often mentioned the great pleasure he derived from sharing the spiritual power of *dhikr* with Americans of different religious backgrounds and from observing the openness and joy they exhibited in response to it. His love for God and all living beings, articulated through his words and deeds, his passion for telling stories and jokes and his exuberant ritual performances left a profound impression on his audiences.

During his visits, Muzaffer Effendi spent much of his time guiding his growing community of followers in Spring Valley. Since many of them lived in New York City, the need for a Sufi centre in Manhattan became evident. In the spring of 1980, the Dia Art Foundation belonging to Phillipa Friedrich and her husband, two of Muzaffer Effendi's Spring Valley followers, offered him a permanent venue in Manhattan. Within six months, the three-storey building was transformed into a mosque and Sufi centre and given the name Masjid al-Farah, in honour of Shaykha Fariha. Thereafter, he divided his time in the USA between Spring Valley and Manhattan. In 1980, Muzaffer Effendi bestowed the crown of shaykhhood on Phillipa Friedrich, Shaykha Fatima Fariha and Lex Hixon, Shaykh Nur al-Anwar Ashki, in Masjid al-Farah, which eventually became the centre for the NAJSO. During Muzaffer Effendi's absence, Shaykh Nur shared teaching and ritual responsibilities with a number of other *khalifas*. After Muzaffer Effendi's death in 1985, Shaykh Nur took over leadership of the NAJSO succeeded by Shaykha Fariha after Shaykh Nur's death in 1995. Like her predecessor, she guides her community through her teachings, leads them in *dhikr*, interprets their dreams and initiates new members. This article explores the divergent approaches of the NAJSO and the HJOD to perpetuating Muzaffer Effendi's legacy based on an exploration of their websites, observations of their rituals and statements by their members.

Statement of mission

The statements of mission of the two branches are articulated through texts and images on their websites. The initial page of the NAJSO website (www.narashki.jerrahi.org) displays a photo of men in white Turkish skullcaps and women with white scarves performing *dhikr* together. The following page, entitled 'Nur Ashki Jerrahi Sufi Order', is divided in half with *As-salaamu 'alaykum*, Greetings of Peace, heading the left side. Under the heading is the following statement:

> The Nur Ashki Jerrahi Sufi Order is a community of dervishes within theHalveti-Jerrahi Tariqat, in the specific lineage and spirit of Sheikh Muzaffer Ashki al-Jerrahi, Sheikh Nur al-Jerrahi, and Sheikha Fariha al-Jerrahi. We are based at Masjid al-Farah in NYC, with various circles throughout the U.S. and Mexico. We joyfully welcome seekers and students of all religious and non-religious paths into our gatherings.

Under this statement is a picture of the Halveti-Jerrahi *tekke* in Istanbul, followed by a list of four links labelled *Khutbas* (Sermons) and *Sohbets* (Talks)/Shaykha Fariha al-Jerrahi, Invitation to Union, *Dhikrullah*/The Sufi Ceremony of Divine Remembrance and Ascension: Basics in *Salat* (five daily prayers), followed by a note announcing the availability of more articles and teachings through a link labelled Teachings, and audio versions of *khutbas*, *sohbets* and spiritual discussions through a link labelled Events. Located on the second webpage, these elements are central to the website visitor's first impression and to the NAJSO's mission.

Equal in importance, on the right half of this page, is a column of quotes with pictures of their authors adjacent to them. Pictured from top to bottom are the NAJSO's guiding figures: Muzaffer Effendi, Shaykh Nur, Shaykha Fariha and Shaykha Amina, the head of the Mexico City subsidiary circle. While Shaykha Amina's hair is completely covered by a white headscarf, Shaykha Fariha is wearing a skullcap with the rest of her hair visible.[18] Muzaffer Effendi's quote, which derives from al-Junayd al-Baghdadi, reads: 'Islam is like clear water poured into different vessels. It takes the color and shape of each vessel.' His acknowledgement of this statement gives authority to its content. It serves as an official justification for the NAJSO's innovations. The other quotes focus on the heart and love as being central to Islam and the Sufi experience.

The pictures and texts communicate the NAJSO's self-definition and mission. It emphasises ritual, love, individuality and gender equality. It establishes its legitimacy by placing itself within the Halveti-Jerrahi Tariqat, in the specific lineage and spirit of Shaykh Muzaffer, Shaykh Nur and Shaykha Fariha. It seeks to proliferate knowledge of Islam, by offering its teachings and participation in its rituals to everyone, including the non-religious. The openness, individuality and gender equality characterizing these statements and pictures constitute adaptations to the American context, and are in stark contrast to the guiding principles of more traditional Sufi orders, such as the HJOD.

The visitor to the HJOD website (www.jerrahi.org) reaches a direct statement of self-definition and mission on the fourth webpage. The initial page is relatively simple, like the welcome page of the NAJSO. It contains verbal messages instead of a picture, a difference that distinguishes the two websites. Beginning with the calligraphic emblem of the mother order, with the words Hazrati Sultan Muhammad Nureddin al-Jerrahi al-Halveti in Arabic, the page contains the words, 'Welcome to the website of the Halveti-Jerrahi Sufi Order of Dervishes, A Traditional Muslim Sufi Order', followed by two links, English and Spanish, to continue.

The second page, entitled An Invitation, contains a collage of quotes from Rumi, the Qur'an and Mahmud Shabistari, a fourteenth-century Persian poet, and statements by Shaykh Tosun, a mixture that is potentially confusing to an uninformed visitor. The quotes and statements articulate some basic perspectives on Sufism, including Sufism as the heart of Islam, the richness of Sufi spiritual life and the beauty of spiritual growth through knowledge and divine union. According to one statement, anyone may visit the HJOD, but joining requires following the Qur'an and *ahadith*. Located on the second webpage, these articulations are significant to the HJOD's self-definition.

The third page focuses primarily on its relief projects. Beginning with pictures from its relief project in Palestine, it continues with links to its other relief projects in Afghanistan, Iraq and Palestine, as well as its Youth for Humanity programme. The page ends with links to other webpages, including Who We Are, Pir Nureddin Al-Jerrahi, Books and Online Reading. There are two links labelled Make a Donation, one at the top and one in the middle of the page.

By clicking on Who We Are, the visitor reaches a more direct statement of mission. After reiterating the fact that the HJOD is a traditional Muslim Sufi Order, the text states that it is a cultural, educational and social relief organisation made up of Muslims from a variety of professional, ethnic and national backgrounds with branches in Turkey, New York, California, Illinois, Bosnia, Germany, Greece, Italy, France, England, Spain, Canada, Mexico, Argentina, Chile and Brazil. Following a reiteration of a statement from the second page that knowledge protects and facilitates one's growth into a gentle, kind and beautiful being are links to two online readings describing 'the endeavour of Sufism' entitled 54 Attributes of the Dervish and 68 Blemishes of the Nafs (soul). Three paragraphs briefly describing the HJOD's projects in Afghanistan, Bangladeshi, Turkey, Palestine, Bosnia, Herzegovina and Kosovo follow. The page ends with a paragraph which reads like a list of achievements. It states that the HJOD has brought distinguished teachers to the USA, organised concerts, published 16 books, offered aid to hungry and homeless people and helped with prisoner rehabilitation, as well as serving on a community partnership clergy committee that raises awareness of substance abuse.

According to its self-definition, the HJOD is both a traditional Muslim Sufi order and a cultural, educational and social relief organisation. In keeping with the first dimension, the website is formal and void of personal information and pictures. The statements and images on the third and fourth webpages emphasise its relief projects to which visitors can contribute. Visitors' donations, in contrast to traditional Sufi donation practices, are made by credit card, making the donor's identity available and the donations tax deductible. The emphasis on its relief projects and the logistics of the activities related to them constitute a central innovation of the HJOD deriving from the American setting.

Based on the above data, the two branches, while very different in their approaches to other aspects of their self-definitions and missions, share a couple of traits and goals. Both promote Islam and Sufism in Europe and the Americas among Muslims and non-Muslims, and both seek legitimacy for their path through Pir Nureddin al-Jerrahi, the founder of the Halveti-Jerrahi Sufi Order in Istanbul. The main feature distinguishing the two branches from each other is the more emotional, open and individualistic approach of the NAJSO as opposed to the more traditional, reserved and discrete approach of the HJOD. This distinction can explain the lack of any mention of *dhikr* on the introductory pages of the HJOD website and a picture of a *dhikr* on the first NAJSO webpage. Moreover, pictures of the leaders are absent from the HJOD website, whereas they figure prominently on the NAJSO website. Furthermore, the HJOD's central goal of carrying out relief work is not shared by NAJSO. By contrast, the NAJSO emphasises its spiritual and educational mission. A further shared goal, the promotion of interfaith dialogue, is pursued more extensively by the NAJSO, through its outreach to the surrounding community and through Shaykha Fariha's ongoing participation in interfaith forums, the transcripts and audio recordings of which are archived on the website. Converting to Islam is not a prerequisite for participating in the NAJSO *dhikr*, as is the case for the HJOD. For newcomers to the NAJSO, deciding to relinquish their former religious affiliation and make the commitment to officially join the community can be a gradual process. The HJOD's sole form of involvement in interfaith dialogue consists in its membership in the community partnership clergy committee, a form that is comparatively limited and reflects the HJOD's rigid approach to its own organisational structure and borders.

Outreach

Outreach encompasses those means by which the branches make their existence known and communicate their self-definition and mission outside their circle of current members. Both branches use their websites as their primary method of outreach, in addition to word of mouth promotion through the personal contacts of members. Both advertise their subsidiary circles on their websites, and include contact information and addresses for these circles. Both reach out to Spanish speakers, the HJOD through Spanish translations of the second introductory page and its online readings, and the NAJSO through a link to the parallel Spanish-language Mexico City centre website. The main distinction between their websites is the HJOD's formality and the NAJSO's openness. The NAJSO website includes pictures of its leaders, while the HJOD website has only small group pictures of the main and some subsidiary circles reachable from links to individual circles found on its Locations page. The pictures make the NAJSO more transparent and approachable.

In addition, the NAJSO's Sufi Book Store located near the mosque also served to advertise the branch and its events until its recent closure. Furthermore, Shaykha Fariha gives public talks at conferences and encourages leaders and members from a variety of religious denominations to visit and participate in ritual gatherings. In addition, the subsidiary circle of the NAJSO in Portland, Oregon performs *dhikr* for inmates in several local prisons. By contrast, the HJOD reaches out to the surrounding community during the month of Ramadan by inviting prominent community leaders to participate in the breaking of the fast. Its two main modes of outreach, however, address two very different audiences. Shaykh Tosun's translation and publication of historical works by Turkish Sufi scholars target English-speaking scholars of Sufism worldwide, and the HJOD's relief projects offer aid to Muslims in a wide variety of contexts internationally.

Both branches seek to spread knowledge of Islam and Sufism in their local context. However, the NAJSO is better equipped to succeed in this goal. Its success is facilitated by the accessibility of the centre due to its location and by its openness. Located in Manhattan, the doors of the Masjid al-Farah are open on Thursday evening to anyone who comes along and is interested in investigating the branch and its ritual. By contrast, the HJOD's Jerrahi Mosque is situated on a rural road with no bus service on Saturday, the day of its *dhikr*. The likelihood that people of a variety of backgrounds will visit the NAJSO *dhikr* is much higher. The HJOD maintains a close-knit and exclusive community in several ways. Many of the members are second-generation participants and their children all attend the nearby Waldorf School together. This exclusivity, together with the branch's rigidity and formality, discourages some visitors. Evidence of the NAJSO's openness and the HJOD's formality also pervades their declarations of lineage.

Declaration of lineage

Lineage is a central aspect of a Sufi order's self-definition and its current leader's means of legitimacy, as well the source of its doctrine and practices. Both branches trace their lineage back to Pir Nureddin al-Jerrahi, the founder of the Halveti-Jerrahi Sufi Order, but their website presentations of lineage varies in a number of significant ways. On one webpage, the HJOD presents the story of Pir Nureddin's initiation into the Halveti Sufi Order and his founding of the Halveti-Jerrahi Sufi Order, including miraculous events occurring before his birth and during his lifetime. The website makes no mention of the link of transmission between Muzaffer Effendi and Shaykh Tosun. Muzaffer Effendi's name appears only as the author of the text '54 Attributes of the Dervish' and of some of the books available for purchase.[19] Shaykh Tosun's receipt of the shaykh crown and his founding of the HJOD are omitted.

The NAJSO webpage entitled Lineage explains the source of the initiatory power, which flows into new members from the current leader Shaykha Fariha. It describes Muzaffer Effendi's transmission of leadership to Shaykha Fariha and Shaykh Nur and the hand-taking ceremony for initiating new members:

> The initiatory power received as one enters the Nur Ashki Sufi Order streams from the Divine Heart and from the heart of the beloved Prophet Muhammad, may Allah embrace him in the peace of perfect union. This light of transmission flows through the incomparable Hazreti Fatima and Hazreti Ali, daughter and son-in-law of the Prophet, and heart to heart through eleven centuries of mystic shaykhs, to the founding pir of our order, Hazreti Pir Muhammad Nureddin Jerrahi, born in Istanbul in 1678 CE. The unbroken chain of transmission continues until it reaches these shores with Nureddin Jerrahi's nineteenth successor, Shaykh Muzaffer Ozak al-Jerrahi. In 1980 in the Masjid al-Farah, Shaykh Muzaffer placed the crown of the order, the taj, upon the head of Lex Hixon, Nur al-Anwar al-Jerrahi, and then upon the head of Fariha al-Jerrahi, who were kneeling side by side. For the remaining fifteen years of his life Shaykh Nur spread the lineage through the Americas. His vision of Universal Islam opens a new era of spiritual flowering. When personally linked with the hand of the shaykh, the dervish becomes an illumined vessel for the light of the lineage, and an outpouring of the Divine Heart.

At the bottom of the page are pictures of Muzaffer Effendi, Shaykh Nur, Shaykha Fariha and Shaykha Amina.[20] Above these pictures are calligraphic representations of Pir Nureddin, Muhammad and Allah. Clicking on Pir Nureddin's name under the representation takes the visitor to a recounting of Pir Nureddin's life and spiritual career similar to the one found on the HJOD website. Here the story is supplemented by explanations of terms and personal interpretations by Shaykh Nur, as follows:

> Nureddin means the Light of the Way of Truth. Al-Jerrahi means the Surgeon. For Shaykh Nur this meant the surgeon of the heart who performs the delicate operations necessary for clearing the heart of obstruction. Nur would also refer to him as 'the whirling diamond'.

Here again the HJOD's discretion and traditionalism and the NAJSO'S individualism, transparency and emotional exuberance distinguish the two branches' websites.

One further aspect of the NAJSO's claim to legitimacy is hair from the Prophet's beard, a relic given to the branch by Muzaffer Effendi. Muzaffer Effendi also gave one to Shaykh Tosun, but it is not mentioned on the website. The story of these relics reads:

> At the time of Sheyk Muzaffer, may Allah sanctify his secret, the Jerrahi Order in Istanbul held 3 relics of the holy beard. Effendi brought 2 of these to the U.S. at the opening of the Masjid al Farah in 1980. One he gave to the Spring Valley Tekke in the keeping of Sheyk Tosun, and one he gave to the Masjid in the keeping of Sheyk Nur. After Sheyk Nur passed, the relic mysteriously disappeared. Last year, through the grace of our brother Mujtaba Ali, the head of the Atlanta Circle, we received another holy relic of the beard. It had been held in his family, through his mother's line, and at some point it split into two. Mujtaba was given the new beard. After holding it for a precious few months – he reports that it was like the sun shining in his house – he was moved to give it to the Nur Ashki Tariqat in replacement of the earlier relic, so that it could be shared and held by all of us. May our gratitude be multiplied by the Divine gratitude, and fill his life, and that of his family with constant blessing.

The NAJSO seeks to enlighten current and potential members about every aspect of Sufi orders in general and specific details of the NAJSO, which are depicted as imbued with love and spiritual power. In pursuit of this goal, the NAJSO divulges many more details about its formation and development than the HJOD website does. The proliferation of details on the NAJSO website, and lack thereof on the HJOD website, also characterises their instructional texts.

Instruction

Both the NAJSO and the HJOD have posted instructional texts on their websites; however, the content and presentation of these texts vary considerably. Referred to as online reading, the HJOD's instructional texts are listed on one webpage as links. The page begins with a note explaining that the texts constitute 'talks and letters given to you and us by the sheykhs of this Tariqa'. Of the 34 in all, 23 are talks and 11 are letters, which bear the title of the month and year of their composition. The talks focus on a variety of topics ranging from *salat* (the five obligatory prayers), *dhikr* and *hajj* to arrogance and humility, death and fear. Each ends with Shaykh Tosun's name, and, in many cases, the date when the text was written. Many contain short quotes or long excerpts translated into English from earlier Sufi works by Turkish scholars. They constitute food for thought for those already initiated into the HJOD or familiar with Sufism. Visitors with no background will benefit to a lesser extent from these texts.

By contrast, the NAJSO's instructional materials, which are labelled Teachings, consist of an organised programme for learning about Islamic and

Sufi doctrine and practice in general, as well as the NAJSO and its approaches and practices more specifically. Included are texts explaining the logistics and meaning of ritual washing, the five pillars, individual *dhikr*, communal *dhikr* and the hand-taking ceremony. Other teachings focus on the mystical path, the Qur'an, the way of the Prophet Muhammad and the seven levels of being. In addition to attending the weekly ritual evenings and experiencing the lessons in person, those interested can consult the teachings, listen to audio versions of weekly lessons or view videos of public lectures by Shaykha Fariha. Some teaching texts are transcripts of talks or lessons given by Shaykha Fariha or Shaykh Nur. Some transcripts include questions addressed to the speaker by those members or guests in attendance. The teachings, whether in written or oral form, are personal, interactive and applicable to the contemporary context of the lives of its members and of potential newcomers, whenever appropriate. They include the perspectives of Muzaffer Effendi, Shaykh Nur, Shaykha Fariha and, to a limited extent, Shaykha Amina, as well as quotes from earlier scholarly and poetic works.

A comparison of Shaykh Nur's and Shaykh Tosun's instructional text on the first of the seven levels of being illustrates the difference in the branches' approaches. Shaykh Nur's description is part of a lesson on the shaykh's duties. After explaining the hand-taking ceremony, he turns to dream interpretation, in particular a dream experienced by Rahima, a 12-year-old member of the NAJSO's Mexico City circle, which he designates as a treasure for the entire community of NAJSO dervishes. In her dream, Rahima was taken through a large house with seven floors with variations in furnishings that suggested that she was being introduced to the seven levels of being. The floor of the first level, according to Rahima, was dirt. There were no signs of human habitation or refinement. After describing all seven floors, Shaykh Nur elaborated the first level of being, as follows:

> The first level is the domineering self, basis for the aggressiveness, territoriality and violent urge for survival that seriously threaten the coherence of our personhood, our society and our planet. There is nothing intrinsically human here. There is no possibility for hospitality. There is not even the cleanliness that is essential for human dignity. Although most human beings experience disconcerting flashes of this domineering ego, very few persons remain focused on this level. Only war criminals and other enemies of humanity could be said to live primarily on the first level of consciousness. Nevertheless, there is nothing intrinsically evil about this first level. It provides a biological ground floor for human reality. Through this consciousness, the lungs breathe and the heart beats.

Shaykh Nur's description presents a vision that is applicable to the broader context of the members' daily life conditions. Consumed by his intense compassion for all of humanity, he envisions this level not as a stage with fixed boundaries but rather as fluid, where no human dwells permanently or exclusively.

By contrast, Shaykh Tosun's online reading entitled 'Seven Levels of Being' is adapted from *Marifetname* of the eighteenth-century scholar Ibrahim Hakki Erzurumi (1703–1780). He describes the first level, referred to as *Nafsi Ammara*, as follows:

> In this first level of the development of man, the rational self and human conscience have been defeated by lust and carnal desires. At this stage, our self does not recognise any rational or moral barriers to get what it wants. It expresses itself in selfishness, arrogance, ambition, stinginess, envy, anger, cynicism, laziness and stupidity. Originally, nafs, one's self, identity, one's own personality and reality, is one of the Creator's gifts to man. But because we allow it to lean towards material values, to take pleasure only in worldly life, and because we succumb to fleshly lusts, it has turned ugly and become almost animal-like, while its shape remains that of a human being. It is a fauve camouflaged in the appearance of man, a mad animal which bites and claws itself as well as others. This ego is our private devil, our worst enemy, who is living inside us, dominating and tyrannizing us and keeping our human soul imprisoned and forgotten in the depths of our subconscious. If we are fortunate enough to be led by a guide to seek a better state, then the devil whispers in our ear: 'What business do you have to be on this path? Don't you see that everyone who was on this path sooner or later died? Now is the time of facts, of science, of prosperity, and of good life. If you want to be religious – all right! Go to the mosques, pray, fast, and pray that the spirits of these holy men of the past help you, for there is no teacher alive worth your while!'...On the level of the evil commanding ego, all these influences are very heavy. To get out from under them, someone strong has to hold you by your hand and extricate you. It is very difficult if not impossible to do it by yourself.

Shaykh Tosun continues by elaborating the fact that only with a shaykh's assistance can one progress to the next level.

The two approaches to the first level vary considerably. Shaykh Nur describes the level as a necessary and integral component of existence having little bearing on the members' lives except as the basis of biological functions. By contrast, Shaykh Tosun depicts it as a state, potentially inhabited by his readers, which is to be feared, despised and overcome with great difficulty. His depiction emphasises the absolute necessity of a shaykh's help. As in the online reading on other topics, Shaykh Tosun draws on the perspective of a scholar from an earlier historical period. His teachings lack the degree of direct, practical applicability to the contemporary context that prevails in Shaykh Nur's teachings.

Ritual

Both branches dedicate one long evening a week to gathering communally to share a meal, pray, learn and perform *dhikr*. The sequence of these activities differs from one branch to the other, as does the day of the week on which the gathering is held. More importantly, aspects of the content, atmosphere and logistics vary in several ways. These variations reflect the differences between the branches mentioned above, as well as their approaches to gender and hierarchy.

On Saturday evenings at 6.30pm, the members of the HJOD gather for their ritual evening at the Jerrahi Mosque in Spring Valley. The mosque consists of the main square-shaped room, which serves as a prayer space for men, with a *mihrab*, or niche, indicating the direction of Mecca, in one corner. Several steps up to the back is a smaller rectangular space for women separated by a low wooden barrier. Next to this space is an adjoining rectangular communal room where the meal is taken and Shaykh Tosun gives his lesson.

The evening events begin with communal prayer with the imam chanting segments of the prayers. Following the prayer, the women take their seats at a table on one side of the adjoining communal room and men at a table on the other side. Women sit at one end of the table in the middle of the room and men at the other end. After dinner, Shaykh Tosun gives his lesson, which is followed by the evening prayer and *dhikr*. The men perform the principle parts of the *dhikr* in the square-shaped room. They chant *ilahis* in Turkish and rotate hand-in-hand in a circle accompanied by drumming, creating an exquisite artistic performance. The women stand in rows, swaying back and forth and repeating some phrases from the *dhikr* in low voices in their separate space. Throughout the evening, the women's heads are covered with scarves. They wear long sleeves and floor-length skirts, dresses or trousers. The men wear white skullcaps, long-sleeved shirts and long trousers, as well as the mother order's traditional green vest in some cases. After the *dhikr*, everyone retires to the communal room for dessert and tea. The evening ends after midnight.

On Thursday evenings in the Masjid al-Farah, the NAJSO members and guests gather for their ritual evening at 6.30pm. The mosque consists of a long rectangular room with the door to the street shielded by a barrier at one end and the *mihrab* in the far left corner at the other end. The evening begins with communal prayer and a lesson by Shaykha Fariha followed by *dhikr*. Men and women take part in all activities together. They stand, bow and prostrate themselves side by side during the prayer with women forming rows behind the men's rows. During *dhikr*, both men and women chant the *ilahis* in unison. As English is the common language of the members, English translations of the *ilahis* are chanted instead of their original Turkish versions to make the experience transparent and more meaningful to the participants. Men and women, joining hands and rotating in a circle, unite in a circle of emotional fervour filled with love.

This gender mixing began with Shaykha Fariha's leadership. For most of Shaykh Nur's leadership, mixed-gender *dhikrs* took place in other NAJSO circles, including Mexico City, but not in Manhattan because of objections raised by some members. Shortly before Shaykh Nur's death, however, the men's and women's circles would begin the *dhikr* separately, but end it together in one circle. Some members could not accept the leadership of a woman and left the NAJSO when Shaykha Fariha took over. During the *dhikr*, prayer and lesson, the women wear scarves, white skullcaps they received in the hand-taking ceremony or skullcaps covered by a scarf, according to individual preference, as well as long sleeves and long skirts, dresses or trousers. The men wear their white skullcaps, long-sleeved shirts and long trousers. After the *dhikr*, everyone retires to the second floor to share a meal as a mixed-gender group.

Gender and hierarchy

The HJOD approach to gender is rigid. Only two references to women can be found on the website. Both are located in the online readings. One, entitled 'True Love', begins with a *hadith* stating that Muhammad said that he was made to love three things: women, perfume and the comfort of his eyes in prayer. An elaboration of this *hadith* is followed by a description of the creation of Adam and Eve. It states that Adam loved Eve as all beings yearn for that which is uniquely divine in themselves. It explains that the love of woman is her yearning for her origin as part of man and that God's love for human beings is the love for the one whom He has created in His own image, namely man. The text suggests that women envision themselves as part of men rather than independent beings and that God's love for the human being is only for man. The second reference to women is a brief discussion of women and power based on a rebellion by Muhammad's wives. The discussion is supported by a Qur'anic verse referring to this event and Shaykh Ibn al-'Arabi's statement that women are the strongest among Allah's creation is cited. The discussion ends with a *hadith* calling on believers to fear women.

Shaykh Tosun maintains gender segregation practices that could be considered liberal in Turkish terms and conservative from an American perspective. The most notable feature of the HJOD's approach to gender is women's marginal participation in *dhikr* as described above. Equally significant is women's exclusion from positions of leadership over men. His intention seems to be to perpetuate the practices of the mother order. However, his spiritual guide Muzaffer Effendi never imposed gender segregation on Western visitors to the Istanbul *tekke*. Instead, he encouraged Western visitors, both men and women, to remain with him and the men's group during *dhikr* and afterwards for tea and conversation. Western women were not expected to join the Turkish women members, who watched the men perform *dhikr* from behind a curtain on a darkened balcony, where they quietly imitated the swaying movements and recitation of the men.

Furthermore, the HJOD takes a conservative approach to hierarchy. The link to the text entitled '54 Attributes of a Dervish' appears twice on the HJOD website, together with the link to '68 Blemishes of the Nafs', on the introductory page 'Who We Are', and at the top of the list of online reading. This prominence underscores its importance. Along with general guidelines, it describes the status of the dervish and his behaviour vis-à-vis his shaykh, as exemplified by the following excerpt:

> A dervish should not stay too long in the presence of his shaykh unless he is asked to do so. When he is in the presence of his shaykh, he should sit on his knees, be extremely careful of unbecoming behavior, and avoid speaking unnecessarily ... He should consider his shaykh's mistakes better than his own best achievements ... A dervish should consider that when he is in the presence of the shaykh, it is as if he were in the presence of Allah, of Allah's Messenger, of the Saints and the Saint of his order, and act accordingly. He should follow his teacher's orders without fail, and with joy.

The text derives from Muzaffer Effendi's book entitled *Ziynet-ul-Kulub*. Through the use of the masculine singular, this text, like other online readings, appears to address only male dervishes. Its guidelines of ideal behaviour serve as a basis for practices regarding hierarchy within the Halveti-Jerrahi Order. They reflect the attitudes and practices of Shaykh Tosun, and some of his community's members, and his intent to preserve this aspect of Muzaffer Effendi's legacy. However, Muzaffer Effendi never imposed these guidelines on the Western followers he encountered in Istanbul or in the USA, realising that they were unaccustomed to this type of behaviour.

By contrast, the NAJSO takes a much more relaxed approach to hierarchy. Some practices regarding hierarchy common to traditional Sufi orders were voluntarily observed by some members during Shaykh Nur's leadership. These members bowed before him and kissed his hands, and stood when he entered, out of love and respect, but not because it was required of them. These practices have become less common during Shaykha Fariha's leadership as a result of her advocacy of absolute equality of status. The members of her community love and revere her immensely, and some of them choose to show their respect through various deferential gestures.

The inclusion of gender in the NAJSO's promotion of equality pervades its dogma and practice. The images of women on its website, articulated through texts and pictures, exemplify this liberal approach to gender. It is explicit in the teaching text on women's historical roles in Islam and Sufism. This text, entitled 'Dome of Prophets and Saints', lists historical figures revered and loved by the NAJSO. It mentions Eve, Hagar, Sarah, Mary, the Prophet's mother Amina, his daughter Fatima and his wives, along with significant men from these time periods. The list is followed by a quote from Ibn al-'Arabi[21] deeming women eligible for any life station available to men, including sainthood, which reads:

> All stations, all degrees, all attributes may belong to whomever God wills equally among women as among men. They share all degrees, including that of the Qutbiyya. The Shaykh al-Akbar, Muhyiddin Ibn al-Arabi.

The lengthy excerpts from the famous work on Sufi women by Abu 'Abd ar-Rahman as-Sulami that follow this quote describe numerous prominent women's contributions to the historical development of Sufism.

This teaching segment provides legitimacy for the gender equality characterising the NAJSO on a practical level. It promotes complete gender equality and women's participation and empowerment at all levels. The pictures of the NAJSO's leading figures on the second page mentioned above include two women and two men. Women participate side by side with men in *dhikr*, hold most of the NAJSO's leadership positions, give public addresses on its teachings and author some of its online foundational texts. The fact that all of its members, both men and women, receive a white skullcap upon initiation further underscores its unconditional equality. Most importantly, the current head of the NAJSO, Shaykha Fariha, as well as the heads of most of the subsidiary circles, is a woman.

Conclusion

Both the NAJSO and the HJOD perpetuate the legacy of their spiritual inspiration and guide Muzaffer Effendi, each through its own interpretation of that legacy. Both branches acknowledge his commitment to *shari'a* through their online teachings and through their practices. While the HJOD makes commitment to *shari'a* a prerequisite for membership, the NAJSO allows new members to make a commitment gradually, in keeping with Muzaffer Effendi's understanding of human nature and tolerance of cultural differences. Both branches exemplify Muzaffer Effendi's openness to change by incorporating innovations linked to the American context, namely the HJOD's relief projects and the NAJSO's individualism, transparency and liberalism in particular with regard to gender and hierarchy. While the HJOD maintains the rigidity and formality with regard to gender and hierarchy, which has traditionally characterised the Istanbul mother order, the NAJSO recognises the fact that Muzaffer Effendi chose not to impose this rigidity and formality on his Western followers. Instead, it places emphasis on creating an atmosphere that nurtures individual spiritual awakening, fostering an environment imbued with the love for God and humanity that pervaded Muzaffer Effendi's being.

Experiencing a sense of home in exile by relocated Muslim members, which constitutes a significant function of some Sufi orders that are currently expanding to Europe and the USA, is a potential effect of belonging to the HJOD or the NAJSO that is appreciated by very few, if any, of their members. For most of the members of both branches, including Shaykh Tosun, Sufism was not part of their life experiences prior to joining these orders. Instead, the HJOD and the NAJSO belong to a very different, but growing, category of transnational Sufi orders. They are among those orders that appeal more commonly to the inexperienced and uninitiated, both Muslim and non-Muslim, one aspect of continuity between these two branches and those historical orders that served to proliferate Islam among non-Muslims in frontier regions.

References

Berkey, Jonathan P. (1992) *The Transmission of Knowledge in Medieval Cairo. A Social History of Islamic Education*, Princeton: Princeton University Press.

Blann, Gregory (2005) *Lifting The Boundaries: Muzaffer Efendi and the Transmission of Sufism to the West,* Nashville: Four Worlds Publishing.

Boogert, Nico van den (1997) *The Berber Literary Tradition of the Sous*, Leiden: Nederlands Instituut voor het Nabije Oosten.

Boyd, Jean and Beverly, Mack (2000) *One Woman's Jihad*, Bloomington: Indiana University Press.

Bunt, Gary R. (2000) *Virtually Islamic: Computer-Mediated Communication and Cyber Islamic Environments*, Cardiff: University of Wales Press.

Eaton, Richard M. (1993) *The Rise of Islam and the Bengal Frontier, 1204–1760*, Berkeley: University of California Press.

ElBoudrari, Hassan (ed.) (1993) *Modes de Transmission de la Culture Religieuse en Islam*, Cairo: Institut français d'archéologie orientale (IFAO).

Ernst, Carl W. (2005) 'Ideological and technological transformations of contemporary Sufism', in Miriam Cooke and Bruce B. Lawrence (eds) *Muslim Networks from Hajj to Hip Hop*, Chapel Hill: University of North Carolina Press, pp. 191–207.

Ernst, Carl W. (forthcoming) 'Sufism, Islam, and globalization in the contemporary world: methodological reflections on a changing field of study', in Azizan Baharuddin (ed.) *Islamic Spirituality and the Contemporary World*, Kuala Lumpur: Centre for Civilisational Dialogue, University of Malaya.

Finkel, Jori (2003) 'Looking for the soul of SoHo. Avant-garde guru Richard Kostelanetz goes off the map', *The Village Voice* (16–23 July) (www.villagevoice.com/news/0329,finkel,45522,1.html).

Haddad, Yvonne (2004) *Not Quite American?: The Shaping of Arab and Muslim Identity in the United States*, Waco (Texas): Baylor University Press.

Haddad, Yvonne and John Esposito (eds) (2000) *Muslims on the Americanization Path?*, Oxford: Oxford University Press.

Halveti Jerrahi Order of Dervishes website: www.jerrahi.org.

Hermansen, Marcia (2000) 'Hybrid identity formations in Muslim America: the case of American Sufi movements', *The Muslim World*, 90(1/2): 158–197.

Hermansen, Marcia (2004) 'What's American about American Sufi movements?', in David Westerlund (ed.) *Sufism in Europe and North America*, London: RoutledgeCurzon, pp. 36–63.

Hermansen, Marcia (2006) 'Literary productions of Western Sufi movements', in Jamal Malik and John Hinnells (eds), *Sufism in the West*, London: Routledge, pp. 28–48.

Kraemer, Annette (2002) *Geistliche Autorität und islamische Gesellschaft im Wandel: Studien über Frauenälteste (otin und xalfa) im unabhängigen Uzbekistan*, Berlin: Klaus Schwarz Verlag.

Lohlker, Ruediger (2000) *Islam im Internet: Neue Formen der Religion im Cyberspace*, Hamburg: Deutsches Orient Institut

Malik, Jamal and John Hinnells (eds) (2006) *Sufism in the West*, London: Routledge.

Nur Ashki Jerrahi Sufi Order website: www.nurashkijerrahi.org.

Phillips, Carter (2000) 'The world is beautiful', *Enlightenment Magazine*, 18 (www.wie.org/j18/bayrak.asp).

Rausch, Margaret (2006) 'Ishelhin women transmitters of Islamic knowledge and culture in Southwestern Morocco', *Journal of North African Studies*, 11(2): 173–192.

Webb, Gisela (1995) 'Sufism in America', in Timothy Miller (ed.) *America's Alternative Religions*, Albany: State University of New York Press, pp. 107–108.

Werbner, Pnina (2003) *Pilgrims of Love. The Anthropology of a Global Sufi Cult*, Bloomington.

Westerlund, David (ed.) (2004) *Sufism in Europe and North America*, London: RoutledgeCurzon.

Sufism in the USA

Creolisation, hybridisation, syncretisation?

Oluf Schönbeck

Traditionally, Sufism has been defined as Islamic mysticism or mystical Islam by Western scholars – a tradition still true today (compare, Schimmel 1975; Werbner 2003; Malik and Hinnels 2006) or, for example, Hermansen 2007: 1:

> Sufism (Arabic: *tasawwuf*) is Islamic mysticism, the quest for a direct experience of the divine or the ultimate on the part of the spiritually inclined Muslims.

Whereas the word Sufism was coined in the late eighteenth century by European Orientalists primarily in connection with the literary products of Persian poets, the so-called 'Soofees' (Ernst 2002: 3f.), the Persian 'Ali b. 'Uthman al-Jullabi al-Hujwiri (d.1071) summed up the etymological musings of previous generations on the corresponding Arabic term *tasawwuf*, concluding: 'The name has no derivation answering to etymological requirements, inasmuch as [it] is too exalted to have any genus from which it might be derived.'[1]

Elusive as the etymology of *tasawwuf* may be, the origins of the various practices and world-views of the Sufis has baffled Western scholars no less. Deemed to contain elements of Greek philosophy, Christian religion and Vedanta philosophy as well as yogic meditation, Sufism has generally been assigned the part of the syncretistic bastard in the family of world religions otherwise in general considered to consist of monolithic entities.[2] But there are signs that the academic study of religion has finally reached a point where it is ready to dislodge the view of religion as an essence, a view dominant in the West since the Protestant Reformation. A similar fate appears to await the use of the term 'syncretism', originally applied derogatively in the post-Reformation period to attempts to accommodate the Protestant and Catholic traditions claimed by the opposition to consist of two essentially different faiths. Ever since, there has been a tendency to view that term syncretistic as being derivative and thus only second best; but the fascination with authenticity and originality so common since the Romantic Movement has finally given way in academia to a more sober recognition of the fact that in the world of religions there are no essences and so 'syncretism becomes a meaningless term if everything is syncretistic' (Ernst 2005: 16).[3] In the globalised market of the twentieth century – globalised in the sense of an unprecedented worldwide migration of ideas, commodities and individuals – the search for authenticity has turned into something of a wild-goose chase. Nevertheless, attempts are still made to map the development of Sufism from the early days of Islam to the beginning of the third millennium CE (for example, Malik 2006), where seven distinct phases are described).

Classifications

Gisela Webb (2006) has identified three major waves of Sufi activity in America:

1) The interest in the early 1900s of Americans and Europeans in the *lumens orientis* – the wisdom of the East – sparked by the contact of the colonial period. As an example of this first wave Webb chooses Hazrat Inayat Khan, a representative of the South Asian Chistiyya Order who in 1910 founded the Sufi Order in the West. Representing a universalistic, theosophist orientation, he wanted to unite East and West and saw the universal truth of Sufism as holding the core of all religions. The worship he promoted included discourse as well as music.

2) The second wave coincided with the anti-establishment movements of the 1960s and 1970s, and saw the flowering of several Sufi groups as part of an alternative religious milieu inspired mainly by Hindu and Buddhist traditions. One example of the Sufism of this wave was the Sufi Order of America, led by Pir Vilayat Inayat Khan, son of Hazrat Inayat Khan, who avoided overt affiliation with institutional Islam. Practices from Sufi/Zen/Yoga/Kabbala traditions were mixed and terms like 'universal' or 'cosmic' flourished.

3) The last decennia of the twentieth century with increasing immigration also from Islamic countries saw the establishment in America of branches of Sufi *tariqas* (paths or orders) originating in Islamic countries, which maintained cherished *silsilas* (chains of succession of Sufi masters) to masters living abroad while being governed by local *shaykhs*. Some of them – like the Halveti-Jerrahi Order originating from Istanbul, or the Bawa Muhaiyaddeen Fellowship founded by an immigrant from Sri Lanka – built mosques where dervishes as well as immigrant non-Sufi Muslims were accommodated. The Sufism practised in such groups is traditional in the sense of identifying with Islam and including the fundamental pillars of Islam. Members apply *ijtihad* (traditional Islamic interpretation) to their daily lives and address global problems (e.g. international charity).

Marcia Hermansen has proposed a 'horticultural' classification of the population of the 'garden' of American Sufi movements (Hermansen 2006). Groups which are founded and (usually) led by immigrants born and raised in Islamic countries and which identify with Islamic source and content she designates 'hybrids' (e.g. the Halveti-Jerrahi Order or the Bawa Muhaiyaddeen Fellowship). Groups entertaining an inclusive, universalistic view, according to which there is an eternal common truth underlying all religions, and not insisting on an Islamic identification, are dubbed 'perennials' or 'universalist'. Implicit in the term 'perennial' is of course also a reference to the *philosophia perennis* – the eternal philosophy as characterised by, for example, the French Sufi René Guenon and not least by Aldous Huxley in his *The Perennial Philosophy* (1944). This philosophy is more or less identical with what is generally understood as 'mysticism' or 'spiritualism'. Examples are the Sufi Order in the West and the Sufi Order of America, led by Pir Vilayat Inayat Khan, son of Hazrat Vilayat Inayat Khan. A third category termed 'transplants' is reserved for groups appealing primarily to small circles of immigrants with only minimal adaptation to the American context.

Obviously, the two terms 'hybrids' and 'perennials' include a highly composite and heterogeneous material, the complexity of which straddles a certain tension concerning the necessity of conforming to traditional Islamic values such as the five pillars, *shari'a*, behaviour, dress code, gender roles, etc.

The relationship to Islam as a classificatory criterion is even more explicit in the classification suggested by Alan Godlas.[4]

Islamic Sufi orders in the West

The common denominator for this category is the avowed adherence to Islam and especially to *shari'a*. Examples are the Shadhiliyya Sufi Center of North America founded by Sidi Shaykh Muhammad al-Jamal from Jerusalem, the Tariqa Burhaniya of Sudanese origin, the Naqshbandi-Haqqani Order, the Chisti Order, the Jerrahi Order and the Qadiriya Order.

Quasi-Islamic Sufi organisations and orders

In most of these organisations, the practice of Islam is not a condition for being instructed in the Sufi path, although the *shaykh* himself or herself usually adheres to the *shari'a* (but not necessarily in the normative Sunni or Shiite manner). These groups include Muslims as well as non-Muslims. Examples are the Bawa Muhayidden Fellowship and the Threshold Society and Mevlevi Order.

Non-Islamic Sufi organisations and schools in the West

The groups in this category teach Sufi doctrines and practices, but have generally cut all ties to Islam and the members are generally non-Muslims. Sufism is considered to be fundamentally universal and prior to Islam. Examples are the Sufi Order International (formerly the Sufi Order in the West), led by Pir Zia Inayat Khan (son of Pir Vilayat Inayat Khan); International Sufi Movement, led by Hidayat Inayat Khan (another son of Hazrat Inayat Khan); Sufi Ruhaniat International (formerly the Sufi Islamia Ruhaniat Society), founded by Murshid Samuel Lewis, also known as Sufi Sam and a disciple of Hazrat Inayat Khan; the Mevlevi Order of America; the Golden Sufi Center; Sufi Foundation of America and Sufism Reoriented.

Organisations or schools related to Sufism or Sufi orders

Included in this category are various organisations which aspire to revive the spiritual dimension of Islam and disseminate knowledge of Sufism by sponsoring seminars and conferences and publishing scholarly journals. Included are such organisations as Islamic Studies and Research Association, International Association of Sufism, American Sufi Muslim Association and the Naqshbandi Foundation for Islamic Education.

Unfortunately, this categorisation is not very precise as far as stating its criteria for defining Islam is concerned, although this clearly is pivotal for the categorisation itself. Nevertheless, one may – with reference to Godlas' categories and thus with some degree of academic legitimacy – consider oneself a practising Sufi or member of a Sufi order without adhering to Islam. This of course makes the traditional characterisation of Sufism as Islamic mysticism somewhat ambiguous, to say the least. Some examples of what is entailed in qualifying to be categorised as an Islamic Sufi order in the West, a Quasi-Islamic Sufi organisation or order, and a Non-Islamic Sufi organisation or order, may illustrate this.

Islamic Sufi orders in the West

The North American headquarters of the Shadhiliya Sufi Center is located in California. The head of the centre is Sidi Shaykh Muhammad Sa'id al-Jamal who has done most of his work in Jerusalem, although he belongs to a Syrian branch of the Shadhili Order. Since 1993 he has been travelling in the West and every year he visits the North American branch in California.

The lay-out of the website of the centre clearly indicates that this is an Islamic organisation. Thus, for instance, when the time of Ramadan is approaching all the appropriate practices are carefully listed.

Among the recurring activities of the centre is *dhikr*, which takes place on Sundays and Thursdays – Thursdays as preparation for Friday's *jum'a* (Friday prayer) – and *zawiya*, i.e. spiritual retreats. Descriptions of activities are elaborate and use the appropriate Arabic terms and the overall impression is a combined introduction to the Tariqa Shadhiliyya including the *shaykh's silsila*, as well as to Islam with the five pillars and all they involve supplied with pages with an Arabic glossary and guide to Arabic pronunciation.

Among the more exotic elements is the so-called 'Healing Intensive' offering 'physical, emotional and spiritual healing' in the form of 'CranioSacral Therapy', 'Healing Massage', 'Shiatsu Massage' or 'Herbal and Nutritional Consultation'. On the website, everyone – irrespective of background – is invited to explore 'our Path along the Sufi way' and it is not mandatory to commit oneself to become a Sufi before being allowed to take part in the activities of the centre. Nevertheless, the answers on the page titled 'Frequently Asked Questions' clearly show that the activities of the centre are undoubtedly Islamic in nature.

In the Arabic glossary, *shari'a* is defined as 'the divine law', which is identified with the way of the Sufi.

Quasi-Islamic Sufi organisations or orders

The Bawa Muhaiyaddeen Fellowship in Boston is a local branch of the national Bawa Muhaiyaddeen Fellowship with headquarters in Philadelphia, which in turn see themselves as a branch of the Quadiri Order. The fellowship was founded by the Tamil Guru Bawa Muhaiyaddeen, who arrived in the USA from Sri Lanka in 1971 and continued going back and forth catering to the two respective Sufi communities until his death in 1986. By then he had acquired sufficient American followers for a mosque to be constructed in Philadelphia. Guru Bawa Muhaiyaddeen was buried west of Philadelphia and his mausoleum has become the first Sufi *mazar* or pilgrimage shrine in the Western hemisphere being visited by members of the Bawa Muhaiyaddeen Fellowship and other Sufis. One member of the fellowship characterised the Sufism of the Guru as 'very Islamic in its principles', while describing Bawa Muhaiyaddeen as progressive in his measures and considering rituals to be secondary.[5] The spiritual guidance of the Guru, who did not belong to any explicit *silsila*, took priority over the ritualistic dimension of Islam. Nevertheless, Bawa Muhaiyaddeen explicitly considered his teaching Islamic.

Every Sunday morning some 6–8 members of the Boston group consisting of 10–14 core members would meet to pray together, watch or listen to video- or audio-taped lectures of the Guru, and perform *dhikr*. The meeting would be led by any member of the group, male or female, who opened the meeting with the *Bismillah*, the traditional Islamic invocation of the name of Allah. After the lecture and the following discussion, members requested particular prayers or, for example, the *fatiha*, the first chapter of the Qur'an, which was chanted in Arabic by the members together. This might be followed by *dhikr*. Most of the members had an Arabic name given by the Guru in addition to their birth name, some but not all observed the five daily prayers, and one female member wore *hijab*. Members considered themselves followers of the Sufi path rather than Sufis, a term reserved for the masters.

Non-Islamic Sufi organisations or orders

As mentioned, the Sufi Order International (formerly the Sufi Order in the West) has its origins in the Chisti-tradition and was founded by the Indian Sufi and musician Hazrat Inayat Khan, who came to the USA in 1910. According to Andrew Rawlinson (1993), it was characteristic of Hazrat Inayat Khan to give up right from the very beginning any ties to Islam and to give women a central part in the activities of the order. This line has been continued by his son, Pir Vilayat Inayat Khan, and his grandson, Pir Zia Inayat Khan.

The website of the order, apart from a quotation of Rumi, is practically free of any references to Islam, and Sufism is described as the road to the truth found in all religions: the divine present in each and every human soul. Sufi Order International is characterised as 'An Inter-Religious Path to Spiritual Growth', and it is the purpose of the order to awaken the divine consciousness in every human individual, to root out suffering and to further a transformation creating a new life of love, harmony, balance and creativity.

The spiritual training takes the form of seminars, retreats and the so-called Universal Worship, during which Holy Scriptures of all the major religions are placed on the altar as a sign of their shared universal essence. Furthermore, collective healing is being practised, as the awakened mind is believed to be endowed with a divine power that may be controlled through concentration, breathing exercises and prayer. Anyone is welcome to contact 'The Healing Order', which is part of Sufi Order International, and may receive free of charge remote healing by the group.

Another central and regularly occurring activity is the so-called Universal Dance of Peace, usually sponsored in collaboration with the Sufi Ruhaniyyat International Order and founded – as mentioned – by Samuel Lewis, a disciple of Hazrat Inayat Khan. According to Marcia Hermansen, along with *dhikr*, alchemistically and hermetically inspired meditation as well as Jungian dream therapy is also practised in the order (Hermansen 2000: 162), although these practices are not mentioned on its website. An estimated 10,000 individuals had by the year 2000 been initiated by the order (Hermansen 2000). At the initiation, the initiate receives a new name which may be of Islamic, Hindu or any other mythological origins. Only a small minority consists of Muslims prior to initiation; in fact, the majority are recruited from American Christian or Jewish traditions, and after initiation they do not consider themselves Muslims but rather Sufis with Christian or Jewish backgrounds (Nguyen 2003). A representative member could be Jeremy, who describes himself thus:

> I was raised Jewish and had a Bar Mitzvah, then took a hiatus from religion for many years. My senior year in college (1998–1999) brought a new interest in spiritual matters, which included my first meditation retreat at Green Gulch near San Francisco (a Zen centre). In 2001 I travelled to India and studied yoga and Vedanta, and then upon returning home decided to connect my spirituality with my Jewish origins. I read about Zalman Schachter-Shalomi in the book *The Jew in the Lotus* and tracked him down in Boulder. Under his tutelage and that of his disciple Nataniel Miles-Yepez (January, 2002 to the present), I learned some basics of Kaballah [sic] and began to weave together the strands of Buddhist, Jewish and Hindu teachings I had learned. As it turned out, Zalman is also a Sufi Sheikh in the lineage of Hazrat Inayat Khan, and had ordained Nataniel. I took initiation from Nataniel in March 2003. (Nguyen 2003)

During his initiation Jeremy learned Sufi meditation, Hatha Yoga and Vipassana meditation. While keeping contact with Zalman and Nataniel via email or phone, the only communal spiritual activity in which he takes part consists in a weekly 'Quaker-style' meditation group where six members from various religious backgrounds come together for half an hour of meditation. He sees himself as belonging to a Sufi lineage (through Nataniel to Zalman and eventually to Hazrat Inayat Khan) and as a practitioner of Sufi meditation, but at the same time as firmly rooted in his Jewish background to which his two preceding teachers were also connected, Zalman being a rabbi. He describes his form of spirituality as a 'crossroads' tradition of which Hazrat Inayat Khan is seen as quintessential. Jeremy considers his connection with Islam as 'rudimentary', he does not practise the rituals nor is he familiar with the scriptures: 'Sufism is, for me, a universalist umbrella over my understanding of God and spirit, one that is formed from personal experiences almost completely disconnected from Islam.'

Concluding discussion

The examples given show that at least in the North American case, the terms 'Sufi' and 'Sufism' are being used to characterise a vast and composite field covering more traditional Sufi orders with an unambiguous and explicit Islamic frame of reference and with close connection to their mother orders in the Islamic part of the world as well as less traditional Sufi groups and movements, which apart from a limited nomenclature and a few practices have nothing in common with Islamic faith. The latter are only less traditional in their choice and combination of elements, since they are quite traditional in the sense that they incorporate elements from many traditions. Ironically, Sufism, which for 200 years of Western scholarship and up until the 1960s was seen as a conglomerate of Greek philosophy, Christianity, Hinduism, Buddhism and Jainism (Ernst 2002), has now become essentialised to the degree that it is seen as the most central quality or the only recurring element in different forms of Western Sufism, Islamic Sufism, Quasi-Islamic Sufism and Non-Islamic Sufism. In other words, this basic Sufism has taken on the appearance of a monolithic entity that to a greater or lesser degree is being copied by or inspires a number of Western new religious movements seen to be derivatives of something, which itself was formerly considered a derivative.

My point is that it does not make much sense to simply characterise Sufism as Islamic mysticism nor is it very helpful to apply terms like 'syncretism', 'hybrids' or 'creolisation' to a situation without any original elements. On the other hand, one might as well accept the fact that terms like Sufism and mysticism are here to stay. Furthermore, to give them up in the academia would mean – at least in the present context – to discredit a long-established methodological tradition of accepting informants' self-ascription, something the author is not prepared to do.

Critical scholars have proposed to replace essentialist models of definition with polythetic ones, which substitute the criterion of family resemblance for identity and thus in a meaningful way would be flexible enough for '... multiple various and even conflicting authoritative positions [to] be included under the rubric of a single religious category' (Ernst 2005: 3). It is a step in the right direction, I believe, but of course there is more at stake than logic in the problem of definition. Were it only a question of scholarly debate within closed academic circles, a simple numerical system might suffice, e.g. $Sufism_1$, $Sufism_2$, $Sufism_3$ or $Islam_1$, $Islam_2$, $Islam_3$. One could even do without the somewhat negatively tinted epithets of Alan Godlas (Quasi-Islamic and Non-Islamic). But with the coming of the electronic age, the democratisation of the media and the rising level of education, the interface between academia and the public has become a highly contested playing field. Power and discourse is the name of the game, and the prize is the right to define. In the present context, the question of how to define Sufism inevitably spills over into the questions of how to define Islam and of who has the right to define Islam.

The post 9/11 situation of Muslims in the USA has seen an increasingly bitter fight for the right to speak on behalf of the Muslim community and to define the correct and orthodox version of Islam. Umbrella organisations and associations like the Council of American-Islamic Relations (CAIR) and the Islamic Society of North America (ISNA), which some may characterise as mainstream, conservative, right-wing or even as Wahhabi and extremist inspired, compete with institutions like the Islamic Supreme Council of America (ISCA) founded by Shaykh as Sayyid Muhhammad Hisham Kabbani of the Naqshbandi-Haqqani Sufi Order in order 'to present Islam as a religion of moderation, tolerance, peace and justice',[6] but seen by others as having close ties to neoconservative circles.[7] While the competition reflects the classical opposition between the Wahhabi/Salafi tradition and the Sufi/Tasawwuf tradition, the key term in the present situation is clearly 'moderate', which indicates genuine attempts at accommodation and co-operation across religious and community lines:

> The Islamic Society of North America has served the Muslims of this continent for well over forty years. During this period ISNA has provided many invaluable services to the Muslim community of North America. Most manifest of course, is the ISNA Annual Convention, which, since its very inception has been a meeting place of people and ideas. In addition to building bridges of understanding and cooperation within the diversity that is Islam in America, ISNA is now playing a pivotal role in extending those bridges to include all people of faith within North America. Less well known, and yet critically important are our efforts that go beyond the Muslim community in North America to include projects that are often more humanitarian than theological, more global than national, and altogether more complex and nuanced.[8]

A key person on the American Muslim scene is Ms Sheila Musaji, who from 1989 to 1995 as founding editor published *The American Muslim* as a quarterly print journal. After 9/11 she allegedly noticed that many 'of the individuals who had represented the Islamic "middle path" and moderate voice in the public dialogue on Islam (…) had faded from the pages of the Muslim media … had been replaced by other voices that promoted a vision of Islam that promotes anger, discord and even violence.'[9] So she decided to reawaken what had in the meantime become an email newsletter with a relatively small circulation, and on 1 January 2002 *The American Muslim* became an online magazine with the goal to provide

> … an open forum for the discussion of ideas and issues of concern to Muslims in America from various points of view (based on the Qur'an Sunnah) representing no one school of thought, ethnic group or organisation (…) a forum for and encourage inter-community dialogue particularly on divisive issues, and to encourage interfaith dialogue (…) a balanced, moderate, alternative voice focusing on the spiritual, dimension of Islam rather than the more often heard voice of extreme political Islamism.[12]

In the eyes of Sheila Musaji, the

> attempt on the part of the various factions within the Muslim community to become 'the voice of Islam in America' was drowning out any real dialogue within the community because all too often those who control any particular organisation or mosque expected (or sometimes demanded) that you agree with their: Shi'a anti Shi'a/Sunni anti-Sunni/modernist anti-modernist/Salafee [sic] anti-Salafi/Sufi anti-Sufi/ethnic/cultural/nationalistic/political … interpretation of Islam completely, to take sides absolutely.[11]

In Sheila Musaji's list of persons who after 9/11 stated unequivocally that terrorist acts are forbidden by Islam and who thus inspired her to take up the task of continuing to publish *The American Muslim*, she mentions first of all Shaykh Kabbani. And it will probably not come as any surprise that the website's search machine presents a substantial number of hits on the topic of 'Sufi'. Nevertheless, in the wake of the 2005 ISNA Convention (an annual event that draws some 30,000–40,000 participants), she chose – in response to an article critical of an ISNA article published on the net[12] – to defend the organisation in which she had been active, and to which she had contributed financially as well as been critical of for some 30 years:

> Over the past 30 years I have been openly critical of some of the policies of ISNA and other national and local Muslim organizations, so I cannot be accused of being blind to the very real problems that need to be addressed. That being said, I have seen over the years a very steady progress towards addressing and solving many problems. At this convention I saw major changes from 30, 20 or even 10 years ago. I personally know many of the brothers and sisters who have been involved with ISNA (some from the beginning) and based on my personal experience, they have been open to suggestions, gave genuine consideration to constructive criticism, and are well-intentioned. ISNA grew out of the earlier

> MSA [Muslim Students Association] and was one of the first organizations attempting to create an association that would give Muslims in America a voice. The ISNA convention is the largest gathering of Muslims in the U.S. (Musaji 2005)

In Sheila Musaji's view, ISNA is generally accepted by Muslims as well as by non-Muslim agencies and organisations as the primary voice of Islam in America. This, however, does not mean that there is not room for improvement. According to Ms Musaji in 2005, the ISNA needed to expand its scope, something which could be done by

> encouraging ISNA to initiate dialogues with Sufi organizations, Shiah organizations, progressive Muslim organizations, African-American organizations, and finding ways that they can all work together. This can be done by encouraging ISNA to be more transparent, and to include representatives of other communities on its board. There is a lot to be done, but such positive developments can only come about by working with and not against the existing organization. (Musaji 2005)

While at times there appears to be instances of rapprochement, at other times there are open hostilities among the various players on the playing field of the American Muslim scene. The future is hard to predict, so many unknown or little known factors being involved: Since the US Census Bureau does not ask questions about religious identity, the actual number of Muslim adults in the country may be anywhere between 2.35 million (PEW Research Center survey 2007) and 6–7 million (CAIR survey 2001).[13] Of these, 2 per cent identify themselves as belonging to a Sufi tradition:

> … the largest segment of the respondents said they consider themselves 'just Muslims,' avoiding distinctions like Sunni or Shia. Another 36% said they are Sunni and 12% said they are Shia. Less than half of 1% said they are *Salafi*, while 2% said they are Sufi'.[14]

Add to this the unpredictability of the state of economic and political affairs in the USA, as well as internationally, and one is left with the feeling that only a kind of cultural chaos theory may perhaps provide answers as to the course of the future development. Where does this leave the scholars to play with their categories and little boxes?

Scholarly attempts to unmask time-honoured traditions of origins and influences are generally seen as – and may indeed be – challenges to well-established structures of power. Anxieties about textual authority (Ernst 2005: 15) are ever present, as the reactions to the attempt of Christoph Luxenberg (a pseudonym) in 2002 to prove that the Qur'an is based on a faulty reading of a Christian text in Syrian-Aramaic have shown.[15] It makes little difference if scholars insist that definitions only have analytical or heuristic purposes and do not necessarily have real-time referents – as soon as the text is published, in print or on the net, it is in play and up for grabs. Sometimes lives are at stake in a process, where a discourse may be used to define, qualify or disqualify groups and individuals in ways that are totally beyond its author's control.[16] What appeared to be primarily an analytical problem has turned out, secondarily, to have ethical, ideological and political aspects as well. What is the effect of the Saudi-financed Wahhabi/Salafi critique of Sufi *tariqas* in the West,[18] and which role may definitions of Sufism play in the process? Which implications may it have for discussions of Sufism and vice versa that the historical division between traditional Muslims with allegiance to Sufi-influenced Islam on the one hand and anti-Sufi reform movements (e.g. the Deobandis and the Ja'mat-i Islami) and educated mosque leaders on the other reflects a rural/urban divide (Geaves 2006: 143)? Do the facts that North American Sufism appeals mainly to Caucasian Americans, and that the few African American Muslims who do join usually favour *shari'a* oriented orders like the Naqshbandi-Haqqani Order (Hermansen 2007: 3), influence the way Sufism is being studied in the academia dominated by Caucasian Americans?

Clearly, in the present situation of growing tension between the East and the West, the North and the South, between the predominantly Islamic and the predominantly Christian nations, and in the USA between the African American and the Caucasian American populations, there is a lot of negative potential involved in the competing bids to define Islam and Sufism. But the positive potential may be equally large and in this game the individual scholar of Sufism needs to be aware of his or her potential contributions. The days of secluded studies in the ivory tower are irretrievably lost.

References

Ernst, Carl (2002) 'Between orientalism and fundamentalism: problematising the teaching of Sufism', in Brannon Wheeler (ed.) *Teaching Islam*, Oxford University Press: Oxford, pp. 108–123. (Page numbers used supra refer to web version.)

Ernst, Carl (2005) 'Situating Sufism and Yoga', in *Journal of the Royal Asiatic Society*, 15: 15–43.

Geaves, Ron (2006) 'Learning the lessons from the neo-revivalists and Wahhabi movements. The counterattack of new Sufi movements in the UK', in Jamal Malik, and John Hinnels (eds) *Sufism in the West*, Routledge: London and New York, pp. 142–159.

Hermansen, Marcia K. (2000) 'Hybrid identity formations in Muslim America: the case of American Sufi movements', *The Muslim World*, Spring, 90(1/2): 158–197, www3.interscience.wiley.com/cgi-bin/fulltext/119036955/PDFSTART (visited 17 September 2008).

Hermansen, Marcia K. (2006) 'Literary productions of Western Sufi movements', in Jamal Malik and John Hinnels (eds) *Sufism in the West*, Routledge: London and New York, pp. 29–48.

Hermansen, Marcia (2007) 'Sufism and American women', in *World History Connected*, 4(1), web edition: www.worldhistoryconnected.press.uiuc.edu/4.1/hermansen.html (visited 25 February 2008).

Malik, Jamal (2006) 'Introduction', in Jamal Malik and John Hinnels (eds) *Sufism in the West*, Routledge: London and New York, pp. 1–27.

Malik, Jamal and Hinnels, John (eds) (2006) *Sufism in the West*, Routledge: London and New York.

Musaji, Sheila (2005) 'Through the looking glass: ISNA? Thugs (2005 ISNA Convention)': www.theamericanmuslim.org/tam.php/features/articles/isna_thugs_2005_isna_convention/ (visited 28 February 2008).

Nguyen, Martin (2003) 'The Alternative Institutionalization and Practices of Sufi Orders in Boston': www.pluralism.org/affiliates/student/nguyen/Boston_Sufi_Orders.pdf (visited 25 February 2008).

Rawlinson, Andrew (1993) 'A History of Western Sufism', DISKUS WebEdition, 1(1) at www.uni-marburg.de/religionswissenschaft/journal/diskus/rawlinson.html (visited 25 February 2008).

Schimmel, Annemarie (1974) *Mystical Dimensions of Islam*, The University of North Carolina Press: Chapel Hill.

Webb, Gisela (2006) 'Third-wave Sufism in America and the Bawa Muhaiyaddeen Fellowship' in Jamal Malik and John Hinnels (eds) *Sufism in the West*, Routledge: London and New York, pp. 87–102.

Werbner, Pnina (2003) *Pilgrims of Love. The Anthropology of a Global Sufi Cult*, Indiana University Press: Bloomington & Indianapolis.

Strategies for concord

The transformation of Tariqa Burhaniya in the European environment

Søren Christian Lassen

The growing wave of research into Sufi *tariqas* in Western Europe has, among other things, shown that Sufism in this new environment has even more variation than it has in Muslim majority countries. The leaders and founders who come to Europe and initiate branches and organisations come with different aims and motivations – some are faithful transmitters of their tradition, others see it as their task to reinterpret it. Some remain focused on the environment they left back home, others reach out across ethnic and national boundaries. Certain organisations partly or fully abandon the attachment to Islam in favour of a universalist approach to mysticism. Several scholars have tried to conceptualise these various shapes of Sufi activity. Marcia Hermansen (2006: 28ff.) has in the North American context proposed the terms 'transplants' for movements that adapt little to the American context, 'hybrids' for movements that engage actively with the changed conditions without leaving their Islamic identity, and 'perennials' for movements that more or less subscribe to the idea of Sufism as a manifestation of universal truths. Ron Geaves (2000: 72), writing about the flourishing Sufi environment in Britain, outlines four categories, comprising shari'a-based as well as universalist groups. Ludwig Schleßmann (2003: 23ff.), who has published the only overview of Sufism in Germany so far, distinguishes between only two: universal and traditional Sufi movements, which correspond to universalist and shari'a-based outlooks, respectively.

The Sudanese Sufi order Tariqa Burhaniya has since *c.* 1980 established branches in several countries in Western Europe, first and foremost Germany, and attracted new groups of followers. Tariqa Burhaniya has in a few decades developed from a regional North African, Arabic movement to a transnational and transethnic organisation with a strong community spirit. The order now has two homelands: original Sudan, which is perceived as the spiritual source, and Germany, which to a large extent has become the organisational centre. This transition from an ethnically homogeneous movement to the present multinational tariqa seems to have been relatively smooth, and the order has reached a remarkable stability in Western Europe. The development of Tariqa Burhaniya in Europe has from its introduction to the present day been characterised by a dynamic interaction between Sudanese and Europeans – primarily

Germans. The outcome today is a community spirit that can be described as concord.

Regarding what can be called the religious identity of Burhaniya, it has during its short history in Germany to some extent crossed the categories outlined above. This can be explained by looking at the original introduction and reception of the order in Germany. The origins here are to be found in a disparate movement involving a small number of young middle-class Germans with little interest in Islam, but in search of experiential religious practices. This is because the introduction of the tariqa coincided with the heyday of what is often summarised as the New Age movement: a broad and heterogeneous wave of alternative spirituality, fascination of Oriental religions, therapy and esoteric ideas among broad parts of the young urban population in Germany as well as in many other countries, evolved out of the counterculture movement and the 'youth revolt' of the late 1960s.

The present article will look at measures and activities in Tariqa Burhaniya that promote concord and community, as well as trace the order's evolution from alternative spirituality to shari'a-based Sufism, concentrated on Germany. This will demonstrate the need to look at the specific context or the reception of a Sufi movement – or any Islamic movement – in Europe. In the present writer's opinion, these circumstances are at least as important for determining a movement's course in its new environment as is its original identity from its homeland. The article mainly builds upon the author's field research in Tariqa Burhaniya since 2003. The material is gathered from participant observation as well as interviews and conversations with a great number of Burhanis, in various cities as well as at the order's European centre Haus Schnede in north Germany. Unless otherwise noted, the information derives from these sources, which are anonymised. The same applies to anonymised quotations in the present text, which are translated transcripts from interviews with various members. I am indeed grateful to Tariqa Burhaniya and its members for the great courtesy and openness that I have met at all times.

History and legends

The history of Tariqa Burhaniya as a religious organisation in Europe is not much older than 25 years. Nevertheless, legends have already arisen concerning the tariqa's origin and early history in the West. These can be seen to assume the place of myth known from older religions in the way they interpret the movement's past history and present shape. This section will describe the salient points in the translocation of Burhaniya to Europe, as well as point to the use of legend in the movement's self-representation.

Established religions often trace their origin and past history through mythical and legendary narratives. The actions believed to have been carried out in mythical time assume paradigmatic qualities for the present, as the myths explain and justify not only the order of the world, but also social structure, etc.

(Paden 1994: 73ff.). This scheme cannot be applied literally in the case of Islam during the historical period from the Prophet Muhammad until the present. The Prophet is not a mythical figure, but the Qur'an contains plenty of stories about former prophets and ancient peoples that are enacted in a mythical-like time and serve to teach the consequences of disobedience towards God, among other things. However, the life of the Prophet Muhammad, as primarily told in hadith, assumes much greater importance for contemporary Muslim life. As Muhammad is an historical person, his actions are not enacted in mythical time, but are narrated as legendary history. The traditions about the Prophet's life in hadith make him an exemplar and a model to be imitated. This procedure is not only applied to the formative period of a religion: religious reformers and leaders – and in particular those who have been instrumental in revivals or significant changes in their tradition – may similarly be the subject of legends. This is seen in religions in general, and likewise in the case of Islam. Analogous to myths in the strict sense of the term, the legends ensure the special status of the person in question by putting his life in a legendary or miraculous light. Such a thing has happened to the founder of the Burhaniya order, Maulana[1] Shaykh Mohammad Osman Abduh al-Burhani. The background of his being elevated in this way lies in his role in bringing the order to Western Europe. Unlike several other religious leaders from Asia or Africa, however, he did not travel to the West himself to win new followers, but remained in his homeland Sudan. After a brief sketch of the origins of Burhaniya's introduction into Europe, this section will show how the process of constructing the legendary history of Shaykh Muhammad Osman and his time is carried out.

The origins of the German attachment to the Burhaniya order go back to the colourful religious environment of the 1970s and early 1980s, when young middle-class people all over Western Europe were attracted to new forms of religion or spiritualism. Burhaniya entered the religious market of Europe through the Egyptian academic Dr Mohammad Salah Eid (1936–1981), who started gathering people for Sufi sessions in some big cities of West Germany from *c.* 1973 (Schleßmann 2003: 250–255). Salah Eid was a trusted disciple of Maulana Shaykh Mohammad Osman, the then head of the Burhaniya order, and passed on his teachings and practices, even though they often formed a part of colourful and composite gatherings. A veteran from that time recalls these gatherings:

> ... I had known different spiritual movements. I was interested in yoga, in tantra, in shamanism, and it was always fine for the people who did it, but not for me. (...) And then I had participated in a Sufi seminar in a therapy centre. It was a mixture of Sufism, retreat, fasting and psychological exercises, and it was an Egyptian disciple of the then head Maulana Shaykh Mohammad Osman from Sudan. I had very deep experiences there.

The 'Egyptian disciple' mentioned above is Salah Eid. His experience-based Sufi practices came to an abrupt end with his demise in 1981 after a car accident. The small groups he had formed were left high and dry: even though Salah Eid was not a Sufi master in the strict sense of the term, to his followers he represented the authenticity of the North African source. His passing is described by veterans from those days as a profound loss. His time can be labelled the *prehistory* of Burhaniya in Europe: it was a period when the order had only a sporadical presence, it lacked most of the organisational features it has now, and the period is not always recalled in full detail by the veterans. The tariqa was about to enter its *historical period*.

The Burhaniya order was, as mentioned, headed by Shaykh Mohammad Osman Abduh al-Burhani, also known as Sidi Fakhruddin (*c.* 1900–1983). Shaykh Mohammad Osman formed the order as a new shape of the Disuqiya order named after the Egyptian Sufi Sidi Ibrahim al-Disuqi (d.1296), with attachment to the Shadhuliya order. The Burhaniya order thus counts as important members of its *silsila* Ibrahim al-Disuqi as well as his uncle, Abu'l-Hasan ash-Shadhuli (d.1258). At that time, the middle of the twentieth century, several branches of the Disuqiya were active in the region, but Shaykh Mohammad Osman established himself as the sole inheritor of the tradition, and his order was named Tariqa Burhaniya Disuqiya Shadhuliya (Frishkopf 2001). Burhaniya, which has become the main name, is derived from the byname Burhan for Sidi Ibrahim al-Disuqi.[2] In Burhaniya's own view, Shaykh Mohammad Osman did not *found* the order, but revived or revitalised the old Disuqiya order that had lain dormant for several centuries. Shaykh Mohammad Osman is said to have been given instructions on a spiritual level from Sidi Ibrahim:

> He held long nightly vigils in prayer during which he had visions wherein he was visited by some of the great saints. During these visions and in his dreams he learned some parts of the awrad – the special prayers of the Burhaniya. (…) In a long vision taking over forty days he learned that his task was to revitalize the order of Sayyidi Ibrahim Desuqi.[3]

The rituals and customs of the tariqa are thus thought to have been transmitted from Sidi Ibrahim Disuqi, not conceived or invented by Shaykh Mohammad Osman. At the same time, the idea of a revival of a dormant line ensures the legitimacy of the current shaykh, as this procedure enables him to trace his line of initiation back to the Prophet through Sidi Ibrahim. The tariqa gained a considerable following in both Sudan and Egypt, and in 1981 it was on the verge of being brought to Western Europe.

After Salah Eid's demise, a group of young Germans from the environment around him decided to travel to Khartoum to seek out the pure source of spirituality embodied by Maulana Shaykh Mohammad Osman. According to several Burhanis, the group consisted of 40, although other sources mention numbers between 40 and 50.[4] Regardless of the exact number, the figure of 40 is filled with symbolism and is part of the legendarisation of this journey. The group of young Germans had different backgrounds, but one thing that they all had in common was that they were not Muslims. Burhaniya was not entirely new to them – most of them were followers of Salah Eid, and many had been practising the order's *hadra* ritual back in Germany for some time. The journey is a turning point in the history of the tariqa and now forms part of its legendary history, as it is believed that Maulana had predicted the coming of a group of Germans who would carry the order back with them to Europe. One of the participants in the journey recalls their arrival:

> The remarkable thing was that when we arrived there were a number of Sudanese – they came to pick us up from the airport – they were all crying, and we thought: Oh, maybe the Sudanese are used to cry so much out of joy or as a welcome. But then we learned that Maulana Shaykh Mohammad Osman already thirty years earlier had said to his disciples: There will come a day when forty Germans come here, and they come as Muslims in order to enter our Tariqa.

The journey symbolically expresses the order's reading of its history: Sufism and Sufi shaykhs in Oriental countries are a repository of spiritual authenticity, and the time has now become ripe for transmitting this to Europe. The construction of the legendary history of Burhaniya thus takes two shapes: first Shaykh Mohammad Osman's own life and initiation into his mission (the word is used on the Burhaniya website: 'A Lifelong Mission'). Second is the German reception of Sufism which is primarily seen in the stories about the prediction of the coming of the Germans. The actual journey at the end of 1981 has thus become a foundation myth for the tariqa.

At the same time, this journey marks the beginning of the *historical* period of Burhaniya in Europe. It brought about the close interaction between Sudanese traditional leaders and European Sufi practitioners that has characterised the movement ever since.

Canonical literature and orthodoxy

The legendary history of Shaykh Mohammad Osman rests on the tariqa's view of him as an authentic master. This is not only preserved in the memory of those who knew him: his writings have acquired an essential importance to the movement. This is not unusual since in many Sufi orders, a semi-canonical status is attributed to the writings and thinking of the group's founder or main figure. The same has happened to Shaykh Mohammad Osman, and the tariqa actively preserves and passes on the crucial status that his person has acquired since his demise. This bond to the founder ensures that the order remains faithful to its own ideals. This section will trace the main points of Tariqa Burhaniya's history in Europe and give an overview of the use of literature in the tariqa, especially regarding the founder's writings.

Since the beginning in the early 1980s, Burhaniya has spread to several European countries, but Germany remains its European centre and the order's dynamic new homeland, beside the spiritual and historic homeland of Sudan.

The founder (or reviver) of the order, Maulana Shaykh Mohammad Osman, passed away in 1983 and was succeeded by his son, Maulana Shaykh Ibrahim.[5] He in turn passed away in 2003 and was followed by *his* son, Maulana Shaykh Mohammad, who thus represents the third generation of the modern order. All three heads – and only they – have carried the honorific title *Maulana*, and as the knowledge is considered to have a divine source, Burhanis maintain that there is no difference between them in reality – they all have the same knowledge. The present Maulana is only in his thirties, but is being supported by his uncle, Shaykh Husayn, who is a younger brother of the late Shaykh Ibrahim and thus the son of the founder. Both of them reside permanently in Germany with their families.

During the time of Shaykh Ibrahim, Burhaniya spread to several European and non-European countries. The most important groups are in Italy, France, Switzerland, Sweden and Denmark – with Germany as the centre. This country became the European heartland of the order from an early stage; it was here that it was introduced, and it is here that we find by far the greatest number of adherents. Up to the mid-1980s the order regularly saw new entrants, but this trend has slowed down, and today comparatively few adults enter the order from outside. For recruitment, the tariqa instead relies on the second generation, the children of the first generation. It seems that most of these young people do not have the urge to rebel or seek out their own way – they tend to remain in the order and see it as fully natural to be German Sufi Muslims. Burhaniya is today present in a number of German cities where it is organised in semi-autonomous city groups, the biggest of which are in Hamburg, Berlin and Munich. Here and in a few other German cities the groups meet in their own community premises, called *zawiya*. This term is known from classical Sufism, and in Egypt it denotes a gathering place for Sufis, often including the tombs of one or more saints. Burhaniya's German zawiyas are located in flats or minor houses and are maintained by the city group in question. An important element in a zawiya is the hadra room, the location of the weekly common ritual, as well as of prayers and social gathering. The groups meet frequently in the zawiya which assumes great importance as the movement's own space and precincts.

Tariqa Burhaniya is an orthodox order in the sense that it stresses the observance of the shari'a and its dependence on the canonical Islamic scriptures, such as Qur'an and hadith. Whether one needs to perform the five daily prayers, fast in the month of Ramadan and so on, is never put into question. Both North African and European Burhanis follow shari'a to the letter, and one can hear German Burhanis tell – with a bit of pride – how, for example, Turkish Muslims in Germany admire them because of their strict performance of the ritual duties. A booklet published by the tariqa in Germany for the use of its members is an indication of this. The title is *Kleiner Leitfaden zur Scharia* (A short guide to the shari'a) and it is an adapted translation of a classical work from the Maliki school, to which Tariqa Burhaniya belongs. Throughout its 116 pages,

From Burhaniya's Berlin zawiya*: the hadra room where the members perform the weekly rituals and meet for lectures and social gathering.*

meticulous and detailed instruction is given on how to perform the prayers, how to fast during Ramadan and a few other issues. This example of functional literature reflects how seriously the tariqa goes about the details of ritual and behaviour.[6] It should be noted here that Burhanis in Europe apply the shari'a only in the field of family law and personal behaviour. There is no mentioning of shari'a as the basis of society, striving for an Islamic state, etc.

Burhanis will often make a point of supporting their views with references to the canonical scriptures. The Qur'an and hadith are fundamental, but the writings of the founder, Maulana Shaykh Mohammad Osman, are in many cases more relevant for the daily life of Burhanis. Shaykh Mohammad Osman did not write prose literature such as introductory material to Sufism; the types of literature that are put to use today are of two kinds: his *qasa'id* and his discourses.

The *qasa'id* (sing: *qasida*)[7] are poems or hymns, composed by the founder and later edited and published by the tariqa in North Africa. There are several print editions available, published in various Arabic cities. No translations are available, but the German Burhaniya has published a transcription into the Latin alphabet of a full qasa'id collection. The qasa'id are put to very frequent use by the Burhanis – they are sung at the weekly hadra rituals and at other religious celebrations and, more widely, whenever Burhanis gather for a function, a marriage or other arrangements. The discourses are another well-known type of

Sufi literature. Maulana Shaykh Mohammad Osman is said to have given talks and question-and-answer sessions every night for a number of years. These discourses were meticulously recorded on tape by his disciples, and Burhanis in Germany are now working on editing and translating this great corpus of material. Senior leaders like Shaykh Husayn and others regularly give lectures where they explain or interpret sayings of the founder. Quotations from Shaykh Mohammad Osman and anecdotes about him are in constant circulation in the movement. Altogether, his writings constitute the main text material for the Burhanis regarding moral training, Sufi practice and religious poetry.

However, there are of course several ways to read and interpret the Islamic scriptures and the shari'a, depending on one's viewpoint and general position within Islam. For Burhanis it is important to stress that they follow the inner meaning of the scriptures, mediated by Maulana. It is believed that the founder had an exceptional understanding of the inner meaning of the Qur'an which he passed on through his writings and discourses. As one Burhaniya leader puts it:

> A person who practices manners [*adab*] on such a high level also has knowledge on a very high level. If you go to another mosque they will not be wrong, but there are limits to their knowledge. They explain from their standpoint, whereas Maulana explains from his standpoint, goes more in depth and gives the background (…) When you are asked some question that you can not answer, most imams will say: The Prophet Muhammad (saas), he did so and so, therefore we do so. But then – *why* did he do so? We are not allowed to ask that. – No, it doesn't matter, he did so, and then it is the best. It is all right on their level, because they may not have the background for these things.

It must be emphasised here that Burhanis as a rule are not polemical or patronising towards imams and Muslims in general, but they feel themselves lucky that they possess the deep religious knowledge that they receive from Maulana Shaykh Mohammad Osman. He is considered to have had a profound understanding of religion and spirituality as well as the Qur'an, all because of his spiritual initiation into the succession by Sidi Ibrahim Disuqi. In the light of these abilities and the way Maulana's writings are utilised in the tariqa, his writings can be called semi-canonical. What is of utmost importance in a living religious tradition, however, is not only *how* the scriptures are interpreted, but *who* is authorised to interpret them. The power in a religious movement to a large extent rests on this. In Tariqa Burhaniya, there are several indications that the Sudanese leaders have not relinquished their monopoly of interpretation. The consequences of this will be dealt with in the following sections.

Religious practice and guidance in transformation

The religious practice in a modern Sufi tariqa like Burhaniya is demanding. It presupposes careful observance of the shari'a and the ritual duties, and it adds a good amount of Sufi practice that is considered required if one wants to make progress. After the initial loose forms of practice in Germany during the 1970s and early 1980s, the rituals have gradually become more orthodox. At the same time, certain indications point in the opposite direction, for example as far as the involvement of new groups in the ritual practice is concerned. This section will focus primarily on three elements: the *aurad* readings, that will just be touched upon; the hadra ritual, the central common practice of the Burhanis; and the religious guidance, *irshad*, that is exceedingly necessary in an environment like modern Germany.

As already indicated, the European Burhaniya originated in Western Europe in the colourful environment of spiritual seekers, religious nomads, syncretists and practitioners of alternative spirituality. This current – which nowadays has not ceased, only slowed down – was broader than the common designation 'New Age' suggests: several established religions were part of this. On a larger scale, the whole scene can be seen within the framework of identity formation in late modernity, where common elements are the importance of the individual choice and a trend towards a universalist approach to religion. Universalism used in connection with Sufism usually designates the conviction that Sufism is a common current running through all religions and not limited to Islam. Although Universal Sufism has been introduced and propounded by religious leaders from the Islamic world – among whom a crucial figure was the Indian Hazrat Inayat Khan (1882–1927) – the followers of this kind of Sufism are mainly persons with a European or North American, non-Muslim background. Burhaniya has in its homeland always been an orthodox order that stresses observance of the shari'a, but the order took a slightly different shape in its early years in Western Europe. The small circles of Sufi practitioners around Salah Eid – and later the first groups following Maulana Shaykh Mohammad Osman – were first and foremost interested in spirituality and the experiential aspects of Sufism, and rarely had a philosophical or literary approach. Furthermore, in general the Sufi practitioners were not Muslims or not even interested in Islam. It was common in the beginning to be initiated into Tariqa Burhaniya without being a Muslim, and several of the members from that time recall that they never would have entered the movement had they known that it would imply becoming a Muslim. Islam had for these people certain connotations that were extremely far from their religious interests. This changed after a few years and, as a rule, before the mid-1980s newcomers would say the *shahada* – confession of faith in Islam – and take the pledge to the tariqa simultaneously. The departure from universalism among Burhaniya adherents can partly be attributed to Maulana Shaykh Ibrahim, the second head of the movement.

The current Sufi practice in Tariqa Burhaniya is a mixture of individual readings and collective rituals. The individual readings consist of prayer formulas and the names of God, called aurad,[8] that are supposed to be read or recited by each individual on a daily basis. Each member has an aurad booklet that is used for the daily readings in so far as they are not learnt by heart. The readings can take several hours daily and are seen as the foundation of the individual's spiritual development and a precondition for the weekly collective hadra ritual. They are not individually given; the same aurad booklet is used by all Burhanis.

The collective rituals are basically the weekly hadra that combines *dhikr*, prayers and bodily movements.[9] Hadra literally means 'presence', and the idea is that various saints are invoked and visit during the initial prayers. The ritual is carried out by all Burhaniya groups every Thursday evening and on a number of other occasions, and a typical sequence will take between one hour and one and a half hours. The participants are divided into the following three groups with different tasks:

a) singers, *munshidin*. A small group sing, and alternately recite, a number of Shaykh Mohammad Osman's qasa'id. The group consists of a lead singer – which changes during the ritual – and the rest who act as choir singers. Musical instruments are not used.

b) clappers, *bust*. The whole sequence is controlled by two men who use powerful handclaps to keep a steady rhythm. At the same time, they keep a watch on the participants to see if someone is making the wrong movements, standing at a wrong place, etc. One of the clappers is usually responsible for the whole performance and it is he who would say the long sequence of prayers and invocations at the beginning of the ritual.

c) the rest of the participants are *dhakirin*, i.e., those who perform dhikr. They will take up positions in two rows opposite each other, at right angles to the singers. During the singing they will swing their bodies from side to side in tune with the singing and repeat short sentences like *La ilaha illa 'llah* ('there is no god but God'), *Allah* and others. During the recited hymns they do not swing, but stand upright and listen. Dhikr in Burhaniya is carried out only in this active, bodily form, not as a sitting practice. The functions of singer and clapper are specialised, and the persons who perform them have chosen and learned this task and will perform it at every hadra.

d) Women and children could be mentioned as a fourth group. Nowadays women do not watch or take an active part in the hadra, but they sit and listen, separated from the men by a curtain or similar. Small children are with their mothers. Boys start taking an active part in the hadra from an early age, whereas girls never have the occasion to take part.

The unorthodox Sufi practitioners of the early years initially followed modern Western social manners, and the hadra ritual was practised together, as a mixed community of men and women standing in a circle. Groups were formed primarily in Hamburg, West Berlin and Munich, and started meeting every Thursday night in various back premises, in a manner similar to the many alternative and spiritual groups at the time. It could be that changes in this pattern were connected to Shaykh Ibrahim, the founder's son's takeover in 1983–1984. The second Maulana frequently visited Europe and in general maintained a closer contact with and supervision of the followers there than his father had been able to during the last few years of his life when the tariqa developed in Europe. Regardless of the exact cause, the groups began separating into men and women during hadra, and later started using two separate rooms. The women were then performing dhikr with bodily movements like the men, while listening to the singing and handclaps in the adjacent room. Shaykh Ibrahim finally decreed – a few years before his demise – that women were no longer allowed to take an active part in the hadra; they should sit and listen and follow mentally. This measure, which has caused some resentment among the German women members, but as far as I know no open protest, goes against the tendency towards contextualisation in the Western environment that otherwise characterises the order. Burhanis often stress that Sufism can be combined with a normal life in Europe, and that Sufi practitioners should not stand out among the public. Some have admitted that this measure does not make it any easier to attract outsiders to the tariqa.

However, new groups are drawn into the ritual. In general, the European converts are a new element in the order, and the fact that they assume almost all positions in the organisational hierarchy as well as the specialised functions in the hadra is in itself a change from the conditions in Islamic countries. But that is not all: the young Burhanis, i.e. the boys, most of whom are sons of the first generation in the order, take an active part from an early age. Some of them opt for the specialised posts of singer or clapper, and one can hear young people of 20 years of age or less sing hymns for hours in good, chaste Arabic. Similarly, the young people who specialise in handclapping have a good command of long prayers said in Arabic. Things have gone so far in this direction that one can witness a hadra directed by young people alone, at least in its first stages. The European tariqa has thus to some extent turned the traditional hierarchy on its head in the ritual context.

For a movement like Burhaniya that operates in a non-Muslim environment, the religious guidance and instruction is of great importance. The usual Sufi designation murshid has a slightly different meaning in Burhaniya from most Sufi orders where it is used synonymously with 'shaykh' or 'master', i.e. the head of a movement. The shaykh in Burhaniya is Maulana, but there are in every city group a number of murshids whose task is to guide members in the correct reading of aurad, introduce newcomers, etc. There are thus scores of murshids in the country, the great majority of whom are ethnic Germans, including the head murshid for all Germany. They are not entitled to give religious or spiritual guidance in the strict sense of the term. Nevertheless, the same can be said here as about the hadra: the very presence of European converts as murshids is a novelty. Here, it is not the young people who take up new positions, but the women. Women murshids are quite common in Burhaniya, which reflects the self-conscious status of women in the European branches of the order.

As a conclusion it can be said that the Burhaniya rituals and practices are not fundamentally changed in Germany, but remain faithfully performed according to guidelines and traditions from Sudan. Nevertheless, the social and cultural context is totally different, and this is reflected in the performance of the practices. The European Burhaniya challenges the hierarchy that is usually strong in Sufi rituals. That this is possible indicates that authority in the tariqa is flexible: it is adjustable when the context is changed – as long as the adjustments do not challenge the prerogative of the Sudanese.

Cultural interaction

The Burhaniya tariqa, which is strongly attached to North African culture, is being naturalised in modern Germany and among Germans who are fully immersed in the modern Western way of life. This process presupposes the previously mentioned interaction between Sudanese leaders and German converts. In this field, compromises are inevitable between the Sudanese – who stand for the attachment to Arabic and Sudanese cultural norms – and the Europeans – who to various degrees insist on contextualising Sufism. With some reservations, this dichotomy can also, following Andrew Rippin's definitions, be viewed along the line of traditionalism and modernism (Rippin 2001: 182 ff.). This might well seem artificial, but it is used as an analytical tool. It must be pointed out that the Sudanese leaders in Germany are very much themselves part of the European modernity; what is implied by the use of this dichotomy is the meeting of cultures taking place in Europe, and an attempt to conceptualise this meeting. The way this is played out in the field of culture gives some ideas about the dynamics of Tariqa Burhaniya. This section will trace the meeting of cultures in the German Burhaniya through selected examples.

The Sudanese represent the traditionalist side of this dichotomy. The Sudanese leaders in Germany – mainly Maulana and his family and a few senior disciples – possess privileged access to the pure source of authenticity. First, it is implied that this access cannot easily be transferred to Europeans. It is an important part of Burhaniya's self identity that the source somehow still springs from the historical founder Maulana Shaykh Mohammad Osman and, through him, from previous Sufis and ultimately from the Prophet. Indeed, according to Burhanis, the founder determined, and wrote in his qasa'id, that the office of Maulana should always run in his own family. Second, the Sudanese in their homeland represent an age-old Islamic and spiritual tradition. There is some admiration for the Sudanese among the European members – they are seen as kind, morally upright, honest people.

On the other hand, the Germans, as 'modernists', represent the possibilities for the order to find its way in modern Europe. It is easy to see that Burhaniya's establishment in Germany creates a lot of new opportunities – publication, technical equipment, communication among other things are very well developed there. Altogether this facilitates the order's outreach to new groups, and in this way promotes its growth, both qualitatively and quantitatively. All this can be seen as a mediation of knowledge from the already mentioned 'pure source' to the new recipients in Europe. This mediation is still today to a large extent in the hands of the traditional Sudanese leaders. Although Europeans, in particular Germans, have important positions in the organisation of the order and also act as spiritual advisers, it is undisputed that the religious or spiritual leadership remains in the hands of the Sudanese. As Burhanis say – there is only one teacher in Burhaniya, which is Maulana.

This mediation or interaction can be seen more clearly by possible fractures, or better, meeting of cultures, from which a few examples will be taken. It was related in the previous section how women were excluded from active participation in the hadra ritual. This touches on the larger question of the relationship between the sexes in Burhaniya. In the ritual sphere, men and women are strictly separated, and whereas an outsider could point to a disadvantage to the women, as they cannot take an active part in hadra, Burhanis in general see no problem in the separation of sexes. It is limited to the ritual sphere, and outside the performance of Islamic prayers and hadra rituals, there is no exclusion of women whatsoever. However, Burhanis tend to separate more into informal male and female company – friendships seem to run more along these lines than otherwise current among Germans. On the other hand, social interaction among Burhanis is frequently cordial and friendly, also across gender. Men and women as a rule shake hands with each other, and it is not infrequent to see men and women who are not in a blood relationship (and thus supposed to keep a

Sharing a common meal during the annual European hauliya *in Haus Schnede.*

distance, according to many Islamic scholars) embrace each other out of joy at meeting. These patterns of social interaction at times cause some resentment from non-Sufi Muslims when they meet Burhanis at various functions.

A related point is dress. In accordance with Burhaniya's general wish to contextualisation into Western Europe, it is not surprising that the order does not promote 'Islamic dress', neither for women nor for men. A few German women members choose to wear headscarves in public, but according to the order's authorities there is no demand on the women to cover their heads; it is not even considered preferable. Maulana is quoted as saying that Burhanis should not stick out in the country where they live. This is also visible on the male members: whereas traditional Muslims tend to wear a full beard in imitation of the Prophet Muhammad, very few Burhanis follow this example. Most members of the tariqa, including the Sudanese and Egyptians, are clean-shaven, and some, including Maulana, wear a small moustache. A double reason for this is given: first, that Muslims should not stick out, as already mentioned; second, that a beard is associated by many Westerners with Islamic extremism and terrorism.

Finally, a detail that shows the differences: on several occasions, Burhanis have a common meal or dinner in their zawiya (centre). Usually, everybody, except the ones who are not physically fit, sit on the floor, either in long rows with the food in the middle, or centred around big round metal trays. The men and the women frequently sit separately, and the food, which is eaten by hand, can be partly Arabic, partly Mediterranean and partly German. There is here a merging of different cultural elements, and the composition is not fixed once and for all. Some German Burhanis, for example, would prefer to sit at tables which they feel is the way to eat in Germany, and therefore Burhaniya could do the same. In their own houses, German Burhanis will invariably sit at tables and eat with knifes and forks.

In the field of culture, there is thus an interaction between North African and European elements that goes both ways. On the one hand the Sudanese and the culture they bring to Germany is being adjusted in certain ways; on the other hand, German Burhanis adopt parts of this culture and internalise it as their own Burhani culture.

Hauliya and communitas

In the study of religion, the religious festivals constitute a time-honoured object of study, as they play an essential part of any religion's inner life. Through festivals and other celebrations, time is ordered and connected to religious dogma, the sacred is restored to its rightful place, the world is re-established and the core values of the religion are spelled out. The big festivals dominate life for their participants: there is no life outside the festival (Paden 1994: 104 ff.). This attendance to big religious festivals can be an experience on several levels; on the social level, a general sense of togetherness and community has often been noted. The anthropologist Victor Turner, writing about pilgrimage as a phenomenon that can easily be compared to a religious festival, was famous for defining this experience as *communitas*, for example:

> A relational quality of full unmediated communication, even communion, between definite and determinate identities, which arises spontaneously in all kinds of groups, situations, and circumstances (…) The distinction between structure and communitas is not the same as that between secular and sacred. (Turner and Turner 1978: 250)

Tariqa Burhaniya, being an orthodox Sufi order, has a range of celebrations from the common Islamic sacred dates to specific Burhaniya occasions. Burhanis celebrate the two *'id* festivals and the *mawlid* of the Prophet, but the focus will be here on the annual European *hauliya* which takes place in August. The Arabic word hauliya can be translated by 'anniversary', and as such it has a crucial importance in Burhaniya. The primary anniversary is here, as in all Sufi orders, the annual saint's day. Every year in April a very large gathering of Burhanis assemble in Khartoum for the hauliya in honour of the founder Maulana Shaykh Mohammad Osman on the occasion of the anniversary of his death.[10] Groups of Burhanis visit Khartoum every year from various countries, and this is in a way a repetition or re-enactment of the initial journey to the shaykh back in 1981. The modern Europeans go on a journey back to the source, a journey that becomes trying in the scorching heat that is prevalent in Sudan at that time. Nevertheless, the hauliya in Khartoum is dominated by Sudanese and Egyptians and is in this way a traditional celebration where the European members come as guests. What is more relevant to the Western branches is the European hauliya at the order's estate in Northern Germany, Haus Schnede, every August.

Haus Schnede is a country estate, built in 1912 in Lüneburger Heide about 40 kilometres south of Hamburg, that has had various uses over the years. In 1981 it was acquired by a small group of Sufi leaders in Germany, including Salah Eid a few weeks before his demise. The idea was to create an open Sufi centre that would be a meeting place for various tariqas and shaykhs in Europe, including the Naqshbandiya-Haqqaniya and the Burhaniya (Schleßmann 2003: 142 ff.). During the 1980s, however, Haus Schnede became mainly a Burhaniya centre, where members could stay for shorter or longer periods. In 1992 the house was purchased by *Tariqa Burhaniya Stiftung*, a foundation established by the tariqa with the purpose of acquiring and running the house as a European centre for Burhaniya. Haus Schnede is now used for various gatherings, for example by the Burhaniya youth groups, and it is rented out to customers outside the tariqa for seminars and meetings, but is not being used by other Sufi tariqas. The main event in Haus Schnede is the European hauliya, which is celebrated every year in the first weekend in August and the week leading up to it. This weekend has no religious significance, but is chosen because this is the only week where schools in all German Lands have summer holidays. The European hauliya is not just a duplicate of the one in Khartoum, but assumes an essential importance as the great gathering of Burhanis from European countries, and under the wings of Maulana and other Sudanese. One can say here that the source has moved to Europe.

The European hauliya, strictly speaking, takes place on the Saturday in question, when the main functions are held. Several hundred people usually participate. A figure of 600 is given as a good estimate, but this probably includes day visitors. The overnight participants are accommodated in Haus Schnede, but for reasons of space, it is usually only the women who sleep in the house itself, whereas the men are lodged in big tents. All meals are provided for the participants and all logistical work is done by volunteers. The majority are Germans who come by their own means of transport. Groups come from France, Italy, Denmark and Sweden, and visitors from other countries, including the USA. The celebration is a mixture of religious functions, social meetings and entertainment.

During the weekdays various activities are held, but the main occasion is on the Saturday. In the afternoon the hauliya is formally inaugurated by a *saffa*, a procession that goes on a short round trip in the forest in the vicinity of the house. This procession, which is the most public function of the hauliya, is led by a number of singers, Sudanese and Germans, who sing qasa'id with an improvised amplification. Many of the participants follow the procession around, clapping their hands and singing in the chorus line. The whole picture is of a joyful celebration and an occasion where women and girls can mix almost freely. The saffa must be seen as a religious ritual, but it is enacted in an informal and cheerful manner by a very mixed group of Burhanis and it brings out the transnational and transethnic character of the tariqa. The singers and the core group around them are male, but men, women and children all take part in the procession with handclaps and enjoyment. Thus, this serves as an outlet for feelings of togetherness and celebration across genders and ethnic borders that cannot be accommodated in the formal hadra rituals.

The main religious occasion during the hauliya is the hadra ritual performed on the Saturday night. This goes along the lines already described: it is carried out in a big tent with a curtain separating men and women. It is often said to last 'all night' until the dawn prayer, but as it is frequently started very late, i.e. after midnight, in reality it may not last more than a couple of hours. For a number of years, one or more weddings have taken place during each hauliya, where German or mixed German–North African couples have been married by Maulana. This further reinforces the importance of the occasion and the concord, as it symbolises the bonds connecting Burhanis. Altogether, the European hauliya efficiently promotes concord among Burhanis, nationally as well as globally, and it is reinforced through the regular annual meetings. Every year, there are groups of Burhanis from other European countries who enjoy the annual reunion, and the ties across borders are strengthened by this. The hauliya does not promote or contain ecstasy or abandon; instead, the picture is of a cosmopolitan and colourful, joyful gathering that can very well be seen through

The procession during the hauliya *in Schnede brings out the multinational character of Tariqa Burhaniya.*

Turner's concept of communitas. This is achieved not least by the saffa and the whole social interaction and togetherness that Burhanis describe as a welcome respite from their everyday life and as an occasion where the brotherhood and sense of community of Burhaniya is strongest.

Conclusion

The present article, presupposing a dichotomy in Tariqa Burhaniya between Sudanese and Germans, or born Muslims and converts, has pointed to a number of fields where the order is changing or adjusting to the new conditions in Western Europe. Tariqa Burhaniya today is a rather small movement within European Islam, but it seems to have a good measure of success with regard to the contextualisation of Sufism in modern Germany. The strategies employed for this could be labelled as a dialogue that promotes concord through a variety of measures that unite the religious and the social spheres for the members. The transformation happening in the new environment empowers new groups, such as women and young people. The history in Europe suggests that authority in Burhaniya is to some extent flexible, but up to now, there has been no sign that the leadership of the Sudanese could be challenged. Through legendarisation and historical myths, among other things, the Sudanese have ensured that the supreme leadership remains with them. The concord and the cordial interaction within the movement, furthermore, can be seen to take two shapes. On the one hand the concord is especially found among the Germans and other Europeans themselves. The Germans share a common culture and language and are in general a very integrated group across the country. Similarly, there is a considerable concord between German Burhanis and members from Sudan, Egypt and other Muslim majority countries. It has been shown, however, that the interaction between Sudanese and Germans is balanced on different forms of superiority: the Sudanese maintain the prerogative of religious leadership, whereas the Germans to a great extent are the leading force in organisational and practical matters.

Until now, this interaction has been by and large fruitful, but the balance may be challenged in the coming years, as the young European generation comes of age in earnest and will tend to take over positions of authority. The young generation, of whom several are now in their twenties and thus no longer 'youngsters', will define the shape of the tariqa during the coming decades. They are not 'converts', as most of them are born and raised as Muslims, nor are they immigrants or 'traditional Muslims'. Instead, they are evolving as a new category of German Sufi Muslims who are at home and content with their religious practice and Sufi education. Only time will show whether this will entail greater integration between Sudanese and Germans in the order.

Finally, the material suggests that the history of Burhaniya in Germany and Europe is strongly influenced by the specific conditions surrounding its original introduction in 1979–1980. As Gritt Klinkhammer has pointed out (2005: 267), the introduction of Sufism in Germany was hardly related at all to the great influx of Muslim Turkish workers from the 1960s, and there is still little interaction between Burhaniya and the big Turkish migrant population in Germany. Similarly, the branch of Tariqa Burhaniya in Denmark almost entirely consists of born Muslims with an immigrant background. This in turn is due to its introduction in Denmark by an Egyptian immigrant who could not easily spread the tariqa to ethnic Danes. I will propose that even greater attendance is given to the processes of the introduction of Sufi movements, as well as the specific social contexts that influence the course these movements will take in the new environment. In any case, indications are that interest in Sufism in Western Europe will increase in the coming years. The ways that Sufism will be spread and the shapes it will take will provide ample reasons and material for further research.

References

Frishkopf, Michael (2001) 'Changing modalities in the globalization of Islamic saint veneration and mysticism: Sidi Ibrahim al-Dasuqi, Shaykh Muhammad 'Uthman al-Burhani, and their Sufi Orders', *Religious Studies and Theology*, 20(1 & 2): 11.

Geaves, Ron (2000) *The Sufis of Britain. An Exploration of Muslim Identity*, Cardiff: Academic Press.

Glasbrenner, Eva-Maria (2001) 'Tanz in der sudanesischen Bruderschaft Tariqa Burhaniya – Beschreibung einer Hadra', in *Acta Orientalia*, 62: 81–91.

Hermansen, Marcia (2006) 'Literary productions of Western Sufi movements', in Jamal Malik and John Hinnels (eds) *Sufism in the West*, London: Routledge.

Klinkhammer, Gritt (2005) 'Traditionalizing Spirituality: the Burhaniya Sufi Order in Germany', in Sigrid Nökel & Levent Tezcan (eds) *Islam and the New Europe. Continuities, Changes, Confrontations* (Yearbook of the Sociology of Islam, 6), Bielefeld.

Paden, William E. (1994) *Religious Worlds. The Comparative Study of Religion*, Boston: Beacon Press.

Rippin, Andrew (2001) *Muslims. Their Religious Beliefs and Practices*, London: Routledge.

Schleßmann, Ludwig (2003) *Sufismus in Deutschland. Deutsche auf dem Weg des mystischen Islam*, Köln: Böhlau.

Turner, Victor and Edith Turner (1978) *Image and Pilgrimage in Christian Culture. Anthropological Perspectives*, Oxford: Columbia University Press.

Sufism contextualised

The Mevlevi tradition in Germany

Gritt Klinkhammer

The following chapter will address the spread of Mevlevi Sufism in Germany, consider its inner dynamics of development and differentiate among the various forms present in the country. Assuming that a contextualisation is in some way necessary for traditions in diaspora, the question arises about what that implies for the adaptation of Sufi Islam to modern secular-Christian society. A fundamentalist attitude would, in contrast, be one of avoiding the contextualisation of religion. A moderate attitude would be one of translating the key features of religion, possibly changing the general set-up of some cultural customs, and definitely changing some traditional dogmatic attitudes into a modern individualised one if the societal background is secularised and pluralised (e.g. ter Haar 1998).

Sufism is often distinguished as the better side of Islam which should be fostered in order to modernise the common religion of Islam. Bassam Tibi (2001), for example, ascribes Sufism the potential for modernisation and renewal of Islam. The common appellation of Sufism as mysticism often implicates this appraisal as well. Looking at the reception of Sufism in Germany, we may diagnose a different development: Sufism seems to be contextualised in a way that shows assimilation into structures and forms of new secularised and individualised religion rather than interference in the Muslim migrant's everyday life. This observation fits the theory of religious change in modern societies by Pierre Bourdieu (1992). He argues that the result of enlightenment and secularisation is the competition between religious fields and secular fields elaborating social and individual meaning. The competition on competences has generated the disbanding of boundaries of each field; for instance, the religious specialists have assimilated into therapy fields and vice versa. This is also true for more aesthetic fields of arts, as we will see in this chapter. The sustained success of the open esotericism market as well as of diverse kinds of spiritual therapies has been produced by this modern market of fields of meaning; Sufism in Germany is in some respects one of it. The disbanding of boundaries of fields within the spiritual, therapeutic and aesthetic market is accompanied by effects on accepted forms of allegiance and authority, as will be shown.

That the reception of Sufism is imbedded into the whole spiritual market is especially true for Germany in contrast to France, Great Britain or other European countries with a colonial history of encounters and experiences with Muslim countries. Germany, in contrast, had neither colonial power in Turkey – where the majority of Muslim immigrants came from[1] – nor is Sufism as vivid among current Turkish immigrants as among Indian, Pakistani, Indonesian, North African and other Muslims in the Western diaspora. The ban of Sufi brotherhoods in Turkey since 1925 has consolidated the decline of this tradition in general.[2] Thus, the spread of mainstream Sufism was hardly related to the immigration of Turkish labourers in the 1960s. While in Muslim countries, the institutionalisation of Islam and folk tradition was deeply influenced by Sufism, in Germany, Sufism has remained a rather separate phenomenon from the Sunni Islam of the immigrant's mosques, even today. The history of Sufism in Germany has been a history of trans-ethnic Sufism which must be identified and investigated as a phenomenon within the scope of the 're-sacralisation' (Bell 1991) of Western societies, which began in the early 1970s. A more experience-based form of Sufism was introduced in Germany by people who did not seek a new religion, but were searching for spiritual (self-) experiences. It is characteristic of the history of the German reception and spread of Sufism that none of its early representatives and publicists committed themselves in the beginning exclusively and strictly to Islam until the 1980s.[3] Instead, the universality of Sufism's 'spiritual psychology' was stressed and mixed creatively with other doctrines. During my survey on Sufism in Germany, early Sufi followers told me that they had met their first shaykhs (spiritual Sufi guides) because of their interest in therapeutic and esoteric courses on physical and/or spiritual (self-) healing. Some of the later members of different orders told me that they came to the movement as a result of their voyage through the spiritual therapeutic market as well.

This chapter will show and analyse how one special form of the German transethnic Sufism, the Mevlevi tradition, has been successfully transformed into today's[4] German fields of the production of meaning – taken as an example of Europe and North America, which is labelled in the following section as 'the West'. As an example of this, a description of several forms of popular Western Mevlevi undertakings will be presented, accompanied by a contrasting focus on a German Mevlevi *tariqa* (Sufi brotherhood), whose shaykh seems to both contextualise as well as retain essential aspects of the Muslim Mevlevi tradition. Then, we will see, Islam is not in the centre of interest and, accordingly, common diaspora Islam has not been changed by this new reception and adaptation of Sufi-Islam in Germany.

The Western reception of Rumi

No other Sufi is as well known in the West as the Persian-Turkish Jalaluddin Rumi (1207–1273). His poetry has been translated into many European languages, the music of the traditional ney-flute has been heard in many Western concert halls, and the whirling dance of his disciples in their wide white robes has been seen by many without their knowing that all this has something to do with Islamic tradition.[5] An American journalist stated that Jalaluddin Rumi

> is the most popular poet in the United States. Barely known there only a decade ago, classes on his work have sprouted up on university campuses throughout the country. Community lectures and public readings of his poetry are announced in the cultural sections of newspapers in virtually every major American city. In perhaps the ultimate measure of his celebrity, a group of movie stars and singers has made a recording of his poems.
> (Holgate 2005: 52f.)[6]

UNESCO declared 2007 the 'Year of Rumi' in the spirit of Mawlana Jalaluddin Rumi, as one of the greatest spiritual and literary figures of all time. In Germany, Rumi has often been compared with the popular German mediaeval mystic Meister Ekhart. Both have been attributed a mindset tolerant of other religions and are masterminds for what is understood as universal mysticism in Islam and Christianity – even if historical traces give different references (Grundmann 1970, Schimmel 1978).

Since the second half of the twentieth century, Western thinkers have sought to turn the colonialist stereotype about the condition of underdevelopment and soullessness of the Middle East on its head, by proclaiming the East as the home of spirituality and mysticism, and the West as the abode of soulless materialism. This position has considerable appeal even today. Thus, Sufism has been assigned a role as a bridge between Eastern spirituality and mysticism and Western rational philosophy. Today this idea has also spread into everyday life and is as such manifested in the way in which Sufism has been turned into a commodity in the West, reflected by a thriving Sufi market – especially of Sufi music and poetry, as well as Sufi rituals for self-experience or therapy.

The popularity of Rumi in this secular, free-floating and economic context is also true for Germany, and is evident not only from the reception of his poems, but also through the general spread of Sufism, such as in books, Sufi music and dance. If one searches for Sufi music titles, the German Amazon website alone lists about 111 titles available as CDs,[7] most of them featuring Rumi's name on the cover.

Sufi ritual dance and therapy are also performed in the West. There is a wide spectrum of workshops tracing themselves back to Rumi. Most of them can be found on the Internet, and some examples are presented below in order to indicate the drift of Mevlevi Sufism into new secular and non-Islamic fields of meaning. The whirling dance (sema),[8] music and poems are integrated in secular kinds of therapy and understood as universal (trans- or pre-Muslim) spiritual practices or expression, or simply presented as possibilities for new aesthetic experiences. The following examples are only a few from a wide field of offerings. They show the secularised and aesthetical contextualisation as well as the special composition of the spiritual meaning of Mevlevi Sufism in the German reception and adaptation. In this context, Islam may only gain importance for legitimising the teacher's authority (by birth/family background), not for the participants' religious belongings.

First, there is a presentation of Whirling (sema) as therapeutic action. The Egyptian Gamal Seif is one of a number of dancers in German-speaking regions offering 'Oriental dance' workshops and shows for private ceremonies and corporate parties in locations. He studied pedagogy of sport and promotes, during his workshops, the notion developed in his doctoral thesis on the therapeutic impact of 'Zaar', an Egyptian purification ritual. In one of his current workshops,[9] Seif teaches the method of the Whirling Dervish dance to participants, and offers to bring the 'original robes' with him. Within the same workshop, he instructs the participants on the 'Zaar-ceremony as an Egyptian spiritual purification ritual of women', although men are also invited to take part. Previous knowledge of dance is not necessary for participation as the workshop aim is to achieve self-experience.

Gamal Seif presents Mevlevi Sufism and its Islamic tradition in a mix with other 'ancient and oriental roots' of knowledge. He creates an oriental spiritual setting and exotic atmosphere combined with his aesthetic freestyle, for example in his costumes.

The dance market is accompanied by the music market around the Rumi tradition. This music market has arisen not only for dhikr (Sufi ritual) music (as world music), but also for musical versions of the translated poems from Rumi. Artists are feeling inspired by Rumi not only to translate his verses but also to write their own.[10] One of these is the Iranian-Jewish Shahram Shiva who emigrated to the USA at the age of 16. He describes himself as a long-time practitioner of Eastern mystical traditions and of yoga, meditation, whirling, Sanskrit/Persian prayers and non-violent living. Shiva has been translating the poetry of Rumi since 1988. From 1992 onwards, he has been presenting Rumi's poems (bilingual English-Persian) at concerts with diverse music groups in the

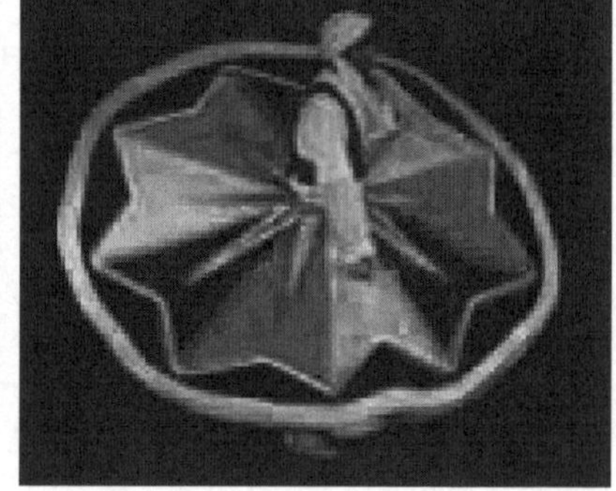

Seif advertising for the workshop in 2007.

USA. Shiva's translations of Rumi have been published in several books (e.g. *Rumi Thief of Sleep*, 2000) and are available on the CD *Rumi: Lovedrunk*. In order to instruct others in 'Transformative Whirling', he also offers an 'Easy-to-follow four-step system', a method that he has published and offered in large-scale workshops to around 350 people. On his website he promises: 'By following this proven method [students] without any prior training can begin whirling immediately.' He claims that 'Whirling is for all of humanity and does not belong to any one part of the world, or a certain religion or spiritual sect', and he argues that 'people from all countries and all faiths have been turning, spinning or whirling since the beginning of time'. In this context, whirling is interpreted as a pre-Islamic, basic human experience.

This universal understanding of whirling can also be found in the more therapeutic application of whirling in the school of 'Kiyana'. Kiyana sought to denote the 'origin' and 'applies to the vital movements that are the source of all corporeal movements and athletic exercises which appeared in ancient Persia' (www.en.wikipedia.org/wiki/Sufi_whirling)

Accordingly, whirling is defined as the 'ancient mystical movements that come from the depth of the centuries (www.whirlingof121.com/E2%20workshop.htm). It is compared with Indian Yoga. On the website, one finds nothing more than another photo of 'Sama'a' (the dance of a whirling dervish) and information for a workshop on 'Sama'a', where you can learn whirling to get 'nourishment for the body, education of the soul, refinement and

'The wind is the mightest when it whirls.' Shahram Shiva, Whirling (www.rumi.net).

The doctrine implies endless breathing, exercises for the eyes, discipline of the body, balanced and imbalanced movements, the method of shared mindfulness and whirling. (www.whirling.de – viewed in 2007).

perfection of living' (www.gurdieff-movements.net). If you are drawn by this and further sophisticated evaluative statements from participants, you are invited to get in contact by email and to read *Sama'a – Light of the Light of the Light*, written by the Iranian Javad Tehranian (2001), which has been published in German, English, French and Farsi.

Finally, there is a more religious interpretation of whirling by 'Gayanshala'[11] a German association for 'Oriental Music and Mysticism' which wants to 'make a contribution to peace by caring for Fine Arts and acceptance of the variety of creation'.[12] In the tradition of Hazrat Inayat Khan, who brought the Indian Chisti Sufi Order to Europe at the beginning of the twentieth century and turned it into Universal Sufism, Gayanshala focuses its interest on the spiritual power of Indian, Persian and other oriental music. Furthermore, their website refers to 'mystical dances of the Bektashi and the Mevlevi dervishes' and the spiritual healing impact of music in the tradition of al-Farabi (d.950) and Ibn Sina (d.1037), instructed and offered by Oruç Güvenç. The association seeks to be a centre for transreligious encounters, based on a part from the Qur'an verse (5: 48): 'If God had wanted, he would have created people as only one community.'

Under the heading of '*sema*' Talip Elmasulu, a member of the Istanbul Galata-Mevlevi Group[13] which is famous for its touring whirling shows in Europe as well as in North America, offers a workshop on whirling dance. Here, the turning movement of the whirling dance is understood as a symbol for the basis of our living – from each small atom to the cosmos. Through this whirling – according to the text – the dervishes are seeking to achieve harmony with nature and the creator. Elmasulu lives in Germany, and may be hired for concerts and other performances. He informs the audience before his performance that he does not want to be acknowledged with applause because he understands his performance to be a public devotion.

Many of the sympathisers of Sufism without a Muslim background appear to be global players: they often travel to workshops, looking for new encounters, learning new rituals, etc. since it enables them to have new spiritual experiences. They often belong to the middle class who are accustomed to consuming books, concerts, art and workshops. These peregrinations seem to be interpreted by the participants as a continuous pilgrimage of the self. Some of them have

Talip Elmasulu whirling on stage.

made this peregrination their lifelong task. The German Susanne G. for instance, describing herself as a musician and healer, lives without a fixed abode. As a musician of the American Mevlevi Order of Jalaluddin Loras and at the same time dance choreographer for 'Sufi Ruhaniat International',[14] she constantly travels the world with her music, giving workshops and concerts, for a minimum support of room and board.

The Norwegian anthropologist Bente Nikolaisen has analysed and interpreted the meaning of the *sema* which is constantly performed abroad by the Mevlevi Dervishes, as being linked to the Sufi idea of the soul on a permanent journey to God (Nikolaisen 2004: 91–104). She points out that the Dervishes' travels to enact the *sema* can be understood as a sacred ritual or a religious pilgrimage in itself, since they are doing it with the desire to achieve spiritual transformation through the *sema*. Nikolaisen has focused her study on the Galata Mevlevi Group and their attempt to transform the secular spaces of the performance such as theatres and sport halls into sacred spaces, by instructing the audience about the behaviour and meaning of the ritual as a religious one. Furthermore, the travels of the Sufi sympathisers, who journey from one more or less secularised Sufi workshop to another, can also be understood as a pilgrimage, given the desire for spiritual transformation through appropriate rituals and guidance.

In contrast to the most popular, hybrid and selected reception of Rumi's ideas and ascribed tradition of whirling mentioned above, the homeland tradition of the Mevlevi Order (see, for example, Gölpınarlı 1983), with its strong rules and hierarchy and the lengthy 1,001-day teaching period for *muridun* (pupils, sing. *murid*) is mostly unknown and not flourishing as well in Europe. It is to this tradition, which can also be found in Germany, I now want to turn.

German Mevlevi orders

The Grand Shaykh of the Mevlevis, traditionally based in Konya, Turkey, is known as Maqam Çelebi, because the Maqam is traditionally a member of the Çelebi family. After the institutional decline of the order due to Atatürk's ban in 1925 and the expropriation of their properties, Maqam Çelebi Muhammad Bakir migrated to the *asitana* (central Sufi house) in Aleppo. But the Mevlevihane there was closed in the 1950s when its last active shaykh (Muhammad Shahu) died (De Jong 1991: 888). The tradition lived on but under difficult conditions and without any official centre where the Maqam could reside. After the increasing popularity in the 1990s of Sufism and of Jalaluddin Rumi abroad, Dr Celaleddin Bakir Çelebi, Maqam at that time, created the International Mevlana Foundation in 1996 'in order to give seekers and lovers of Mevlana the possibility of officially becoming a member of a cooperation'.[15] The Foundation is acknowledged by the Laicist Turkish government as a cultural association of Turkish folk tradition. The Foundation is only permitted to show the whirling dance for tourists outside of religious buildings (like in sport halls in Konya) and to present the 'show' in English – although the show in Istanbul is presented in the old Galata Mevlevihane. Not only are foreigners present amongst the spectators, but so are Turkish followers, who pray during the ceremony and therefore consider it a serious religious ceremony. Additionally, the members of the dance group conceive it as a religious event too. Their current Maqam is Faruk Hemdem Çelebi, the twenty-second great-grandson of Mevlana. Under the supervision of this Foundation, further branches in Turkey and worldwide branches with their own respective shayks as instructors have been appointed – for example, in Iran, the USA, Switzerland and Germany.

The German branch of this foundation is represented by Shaykh Süleyman Wolf Bahn Efendi. Wolf Bahn, born in 1944, studied as a Mevlevi *murid* in Turkey for 30 years and opened a *dergah* (Sufi house) in southern Germany in 1991. He still lives there, leading a group of around 40 members, male and female. As is the case for the other branches of the International Mevlana Foundation, he is well known for the public *sema* ritual. Bahn regularly organises such public *sema* 'shows' in different regions of Germany and his group is invited to perform at various venues, such as religious encounter group meetings, among others. His idea of Mevlevi Sufism, which is also that of the 'International Mevlana Foundation' in general, is that Sufism aims at being 'the religion behind religions'. So he, like the Foundation in Switzerland and the USA, introduces non-Muslims to the whirling dance of *sema*.

There are other Mevlevi orders in the Arab world, such as in Syria and Egypt, as well as in the USA and Europe, which are not members of the 'International Mevlana Foundation' and therefore are not acknowledged by the Maqam Çelebi of the 'International Mevlana Foundation'. The Foundation reveals that they do not want to see others establish Mevlevi orders without their permission –not even those shaykhs who got their endorsement from a Mevlevi shaykh, in times when the political turbulence in the Middle East was so great that they could not go to the Maqam Çelebi in order to obtain the *ijaza* (shaykh's authorisation). The turbulent times in Turkey, Syria and elsewhere have long been over and therefore – the Foundation argues – the approval of the current Maqam is required to lead a Mevlevi order anywhere in the world. The Foundation has announced on its website that each shaykh should have his *ijaza* re-issued by the current Maqam Faruk Hemdem Çelebi. The Foundation understands its role as being the protector of the 'intellectual property' of the Mevlevi order, since with the increasing popularity of the whirling ritual of the Mevlevi, the market is full of different parties offering their knowledge of the ritual - some are from the Foundation but others are 'non-authorised' people.[16]

One of these Mevlevi shaykhs who is not authorised by the International Foundation is the German shaykh Abdullah Halis. He built a *tekke* (place of gathering for Sufis) in northwest Germany, and offers courses on Mevlevi Sufism. He has claimed to be a Mevlevi shaykh, authorised by the Syrian murshid Hazrat Mustafa Kemal El-Mawlawi, since the mid-1970s. We will now

The Shaykh: Abdullah Halis al-Mevlevi.

take a closer look at his Sufi order in order to portray the development, success and appeal of a Sufi order in Germany. It is currently a small order with fewer than 50 followers.

El-Hajj Shaykh Abdullah Halis al-Mevlevi (Dornbrach) was born in 1945 in Berlin to Christian parents. There is no written biography or hagiography of Abdullah Halis, but he has related some incidences of his life (Schleßmann 2003: 151f.).[17] As a teenager, he was already fascinated by Islam and learned Arabic somewhere between the ages of 16 and 20, converted to Islam at the age of 20 and then married a Turkish woman. He visited her family in Turkey and there, for the first time, he met Sufis without being aware of their condition.[18] Later he travelled through Turkey for several years, studied Islamic law in Aleppo (Syria) and lived in an old Mevlevi tekke, as one of the last *muridun*. After the fall of the Ottoman Empire, Syria, like most of the Arab world, politically diverged from its Islamic heritage and turned to nationalistic (pan-Arabism) and socialistic ideas until the 1940s, and thereafter to salafiya-Islam,[19] which denies Sufism as a legal source of Sunni Islam. Thus, at that time, Sufism in these countries was declining and survived under these difficult political conditions only in small, more or less private circles. Most dergahs were closed and shaykhs' practices were restricted (De Jong 2000: 137–143).

During his travels, Halis got to know various Sufi orders and learned from different shaykhs. Between 1968 and 1972, he lived in Istanbul with members of the Naqshibendi tradition of Shaykh Dörter and the Qadiri tradition of Shaykh Vehbi. In Bursa, he learnt from the Mevlevi shaykh Ali Baris. After the shaykh's death, Halis went to the Aleppo Mevlevi branch. There he obtained the authorisation (*ijaza*) to teach Mevlevi Sufism from the Grand Shaykh Mustafa Kemal in 1975. In 1976 he made a pilgrimage to Mekka and in 1979 he was authorised to teach Rifa'i Sufism. After a few short sojourns in Berlin at the end of the 1970s, he returned to Berlin for several years and established a tekke in Kreuzberg with the help of youngsters and alcoholics living on the streets. According to one of his early followers, Halis did 'social work' during this time, taking kids from the streets and helping them to survive, teaching the Qadiriye and the Rifa'iye traditions. Together with the Egyptian Salah Id, who taught the Rifa'i and the Egyptian Burhani traditions, and the German Abdul Fatah, who taught the Naqshbandi tradition, they founded the 'Sufi-Tariqat-association'. They gave lectures on Sufism, and organised *dhikr* (remembrance of God) evenings and courses about self-awareness where they integrated *dhikr* and *khulwat* (Sufi desolation ritual). They provided access to therapeutic courses, where they offered *dhikr* as a body/somatic-therapy. Some participants of these therapy courses became followers of these shaykhs.

In addition, they founded the 'Institute for Sufi Research' as a platform to explain and offer Sufi practices from several traditions and make contact with Sufi shaykhs in the Muslim world, as well as with healers from Europe and North America who also worked with breathing and dance (Klinkhammer 2005, 2008). In 1980, Id and Fattah bought a house in the northern part of West Germany, where they wanted to establish a Sufi healing school. In the beginning, Halis was also present and offered courses in Sufism and *dhikr*. But their success lasted only briefly: Salah Id died in a car accident in 1981, and around two years later Fattah and others had to leave the house because they could not fund it any longer just by offering workshops. Abdullah Halis went back to Turkey with his new German wife Nuriye. He wanted to recover from the turbulent times in Berlin. He related that in 1988, while in Turkey, he received the holy mission to return and establish a tekke in Germany, and he also mentioned that he still stays in close spiritual contact with his Mevlevi tutor, the Syrian shaykh Farhad Dede (who died in 1977).

In fact, on his return, Halis did not have the chance to go back to Berlin, but went instead to the vicinity of Jünkerath Eifel, Northrhein-Westfalia, where he opened a tekke and offered *dhikr* evenings of all five traditions he had learned. Perhaps he went there because during his absence, the Sufi scene in Germany had separated into different *turuq* (sing. *tariqa*, which means the way and is a notion for the Sufi Orders), for example, the Burhanis and the Naqshibandis of Shaykh Nazim had themselves become established. In the beginning, the

Naqshibandiyya settled near Jünkerath Eifel, but Halis did not feel comfortable there. It was most likely due to the fact that a lot of changes had occurred on the scene: there was more competition between the *turuq*, there were already established *turuq* which made claims to be the best or the only true one. And yet, Halis was offering several kinds of parallel Sufi traditions.

After Halis' journeys during which he followed and taught different traditions of Sufism, he bought a house near Berlin in 1992 in order to establish a centre of Sufism, but soon he focused only on the way of the Mevleviye. He developed this centre into a Turkish tekke – as he called it – and offers a wide variety of Sufi courses (see below).

Since there is considerable global competition between Sufi orders in the West, a German shaykh does not find it easy to be acknowledged as authentic. In principle, there are two ways of getting acknowledged as an authentic, genuine Sufi leader: you can be the *murid* of a shaykh who, at the end of the training, gives you the right to train other dervishes. This is noted down in the *ijaza*, the certificate from a learned shaykh. The other common practice is to claim a mission or calling by Muhammad (or a shaykh) in a dream, which then becomes evident through the person's charisma, knowledge and spiritual and healing skills. Abdullah Halis claims that he received both.

Despite the widely shared idea that Sufism is a universal philosophy, each branch and each shaykh has his own *muridun*. To gain acknowledgement as a shaykh by German sympathisers, it appears to be important to be a native Muslim, embodying the origin of a Muslim-Sufi life. Authenticity seems to be bound by ethnicity. The large number of members and sympathisers of branches like that of Shaykh Nazim (Turkish Naqshbandiyya) or Shaykh Muhammad (Sudanese Burhaniyya) demonstrates this. Although, at the very beginning, Abdullah Halis had been a central figure in organising Sufism in Germany, and he had many pupils – some of whom are now members of the mentioned branches – he now has just a small number of adherents. He still seems to have good connections to Sufis in Turkey, enough skill and money to buy and build the German *tekke*, and the know-how of an educated Muslim and Sufi shaykh. Since there were problems regarding the question of succession in Nazim's branch in Germany in 2007, Nazim assigned Halis as the legal successor to his branch. Consequences of this will be seen in the future. As far as I was able to ascertain, the number of interested Turkish people in Halis' tekke has increased since then. But still, for most of the Turks and Arabs, the co-educative practices of the rituals and the meetings are a bit strange, especially since there are more German female adherents than men.

Time and again, it is a controversial subject of discussion for Sufis (and sometimes even for scientists) as to whether Halis' Mevlevi *ijaza* – and that of other Western shaykhs – is authentic.[20] His charisma, his dreams and knowledge do not appear to be sufficient proof – even for him, in fact. In order to become established as a Sufi order, at least in an official manner, he wishes to be recognised as a religious order by German law. He told me that he has dreamed of the commission bringing the dead body of his Syrian Mevlevi tutor, Farhad Dede (1882–1977), to the German tekke. The implication of this is apparent: the place where the body of a grand shaykh or Sufi is buried is traditionally the domicile of a Sufi order, a mosque or tekke. Furthermore, it could possibly turn into a place of pilgrimage for Muslims from Syria and Turkey, and Western Mevlevis and other Sufis as well. Thus, it appears that nowadays it is better to have a dead Muslim-born Dede, than to just be a living German shaykh.

The Mevlevi tekke in Trebbus, Germany[21]

Tekke or *tekye* is the Turkish word for the place where Sufis gather. The *dhikr* ceremony is practised there, and sometimes it also serves as a place of study or work. While most places of Sufi gatherings (*zawya, dergah* and other) of several *tariqa* or brotherhoods in Germany are integrated within regular residences, the tekke of Shaykh Halis in Trebbus is an old farm which he has rebuilt in a way that brings a closed convent to mind. There is a main house where the shaykh lives, with a big kitchen and dining room, a mosque with two rooms for the retreat of the 40-days-*khulwat*, rooms for lectures, a guesthouse for around 40 people and a house with two apartments for *muridun* who want to do the 1,001-day Mevlevi-training. The house also includes a library and archive for literature on Sufism, including flyers and other materials tracing the very beginning of German Sufism, a bazaar, a print room and an office. Outside, there is a nice garden with a fountain and a pond, a barbecue area and a vegetable garden, as well as a lot of cats.

Abdullah Halis built the tekke with the help of the people from the village, and in the mid-1990s he was nominated and elected as a candidate for the

Main house of the tekke in Trebbus.

Mosque of the tekke in Trebbus.

municipal council. Astonishingly, despite his peculiar outlook and activities, he has been accepted into this small East German village.

Workshops and courses

Abdullah Halis can be primarily characterised as a 'teaching shaykh' (Buehler 1988).[22] His followers claim to have a spiritual relationship to and through him, so that he is also a 'directing' and a 'mediating shaykh'.

Halis offers a variety of Sufi courses, weekends of meditation, *dhikr* and other topics for people who are interested. Since Trebbus cannot be reached by public transportation, he regularly offers *dhikr* in a Berlin mosque and an intensive long-term home-course via the Internet on Islam and Sufism. His workshops about the introduction into Mevlevi-Sufism are divided into six grades. The first-grade workshop begins with an introduction to Rumi's main work. Participants read his stories and learn to interpret them from a Sufi perspective. They learn the basics about the *lata'if* theory about the centres of body energy; they get to know some forms of *dhikr*, some of Mevlevi *adab* behaviours and the daily *wird* (e.g. recitation of God's names). This teaching programme reflects Halis' perception of Sufism as a universal spiritual psychology of the human being. This psychology is, he says, also understandable, although ultimately not practicable, without Islam. Therefore, during the courses he urges the participants to learn and practise Sunni rules of Islam like

Guesthouse of the tekke in Trebbus.

wudu' (ritual washing), the prayer, wearing a headpiece as well as covering one's arms and legs for prayer and *wird*, renunciation of eating pork, etc. Nevertheless, Abdullah Halis also teaches non-Muslims in his workshops. But he emphasises the importance of knowing what Sufism is and how it is connected to Islamic tradition and ritual practices. Since most of his *muridun* live some hundreds of kilometres away, he has established an additional distance-learning course where each person can learn step by step from month to month about Sufism, self-experience and Islam. These are supported by texts with corresponding exercises, as well as instructions on observing one's own special behaviour, all sent by post.

The workshops are often at weekends, where participants learn, pray, cook and eat together, guided of course by the shaykh and his wife. It has traditionally been handed down that the training of the *murid* and the training for the *sema* both take place in the kitchen, although *sema* is neither the content nor the aim of Halis' workshops, in contrast to most other Mevlevi branches. This may be due to the fact that he may have set a special standard for the learning of *sema*. The only one whom he has instructed in *sema* is – as far as I know – his wife Nuriye, the shaykha of the *tariqa*.

The workshops have a more personal ambience, even if he sets a high value on Mevlevi rules of *adab*[23] towards the shaykh and among the group members, but at the same time he is very present, in direct contact with the people and humorous in handling the group.

Shaykh Halis calls his *tariqa* the 'Kubrevi-Mevlevi-tariqa' in distinction to the 'International Mevlana Foundation' and in respect of the Mevlevis ancestry. (The father of Rumi is supposed to have been a devotee of its founder Najmuddin Kubra, 1145–1220.) Kubra is known for his description of the

Shaykh Abdullah Halis during a workskop with a murid.

Female muridun *during the workshop with Abdullah Halis; Shaykha Nuriye sits in the middle.*

'colourful light' during mystical trainings.[24] Shaykh Halis is currently instructing around ten people in a two-year course on 'Light-Glance Meditation', which contains a specific theory of interrelation of experience of light and the *lata'if* energy. *Lata'if*, within the frame of Sufism, means subtle energy fields in human beings. According to this method there are 42 centres in the body, each with a different impact. The meditation activates these centres and thereby trains spiritual as well as physical self-healing. Therefore, the students also learn meditation techniques which focus the concentration on their spiritual relation to their Shaykh Abdullah Halis and his tutor Farhad Dede, who introduced

A public dhikr *meeting with Shaykh Halis.*

Abdullah Halis into this 'Light-Glance' meditation and its impacts on spiritual as well as physical healing of body and mind by activating the centres of energy.[25] The idea is that the experience of God is possible at every level of existence. And one of the aims is to experience and differentiate one's feelings. For this, the direct instruction and guidance of Shaykh Halis is necessary and no distance-learning course instruction is possible (Krieg-Dornbrach 1997: 58).

The followers

None of his followers live in the tekke, except for Halis' wife Nuriye. Most of Halis' followers are women living in different cities in Germany – which is also true for the other German transethnic Sufi groups. Their relation to Islam is heterogeneous. Complying with the daily Mevlevi *wird* at home is difficult, as is the praying ritual which would require strict discipline. Some of them also try to wear a headscarf in public. They do so more as a form of spiritual retreat and as a way to protect their spiritual energy during everyday life, based on the theory of the *lata'if*, and less because they do not want to attract the opposite sex. Most of the followers are not only women living in Germany, but also native Germans with a Christian background. There are only a few Turks and other native Muslims in Germany who follow Halis as a shaykh, although he is very familiar with Turkish culture and fluent in Turkish. However, since Shaykh Nazim proclaimed that Shaykh Halis would be his true successor and *khalifa*

(Muslim leader), and this for his own followers as well, more Turkish men and women have become Halis' adherents.

The training and guidance of Shaykh Halis not only include intellectual teaching and traditional training, but also spiritual guidance and mediating. His followers praise the intensive spiritual contact they have to him during the times when they are absent from the tekke. If they have problems and cannot reach him on the telephone, they contact him by meditating and praying. The spiritual power of Abdullah Halis is not restricted to his mental abilities. His followers are convinced that his spiritual power leads to mental and physical healing. For example, it is said that he has healed a female follower's glaucoma when she was told that she would be blind in six months.

Contextualised Mevlevi Sufism and the religious market

As has been shown, the contemporary forms of Mevlevi Sufism in Europe and North America vary between the presentation of religion, poetry, body work and spirituality. This adaptation aims to present a relatively fast and individually consumable form of Mevlevi Sufism. The Western market for books, CDs and weekend workshops is continually increasing. The workshop contents focus on whirling, as a foundation of general spiritual and aesthetical experiences. The books and CDs feature Rumi's name on the cover, often without providing any information on who he was. Islam is not an issue. Some of the described examples are even expressly declared pre-Islamic and/or universal non-confessional offerings. Only the exotic and/or elusive Islamic ancestry of the teacher refers to it. Accordingly, there is no expectation of conversion or approximation to Islam for participants.

On the other hand, the review of Shaykh Abdullah Halis' Mevlevi *tariqa* reveals a different presentation of Mevlevi Sufism, namely as an Islamic tradition with rules, intellectual ideas, different practices and hierarchies. At the same time, the teachings of Abdullah Halis are greatly contextualised to the German-identity market, insofar as he provides workshops which fit the modern concept of 'lifelong work on identity', as a continuous process of matching the inner and outer experience of reality.[26] Shaykh Halis' Sufi workshops, as well as the Light-Glance meditation course, foster this attitude. Halis offers these courses not only in his own tekke in Trebbus, but also in the centres of other Sufi orders, such as Nazim's *zawiyas,* among others. Although Abdullah Halis has many participants in these other orders, his direct followers are a comparatively small group. Even though he has also trained non-Muslim people, he emphasises that conversion to Islam is necessary in the long run because Sufism cannot be practised without it.

Beside the argument of the accommodating character of the new spiritual offerings on the Internet as well as of some Sufi groups, these offerings are also based on new forms of allegiance and authority. So, it is interesting to note that Shaykh Halis' character as a 'teaching shaykh' is in contrast not only to the above-mentioned popular commodities available on the market, but also to other larger orders in Germany, such as that of Shaykh Nazim or the Burhani order,[27] none of which attach a comparable importance to the intellectual and religious schooling of their followers. Rather, it appears that the followers are more attached to the spiritual group experiences, such as the spontaneously felt spiritual contact to the shaykh and the absorption of unfamiliar emotions. Nazim and others are more acknowledged as 'directing shaykhs', relying on the exotic charisma and 'ethnic capital' of being born Muslims. Abdullah Halis' charisma, on the other hand, is more familiar and German-like. With their emphasis on charisma and spontaneous experiences, a larger proportion of orders enshrine a variety of exotic and unusual elements in their German branch. And indeed, being a Muslim-born shaykh doubtlessly strengthens this ability. To the German followers, this might secure the uniqueness and authenticity they seek in their search for individuality and identity.

This may also be true for the described examples of whirling offerings on the Internet. The teachers' as well as the shaykhs' authority is legitimised by their Muslim family background. Expertise and authority is based on authenticity and charisma, not on professionalism. Authenticity and charisma are apparently associated with experience and exoticism. The competences of the teachers and of the shaykhs may be transmitted only by experiences and emotions, not by cognitive expertise. The American scientist of India and religions, Daniel Gold, constitutes therein the attractiveness of Asiatic concepts in the West. He argues that the intellectualism of the Jewish-Christian tradition and its critical readings of holy texts have produced a new generation of sceptics in terms of written words. Only experienced-based, practical and body-related forms of teachings are accepted, since they produce immediate perceptible results. Gold relates his argument to all Westerners which means to Indians living in the West as well (1988: 121). This may strengthen the presumption that the ignorance of the German (and Western) revival of Rumi and the renewal of Mevlevi Orders by most of the Turkish immigrants is only temporary. Currently, one can find only a few Turkish or Muslim-born people who are interested in these new approaches. And the contact between the Sufi groups mentioned and conventional immigrant mosques is marginal too. Only a few people from the younger generation, who for example have no problem with mixed gender meetings for *dhikr*, sporadically take part.

In general, the existing data on the development of religion(s) in Germany seems to confirm the above study. Secularisation does not mean the decline but rather the fundamental change in the perception and practice of religion in the contemporary German society. Individuality, against the backdrop of an open mass market, is achieved through authenticity and exoticism. The new reception of Mevlevi Sufism in Germany, therefore, has less to do with a new integration of Islam, but rather with the contextualisation with the new field of the (religious) identity market.

References

Bell, Daniel (1980) 'The Return of the Sacred', in D. Bell (ed.) *The Winding Passage: Essays and Sociological Journeys 1960-1980*, USA: Transaction Publishers.

Bourdieu, Pierre (1982) *Rede und Antwort*, Frankfurt am Main: Suhrkamp Verlag.

Buehler, F. Arthur (1988) *Sufi Heirs of the Prophet. The Indian Naqshibandiyya and the Rise of the Mediating Sufi Shaykh*, Columbia: University of South Carolina Press.

De Jong, Frederick (1991) 'Mawlawiyya', in *Encyclopaedia of Islam*, vol. VI, Leiden.

De Jong, Frederick (2000) 'The takiya of the Mawlawiyya in Tripolis', in Frederick De Jong (ed.) *Sufi Orders in Ottoman and Post-Ottoman Egypt and the Middle East*, Istanbul: The Isis Press.

Fleischer, Heinrich Leberecht (1862) 'Über die farbigen Lichterscheinungen der Sufis', in *Zeitschrift der Deutschen Morgenländischen Gesellschaft*, 16: 235–241.

Gold, Daniel (1988) *Comprehending the Guru. Towards a Grammar of Religious Perception*, Atlanta: Scholars Press.

Gölpınarlı, Abdülbaki (1983 [1953]) *Mevlânâ'dan sonra Mevlevîlik*, Istanbul: Inkilab Kitabevi.

Grundmann, Herbert (1970) *Religiöse Bewegungen im Mittelalter*, Darmstadt: Wissenschaftliche Buchgesellschaft.

Holgate, Steven (2005) 'Persian Poet Rumi conquers America', in U.S. Embassy (ed.) *Sufism in America*, New Dehli.

Jonker, Gerdien (2002) *Eine Wellenlänge zu Gott. Der 'Verband der islamischen Kulturzentren' in Europa*, Bielefeld: transcript Verlag.

Keupp, Heiner et al. (1999) *Identitätskonstruktionen. Das Patchwork der Identitäten in der Spätmoderne*, Reinbek bei Hamburg: Rowohlt-Taschenbuch Verlag.

Klinkhammer, Gritt (2005) 'Traditionalising spirituality. The Burhaniya Sufi Order in the West', in S. Nökel and L. Teczan (eds) *Islam in the New Europe: Challenge of Continuity, Chance for Change*, vol. 6 of Yearbook of the Sociology of Islam, Bielefeld: transcript.

Klinkhammer, Gritt (2008) 'The emergence of transethnic Sufism in Germany: from mysticism to authenticity', in M. Dressler, R. Geaves and G. Klinkhammer (eds) *Global Networking and Locality: Sufis in Western Societies*, London and New York: Routledge.

Krieg-Dornbrach, Nuriye (1997) *Tibb-i Nuraniyya: Das heilende Licht*, Trebbus: Sufi Archiv Deutschland e.V.

Lewis, Frankling D. (2000) *Rumi. Past and Present, East and West. The Life, Teaching and Poetry of Jalal al-Din Rumi*, Oxford: One World.

Nikolaisen, Bente (2004) 'Embedded motion: sacred travel among Mevlevi Dervishes', in Simon Coleman and John Eade (eds) *Reframing Pilgrimage: Cultures in Motion*, London: Routledge.

Schimmel, Annemarie (1980) *Triumphal Sun: Study of the Works of Jalalud-Din Rum,* New York: State University of New York Press.

Schimmel, Annemarie (1995) *Mystical Dimensions of Islam*, Chapel Hill: University of North Carolina Press.

Schleßmann, Ludwig (2003) *Sufismus in Deutschland. Deutsche auf dem Weg des mystischen Islam*, Köln: Böhlau.

Shiva, Shahram (2000) *Rumi Thief of Sleep*, Prescott: Hohm Press.

Tehranian, Javad (2001) *Sama'a – Light of the Light of the Light*, Noure Ala Nour Society.

ter Haar, Gerrie (ed.) (1998) *Strangers and Sojourners. Religious Communities in the Diaspora*, Leuven: Peeters Publisher.

Tibi, Bassam (2001) *Islam Between Culture and Politics*, New York: Palgrave.

Notes to Chapters

Translocal mobility and traditional authority

1 For an orientation in the vast discussions on digital Islam and the Internet, see Eickelman and Anderson (1999); Bunt (2002, 2003).

2 For the sake of a short clarification of these two highly debated terms, see Julian Johansen's overview and Olivier Roy's discussion in *Globalized Islam* (Roy 2004). Roy was one of the first to give a more systematic analysis of the political dimensions (and links) of contemporary Sufi groups and their impact on political life. Radical interpretations of Islam have, like Sufism, been defined in a number of ways. A workable understanding of the phenomenon is formulated by Roy: 'A post-Islamist society is one in which the Islamist parenthesis (in the sense of a temporary experiment) has profoundly altered relationships between Islam and politics by giving the political precedence over the religious in the name of religion itself. The paradoxical result of the overpoliticisation of religion by Islamism is that Muslim religious sentiment is seeking, beyond or beneath politics, autonomous spaces and means of expression, feeding contradictory and burgeoning forms of religiosity, from a call for wider implementation of *sharia* to the revival of Sufism' (2004: 3). The articles in *Sufism Today* provide many examples of the revival of Sufism and its political implications. The complex relationship between Sufism and politics is further illustrated in Heck (2007) and Yemelianova (2007).

3 Examples of websites expressing this universalist approach to Sufism include: www.nimatullahi.org/us; www.sufismjournal.org; www.sufismsymposium.org; www.sufiyouth.org; www.sufiwomen.org; www.superluminal.com; www.sufis.org. For critical discussions, see Stenberg (1996: 97ff., 2004); Wasserstrom (1999: 70ff., 88ff.); Raudvere (2002: 13ff).

4 For studies of how worldly and spiritual dimensions blend in contemporary Muslim piety, see Kafadar (1992); Metcalf (1996); Clarke (1997); Ernst (1997: 205ff.); Manger (1999); Schiffauer (2000); Werbner (2003); Stjernholm (2007); Bruinessen and Howell (2007); Louw (2007); Raudvere and Gaši (in press).

5 This is further developed on SMC's homepage: www.sufimuslimcouncil.org

6 For a recent survey of the relationship between Sufi studies and social theory, see Voll (2007).

7 The richness of this developing trend is visible in recent collections of Sufi studies which emphasise contextual analyses: Geaves (2000); Westerlund (2004); Malik and Hinnells (2006); Heck (2007); Bruinessen and Howell (2007).

8 Or expressed from Lefebvre's more philosophical point of view: 'And what of everyday life? Everything here is calculated because everything is numbered: money, minutes, metres, kilogrammes, calories … and not only objects but also living thinking creatures, for there exists a demography of animals and of people as well as of things. Yet people are born, live and die. They live well or ill; but they live in everyday life, where they make or fail to make a living either in the wider sense of surviving or not surviving, or just surviving or living their lives to the full. It is in everyday life that they rejoice and suffer; here and now' (2002: 21). For a complementary view on how to approach everyday life as an analytical concept, see also Heller 1970/1984.

9 Roy writes when discussing the relationship between homeland, origin and fellowship: 'Relations between militants and their country of origin are weak or non-existent; we are facing not a diaspora but a truly deterritorialised population' (2004: 305).

The politics of Sufism

1 See Mu'ayyid al-'Uqbi (2002) and Zelkina (2005).

2 See Van Den Bos (2002).

3 Zarcone (2004).

4 See Heck (2006a).

5 For a brief overview of Sufism, see Heck (2006b).

6 This term is not limited to Sufism but has a special relationship to it. The task of renewing religion, i.e. the way of the prophets, can be advanced through rational argumentation, consensus-building and public lobbying, but it often coalesces around a public figure with charismatic appeal and rhetorical talent and thus the ability to bring a spiritual viewpoint to the ethical challenges of Muslim society. There are today different conceptualisations of renewal (*tajdid*) in Islam, spiritual renewal being just one of them. Renewed understanding of the purposes (*maqasid*) of shari'a – often inspired by the work of al-Shatibi's *Muwafaqat* – is another prominent kind of renewal in Islam today. A proponent of this approach to renewal is Ahmad al-Raysuni, leading scholar in the Movement of Monotheism and Reform (*Harakat al-Tawhid wa-l-Islah*), the largest Islamist movement in Morocco.

7 Kuftaro was Mufti of Syria (1964–2004) and sheikh of the Naqshbandiyya. It is important to note that al-Habash draws many of his ideas of renewal from Kuftaro. He thus seeks to assume the mantle of Kuftaro's legacy, claiming that other sheikhs in Kuftaro's circle have actually betrayed his programme of renewal for the sake of a reactionary agenda. See Heck (2004).

8 Articles arguing for a definition of Islam as a moderate religion, capable of rational reform, occasionally appear in Syria's state-sponsored press. One example is 'Adnan al-Rifa'i, 'Mu'awiqqat al-islah al-dini fi l-fikr al-mahsub 'ala l-Islam', *Tishrin*, 16 June 2005, p. 15.

9 For the Moroccan context, see Zeghal (2005). For background on Syria, see Weismann (2001; 1997) and Teitelbaum (2004). There are no scholarly publications on the Syrian Muslim Brotherhood today. It exists on the ground as a quasi-social movement but is banned from organising as a political party. Were free and

fair elections to be held, it would be a significant, if not dominant, player in national politics.

10 Both countries have parliaments and thus a measure of popular representation but are in actuality ruled more or less autocratically: a royal dynasty in Morocco and a life-term presidency with dynastic ambitions in Syria.

11 Networks of Sufism can also become an object of international competition, as in the role of the Tijaniyya in Moroccan-Algerian rivalry. See Hamada (2006).

12 For records of his writings, lectures and conferences, see his website: www.altajdeed.org/web.

13 This goal, which is supported by the Syrian state, is also a key goal of the Moroccan state in its management of the nation's religious field (*al-haql al-dini*).

14 Even if lambasting what he sees as the Zionist mindset of US policy (*al-Thawra*, 23 June 2006), he remains ready for dialogue with the West and is respectful of its intellectual and cultural heritage (*al-Thawra*, 14 July 2006). See also the interview conducted by M. al-Hurani in the January 2004 issue (vol. 13, no. 152, pp. 32–35) of *al-Nur* (not to be confused with the communist newspaper in Syria; see www.annoor-magazine.com).

15 See Heck (2004).

16 Lecture on Sufism in a series of lectures on the unity of Islam and the legitimacy of all of its eight confessional groupings, available on his website. In Morocco, in contrast, only one *madhhab* in Islam has official recognition, the Maliki one as adjudicated by the king as 'commander of the faithful' (*amir al-mu'minin*).

17 I use this term in the monolithic sense commonly given to it today by Muslim spokesmen. We recognised that the concept of the West is a construct. However, its construction is closely connected to equally simplistic constructions of 'Islam' in both non-Muslim and now Muslim discourse. The phenomenon is, of course, an ancient one. See, for example, Scarfe Beckett (2003).

18 Again, Muslims who limit Islam to literal wordings of religious texts with no consideration of the common good (*tatbiq zahir al-nass bi-dun i'tibar al-masalih*) miss the essence of Islam (*al-Thawra*, 9 March 2007). Human comprehension (*fiqh*) of religion is the register of the believing intellect (*diwan al-'aql al-mu'min*) and does not end at the limits of the text (*la yatawaqqaf 'inda hudud al-nass*), but includes efforts (*ijtihad*) to comprehend the import of the text.

19 Muhammad al-Habash, *Dirasa fiqhiyya lil-tahaffuzat allati wada'aha al-marsum al-tashri'i 330 li-'am 2002 'ala ittifaqiyyat mukafahat kull ashkal al-tamyiz didd al-mar'a*, published jointly by the Syrian Organization for Family Affairs and the Center for Islamic Studies, Damascus 2005. For a brief summary of its contents, see Heck (2007).

20 At times, he also defends specific state interests. For example, in the wake of the 2006 war between Israel and Hizbullah, he was quick to support Hizbullah and castigate Muslim leaders who issued *fatwas* calling for the withdrawal of Muslim support for Hizbullah (*Syria News*, 16 August 2006).

21 See Heck (2005a).

22 Haddad (2004).

23 Such calls garner public support, enhancing his popularity, and may reflect his own ambitions rather than a future reality. He does recognise the precariousness of religiously based parties and their potential for confessional polarisation, which would be a national disaster for Syria. There are now several members of parliament who represent the concerns of Islam, but they run as independents and see their work as

a way Islam can coexist with others within modern realities. This is, of course, of use to the state, but it also offers Islam a national platform. These PMs have mixed feelings about the possibility of religiously based political parties. The general feeling is that they would harm Islam, leading to its fragmentation across a multitude of parties that represent confessional and not general public interests.

24 For example, he seeks to promote Syria as a centre for global religious tourism and a source of global religious knowledge. His trips to Muslim-majority countries, such as Pakistan, Indonesia and Malaysia, may be useful to a state in search of allies but also serves his interests in recasting Syria's foreign relations in terms of Islam.

25 See www.yassine.net, e.g. 'al-Muhaddithun wa-l-Sufiyya' and 'al-Fuqaha' Talamidhat al-Tasawwuf'.

26 Sufism has never been immune to militancy. It is best to describe Yasin's religiosity as Sufism not Islamism or post-Islamism. See Lauzière (2005).

27 Interestingly, Sa'id Hawwa (d.1989), Naqshbandi affiliate and spiritual guide of the Muslim Brotherhood, saw himself in a similar role, see Sa'id Hawwa (1998).

28 This is not to overlook the fact that a sense of democratic authority is rapidly being introduced into the religiosity of Moroccan society especially via Islamist movements, notably the Movement of Monotheism and Reform (*Harakat al-Tawhid wa-l-Islah*) and its political wing, the Party of Justice and Development (*Hizb al-'Adala wa-Tanmiyya*), which operate within the parameters set by the monarchy.

29 Illustrative of this approach is one of his recent works, see 'Abd al-Rahman, Taha (2005).

30 'Le soufisme: un pilier pour le royaume du Maroc. Allocution de Sa Majesté Mohammed VI, roi du Maroc', as posted at www.soufisme.org.

31 See 'Nida' min Sidi Hamza b. al-'Abbas', www.tariqa.org/ar/appel.pjp.

32 This is not at all to suggest that Yasin's group seeks to claim the title of Butshishiyya or uses it at all.

33 Islamist movements can also present themselves as an alternative society, but the difference lies in their political vision. For a study of Islamism as a social movement, see Rosefsky Wickham (2002).

34 This term, of course, is also used by the Muslim Brotherhood. Yasin is certainly very aware of the writings of Hasan Banna and Sayyid Qutb (and other members of the Muslim Brotherhood). He may have borrowed this concept from the Brotherhood, but this is hardly sufficient evidence of institutional overlap.

35 See S. Hamimanat, 'Sanat Imtihan Nubuwwat al-'Adl wa-l-Ihsan', in *Halat al-Maghrib 2005-2006*, annual of Moroccan life published by Wajhat Nazar: Rabat, pp. 119–148.

36 Analysis of Yasin's political thought comes largely from our reading of *al-'Adl: al-Islamiyyun wa-l-Hukm*, which is available at www.yassine.net/yo12/Default.aspx, along with short articles on his idea of the Islamic state, e.g. 'Bana' al-Dawla al-Islamiyya', also available on his website.

37 Yassine (2000).

38 On early Kharijism, see Heck (2005b).

39 For polemically driven analysis of his claims to saintly stature, see 'Abd al-Rahman Dhu al-Fiqar (2004).

40 The statement of his daughter, Nadia Yasin, on behalf of a republican form of government, cannot be associated with the political outlook of the Justice and Charity

Group, which is saintly first and last, thus accepting the hierarchical notion of authority advanced by the monarchy even if contesting the king's qualifications to rule as supreme authority. See al-Hamimanat, 'Sanat Imtihan'. A leading member of Yasin's group, Munir al-Rakraki, formulated ten conditions that would qualify a person to assume caliphal leadership over the *umma* and claimed that they are all amply represented in Yasin; see his interview with Yasin, recorded on 9 August 2005 and posted on Yasin's website.

41 This project is mapped out in the first book of al-Ghazali's *Ihya' 'Ulum al-Din* (*Revivification of the Religious Sciences*).

42 Yasin is not alone in the Moroccan context in privileging spiritual instruction of the soul over and even against the political implementation of Islam. Other prominent voices, such as Farid al-Ansari, would also privilege the missionary and educational aspects of Islam over political ones, but in contrast to Yasin would not deploy the religion in such a way for the sake of an alternative realm but instead would integrate it with the course of national life as set by the monarchy.

Transnationalising personal and religious identities

1 See Vanly (1992: 170).

2 A general introduction to his life and work is in Christmann (1998).

3 See Böttcher (1998).

4 See Stenberg (1999: 101–116).

5 See Lobmeyer (1995), Abd-Allah (1983) and Hinnebush (1982: 138–169).

6 A short introduction to the work, as well as an overview of existing translations from Kurdish to date, can be found in Shakely (1992: 5-15). There is currently still no detailed account of the life and work of Ehmedê Xanî in a European language. Individual references to specific aspects of his work (nationalism, mysticism, folklore) will be made below.

7 'Al-Boti translated the epic in prose and turned it into a love novel that does not contain any of the philosophical, religious or political view-points of Khani' (Shakely 1992: 10).

8 These circumstances led to al-Buti's integration into the modern and secularly oriented education system, as well as into the centrally administered, state-governed and completely modernised religious world of Syria, as introduced under the military governments of Husnī al-Zaʿīm (1949) and Adīb al-Shīshaklī (1949–1954) (Reissner 1980: 294f.; Seale 1986: 58). Such integration did not happen without resistance and substantial moral reservations – e.g. against a society that produced religious administrators who are being remunerated by the state for spreading their faith – and this becomes apparent in several passages in al-Buti's biography of his father, Mullah Ramadan al-Buti (al-Buti 1995: 62ff. and 41–42).

9 He was born in 1929 on the Turkish side of the Kurdish Jazeera (in the ancient Bohtan principality of Kurdistan), but lived in Damascus from the age of five (1934) onwards. For more detailed information see Christmann (1998).

10 For example, in *Hadha Walidi*, al-Buti refers to Mullah 'Abd al-Majid, Mullah 'Ali, Mullah Saʿid, Muhammad Jazu, Mullah 'Abd al-Jalil, and Mullah Khalid (al-Buti 1994: 40).

11 In addition, his father also edited such books, e.g. Ehmedê Xanî's *NuBihar* (The New Spring), as well as *Nahj al-Anam*, a manual containing Islamic doctrines and *Adab* precepts. He also selected and printed material from the oral tradition, which had not been written down before, e.g. stories, fairy tales, poetry, songs and religious liturgies. It is also likely that al-Buti's father encouraged the translation and editing of E. Xanî's *Mem û Zîn*. (al-Buti 1995: 47, cf. fn.1).

12 al-Buti (1995: 45).

13 al-Buti (1995: 56–61).

14 Also see Christmann (2003).

15 *Hadha Walidi* shows al-Buti's rejection of the 'superstition' and 'backwardness' of the Sufi brotherhoods based in Kurdistan at that time, in particular the Naqshbandiya order, whose teaching methods and cult practices al-Buti condemned as *bid'a* and therefore illegitimate (al-Buti 1995: 14f.).

16 al-Buti, 'Al-Wa'l', in *Min al-fikr wa'l-qalb* (1972: 210–218 (210)).

17 See my analysis of al-Buti's biography of his father which revealed similar patterns of legitimisation: Christmann (2005).

18 al-Buti, 'al-Islam bain al-'aql wa'l-qalb au: al-iqtina' wa'l-hubb' (1960), in *Min al-Fikr wa'l-Qalb* (1972: 96–104).

19 al-Buti, 'Lughat al-hubb', in *Min al-Fikr wa'l-Qalb* (1972: 199–202).

20 al-Buti, 'Layla ma' rawa'i Iqbal', in *Min al-Fikr wa'l-Qalb* (1972: 234–236); for an analysis, see Christmann (2003: 1-8).

21 al-Buti, 'Hajat al-maktaba al-islamiyya ila'l-adab al-islami' (1968), in *Min al-Fikr wa'l-Qalb* (1972: 142–149 (147)).

22 See Conermann (1996).

23 A comprehensive overview of the written tradition of oral versions was carried out by Michael L. Chyet (1994). In this context, reference should also be made to Chyet's commentary (1991) on a written version in the Kurmanji dialect.

24 Roger Lescots' study (1942) gives a partial overview of the important differences between the oral versions and E. Xanî's literary adaptation.

25 al-Buti (1972: 145).

26 al-Buti (1992: 8).

27 For a classification of 'Mem û Zîn' in the context of the propagation of a Kurdish national state, see chapter 4 in Hassanpour (1992: 83–90).

28 The English translation was made by the author of this article. It is based on the Kurdish original (in the edition by Margarita Borisovna Rudenko, 1962), and with the help of the Russian translation by Rudenko (1962), as well as the French rendition by Sandrine Alexie and Akif Hasan (2001). The numbering for the hemistiches follows the French edition.

29 For more information on the handling of topics such as love and sexuality within Kurdish oral folk poetry, see the analysis by Allison (2001).

30 'Tears interrupted Mem's speech. He was about to collapse completely once again, devoid of any strength, when the fire of his tears reached Zîn's heart. She took his hand and moistened it with her tears, and said: "I swear to you, oh Mem, on my tears, which extinguished the flame of the evening light, on my sighs, which diminished my beauty, on my loneliness, brightened by your gaze; I swear that only the solitude of the grave will be able to replace you. Instead of you, only death will be able to embrace me, so that both of us shall be united – whether it be now, at this very moment, or in the hereafter." They then went to the pavilion, afraid that

someone might hear them in the garden. There they sat down and comforted one another, talked about their anguish and sorrow, and complained about the cruelty befalling those chosen by fate. Their utterances created a trance-like state, in which they became completely oblivious to the world around them' (al-Buti 1992: 123).

31 al-Buti (1999a: 241).

32 Christmann (2003: 1–8).

33 See, for example, al-Buti (1988: 189–211); also his *Shaksyāt Istawqafatnī* (1999b). (Here, al-Buti defends prominent Sufis, such as Fudayl Ibn 'Iyyād; 'Abdallāh al-Mubārak; Abū Hamīd al-Ghazālī; and Jalāl al-Dīn al-Rūmī against accusations of *Kufr* and *Ilhad*); similarly apologetic is his three volume commentary of Ibn 'Atā's Aphorisms (al-Buti 2000–2002).

34 Analyses of mystic examples in E. Xanî's work are currently only available in two works published in Kurdish and Arabic; see Durre (2002) and Rasul (1979).

35 Xanî's proximity to Ibn al-'Arabi's concept of the 'perfect human being' [*al-insan al-kamil*] becomes clear in the following passage:

> *The first one, a ray of eternal beauty, was the light in which Muhammad was created.*
> *On God's command, this light became the inexhaustible source of the invisible world.*
> *This prophetic light, like the plants and the sugar they produce, created all our souls.*
> *It became the origin* [asl] *of all Being, both felicitous and infelicitous.*
> [105–108]

36 Al-Buti distinguished between a philosophical, i.e. objective and rational, strand of the unity problem, and the mystical, i.e. subjective and emotional experience of the *unio mystica*. In this regard, he relied on Ahmad Sirhindi's dictum that mystical expressions in relation to *wahdat al-wujūd* should not be understood ontologically, but instead as *wahdat al-shuhud*, i.e. a unity in the *perception* of God. Therefore, perceiving God may indeed be a *feeling* of unity, but it still is no admission of the actual oneness or *being*-one with God, nor a dogmatic statement made while being in a 'sober' state. In this way, al-Buti wanted to avoid any accusation of heresy against ecstatic mysticism. He portrayed ecstasy in such a positive light that an objection could in fact no longer be made: 'Logic itself dictates that human beings, who sense such love, are divine (*yuqaddas*), and that they cannot be condemned for such love (*yu'atab*). After all, such love will ultimately lead them to its source and roots, not to its rivers and branches. [...] I remember that my father often entered such a state, while communicating at the same time with others. Words flowed from his lips when he was completely overcome by this state (*hal*). When he returned from it, he would utter a loud scream that frightened those around him. He later commented that his words [uttered during his ecstasy] would only be understood by those whose hearts were burning with Allah's love and an immense desire to be close to God.' (al-Buti 1994: 119–120).

37 A similar normative reinterpretation can also be observed in al-Buti's later work, e.g. in his reworking of biographies, which he took from such classical works as the *Tarajim*, *Tabaqat* or *Hilyat al-Auliya'* literature (see his *Shaksyāt Istawqafatnī*, 1999b). Rather than the very complex historical personalities, al-Buti's versions contain quite sketchy examples of orthodox and devout Muslims. Similar to his

characterisation of Mem, al-Buti's portrayals mainly include eccentric loners, who remain strong in their faith regardless of the pain and suffering that they experience, who persist in their love of God, and who see their destiny as a test of faith by God (and which can be traced back to such early mystics as Fudayl Ibn 'Iyyad, Abu Hamid al-Ghazali, and Jalal al-Din al-Rumi). Parallels with al-Buti's later biographies can also be found for the 'role-model' presentation of Taj al-Din, Mem's best friend, e.g. 'Aballah al-Mubarak, Hasan al-Habannaka, or Mustafa al-Siba'i (i.e. like Taj al-Din, all of them are noble characters, distinguished by their wealth, political influence and social status, who – for the love of God – sacrifice their lives and property for religion or for the protection of *Auliya' Allah*). Furthermore, the doctrine about fate (*dahr*) and predestination (*qada'*), parts of which are used by al-Buti in his presentation of Zîn, can also be found in some of his other writings (e.g. his *Insan wa-'adalat Allah fi'l-'ard* (Damascus, 1972), or *Man huwa sayyid al-qadr fi hayat al-insan?* (Damascus, 2nd edn, 1976). Finally, al-Buti's description of the negative character, Bakur, who appears in the text as the devil incarnate, recalls al-Buti's polemic against 'the enemies of Islam and against the adversaries of true believers', which appears in many instances of his writings.

38 For example:

You were the one, who created the mirrors, one after the other,
in which Your Beauty could shine.
You were the one, who placed the parrots in front of the mirror,
who caught the wild animals with snares.
This mirror appears to them like water, which reflects light onto them.
In the water, they see Your Adornment, and forget to pay
attention to the snares. [70–73]
You were the one, who grew the soft line of the lily;
You let it fall in love with the sun.
You were the one, who gave the cypresses their high growth and
shackled the pheasants.
You were the one, who gave the roses their thorns, and let the
nightingales sing a thousand (romantic) melodies.
You were the one, who gave the desert lilies their strong colour,
and the nightingales their eloquent voices.
You were the one, who projected the light onto the candle's image,
which destroyed the moth that threw itself into its flame.
You make attractive those who are beautiful, and the ones in love
crazy about them.
This love and this passion of the soul, this seducing of languor and
pulling of hair.
Through you we exist and behold them: one adorned
for the other. [62–69]

39 al-Buti (1992: 44–45).

40 [Chapter 1: 7–10]

You are the loved one of the prudent heart, as well as the
one that attracts all hearts.
You are the loved one, proud and suffering;

You are the one who loves, unconditionally.
You are both saviour and salvation, and surely at the same time also the one who wishes and is wished for.
You are the radiance on beauty's face, but also the fire that burns in the hearts of those who suffer in love.

41 [Chapter 1: 16; 23-24]

Thus both worlds are united in human beings, He is a letter of 'Kun!'
Both the visible and invisible world are united in Him, as well as perfection and imperfection.
Light and darkness exist in Him at the same time, and human beings are at once near and far from You.

42 [Chapter 2: 50-54]

All that has been created, from the beginning to the end of the world, believers and disbelievers,
Everything reflects Your Majesty and Your Divinity, the whole of creation contains Your Essence.
Nothing exists without Your Beauty, nothing would be visible without Your Light.
Your secret lies in things hidden and visible, You are at once present and absent.
For You, there is neither separation nor a permanent location, since You are omnipresent.

43 [Chapter 3: 101-104]

Everything created by God has been recorded, hence the stylus was his first creation.
It contained: the First [qalam]*; the Spirit* [ruh], *the Primary Intellect* ['aql awwal], *and all three manifested the First* [ula mu'awwil].
They should not be separated, but instead combined.
In the words of the Wise: all three are one, but infinite in their manifestations.

44 al-Buti (1992: 39).
45 However, a third edition was allowed only in 1977 (5th edition already in 1982), after a pause of almost 20 years, because of anti-Kurdish policies in the 1960s and 1970s.
46 al-Buti, 'al-Din wa'l-hubb' (1959), in *Min al-fikr wa'l-qalb* (1972: 175–181).
47 al-Buti ,'Li-madha la aktub fi'l-hubb', in *Min al-fikr wa'l-qalb* (1972: 172–174); see also his introduction to the second edition in 1972, pp. 9–11.
48 Summarised at a later stage as: al-Buti, *al-Jihad fi'l-Islam: kayfa nafhamuhu wa-kayfa numarisuhu?* (Damascus, 1993); also see al-Buti's reply to the large number of critiques of his book *Zawabi' wa-asda' wara' kitab: al-jihad fi'l-islam* (Damascus, 1994).

Between home and home

1 Catharina Raudvere's project, 'Between Home and Home: Informal Sufi Networks in Sweden and Bosnia', is further reported in Raudvere and Gaši (forthcoming) and in a forthcoming monograph, 'Between Home and Home. Muslim Bosniak Diaspora in Sweden'.

2 It must be noted that the revival of the term Bosniak (*Bošnjak*) was part of a conscious ideological strategy in the early 1990s in order to institute a clear bond between nation and religion to be used in everyday language. It has turned out to be a successful policy and now most pious organisations and activities use the adjective when referring to the Muslims of Bosnia-Herzegovina (Greenberg 2007). Muslims from parts of the former Yugoslavia other than Bosnia-Herzegovina who have Bosnian/Serbo-Croatian as their mother tongue are usually also included in the term. In religious circles Bosniak has become *the* self-defining term.

3 The more than 25 Bosniak congregations active today in Sweden are united in a national body (Islamska Zajednica Bošnjačka u Švedskoj) with one head imam with pastoral responsibilities, as well as the obligation to take the role as a spokesperson in relation to Muslim and non-Muslim counterparts.

4 Diasporic is in this chapter used according to Mandaville's discussion of the term (2001). On the conditions of life in diaspora, Peter Mandaville writes with a hint at islamophobia and the seemingly persistent segregation of Muslim communities in Europe and North America: 'Giving up on belonging is not easy when constantly confronted with antagonism which labels one as "other", thus continually forcing the politicisation of identity. In the absence of this antagonism hybridity is more easily celebrated. Once the political enters the picture, however, forcing one to define oneself (or defining one on one's behalf), it becomes much more difficult to retreat behind a negative, ironic sense of identity, or "violate the system of naming". What is engendered is the need to speak oneself in terms which transcend the (trans)locality of migrant dwelling, to posit something that is not *of* (and hence cannot be domesticated by) the nation-state' (2001: 103).

5 I would like to express my gratitude to Ašk Gaši who has been most helpful to me during these and previous periods of fieldwork.

6 The first statutes for an Islamic community were decided on in 1930. Since then the Islamic Community of Bosnia-Herzegovina has been a part of the state administration – through all the political and social changes over almost 80 years. Its power is undeniable, but it has also raised a suspicious attitude from those whose views are not recognised by the Community's mainstream theology, be it of radical or liberal orientation.

7 The closure of the Yugoslav *tekije* could be compared with the much harsher Turkish act no. 677, effective from 1925, where all outward signs of Sufi presence in social life were outlawed: places for gatherings, Sufi costumes and garments, honorary titles.

8 The Faculty of Islamic Sciences was established in 1977. It is not a fully integrated part of Sarajevo University, but a confessional educational institute with close links to the Islamic Community of Bosnia-Herzegovina.

9 A detailed discussion on ritual life and pious education in the Malmö Bosniak community can be found in Raudvere and Gaši (forthcoming).

Continuity and transformation in a Naqshbandi *tariqa* in Britain

1 The Barelwi movement has been written about by a number of scholars including Metcalf (1982); Malik (1998); Sanya (2005); Geaves (2002); and Werbner (2003).

2 Deoband *dar al-ulum* was founded in 1867 in North-East India with the intention to train *ulema* who would be dedicated to the cause of reforming Islam through purifying the faith from cultural accretions along the lines initiated by Shah Waliallah (1702–1763). The members have never considered themselves as an educational institution but rather a school of thought within South Asian Islam representing a form of orthodoxy. In 1967, there were nearly 6,000 Deobandi schools in the subcontinent. Tabligh-i Jama'at was founded in 1920 by a Deobandi graduate, Muhammad Ilyas. Unlike Deoband, Ilyas did not feel that it was necessary to belong to the professional *ulema* to reform Islam and instead created a grassroots movement that has gone on to become a worldwide Muslim missionary organisation.

3 For a detailed ethnographic account of a South Asian first-generation Sufi's struggle with micro-politics and regional community leadership, see Pnina Werbner's study of 'Maulana Sahib' in Werbner (2002).

4 Taken from earlier research undertaken in 1997 and first recorded in Geaves (2000).

5 The branch of the Naqshbandi is known as Hijazi because the family claim that their descendants came to Sind with Muhammad Qasim when that region was first invaded by Arabs from Hijaz. However, the family have lived for generations in the village of Ghosuhr, near Lahore. The spiritual lineage is traced back through Shaykh Ahmad Sirhindi (d.1624), known in the subcontinent as the *Mujaddid*, to the founder of the Indian branch of the Naqshbandiya, Khwaja Nasir'd-Din 'Ubaidu'llah Ahrar (1404–1490). The present *shaykhs* are proud of their lineage which includes the famous Shaykh Hazrat Khwaja Mu'inu'd-Din Huzuri Qusuri, who is renowned for having passed 24 hours with the Prophet in a vision, but it is the work of their grandfather, Munazira Azam Hazrat Muhammad Umar Siddiqi Icharvi, and their father, Hazrat Allama Pir Muhammad Abdul Wahhab Siddiqi, to whom they constantly refer for their inspiration. However, it is not surprising that the present *pir*s are keen to acknowledge their eminent spiritual ancestor, Ahmad Sirhindi. Shaykh Sirhindi was well known for his scholarship as well as his spirituality.

6 Interview with Hazrat Allama Pir Faisul Aqtab Siddiqi, 14 May 2007, Hijaz College.

7 Interview with Hazrat Allama Pir Faisul Aqtab Siddiqi, 20 August 1998, Hijaz College.

8 See Geaves (1996: 169–192).

9 Geaves (2000: 131).

10 Geaves (2000: 132–133).

11 The General Certificate of Secondary Education (GCSE) is the name of a set of qualifications, generally taken by secondary school students at age of 14–16 in England, Wales, and Northern Ireland. GCSEs are often a requirement for taking AS/A-levels (normally at 17/18 years respectively), the common type of university entrance requirement. RE stands for Religious Education, a compulsory subject for

all British state school children, in which Christianity and at least two other religions must be taught. RE examinations can be taken at GCSE and AS/A level.

12 See Asif (2006). Asif interviewed students and the Principal of the College. She recounts the students' relationship with the shrine and its impact on their studies.

13 This fotnote should read The Muslim Action Committee (MAC) maintains a blogspot to facilitate news, updates and debates for its supporters and the Campaign for Global Civility on www.muslim-action-committee.blogspot.com (accessed 3rd September 2008). There is also a Wikipedia entry which summarises the activities of the MAC on www.en.wikipedia.org/wiki/Muslim_Action_Committee (accessed 3rd September 2008). All earlier webites containing the Charter for Global Civility are no longer current.

14 A number of first-generation British *pirs* originating from Pakistan and Bangladesh attempted to create national umbrella organisations that claimed leadership of the Barelwi community. These organisations tended to duplicate political leadership amongst the various factions of *ulema* in Pakistan and Bangladesh. The first to be established in the UK was the World Islamic Mission. The International Muslim Organization was an offshoot of this organisation. In reality such bureaucratic and political bodies became the personal tools of various prominent *pirs* and used to supplement their status and promote their activities (see Geaves 1996: 102–103).

15 Geaves (2000: 131).

16 The Internet is an essential aspect of the globalisation of Sufism. Epitomising the new Sufism are websites such as www.masud.co.uk and www.deenport.com. The two websites address themselves to British Muslims and are the vehicles of dissemination for the views of Shaykh Abdul-Hakim Murad and Shaykh Nuh Ha Nim Keller. The latter is a high-profile American convert educated in philosophy and Arabic at the University of California, UCLA and a *shaykh* in the Shadhili *tariqa*. He describes himself as a specialist in Islamic law, especially the traditional sciences of hadith and Shafi'i and Hanafi fiqh which he studied in Syria and Jordan. Shaykh Abdul-Hakim Murad describes himself as a commentator on Islam in Britain. The websites function as online information sources to resolve questions posed by young Muslims that arise from living in a non-Muslim environment. The answers provide erudite explanations based on classical fiqh. Most of the websites are owned by educated young Western Muslims with allegiance to traditional Islam and Sufism and skilled in the traditional Islamic sciences (see Geaves 2008).

17 For a detailed analysis of convergence between Sufis and Islamic reform movements, see Geaves (2006).

18 See Gaborieau (2006: 63). Gaborieau observes that the founders of Tabligh-i Jama'at are also buried in tombs within the grounds of the movement's headquarters in Nizamuddin, New Delhi, but have not become objects of worship.

19 See Asif (2006: 26).

A translocal Sufi movement

1 The ethnographic material in this article is derived from fieldworks in London during the winter of 2004, the autumn of 2006 and the spring of 2007. I wish to express

my gratitude to 99-klubben and Stiftelsen Landshövding Per Westlings minnesfond for providing financial support to make these fieldworks possible.

2 *Tariqa*: lit. 'way' or 'path', yet in Sufi terminology it refers to a particular Sufi order.

3 For more information on the Naqshbandi tariqa's historical development, see Gabourieau, Popovic and Zarcone (1990).

4 *Derga*: a Sufi lodge, sometimes built over the grave of a Sufi saint and therefore a place of *ziyara*, 'pilgrimage'. My spelling of this word is taken from that which is used in several publications of the tariqa. I have seen attendees to the priory use various spellings, and this spelling might well be anglicised. Other spellings can be, for example, *dargah*, *derghai* and *durgah*.

5 www.sufimuslimcouncil.org (accessed 16 August 2007).

6 The conference report can be viewed at www.nixoncenter.org/publications/monographs/Sufism.pdf (accessed 11 August 2007).

7 Mr Reid's speech can be read at www.publicsectorreview.com/?pid=4303&lsid=4303&edname=23911.htm&ped=23911 (accessed 21 May 2007).

8 The debate can be viewed at www.youtube.com/watch?v=uv704B93EZU (accessed 15 May 2007).

9 See, for example, www.craigmurray.co.uk/archives/2006/08/the_ neoconserva.html (accessed 21 May 2007).

10 Videoclips from the meeting at the House of Commons can be viewed at www.youtube.com/watch?v=D_jQFJZURdo and at www.youtube.com/watch?v=n4jaAA37ZUA (accessed 15 May 2007). When I wrote a letter to the Secretary of State in which I asked about the relationship to SMC and how it is viewed as Muslim representatives by the government, I received a reply from the Secretary's office stating the following: 'The Secretary of State has not met with the SMC formally, although she has attended a number of events which were also attended by the SMC. Therefore, I am unfortunately unable to detail the exact content of her dialogue with them.' Personal e-mail correspondence, 16 April 2007.

11 The first issue of *Spirit the Mag* could earlier be read at www.spiritthemag.com (accessed 15 May 2007).

12 I have previously described the 'Celebrating Spirituality' event in November 2006 at www.islamologi.se/?p=199, where pictures from the event can be viewed as well.

13 The programme for this event can be viewed at www.suficinema.com/celebratingspirituality.html (accessed 15 May 2007).

14 The guidebook is titled *The Naqshbandi Sufi Tradition: Guidebook of Daily Practices and Devotions*, and can be bought in the priory.

15 Silat, or Pencak Silat, is also practised in Indonesia, e.g. under the umbrella of the Muhammadiyah organisation. See, for example, Syamsiyatun (2007: 85).

One foot rooted in Islam, the other foot circling the world

1 Compass here refers not to the needle that points towards north but to the two-legged instrument that draws a circle. The analogy is frequently quoted in many variations (for instance, Gürdoğan (1996). I have not yet managed to find it in any standard compilation of Rumi's work.

2 *The Daily Liberal* (web edition), 5 and 6 February 2001.

3 Counts vary from around 40,000 to more than 100,000 participants depending on whether one consults the 'secularist' newspaper *Hurriyet* or the 'Islamist' newspaper *Akit*.
4 Gaboriean et al. (1900) and Özdalga (1999) provide resourceful collections concerning the past and present of Naqshbandi Sufism. See especially H. Alger (1990a, 1990b, 1989), Manneh (1990) and Yavuz (1999). An interesting rendering of the silsila is given by Korkut Özal, one of the cemaat's most prominent members (Özal 1999). See also his account of his relationship to sheikh Kotku.
5 See Yavuz (1999).
6 For other examples of 'Islamic consumption', see White (1999) and Navarro Yashin (2002).
7 Ersin Gürdoğan (1987). Gürdoğan (b.1945) is an engineering professor and prolific public intellectual.
8 As one of many examples one could mention a programmatic article by Ersin Gürdoğan from 1994 in the cemaat's flagship publication *Islam* where he interprets recent Turkish history as a 'culture war' between Muslims and secularists, see Henkel (2004).
9 In the early 1990s, 100,000 copies of *Islam* apparently circulated. Today the cemaat continues Internet and radio service on a smaller scale.
10 They are thus quite different from the figures Oliver Roy describes as Muslim lumpen intellectuals because of their (in his view) shallow understanding of the Islamic tradition.
11 See Algar (1990a) and Özal (1999).
12 Numerous post-Sufi cemaats in Turkey, like the Nurcu cemaats and the Süleymancilar, have been founded by Naqshbandi sheikhs but have abandoned the great emphasis on the silsila central to Sufism. See Yavuz (1999).
13 See, for example, Coşan (1996: 299–322, 323–327).
14 See Schimmel (1985: 53).
15 My translation. See Schimmel (1985).
16 For a table showing the sequence of steps in this endeavour, see Özal (1999: 182–183).
17 See Yavuz (1999) for a perceptive discussion.
18 Sufi organisations were made illegal and their possessions confiscated as part of the Republic's early project of secularisation. Strictly speaking, they remain illegal today.
19 Some of these are recorded on audio and video tapes.
20 See also Henkel (2004).

Creativity and stability in the making of Sufi tradition

1 The transliteration of Arabic words follows the system of the *International Journal of Middle East Studies* (*IJMES*). The plural of the Arabic words in the text is done by adding an 's' to the end of the word. The Arabic plural is given within brackets.
2 Two among the most influential analyses were those of J. Spencer Trimingham (1998 [1971]) for the history of Sufism, and Michael Gilsenan (1973, 2000 [1982]) for the anthropological study of Sufi communities.

3 The Arabic word *zāwiya* (pl. *zāwāiyā*), which literally means 'corner', refers to a Sufi ritual lodge. In Syria this word is also used to designate the local Sufi community.

4 The ethnographic data analysed in this article was collected during a period of 18 months doing fieldwork research among the Sufi communities in Aleppo from 1999 to 2001, as well as during shorter stays in the field during May 2002, May/June 2006 and April/May 2007.

5 Ritual evocation/recollection of God's names. In the Sufi communities in Aleppo where I did my fieldwork this ritual practice aimed to produce a mystical experience of the divine reality (*haqīqa*) through the evocation of the names and the presence of God, Muhammad and the Sufi saints.

6 Pnina Werbner (2003: 157–182) described what she defined as '*deliberate and conscious acts of mimesis*' structuring the expansion of a transnational Sufi cult from Pakistan to Britain. However, she also noticed that this process happened in tandem with the efforts of distinction and self-assertion from the part of the *khalifas*, who aimed to establish themselves as both local leaders and true heirs of their *shaykh*.

7 On the historical cycles of expansion and decline of the Sufi orders and religious institutions, see Trimingham (1998 [1971]: 166–193).

8 The centrality of the *shaykh* and the local community over which he presides in the definition of Sufi identities was also observed in ethnographic studies of Sufi communities in Egypt. See Chih (2000: 171); Hoffman (1995: 123).

9 During my fieldwork, it was not uncommon to meet Sufi *shaykhs* who claimed to master more than one *tarīqa*. Some claimed to be *shaykhs* of up to ten *tarīqas* and expressed it by fusing ritual and doctrinal elements of all of them in the religious activities of their *zawiyas*.

10 These are the *zāwiyas* that were created in Ottoman times, which are the *zāwiya al-Hilāliyya*, *zāwiya al-Badinjkiyya* and *zāwiya al-Maktabiyya*. There are many Qādirī *zāwiyas* in Aleppo that were created in the last two decades and are not part of this hierarchical organisation.

11 Fredrik Barth (1987) showed how the metaphoric character of religious idioms allows the emergence of dynamic forms of articulation between shared understandings and individual creativity in the processes of communication and transmission of religious ideas in New Guinea.

12 In this sense, Sufism combines the doctrinal and imagistic forms of religious codification that were highlighted by Harvey Whitehouse (2000) in his analysis of the modes of religiosity in New Guinea.

13 Talal Asad defines disciplinary practices as 'the multiple ways in which religious discourses regulate, inform and construct religious selves' (1993: 125).

14 See Barth (1990).

15 See also Hilālī (2006: 167).

16 See Bourdieu (1997: 183–184).

17 For the efforts of the Ottomans in transforming the *tarīqas* into centralised 'orders', see Trimingham (1998 [1971]: 238–241). For a similar process of bureaucratic centralisation of the *tarīqas* in Egypt since the nineteenth century, see Luizard (1990: 44–47).

18 This building dates from the thirteenth century and includes a mosque and a *madrasa*, which were already being used in the early twentieth century as premises for the *dhikr* and the *khalwa arba'īniya* (solitary retreat for 40 days) of the *zāwiya al-Bādinjkiyya* (al-Ghazi 1999: 274-275).

19 *Shaykh* Bādinjkī used a similar narrative element in the interview that he gave to 'Abud 'Abd-Allāh al-'Askarī (Bādinjkī 2006: 145–146).

20 The *khalwa* was performed for a period of 40 days (*arba'īn*), during which the *shaykh*'s disciples would stay in the wooden cells that are still visible in the main hall of the *zāwiya al-Hilāliyya*. The disciples remained most of the day in their cells fasting and performing silent *dhikr*. During this period they also listened to lessons ministered by the *shaykh* on religious and secular topics (Hilālī 2006: 168).

21 In reality this shift towards the popular strata was more visible in the Qādirī *zāwiyas* in Aleppo other than the Hilāliyya, where still today the majority of the members are issued from the commercial middle class linked to the merchant families of the *sūq* (bazaar).

22 The discourse about the decline or disappearance of the 'true Sufism' should not be taken literally, but rather as a rhetoric device that is conjured up by many Sufi *shaykhs* in order to claim the monopoly of legitimacy to their particular codification of the Sufi tradition and explain why it is not recognised as a universal model for all forms of Sufism.

23 For the role of religiously expressed 'tradition' in the definition of Aleppo's urban identity, see Seurat (1989: 103–109). For the importance of the notion of 'tradition' among the traders in the *sūq al-medīna* see Rabo (2005: 97–101).

24 *Shaykh* Badinjki even declared in an interview that the only Qādiri *zawiyas* in Aleppo were the *Hilaliyya* and the *Bādinjkiyya* (Badinjki 2006: 147).

25 *Shaykh* Badinjki (2006: 147) claims that his family received a Qadiri *ijaza* from the *zawiya al-Kaylaniyya* in Hama. This was the most prestigious Qādiri *zawiya* in Syria, as the Kaylanī *shaykhs* were considered as being direct descendants from 'Abd al-Qadir Jaiylani, the founding-saint of the *tarīqa*. This *zāwiya*, together with most of Hama's old city, was totally destroyed during the brutal military confrontation between the Syrian army and the Islamic militants led by the Muslim Brothers in 1982.

26 In 2006, *shaykh* Bādinjkī had 30 disciples in various stages of the initiation process.

27 While I had no access to the female members of the *zāwiya al-Bādinjkiyya*, I noticed their presence in the areas reserved for them. See Bādinjkī (2006: 147). *Shaykh* Hilālī does not accept women as participants in the activities of his *zāwiya*. See also Hilālī (2006: 167).

28 The period of *khalwa* in the *zāwiya al-Bādinjkiyya* has been shortened from 40 to four days.

29 Harvey Whitehouse (2000) highlighted the role of discursive and doctrinal codifications of religious traditions in creating egalitarian moral and political communities.

30 The word *hadra*, which means 'presence', has several cognitive and experiential meanings as it refers to the members of the Sufi community who are present in their devotion to God, the *shaykh* who is presiding the ritual and facilitating its mystical effects through his *baraka*, the Qādirī *shaykhs* who constitute the chain of initiation (*silsila*) that connects the *shaykh* with the Prophet, the great saints of Sufism, 'Ali who transmitted the esoteric aspects of the revelation, the family of the Prophet (*ahl al-bayt*), the Prophet, and, as the ultimate reality to be unveiled in the ritual, God.

31 I will present here the ritual model that is followed by both *shaykh* Hilālī and *shaykh* Bādinjikī. A detailed description and analysis of the ritual performance in each *hadra* can be found in Pinto (2006).

32 The *hadra* in the *Hilāliyya* attracts from 70 to 100 men and the one at the *Bādinjikiyya* gathers circa 250 men. I could not estimate the number of female participants in the *hadra* of the *Bādinjikiyya* as I had no access to the room where they performed the ritual.
33 For the concept of a dominant symbol, see Turner (1967: 29–32). See also Douglas (1996) on the uses of the body to communicate symbolic meanings.
34 While the esoteric dimension of religious experience is undercommunicated in the public discourses that circulate in the *Hilāliyya*, it is eagerly searched by the participants in the ritual as a higher existential state of their Sufi identity.

Sacred spaces, rituals and practices

1 The term *mazār* literally means a place of visit. In the South Asian context, it commonly refers to shrines of Muslim saints. However, it is also used to describe the tombs of distinguished persons such as rulers, political leaders, national heroes, etc. Other terms used for Sufi shrines are *dargāh* (lit., a 'royal court'), *darbār* (lit. a royal court), *āstāna* (lit. an abode of a venerable person). The analysis in this essay is based on the ethnographic data from the *mazārs* of Shāh 'Abdu'l Latif Bhitai and Saiyid Pīr Wāris Shāh generated through fieldwork during January–April 2005 and February–April 2006 in Bhit Shah (Sindh, Pakistan) and Jandiala Sher Khan (Punjab, Pakistan), respectively, and is a part of my PhD thesis (Rehman 2007).
2 I use the term '*dargāh*' for the shrine of Shāh Latīf and the term '*mazār*' for the shrine of Wāris Shāh because these terms are the ones used locally to describe the shrines. However, I use the plural term '*mazārs*' throughout the thesis when referring to both shrines as well as Sufi shrines in general.
3 Master-disciple relationship. For a detailed discussion on *pīrī-murīdī* tradition in the *dargāh* of the thirteenth-century saint Nizāmuddīn Auliyā in New Delhi, see Pinto (1995).
4 I will not use the *qaumic* dimension for my analysis of the rituals performed at the *mazārs* of Wāris Shāh and Shāh Latīf since it is mainly related to the politicisation of identities by putting people in sharp categories such as Muslim, Hindu and Sikh, which does not seem to happen as a result of ritual practices performed at the *mazārs*.
5 Some devotees interpreted the thumping of the ground with feet in the *dhammāl* dance as a symbol of mourning related to the seventh-century massacre of Prophet Muhammad's family at Karbala. Others expressed their views that the beating of drums every evening symbolised the saint's presence in the courtyard just like in the Mughul courts announcement was made for kings seating on their thrones.
6 Here, I use the term communion as spiritual contact or telepathy.
7 A middle-aged female pilgrim visiting the *mazār* of Wāris Shāh from Bahawalpur: 20 February 2006.
8 For details on healing rituals among Pakistani *pīrs* and *mazārs*, see Ewing (1984).
9 The belief in the healing properties of the leaves of a tree is shared among the devotees of the *mazārs* of Wāris Shāh and Shāh Latīf. Similarly, the practice related to prescribing two-and-a-half leaves from the tree for healing purposes is also shared among the devotees of both saints.

10 Translation from Sindhi, taken from Allana (1980: 44).
11 There are several categories of *faqīrs* in Shāh Latīf's *dargāh*; namely, *tamrānī*, *autāqī* and *rāgī faqīrs*.
12 The *rāgī faqīrs* told me that they are frequently asked by pilgrims to pray for them since the latter believe that their prayers are more effective.
13 Elderly male pilgrims visiting Wāris Shāh's *mazār*: 11 January 2006.
14 The term *langar* (also called *tabarruk* or *niyāz*) is used for all food distributed at the *mazārs* or saints' *khanqahs*. The practice of food distribution in the Sufi *mazārs* is similar to the distribution of *prasād* (blessed food) given out in Hindu temples. In her analysis of the *langar* at the Sufi cult of Zindāpir, Werbner (2003: 121) uses the term 'good-faith economy'.
15 When pilgrims and devotees bring food offerings, they first take them to the saint's tomb and get them blessed by him before they distribute them among fellow pilgrims either by themselves or with the help of the *mazār*'s servants or *faqīrs*.
16 On the 2005 '*urs* of Shāh Latīf, the Sindhi government announced more than Rs. 2 million (approx. US$ 25,600) for the upkeep of the *dargāh*.
17 The information about the '*urs* ceremony at Shāh Latīf's *dargāh* is based on personal attendance and participant observation during 13–19 March 2006.
18 During the ritual of mourning performed during the '*urs* at Shāh Latīf's *dargāh*, the police constables were not reluctant to show their emotion while they performed their duty. While standing in the outer circles of the mourners some police constables were seen crying and expressing their sorrow side by side with other pilgrims and mourners.
19 To emphasise their association with the *dargāh*, the young scouts were called 'Shāh Latīf Scouts'.

Encountering Sufism on the Web

1 The crossing of borders has been integral to the spread of Sufism and to the formation and expansion of Sufi communities, historically and more recently (Werbner 2003).
2 For details on the spread of Islam and Sufism within and beyond the heartlands, see Boogert (1997), Eaton (1993) and ElBoudrari (1993).
3 For a treatment of these patterns of Muslim migration and the transnational expansion of Sufism to the USA, see Haddad (2004) and Haddad and Esposito (2000). For similar patterns in Europe, see Westerlund (2004) and Malik and Hinnells (2006).
4 For two examples from the American context, Hazrat Inayat Khan and Bawa Muhaiyaddeen, see Webb (1995).
5 For a description of women's roles as educators in women's ribats in medieval Cairo, see Berkey (1992). Examples of Sufi women participating in the spread of Islamic knowledge have been documented for northern Nigeria (Boyd and Mack 2000), Central Asia (Kraemer 2002) and Morocco (Rausch 2006).
6 Beyond the practical, a similar process of adaptation was and is observable on an intellectual level through the interaction among scholars from a variety of schools of thought.

7 For an examination of the effects of globalisation and technological transformations on contemporary Sufism, see Ernst (2005 and forthcoming).

8 In keeping with the spelling on the branches' names on their websites, as well as in the scholarly literature about them, the letter j instead of the letter c, which is pronounced like j in Turkish, will be used in this article for the spelling of the word Jerrahi.

9 Part of the data presented in this article derives from preliminary fieldwork conducted in May 2007. This fieldwork was funded by an internal grant from the University of Kansas.

10 The branch's name derives from the name of its founder, Lex Hixon, who was given the Muslim name Nur al-Anwar by his teacher Shaykh Muzaffer Ozak (see below). Shaykh Nur added Ashki, meaning lover, a nickname given to Shaykh Muzaffer Ozak in recognition of his intense love for God and creation, which he articulated in his Sufi love poetry. Like the names of many offshoot branches of other Sufi orders, it recognises its origin in the Halveti-Jerrahi Sufi Order with the word Jerrahi, as well as its founder with the name Nur. The name Ashki can be seen as referring both to Shaykh Nur, as well as to his spiritual guide, Muzaffer Ozak, emphasising the branch's link to the mother order.

11 Muzaffer Ozak was most commonly referred to as Muzaffer Effendi, and will be designated in this way throughout this chapter. The term effendi is a title of respect equivalent to the English title sir. It is placed after the person's name.

12 The scholarly literature exploring the use of the Internet as a tool or object of research on religion is expanding rapidly. Examples for Islam include Bunt (2000) and Lohlker (2000).

13 The details in this section derive from the only existing publication on Muzaffer Effendi's life (Blann 2005) and statements by members of the NAJSO.

14 As a result of the warmth and enthusiasm Muzaffer Effendi displayed in welcoming them, the tekke became a popular destination in Turkey among Western tourists and scholars alike.

15 This visit was made possible by the generosity of Phillipa Friedrich's mother, Dominique de Menil, who, together with her husband, opened the Rothko Chapel in Houston, Texas. Dominique and John de Menil are remembered for their generosity in supporting artists and their pioneering efforts to promote interfaith dialogue.

16 An online search for information about his art brought up only the following text: Kostelanetz remembers …Tosun Bayrak, who worked with blood, rats, and excrement. Bayrak's pieces inspire some of his most colorful prose. 'Recognizing in the early seventies that SoHo itself was an art gallery,' he writes, 'a Turk named Tosun Bayrak, scarcely young at the time, did radical performance pieces – "actions" they could be called – whose audacity remains unrivaled. When his wife was evicted from a West Broadway building that was sold to a new owner, Bayrak embedded bags of bovine blood and entrails in the walls and ceiling of her loft and replastered them. Inviting people into the loft one Saturday afternoon, he chopped at the walls with an ax to "free" the gore, so to speak. White pigeons, very much a symbol of peace at the time, were released from beneath the floorboards. This piece he called *The Living Loft* (Finkel 2003).

17 In an online interview, Tosun Bayrak explains his decision to give up his career as an artist as follows:

> Actually, both my wife and I were artists, and we felt very strongly that it was feeding our egos. Art, art exhibitions, and the consequences of being accepted and successful are incredible food for your ego, which is the Sufi's enemy. The final straw was when we went to Rome to visit a friend, a sculptor, and there was a very pretty young girl there whom my friend introduced me to. And she was so adoring to me. She said, 'Ohhh, I know you. I *love* your art.' She was completely praising me, and I saw the ego suddenly rise up and say, 'Aha! This beautiful, spiritual girl is telling you that you are a great artist.' So I said, 'Oh, my God! That's it. It's over.' I hit the ego on the head and decided I was finished with it all.

Evidence of Shaykh Tosun's approach to gender, which pervades the HJOD, can be found in this passage. It would be interesting to know the age of this 'girl', on what basis Shaykh Tosun chose to characterise her as 'beautiful' and 'spiritual' and if he 'saw the ego suddenly rise up' when men or women who were not 'beautiful' and 'spiritual' expressed their admiration for his artist productions. Learning humility through Sufism while continuing to pursue a career in art would have been another option (Phillips 2000).

18 The current picture of Shaykha Fariha appeared in early November replacing an earlier one in which she was completely veiled. According to statements by a member with administrative functions within the branch, this change took place for the sake of variety.

19 The links for purchasing books connect the visitor to Amazon.com, but it is explained that a portion of the money spent on the publications nonetheless goes to the relief projects maintained by the HJOD.

20 Until very recently, the picture of Shaykh Tugrul al-Jerrahi, the current leader of the Halveti-Jerrahi Order in Istanbul, could be found in the middle of this row of pictures.

21 It is interesting that both branches quote Ibn al-'Arabi as making two opposing statements about women: that God can grant women access to all stations including sainthood; and that one should fear women and their ability to usurp power.

Sufism in the USA

1 Citation of excerpt from 'Ali b. 'Uthman al-Jullabi al-Hujwiri: *Kashf al-Mahjub. The Oldest Persian Treatise on Sufiism,* trans. R. A. Nicholson, Lahore, 1953, quoted in Malik (2006: 4).

2 For an illustrative example, see *Encyclopaedia of Religion and Ethics* (Edinburgh & New York, 1908–1926).

3 For a useful discussion of this topic, see Ernst (2005).

4 www.uga.edu/islam/Sufism.html (visited 25 February 2008).

5 Information collected in 2003 by Martin Nguyen during fieldwork in the Boston group of the Bawa Muhaiyaddeen Fellowship meeting weekly in Cambridge; see www.pluralism.org/affiliates/student/nguyen/Boston_Sufi_Orders.pdf (visited 25 February 2008).

6 www.islamicsupremecouncil.org/bin/site/ftp/activities_goals_april2002.pdf (visited 28 February 2008).

7 www.sufimuslimcouncil.blogspot.com/ (visited 28 February 2008). For a further selection of information on the opposing views, see www.worldnetdaily.com/news/article.asp?ARTICLE_ID=36457, www.wrmea.com/backissues/0499/9904071.html, www.judiciary.senate.gov/testimony.cfm?id=960&wit_id=2719, www.muslimwakeup.com/main/archives/2005/09/002896print. php (all visited 28 February 2008).
8 www.isna.net/ISNAHQ/pages/About-Us.aspx (visited 16 September 2008).
9 www.theamericanmuslim.org/tam.php/tam/about/ (visited 16 September 2008).
10 Ibid.
11 Ibid.
12 www.muslimwakeup.com/main/archives/2005/09/002896print.php (visited 16 September 2008).
13 Muslim Americans. Middle Class and Mostly Mainstream, 2007, p. 9, www.pewresearch.org/assets/pdf/muslim-americans.pdf and The Mosque in America: A National Portrait. A Report from the Mosque Study Project, 2001, p. 6, www.cair.com/Portals/0/pdf/The_Mosque_in_America_A_National_Portrait.pdf (both visited 15 September 2008).
14 American Muslim Voters: A Demographic Profile and Survey of Attitudes, CAIR 2006, p. 10, www.cair.com/Portals/0/pdf/American_Muslim_Voter_Survey_2006.pdf (visited 15 September 2008).
15 Luxenberg's work made the front page of New York Times (2 March 2002) and was also mentioned in Newsweek International (28 July issue, 2003), an issue that was later banned in Pakistan by the Information minister, according to whom the article was insulting to the *Qur'ān* (under Pakistan's blasphemy law, it is an offence punishable by death to offend Islam, its prophet or its holy book).
16 See the article 'Radical New Views of Islam and the Origins of the Koran' by Alexander Stille. Originally published in New York Times, 2 March 2002, www.holycrossmonastery.org/articles/radical.htm (visited 15 September 2008).
17 See Geaves (2006) for a discussion of the case of Britain.

Strategies for concord

1 *Maulana*, Arabic for 'our master', is an honorific title that is applied with various meanings in Islam. In Tariqa Burhaniya it is used solely for the supreme head of the order.
2 Taken from the order's website: www.burhaniya.info/intranet/I_welc_e.htm (accessed 16 July 2007).
3 Taken from the order's website: www.burhaniya.info/intranet/I_welc_e.htm (accessed 16 July 2007).
4 Gritt Klinkhammer gives the figure of 46 (Klinkhammer 2005: 264).
5 The issue of succession may not have been so smooth in reality. Some sources mention several claimants to authority after the demise of Shaykh Mohammad Osman. According to Gritt Klinkhammer, Shaykh Ibrahim was able to establish his authority only after a year-long strife with non-family claimants (Klinkhammer 2005: 274 f.).
6 Tariqa Burhaniya Disuqiya Shadhuliya Deutschland (hrsg.) 2001.
7 *Qasida* (plural *qasa'id*) is a very common form of Arabic poetry with end rhyme, often used for religious and mystical poetry.

8 *Aurad* is plural of the Arabic *wird*, and can be translated as 'special prayers of a certain order'. In Burhaniya *aurad* refers to a definite body of prayers and recitations laid down by the order's founder and utilised as personal practice for each member. Could also be translated as 'litany'.
9 A detailed description of a hadra ritual in Munich is found in Glasbrenner (2001: 81–91).
10 The anniversary of the death of Maulana Shaykh Mohammad Osman is celebrated on 5 April, i.e., according to the Gregorian calendar.

Sufism contextualized

1 Today there are approximately 3–3.5 million Muslims in Germany; 80 per cent of them have Turkish roots. Most of the Muslim immigrants live in the west of Germany.
2 This led, of course, to new Muslim forms of Sufism such as the tradition of the Suleymancis (Jonker 2002).
3 This observation is based on conversations with members of the Burhaniyya and disciples of the Naqshbandiyya of shaykh Nazim and the 'Mevlevi-Kubrevi Order' of Shaykh Halis.
4 For details about the German history of reception of (Mevlevi) Sufism, see Klinkhammer (2008) and also Lewis (2000: 566–569).
5 The ceremony can be viewed on the Internet, for instance. under: www.whirling dervishes.org/multimedia.htm. This site is not presented by a Mevlevi Order but by Fetullah Gülen, representing a blend of Turkish nationalism and Muslim spiritual tradition. In order to carry out global missionary work among Turkish secular Muslims living in the 'diaspora', he 'advertises' with his websites for a connection of Turkey and spiritual and peaceful as well as educated Islam.
6 Since the poet Colman Barks published an English translation of Rumi's poems in 1995, the popularity of Rumi has increased in the USA. More than 500,000 books have been sold – a huge popular success for a poet. For an historical review on the Western reception of Rumi in literature and art, see Lewis (2000).
7 www.amazon.de (2007).
8 *Sema* is the Turkish form for the Arabic word *sama* which means 'listening', and designates the Sufi ritual of listening and whirling to music. In the following, I will use the Turkish form because it is common in Germany and I would rather refer in the text to its Turkish tradition.
9 www.chiftetelli.at/gallerie.htm.
10 During my fieldwork among German Sufis I also met some Sufis who are non-professionally writing poetry and/or compose Sufi poems.
11 The name Gayanshala refers to the early music school in Beroda, today the music faculty of the University of Baroda. The founder of this school was the grandfather of Hazrat Inayat Khan (see above).
12 www.gayanshala.sufismus.de.
13 Officially titled 'Mevlânâ Eğitim ve Kültür Derneği' Istanbul.
14 This is a foundation in the tradition of Inayat Khan and his universal 'Sufi Order'.
15 See www.mevlana.ch.

16 See www.mevlana-ev.de and www.mevlana.ch.
17 He talked to me about this during various visits in the tekke and on workshops in 2003–2007.
18 It should be remembered that Sufi orders have been banned in Turkey since 1925.
19 As, for instance, the popular Syrian branch of the Muslim brothers, which were active as a resistance movement against the ruling secularist Baath party until 1980.
20 I never heard anyone (among Germans) ask whether the Sudanese Burhani shaykh Osman was legitimated (he was shaykh only by a calling, not by training) or if someone has seen Nazim's *ijaza*.
21 See Halis' website: www.mevlevi.de.
22 According to Buehler, the 'teaching shaykh' who gets authority through his action and the 'directing shaykh' who gets authority through his charisma were early forms of Sufism. The 'mediating shaykh', who lives in seclusion and functions only as mediator to God for his adherents, is a new phenomenon from the nineteenth century.
23 *Adab* means respectful ritualised behaviour. The Halis group, for instance, must avoid speaking in the first person singular, instead always using the plural (saying 'we' instead of 'I'). They kiss their hand before and after they use an object. Both saying 'we' and kissing symbolically are a show of devotion. They stand up when the shaykh does and they do not speak during the meal, at least not until the shaykh allows it; and so on.
24 'Kubrevi' is the Turkish notation for 'Kubrawi' Order. For historical details on the Kubrawiyya and its theory of the light, see Fleischer (1862: 235–241) and Schimmel (1993: 360–364).
25 Halis says that he learned this meditation form from Farhad Dede during his stay in Aleppo as the murid of Mustafa Kemal; see Krieg-Dornbrach (1997: 20–25).
26 See authors who reflect this new identity building in the 'reflexive modernity', like Keupp et al. (1999) and others.
27 A Sudanese order, 'refounded' by Shaykh Osman Burhani (d.1983), which is vividly present in Germany; see Klinkhammer (2005).

Index

Introductory note for readers

Page numbers in italics show illustrations. Page numbers with 'n' show page number first, then the number of the note on that page.